GREENWOOD
GUIDES

The Team

Simon Greenwood

Vicky Norman

Steve Vince

Lily Yousry-Jouve

Charlotte Turner

First published in 2000 by Greenwood Guides,
43a Waldemar Avenue, London SW6 5LN, UK.

Fifth edition

0-9551160-0-7 and 978-0-9551160-0-1
Printed in China through Colorcraft Ltd., HK

THE GREENWOOD GUIDE TO

SOUTH AFRICA

NAMIBIA AND MOZAMBIQUE

hand-picked accommodation

Including Phophonyane Lodge in Swaziland and Malealea Lodge in Lesotho.

fifth edition

www.greenwoodguides.com

Acknowledgements

Series Editor: Simon Greenwood

Writing collaboration and inspections: Simon Greenwood, Vicky Norman, Charlotte Turner and Steve Vince (South Africa and Mozambique); Lily Yousry-Jouve (Namibia). Thanks too to Susan McLaren for her translations from Lily's French.

Map data provided by Collins Bartholomew Ltd.

Production, DTP and design: Tory Gordon-Harris and Jo Ekin

Printing: Colorcraft, Hong Kong

UK Distribution: Portfolio, London

SA Distribution: Quartet Sales and Marketing, Johannesburg

The cover image is of Ant's Nest, page 282 in Limpopo Province. Cover design and digital manipulation by Tory Gordon-Harris.

Serra Cafema (entry page 360): lodge from the Kunene, image by Michael Puliza; and interior of tent, image by Dana Allen.
Ongava Tented Camp (entry number 352): tent and deck, image by Dana Allen.

Province intro images: Title page Porcupine Pie, Western Cape, Northern Cape and Free State Charlotte Turner, Eastern Cape Bartholomeus Klip, KwaZulu Natal Thonga Beach Lodge, Gauteng Rietfontein, North West Province Okambara Lodge, Limpopo Lesheba, Mpumalanga Bufffalo Hills, Mozambique Nkwichi Lodge, Namibia Lily Yousry-Jouve.

Symbols
and what they mean

No credit cards accepted.

Meals can be provided, often by prior arrangement.

Rooms all have TVs.

Stocked wild game can be seen. This does not include naturally occurring wild animals like springbok and waterbuck.

Children are welcome without proviso.

Working farm.

Off-street car parking.

Access only for wheelchairs.

Full wheelchair facilities.

Swimming available in pool, sea, dam or river.

No smoking inside the buildings.

Good hiking or walking direct from the house.

Contents

Introduction

Since we visit each place we feature each year and since we have to turn down so many applications from places that didn't quite appeal enough - or which, frankly, we just didn't like at all - I have been able to calculate that we have now made about 3,000 visits to South African or Namibian places to stay over the last 6 years. I don't like to claim too much, but really if I am an expert in anything it must now be this! Can't think of anything else I excel at... perhaps something fun like database management... or Photoshopping images... some people praise my omelettes....

Anyway, we are ever more stringent about whom we accept into the guide and I think long-standing GG-watchers will agree that the book has got better as well as bigger. I receive a great deal of mail from travellers, which I encourage. It gives us a good idea of how our choices are being received out there in the field. And since we live or die on the happiometer of our travellers, i.e. you, then this info is vital.

We have made genuine human hospitality our common denominator rather than the sterile but safe judgement of a place's worth according to its facilities. We do not give out stars or tiaras as a result. A place is either a lovely place to be or it isn't. That is our simple approach. Beyond that each traveller will need to look at location, rates and exactly what sort of place it is and make their own decisions.

We describe each place ourselves so I hope you will find the text accurate and appropriate as well as lively and at times even humorous.

The job of Greenwood Guides is first and foremost to assess the people running the accommodation and choose only those for whom looking after others, whether they be friends, family or paying guests, is a natural pleasure. Taste, furnishings, facilities, views, food, beds, bathrooms... all these things are important too, but only if they are provided by friendly people.

Thank you for choosing our guide. We do put in an enormous amount of effort each year, revisiting each place each edition, weeding out places that have lost their energy as often happens in the world of accommodation and sounding out all the new great, good and ordinary places that open each year.

As I always say we would be delighted to hear from you when you get back from your travels.

NEW THINGS

This year saw the publication of our new guide South African Highlights, a companion for this book containing recommended things to do and places to eat. If you haven't yet heard of this guide it would be well worth getting hold of a copy before setting off on your travels. "Essential packing'" as travel publisher blurbs so often have it. All the entries have been personally recommended either by GG writers or by owners of places to stay within this guide, i.e. the book contains only absolute favourite restaurants, wineries, cafés, tour operators in many different fields, things to do with the kids, outdoor activities etc. The final list of entries was whittled down to 550 odd from some 1800 recommendations in all. All have been tried and tested, often many times, by people whose opinion we trust. Between the two books you really shouldn't need much else besides your wallet, driving licence, mobile phone and winning smile to have a really fantastic holiday in South Africa.

Also new this year is the section on Namibia. You will find 39 places to stay across the whole country, including the Caprivi Strip, at the back of the book. There is a separate introduction introducing the country there. There has never before been such a collection of great places in that country published with the independent traveller in mind. And I think you will agree that if you hadn't thought there were enough good places in Namibia to whet the appetite before... well, you will now.

THE GREENWOOD GUIDES APPROACH

There are essentially three types of place to stay. There are those that fulfil their obligations in a commercial way and leave you feeling throughout your stay like the paying customer that you are. And there are those few great places where you are welcomed in and treated as a friend, cliché though this may now have become, and where paying at the end of your visit is a pleasurable surprise. And of course there is a third category where paying for your stay is a disagreeable inevitability!

It is a particular irony of the accommodation world that no price is ever put on the essential qualities of a place – people, atmosphere, charm. These ideas are too woolly perhaps to quantify, but this is where one's real enjoyment of a place to stay stems from. You are asked to pay instead for tangible facilities like marble bathrooms and en-suite showers.

This is a fallacy that we try to dismantle in all our guides, which is why you will find places at all reasonable price levels. Expensive does not mean good. And nor does cheap (however appealing the word may sound!). If a place costs plenty then it will probably offer facilities in keeping with the price. But that does not mean you will have any fun. Some very expensive places forget that they are providing a service and look down their noses at their own guests. At the other end of the spectrum, the very cheapest places are often cheap for good reasons. Sometimes for spectacular reasons!

Character and genuine hospitality, the extra qualities we search for, are found spaced evenly across the price spectrum. Nowhere in this guide cuts corners at the risk of your displeasure. We give equal billing to each place we choose, no matter if it is a gorgeous lodge or a home-spun B&B.

At the top end, the most jewel-encrusted, nay 'boutique' places may drip with luxurious trimmings, but have retained their sense of atmosphere and humour, are friendly and informal and nearly all are still owned and managed by the same people. ('Boutique' always used to mean a 'small clothes shop in France', but it has sneaked into accommodation vocab somewhere along the line.)

Equally, there are places in the book that do not have much in the way of luxury, but easily compensate with unique settings, wonderful views and charming hosts.

We are hoping that those of you who normally only plump for luxury at a price will use this guide to vary their holiday a little and stay at a few of the wonderful family-run farms and B&Bs. And that those who usually go cheap as possible will splash out once in a while on a more luxurious option. This book allows for great flexibility in terms of price and style of accommodation. We do not wish to divide the world into budget and luxury, only great and not great enough.

It is the quality of experience that draws us in and this is not determined by how much you pay. In the end I know that you will really like the owners in this book, many of whom we now count as friends. And you will certainly make friends yourselves if you stick to the Greenwood trail.

SOUTH AFRICA

(There is a separate introduction for Namibia at the start of the Namibian section.)

DRIVING

There is nowhere in South Africa that would make a 4-wheel drive a necessity. However make sure you confirm this issue if booking into Mozambiquan or Namibian places.

CAR HIRE

Make sure that you have considered the amount of daily mileage your car hire company gives you. 100km or even 200km a day is virtually nothing and the final cost can be far higher than you estimated. Try and work out roughly what distances you will be covering and ask for the correct daily allowance. There is usually a surcharge for taking your car across the border from SA into Mozambique or Namibia.

MOBILE/CELL PHONES

Airports all have shops that provide mobile phones. They are invaluable and we recommend that you get one. You can buy a cheap handset or just rent one for the duration of your stay and then pay for calls as you go with recharge cards.

TELEPHONE NUMBERS

To call South Africa from the UK dial 0027 then drop the 0 from the local code.
To call the UK from South Africa dial 0944 then drop the 0 from the local code.

The numbers printed in this book are all from within South Africa or Namibia. To call Mozambique from abroad dial +58 then drop the 0 from the local code. To call Namibia from abroad dial +264 then drop the 0 from the local code.

TORTOISES

Look out for tortoises. They are slow, but seem to spend a lot of time, completely against the tide of advice put forward for their benefit, crossing roads.

TIPPING

* In restaurants we tend to give 15%.

* At a petrol station my policy is to give no tip for just filling up, 3 rand for cleaning the windows, and 5 rand for cleaning the windows and checking oil and water. If you really don't want the attendant to clean your windows you need to make this a statement when you ask for the petrol... or they will often do it anyway.

* At a guest-house I would typically give R15 per person staying for up to two nights. If you are staying longer than two nights then you might feel like adding more. If there is obviously one maid to whom the tip will go then give it to her direct. If there are many staff members who will be sharing the tip then give it to your host.

TIME OF YEAR

I got in a bit of a tangle in the first edition trying neatly to package up what is really quite complicated. So I will limit myself to one observation. It seems to me that most Europeans come to South Africa in January, February and March to avoid their own miserable weather and write taunting postcards home from a sunny Cape. I've been doing this myself for the last few years.

However, the very best time of year to visit the Northern Cape, Mpumalanga, Limpopo, North-West Province, KwaZulu Natal and the Karoo, i.e. the whole country except the southern Cape, is from May to October. The air is dry and warm, game viewing is at its best and there are fewer tourists keeping the prices higher. It's worth mentioning.

PAY FOR ENTRY

We could not afford to research and publish this guide in the way we do without the financial support of those we feature. Each place that we have chosen has paid an entry fee for which we make no apology. It has not influenced our decision-making about who is right or wrong for the guide and we turn down many more than we accept. The proof of this is in the proverbial pudding. Use the book and see for yourself. It is also very hard for us to write up a place that we are not enthusiastic about.

THE MAPS SECTION

The maps at the front of the book are designed to show you where in the country each place is positioned, and should not be used as a road map. There are many minor and dirt roads missing and we recommend that you buy a proper companion road atlas.

Each place is flagged with a number that corresponds to the page number below each entry.

Some have complained that it is hard to find detailed road maps of South Africa in the UK, so I suggest you buy one at the airport when you arrive in SA.

CANCELLATION

Most places have some form of cancellation charge. Do make sure that you are aware what this is if you book in advance. Owners need to protect themselves against no-shows and will often demand a deposit for advance booking.

PRICES

The prices quoted are per person sharing per night, unless specifically stated otherwise. Every now and then complications have meant we quote the full room rate. Single rates are also given.

We have usually put in a range within which the actual price will fall. This may be because of fluctuating prices at different times of year, but also we have tried to predict the anticipated rise in prices over the book's shelf life. Obviously we cannot know what will happen to the value of the rand and prices might fall outside the quoted range.

Most game lodges quote an all-in package including meals and game activities.

Although South Africa has become substantially more expensive since the first edition of this guide came out 6 years ago, it is still great value on the whole. The value-for-money increases significantly the more off-the-beaten-track you wander.

Mozambiquan places tend to quote in US dollars.

CHILDREN

We have only given the child-friendly symbol to those places that are unconditionally accepting of the little fellows. This does not necessarily mean that if there is no symbol children are barred. But it may mean chatting with your hosts about their ages, their temperaments and how suitable a time and place it will be. Most owners are concerned about how their other guests will take to kids running wild when they are trying to relax on a long-anticipated holiday… from their own children. Places that are fully child-friendly are listed in the activities index at the back of the book.

DISCLAIMER

We make no claims to god-like objectivity in assessing what is or is not special about the places we feature. They are there because we like them. Our opinions and tastes are mortal and ours alone. We have done our utmost to get the facts right, but apologize for any mistakes that may have slipped through the net.

Some things change which are outside our control: people sell up, prices increase, exchange rates fluctuate, unfortunate extensions are added, marriages break up and even acts of God can rain down destruction. We would be grateful to be told about any errors or changes, however great or small. We can always make these editions on the web version of this book.

DON'T TRY AND DO TOO MUCH. PLEASE.

It is the most common way to spoil your own holiday. South Africa is a huge country and you cannot expect to see too much of it on one trip. Don't over-extend yourself. Stay everywhere for at least two nights and make sure that you aren't spending your hard-earned holiday fiddling with the radio and admiring the dashboard of your hire car.

PLEASE WRITE TO US

Our email address is simon@greenwoodguides.com for all comments. Although we visit each place each edition many of the places featured here are small, personal and owner-run. This means that their enjoyability depends largely on the happiness, health and energy of the hosts. This can evaporate in double-quick time for any number of reasons and standards plummet before we have had a chance to re-evaluate the place. So we are also very grateful to travellers who keep us up to date with how things are going. We are always most concerned to hear that the hosting has been inattentive.

We also have guides to Australia, New Zealand and Canada. These books are available in bookshops or by emailing us direct or mailing us the order form at the back of this book.

So that's about it for another year. My great thanks this time to Charlotte, Vicky, Steve and Lily for all their efforts in researching and updating the guide.

I hope all of you who travel under the auspices of the Greenwood Guide have a wonderful time. I hope this book will be seen as the main reason why you enjoyed your holiday as much as you did.

Simon.

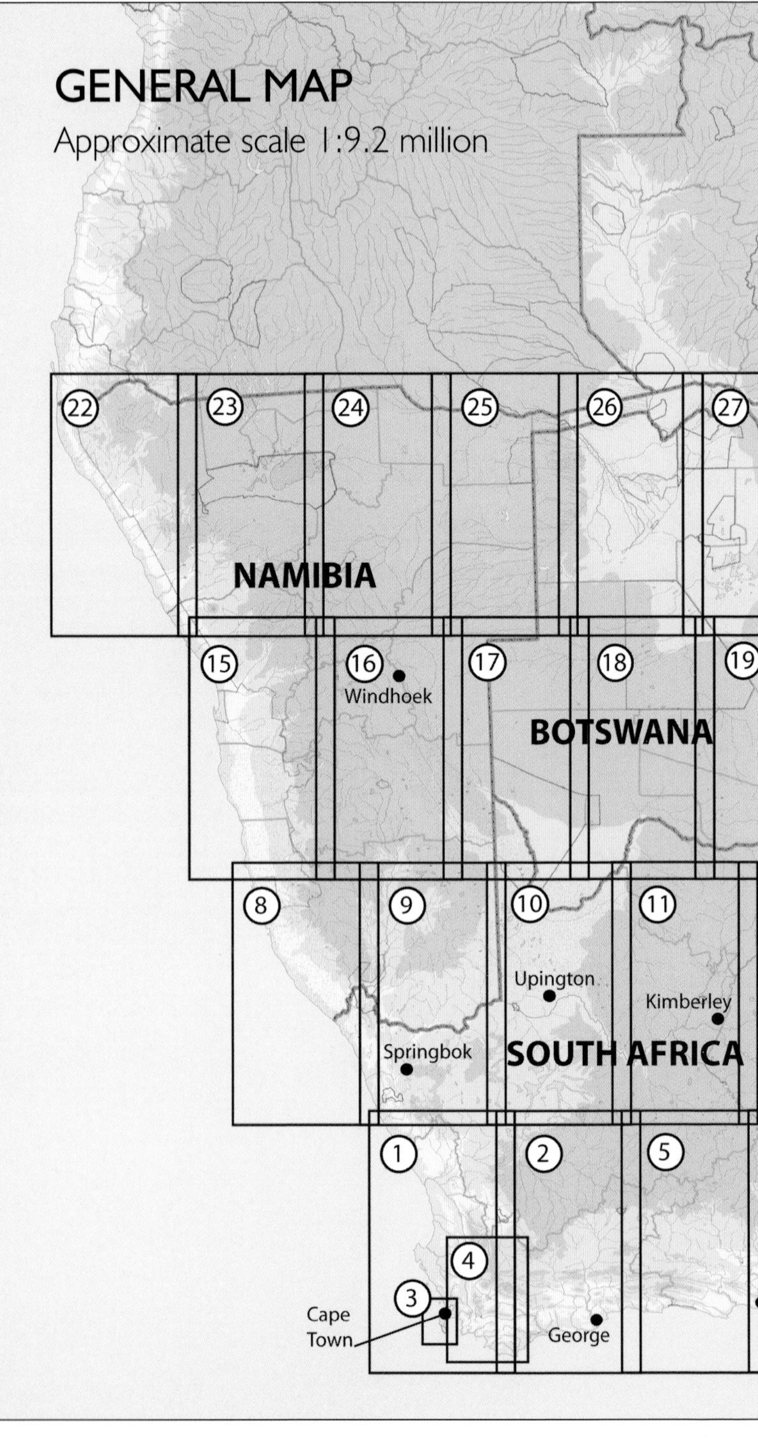

GENERAL MAP
Approximate scale 1:9.2 million
22
23
24
25
26
27
NAMIBIA
15
16
Windhoek
17
18
19
BOTSWANA
8
9
10
11
Upington
Kimberley
Springbok
SOUTH AFRICA
1
2
5
4
3
Cape Town
George

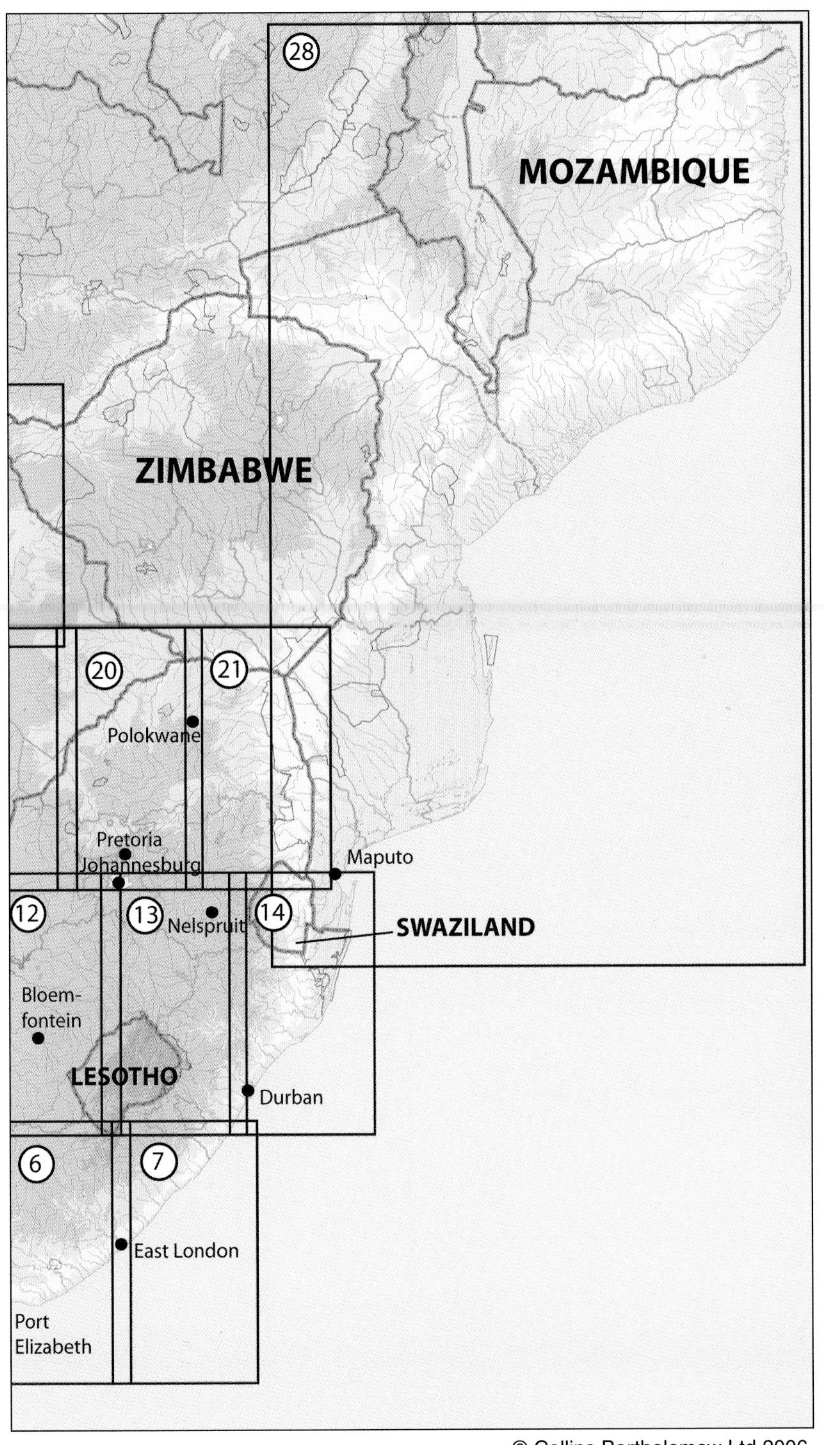

28
MOZAMBIQUE
ZIMBABWE
20
21
Polokwane
Pretoria
Johannesburg
Maputo
12
13
Nelspruit
14
SWAZILAND
Bloem-
fontein
LESOTHO
Durban
6
7
East London
Port
Elizabeth

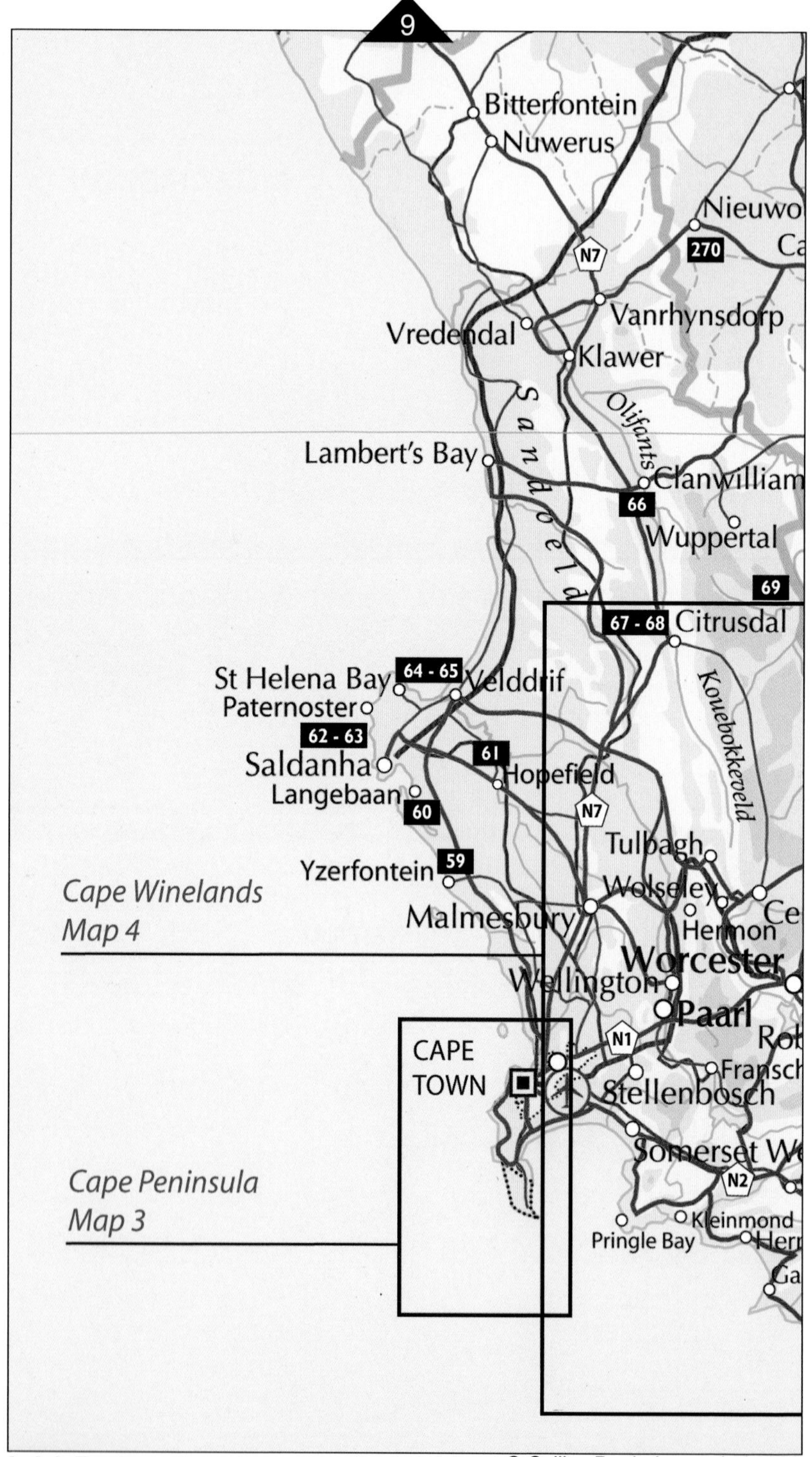
9
Bitterfontein
Nuwerus
Nieuwo
270
N7
Vanrhynsdorp
Vredendal
Klawer
Sandveld
Olifants
Lambert's Bay
Clanwilliam
66
Wuppertal
69
67 - 68
Citrusdal
Koue bokkeveld
St Helena Bay
64 - 65
Velddrif
Paternoster
62 - 63
61
Saldanha
Hopefield
Langebaan
60
N7
Tulbagh
59
Yzerfontein
Wolseley
Cape Winelands
Map 4
Malmesbury
Hermon
Worcester
Wellington
Paarl
N1
CAPE
TOWN
Stellenbosch
Somerset W
N2
Cape Peninsula
Map 3
Kleinmond
Pringle Bay

MAP 1

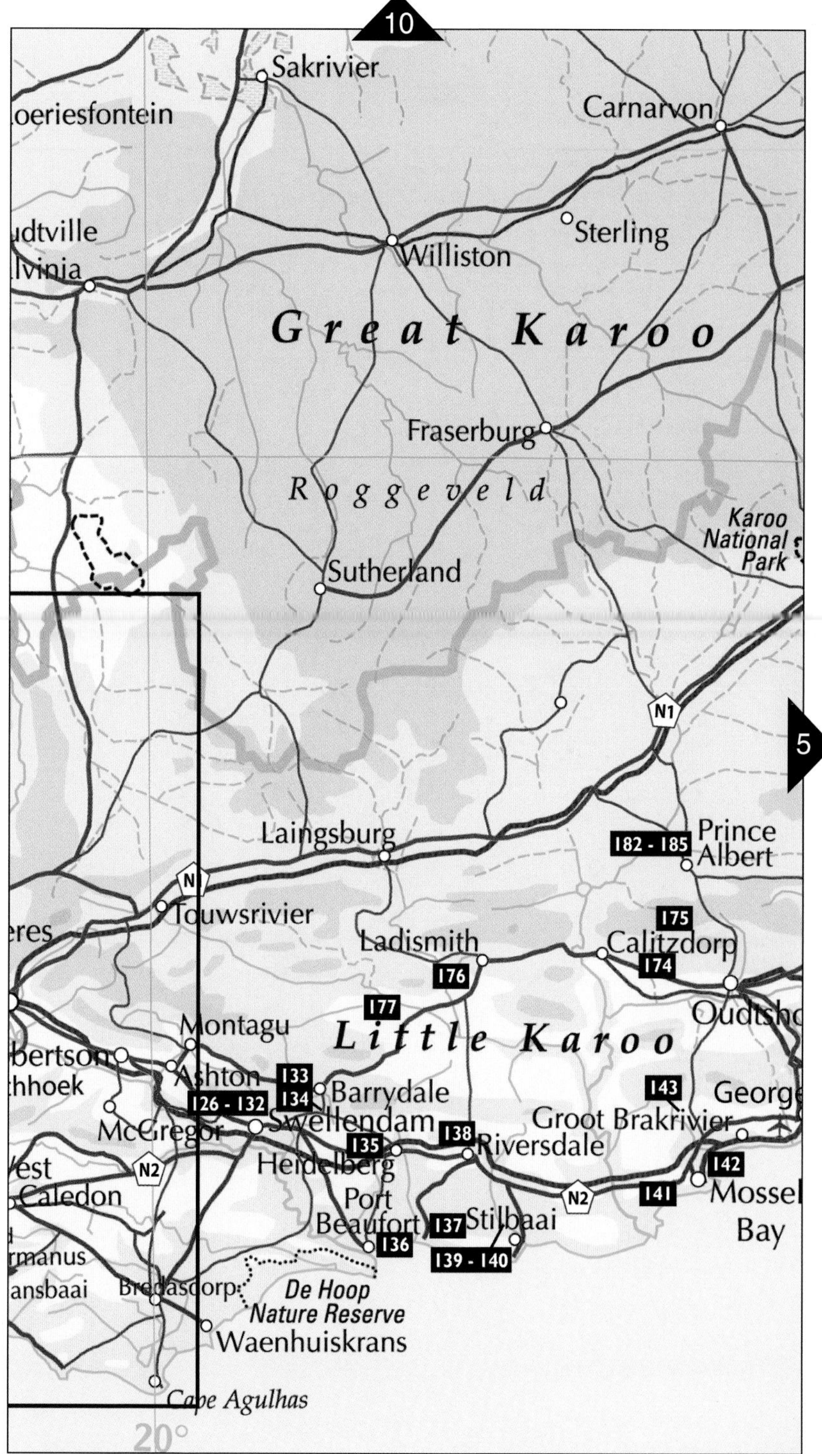
10
Sakrivier
oeriesfontein
Carnarvon
udtville
lvinia
Sterling
Williston
Great Karoo
Fraserburg
Roggeveld
Karoo
National
Park
Sutherland
N1
5
Laingsburg
Prince
Albert
182 - 185
N1
Touwsrivier
eres
175
Ladismith
Calitzdorp
174
176
Oudtsho
177
Montagu
Little Karoo
bertson
Ashton
133
134
Barrydale
143
George
hhoek
126 - 132
Swellendam
138
Groot Brakrivier
McGregor
135
Riversdale
Heidelberg
142
West
N2
Mossel
Bay
Caledon
Port
Beaufort
137
Stilbaai
N2
141
rmanus
136
139 - 140
ansbaai
Bredasdorp
De Hoop
Nature Reserve
Waenhuiskrans
Cape Agulhas
20°

MAP 2

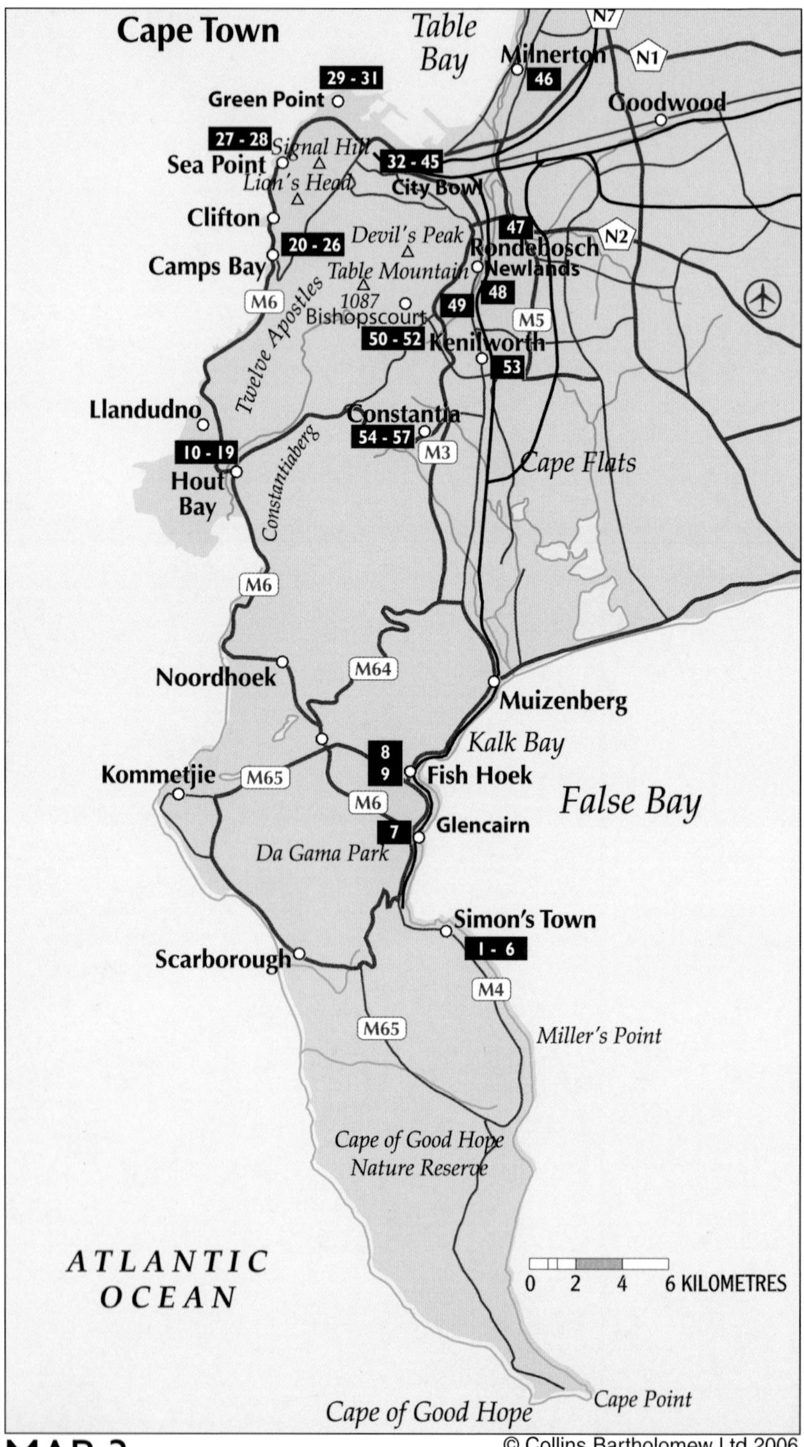

Cape Town
Table Bay
Milnerton
46
N7
N1
Goodwood
29 - 31
Green Point
27 - 28
Signal Hill
Sea Point
32 - 45
Lion's Head
City Bowl
Clifton
47
N2
Devil's Peak
20 - 26
Rondebosch
Camps Bay
Table Mountain
Newlands
1087
48
M6
Twelve Apostles
Bishopscourt
49
M5
50 - 52
Kenilworth
53
Llandudno
Constantia
54 - 57
M3
10 - 19
Hout Bay
Constantiaberg
Cape Flats
M6
Noordhoek
M64
Muizenberg
Kalk Bay
8
9
Fish Hoek
Kommetjie
M65
False Bay
M6
Glencairn
7
Da Gama Park
Simon's Town
1 - 6
Scarborough
M4
M65
Miller's Point
Cape of Good Hope Nature Reserve
ATLANTIC OCEAN
0 2 4 6 KILOMETRES
Cape Point
Cape of Good Hope

MAP 3

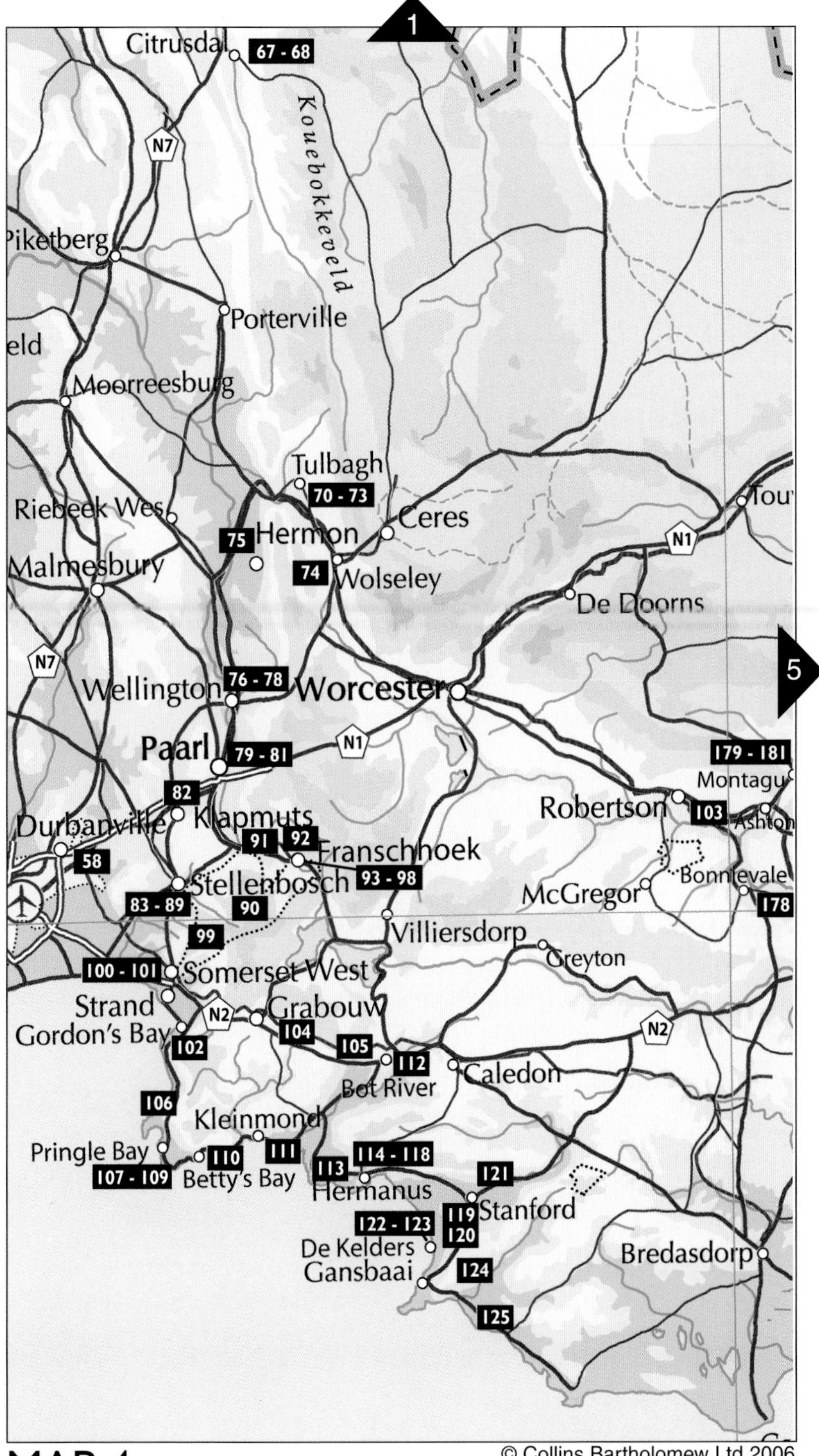

1
Citrusdal
67 - 68
N7
Kouebokkeveld
Piketberg
Porterville
eld
Moorreesburg
Tulbagh
70 - 73
Riebeek Wes
Ceres
75
Hermon
Tou
N1
Malmesbury
74
Wolseley
De Doorns
N7
76 - 78
Wellington
Worcester
5
N1
Paarl
79 - 81
179 - 181
Montagu
82
Robertson
103
Ashton
Klapmuts
Durbanville
91
92
Franschhoek
58
Bonnievale
Stellenbosch
93 - 98
McGregor
178
83 - 89
90
Villiersdorp
99
Greyton
100 - 101
Somerset West
Strand
N2
Grabouw
N2
Gordon's Bay
104
102
105
112
Caledon
Bot River
106
Kleinmond
111
114 - 118
Pringle Bay
110
113
121
107 - 109
Betty's Bay
Hermanus
Stanford
119
122 - 123
120
De Kelders
Bredasdorp
Gansbaai
124
125

MAP 4

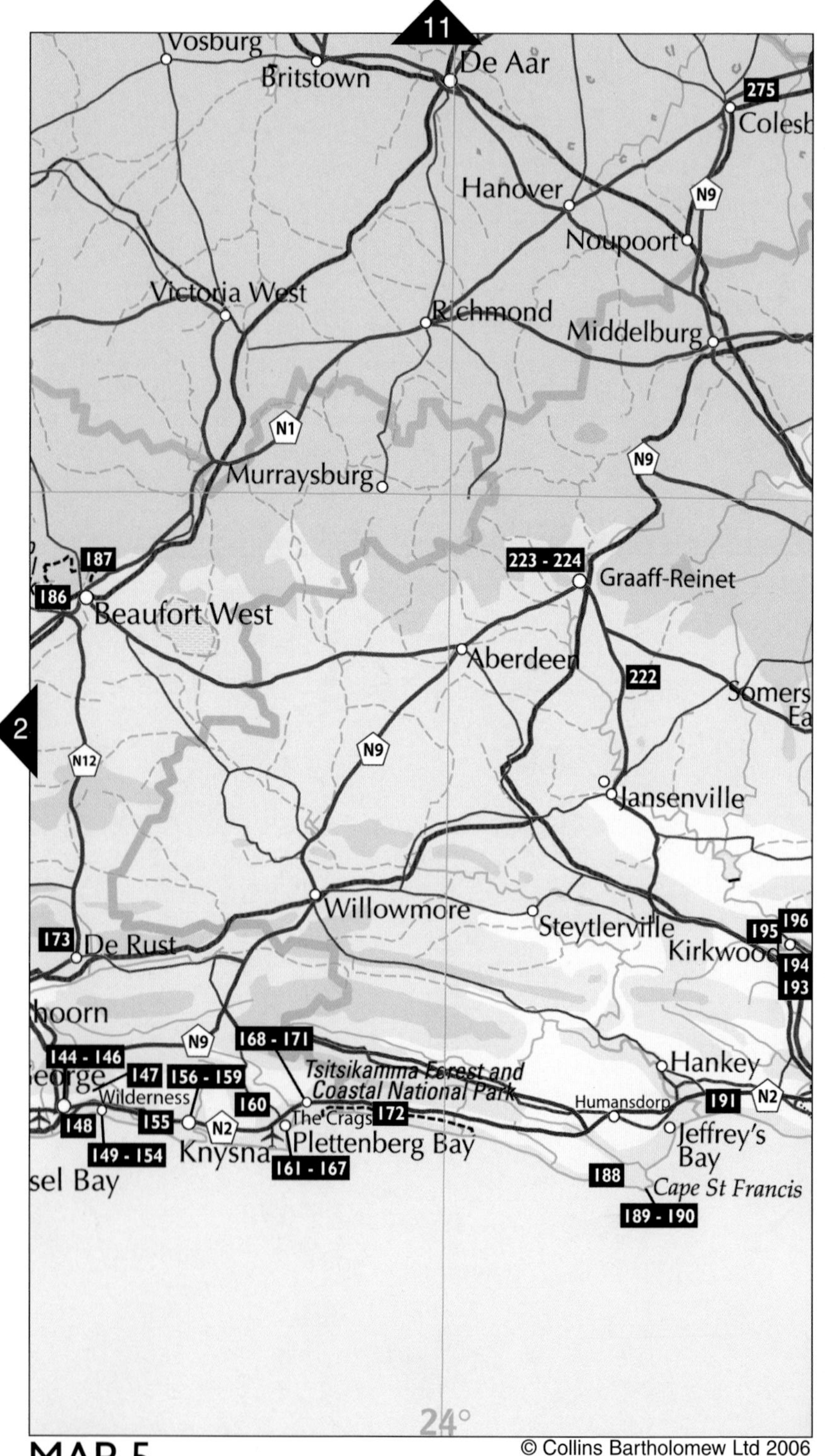
11
Vosburg
Britstown
De Aar
275
Colesb
Hanover
N9
Noupoort
Victoria West
Richmond
Middelburg
N1
Murraysburg
N9
187
186
Beaufort West
223 - 224
Graaff-Reinet
Aberdeen
222
Somers
Ea
2
N12
N9
Jansenville
Willowmore
Steytlerville
173
De Rust
195
196
Kirkwood
194
193
hoorn
N9
168 - 171
144 - 146
eorge
147
156 - 159
Tsitsikamma Forest and
Coastal National Park
Hankey
Wilderness
160
148
155
N2
The Crags
172
Humansdorp
191
N2
Jeffrey's
Bay
149 - 154
Knysna
Plettenberg Bay
161 - 167
sel Bay
188
Cape St Francis
189 - 190
24°

MAP 5

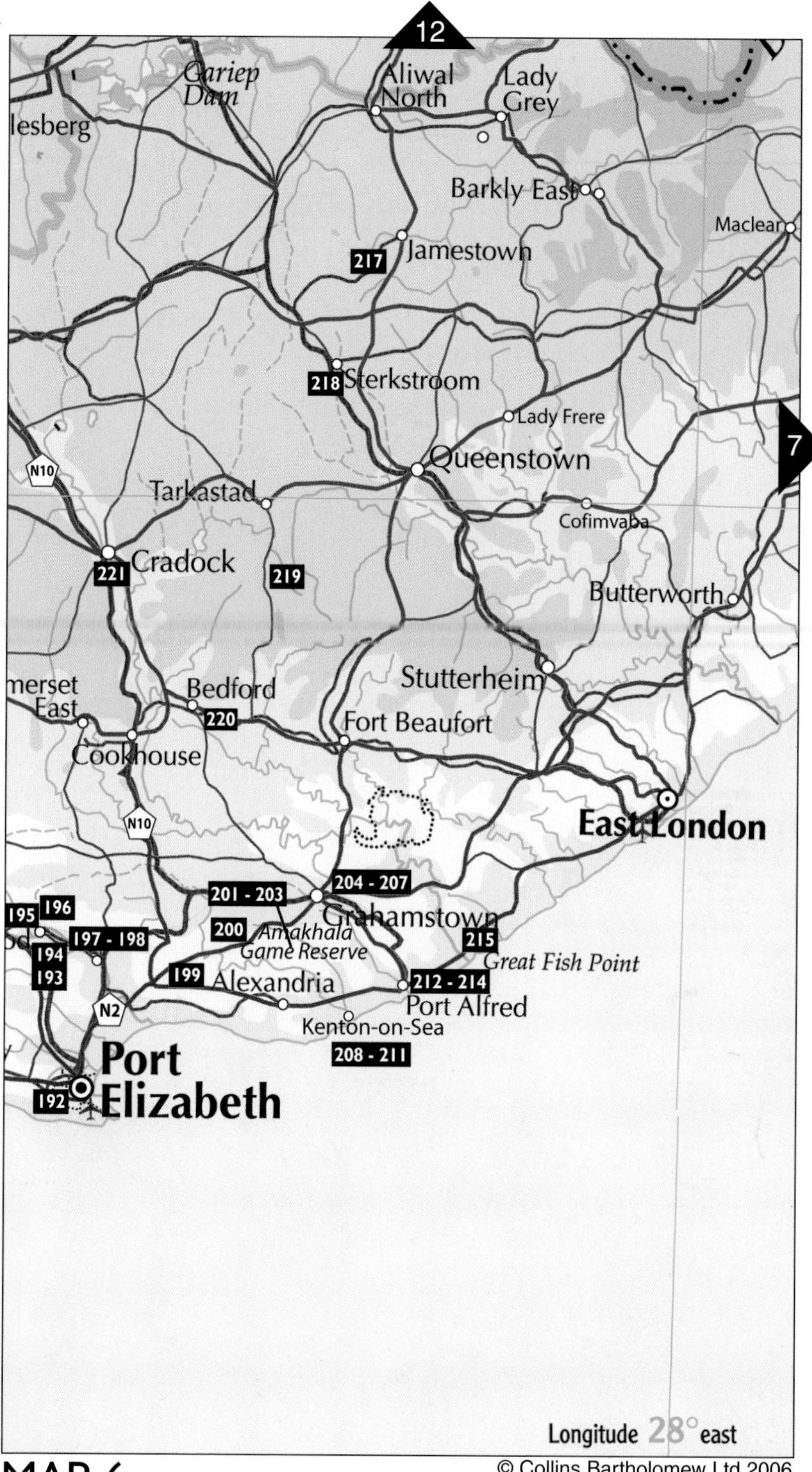
12
Gariep Dam
Aliwal North
Lady Grey
lesberg
Barkly East
Maclear
Jamestown
217
218
Sterkstroom
Lady Frere
7
N10
Queenstown
Tarkastad
Cofimvaba
Cradock
221
219
Butterworth
Stutterheim
merset East
Bedford
220
Fort Beaufort
Cookhouse
N10
East London
201 - 203
204 - 207
195
196
200
Amakhala Game Reserve
Grahamstown
197 - 198
194
215
193
Great Fish Point
199
Alexandria
212 - 214
N2
Port Alfred
Kenton-on-Sea
208 - 211
Port Elizabeth
192
Longitude 28° east

MAP 6

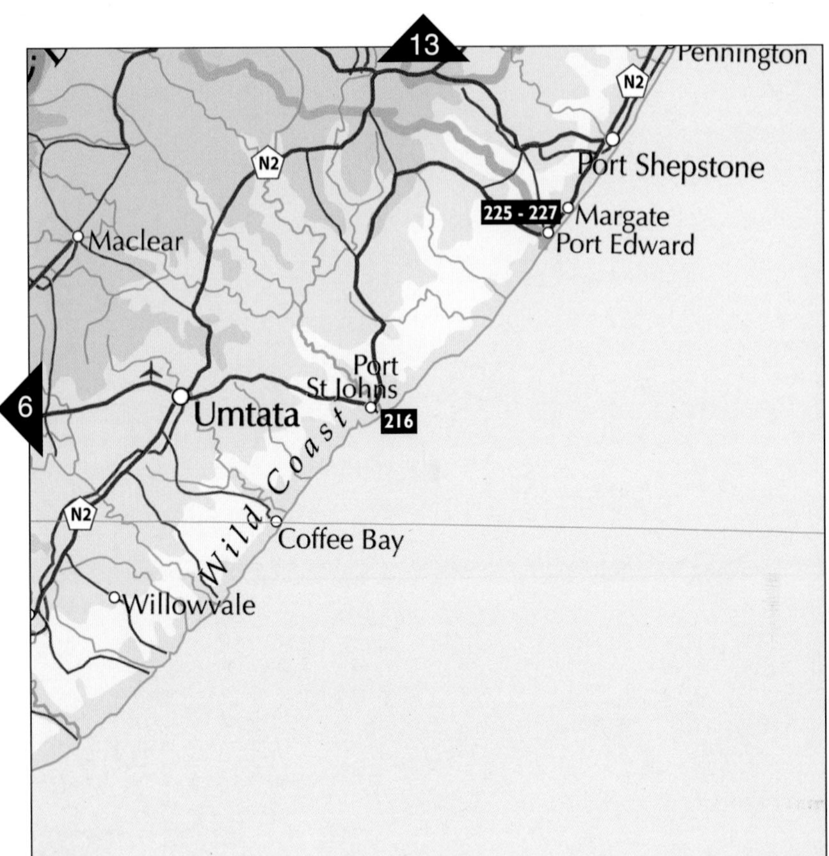
13
Pennington
N2
Port Shepstone
225 - 227
Margate
Port Edward
N2
Maclear
Port
St Johns
6
Umtata
216
Wild Coast
N2
Coffee Bay
Willowvale
INDIAN
OCEAN

MAP 7

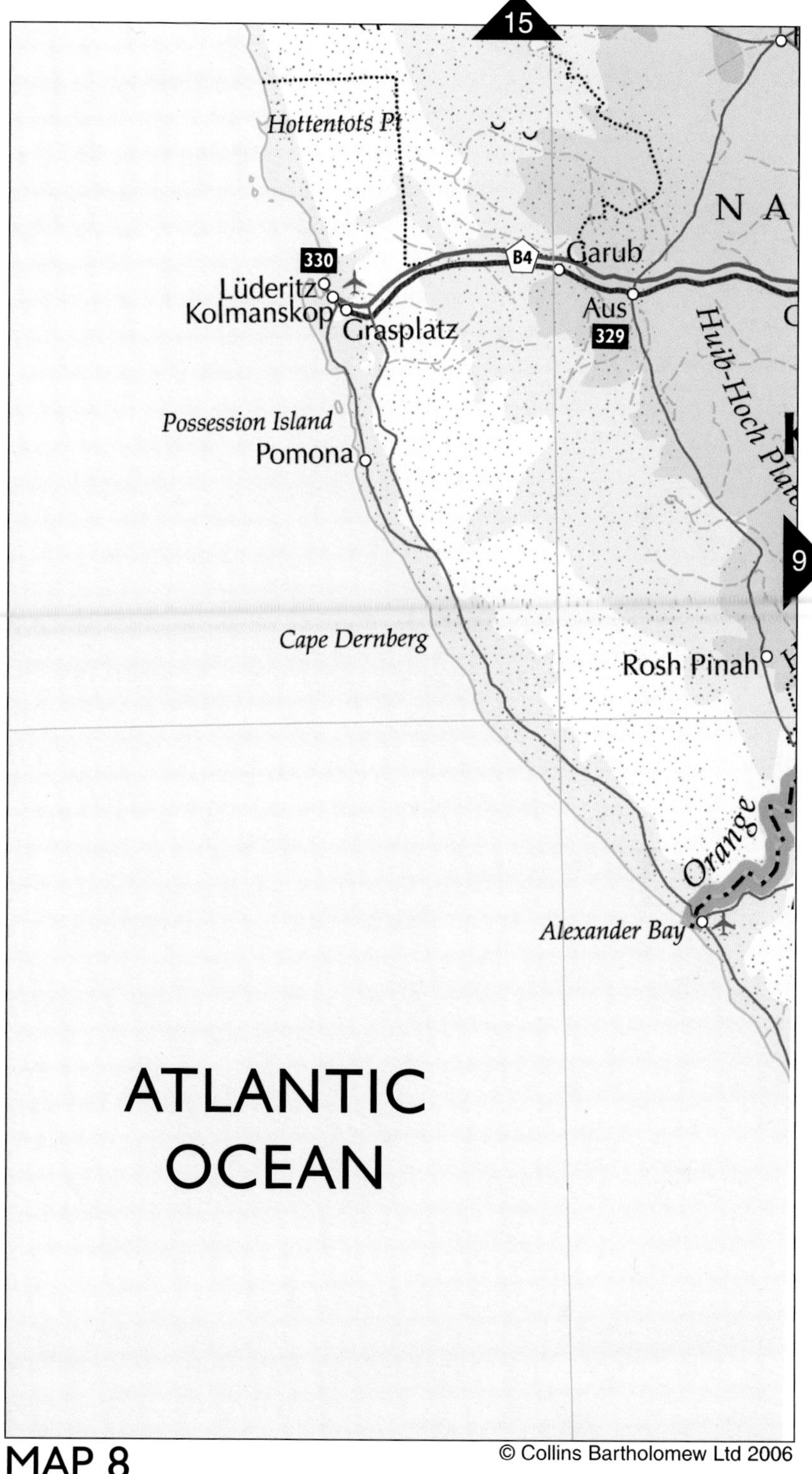
15
Hottentots Pt
N A
330
B4
Garub
Lüderitz
Kolmanskop
Grasplatz
Aus
329
Huib-Hoch Plat
Possession Island
Pomona
9
Cape Dernberg
Rosh Pinah
Orange
Alexander Bay
ATLANTIC
OCEAN

MAP 8

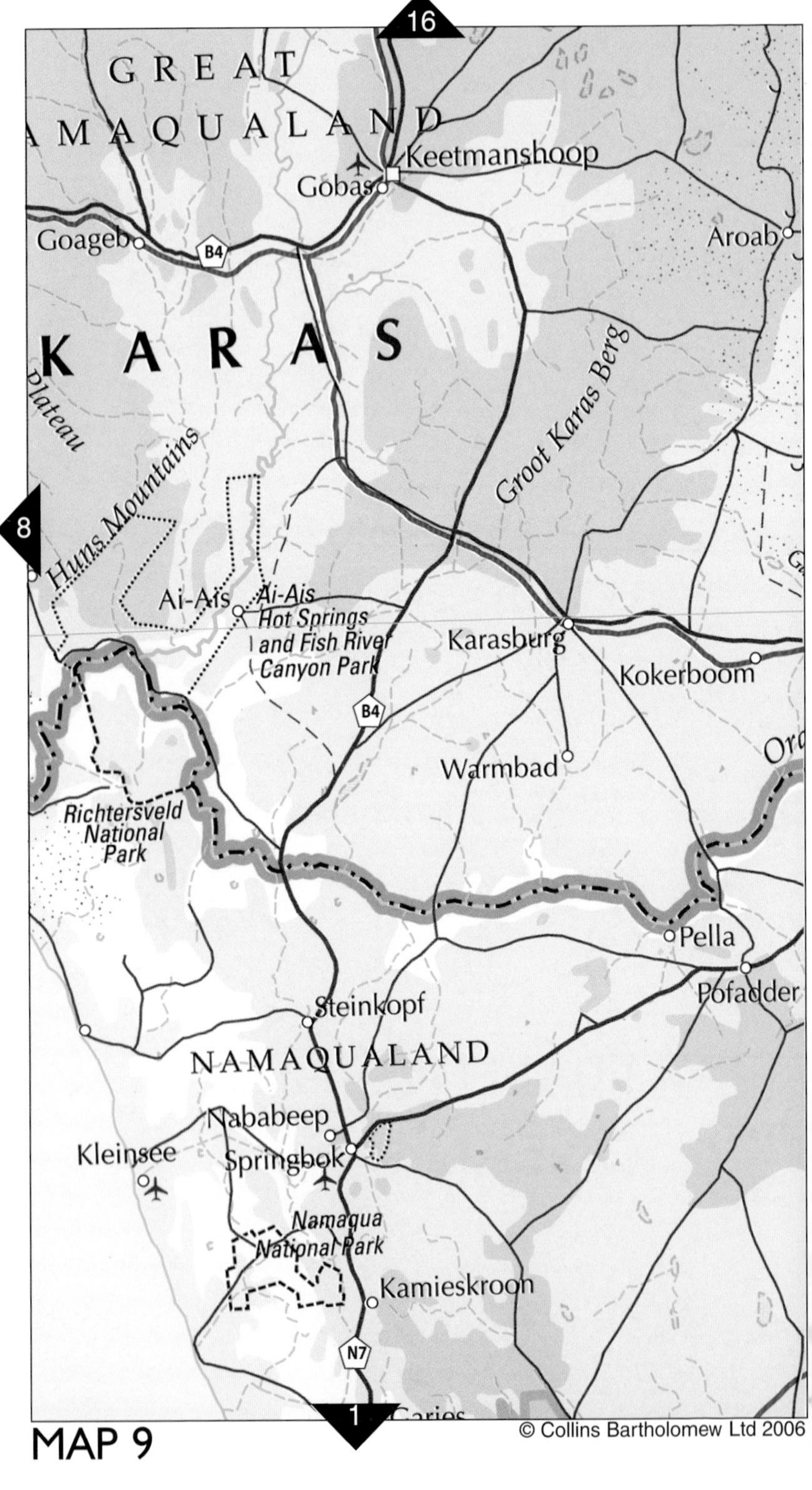
16
GREAT
NAMAQUALAND
Keetmanshoop
Gobas
Goageb
B4
Aroab
KARAS
Plateau
Groot Karas Berg
Huns Mountains
8
Ai-Ais
Ai-Ais
Hot Springs
and Fish River
Canyon Park
Karasburg
Kokerboom
B4
Warmbad
Richtersveld
National
Park
Pella
Pofadder
Steinkopf
NAMAQUALAND
Nababeep
Kleinsee
Springbok
Namaqua
National Park
Kamieskroon
N7
1

MAP 9

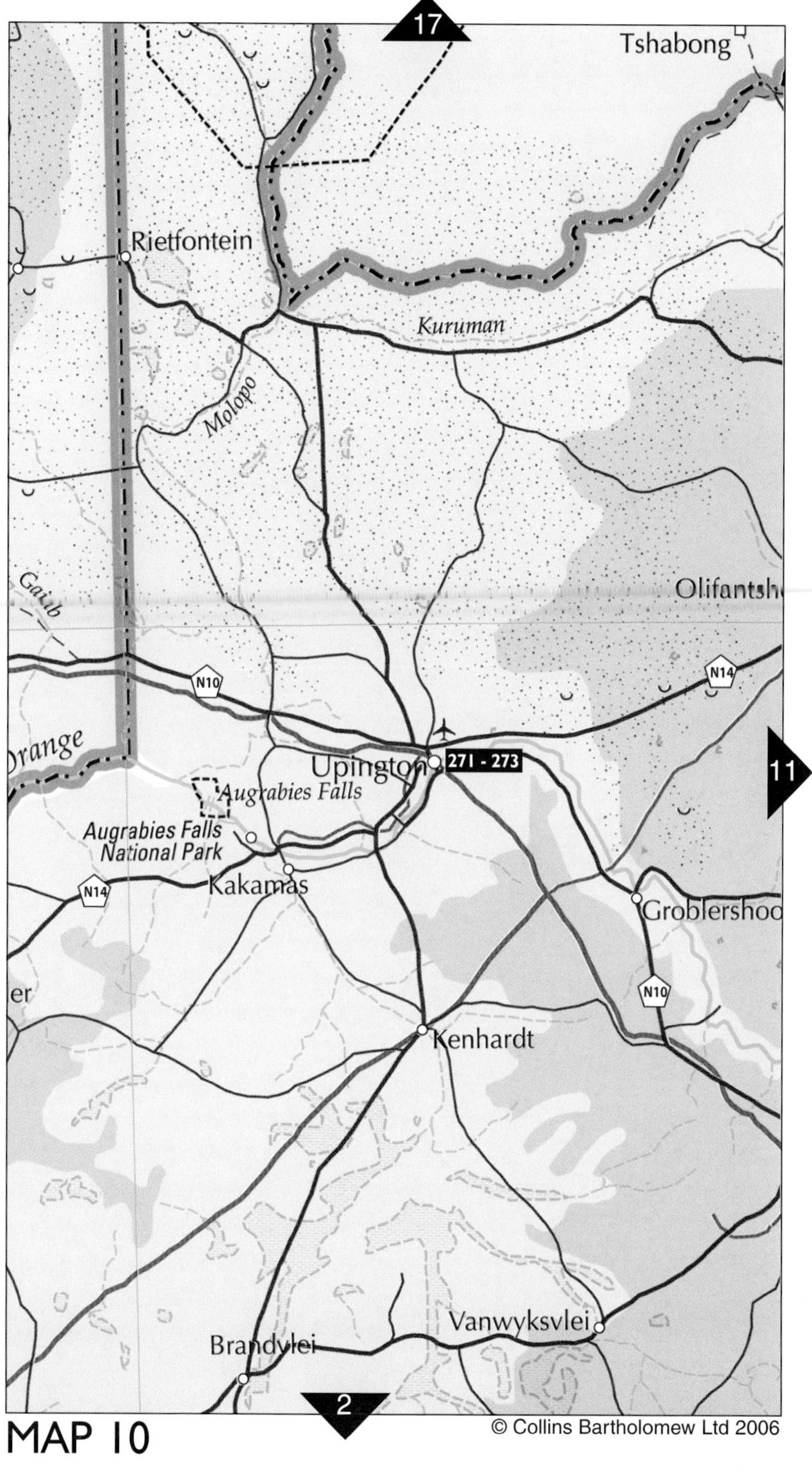
17
Tshabong
Rietfontein
Kuruman
Molopo
Gaib
Olifantsh
N10
N14
Orange
Upington
271 - 273
11
Augrabies Falls
Augrabies Falls National Park
Kakamas
N14
Groblershoo
N10
er
Kenhardt
Vanwyksvlei
Brandvlei
2

MAP 10

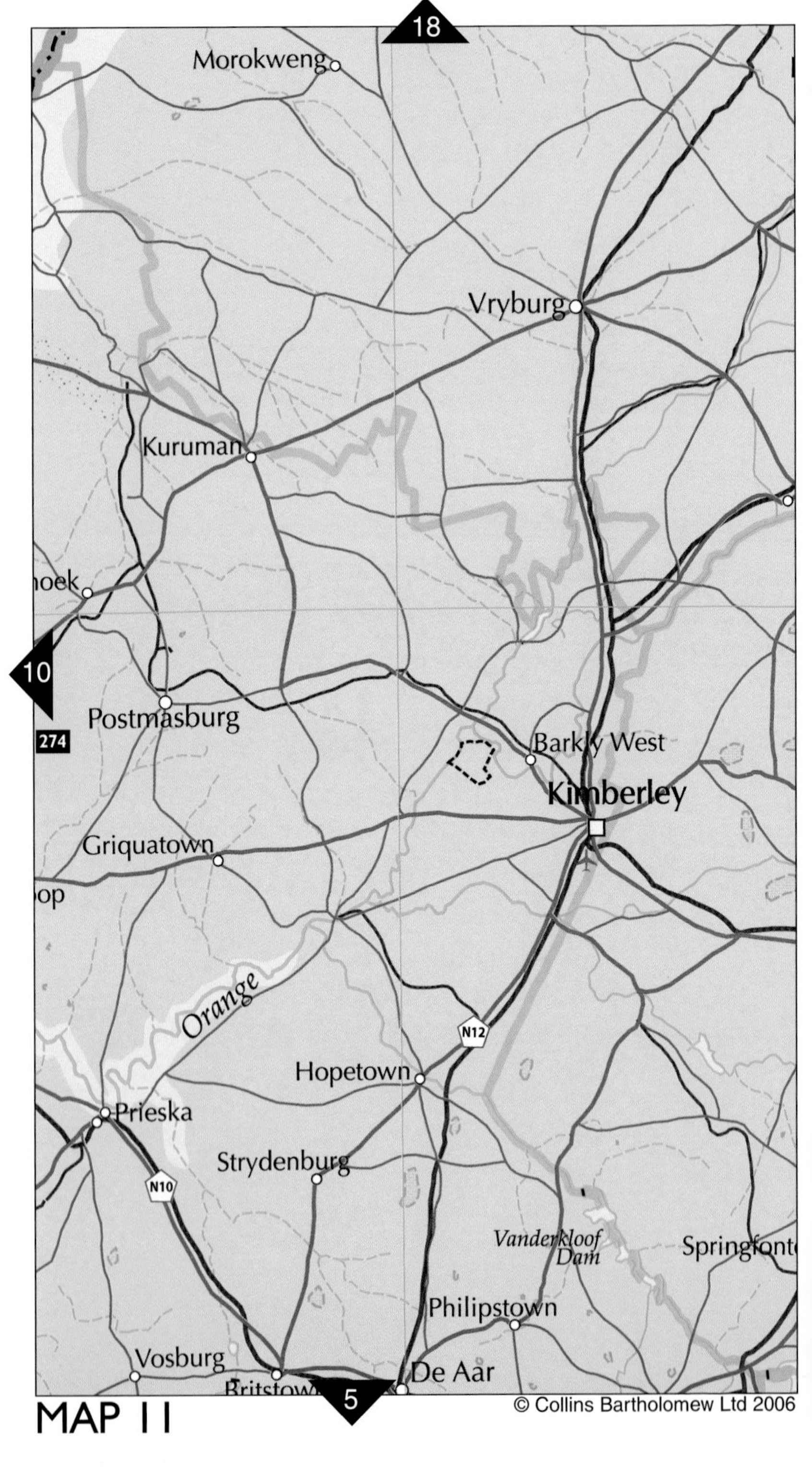
18
Morokweng
Vryburg
Kuruman
hoek
10
274
Postmasburg
Barkly West
Kimberley
Griquatown
op
Orange
N12
Hopetown
Prieska
Strydenburg
N10
Vanderkloof Dam
Springfont
Philipstown
Vosburg
De Aar
Britstown
5

MAP 11

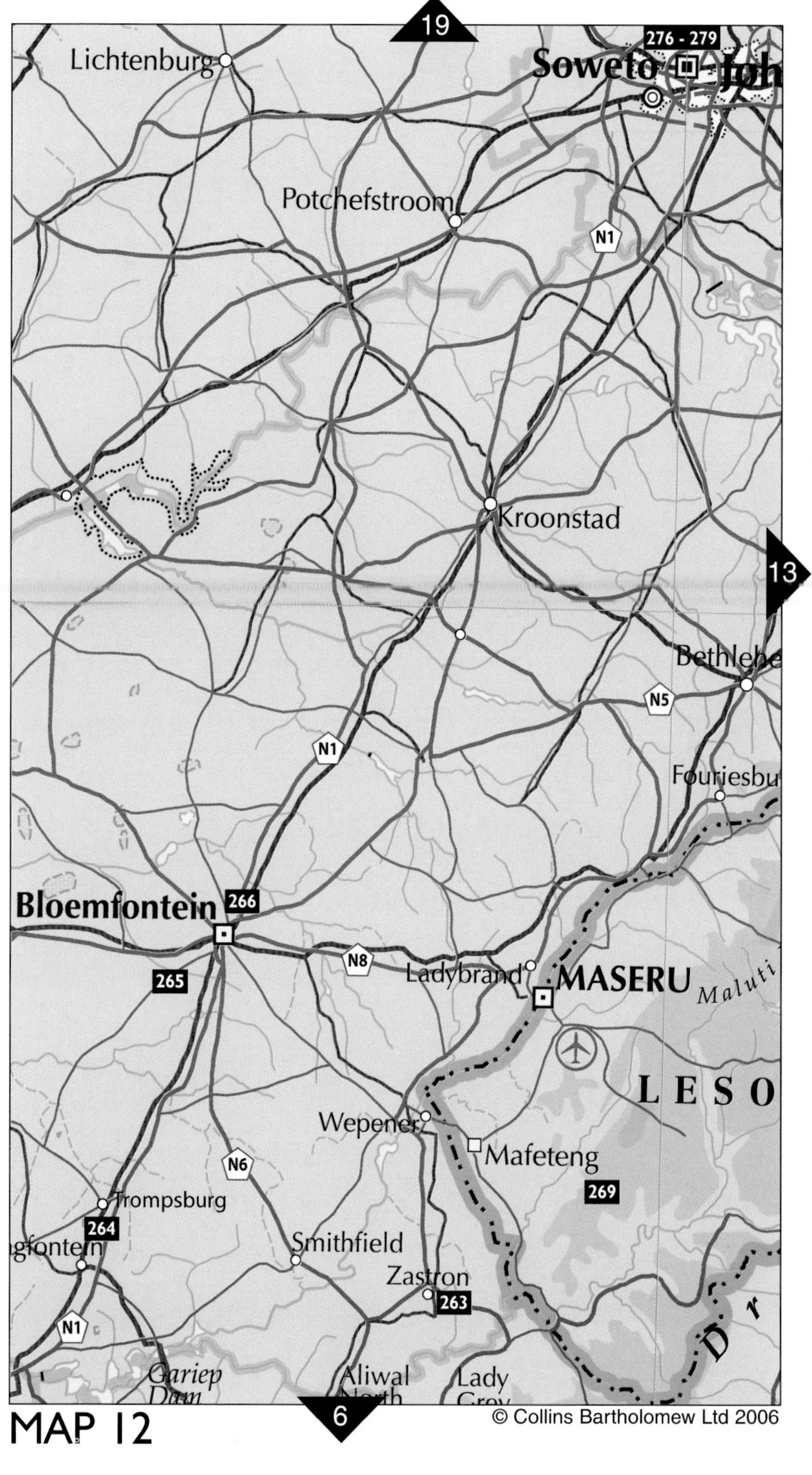

19
276 - 279
Lichtenburg
Soweto
Potchefstroom
N1
Kroonstad
13
Bethlehe
N5
N1
Fouriesbu
Bloemfontein
266
N8
Ladybrand
MASERU
Maluti
265
LESO
Wepener
Mafeteng
269
N6
Trompsburg
264
gfontein
Smithfield
Zastron
263
N1
Gariep Dam
Aliwal North
Lady Grey
6

MAP 12

20
276 - 279
Johannesburg
Ermelo
Amsterd
Standerton
Piet Ret
N11
284
Wakkerstroom
N3
Newcastle
Vryheid
Bethlehem
N5
Golden Gate Highlands National Park
268
Harrismith
Dundee
249
248
247
Elandslaagte
Isandlwana
250
Van Reenen
Ladysmith
Clarens
267
Fouriesburg
251
Tugela Falls
253
Bergville
Winterton
Tugela Ferry
255
12
252
Champagne Castle
254
Estcourt
Greytown
N3
256
Mooirivier
Maluti Mountains
Natal
257
Rosetta
Drakensberg Park
258
260
Howick
259
Pietermaritzburg
LESOTHO
Underberg
228
229
262
Durban
261
Ixopo
Amanzimtoti
N2
Scottburgh
Pennington
Drakensberg
7

MAP 13

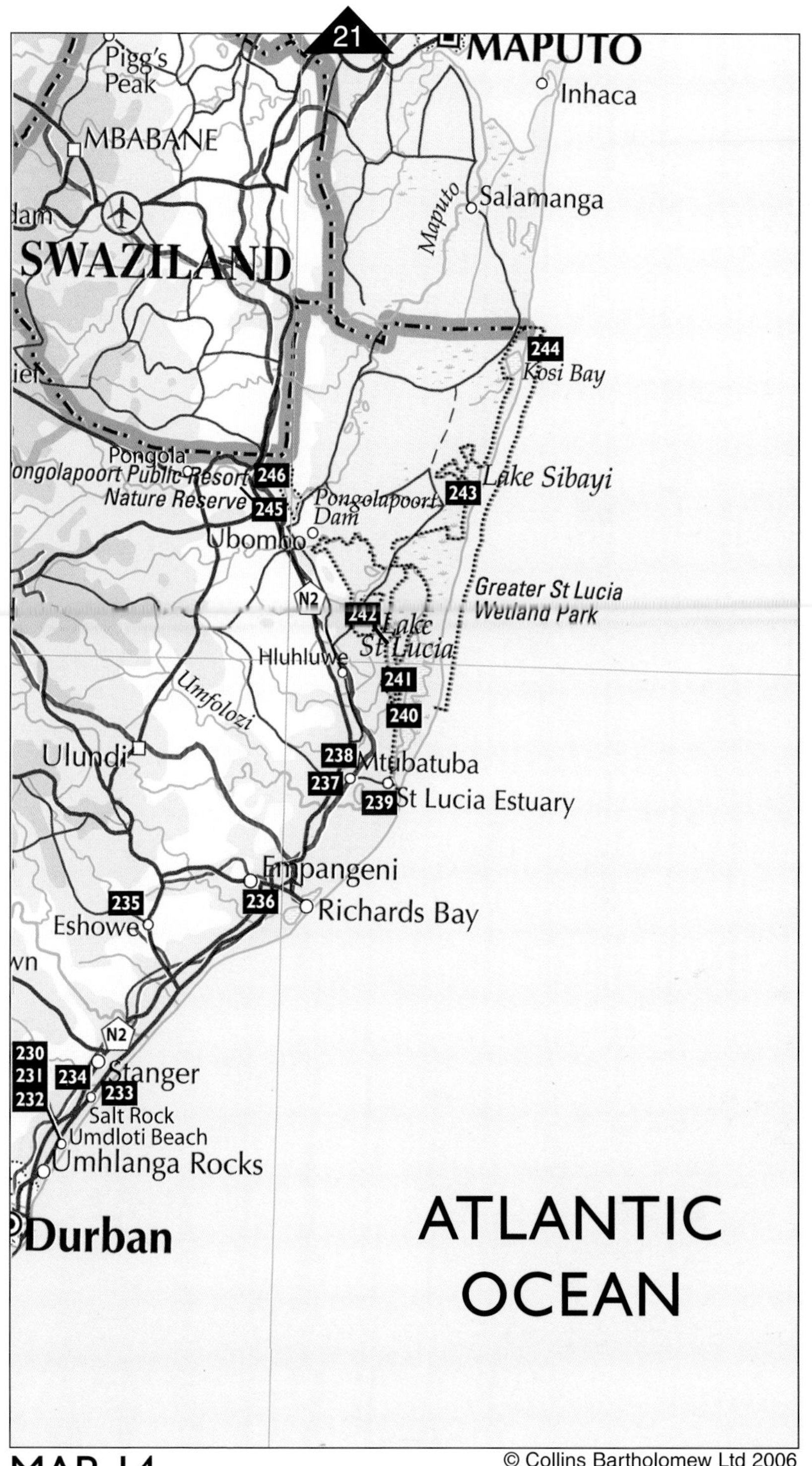
21
MAPUTO
Pigg's Peak
Inhaca
MBABANE
Salamanga
Maputo
SWAZILAND
244
Kosi Bay
Pongola
Pongolapoort Public Resort Nature Reserve
246
245
Pongolapoort Dam
243
Lake Sibayi
Ubombo
Greater St Lucia Wetland Park
N2
242
Lake St Lucia
Hluhluwe
241
Umfolozi
240
Ulundi
238
Mtubatuba
237
239
St Lucia Estuary
Empangeni
235
236
Richards Bay
Eshowe
N2
230
231
232
234
Stanger
233
Salt Rock
Umdloti Beach
Umhlanga Rocks
Durban
ATLANTIC OCEAN

MAP 14

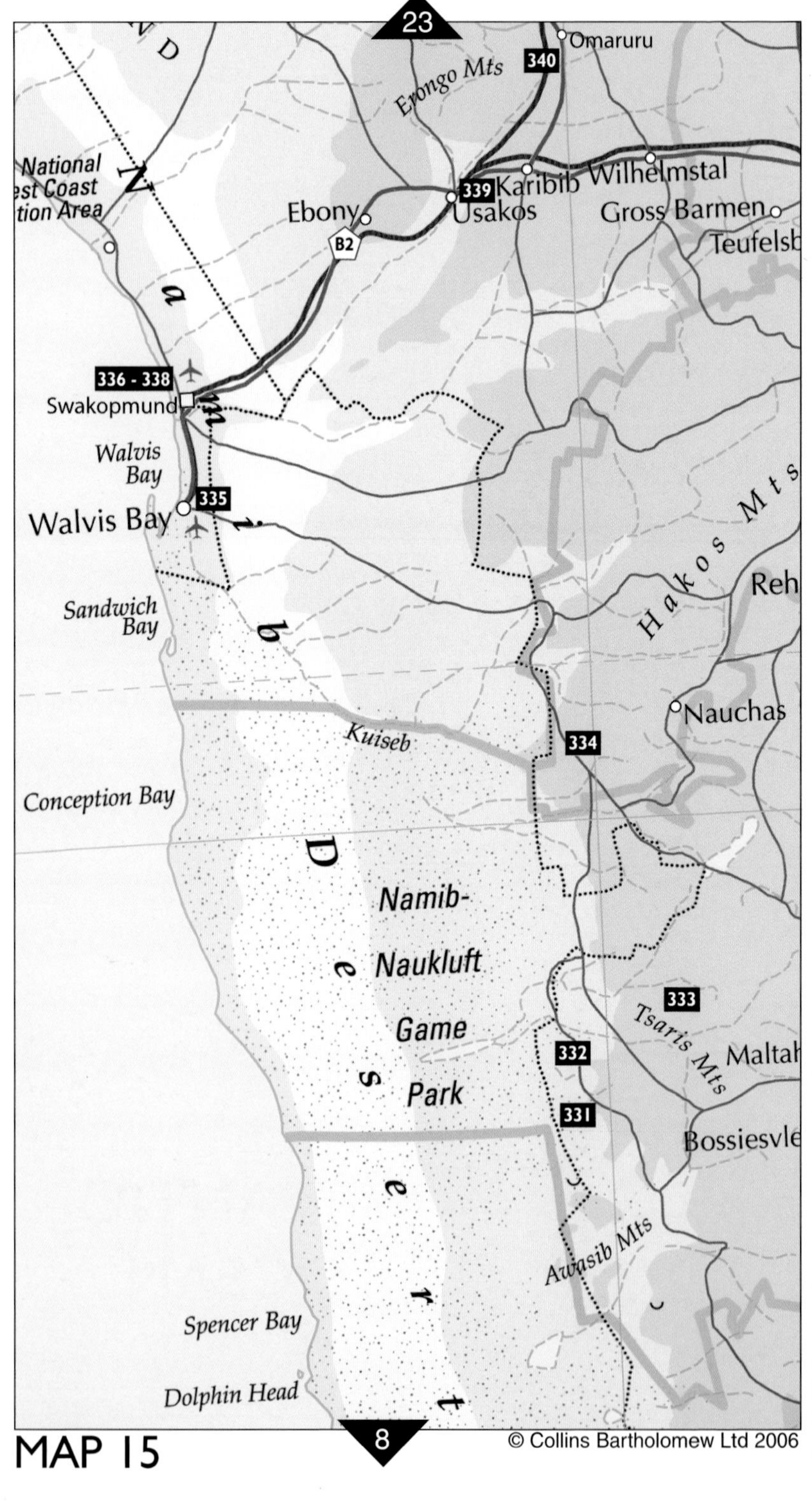

23
Omaruru
340
Erongo Mts
National
est Coast
tion Area
Karibib
Wilhelmstal
339
Usakos
Ebony
Gross Barmen
B2
Teufelsb
N
a
m
i
b
D
e
s
e
r
t
336 - 338
Swakopmund
Walvis
Bay
335
Walvis Bay
Hakos Mts
Reh
Sandwich
Bay
Nauchas
Kuiseb
334
Conception Bay
Namib-
Naukluft
Game
Park
333
Tsaris Mts
Maltah
332
331
Bossiesvle
Awasib Mts
Spencer Bay
Dolphin Head
8

MAP 15

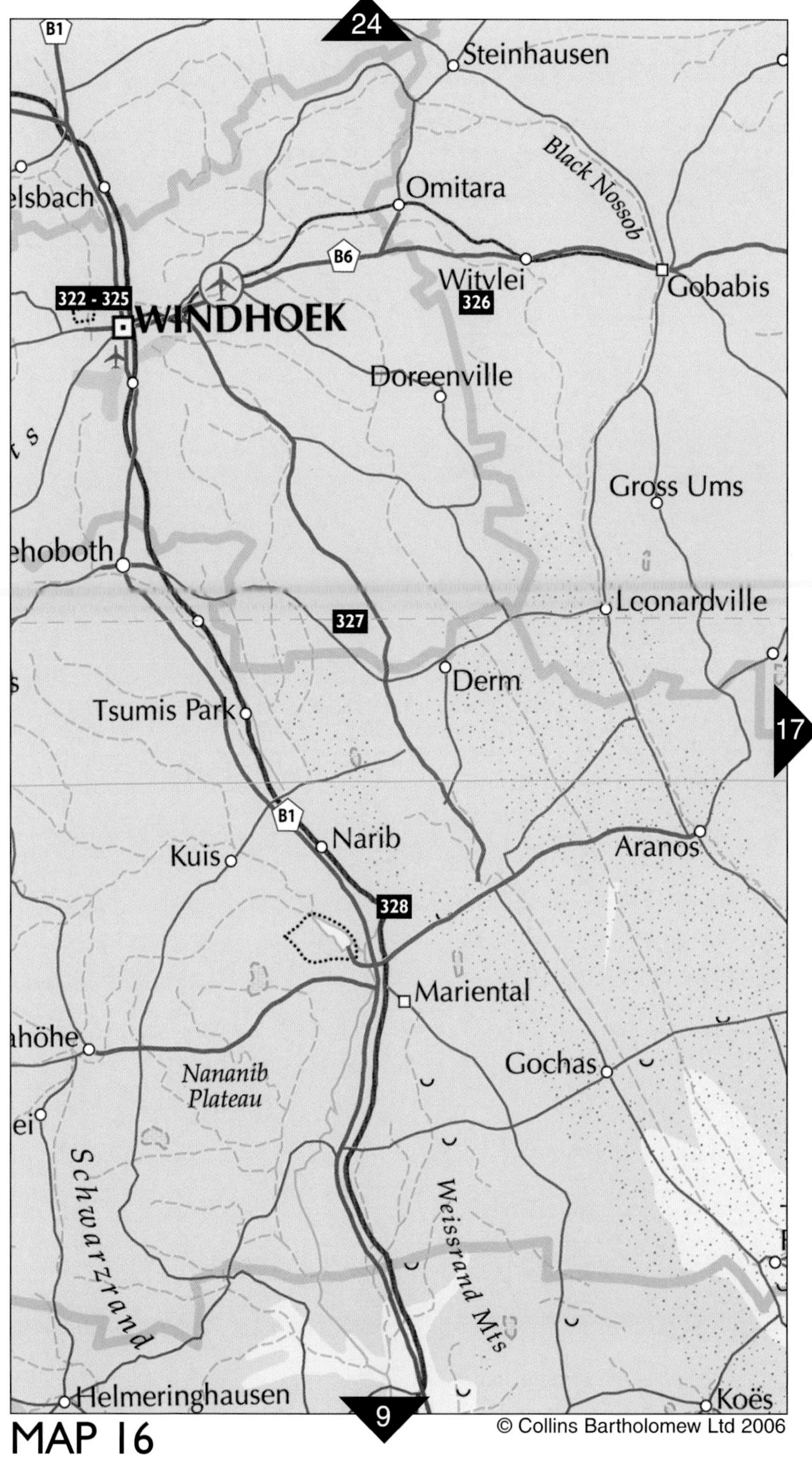

24
B1
Steinhausen
Black Nossob
Omitara
elsbach
B6
Witvlei
Gobabis
322 - 325
326
WINDHOEK
Doreenville
Gross Ums
ehoboth
Leonardville
327
Derm
17
Tsumis Park
B1
Narib
Kuis
Aranos
328
Mariental
ahöhe
Gochas
Nananib
Plateau
ei
Schwarzrand
Weissrand Mts
Helmeringhausen
Koës
9

MAP 16

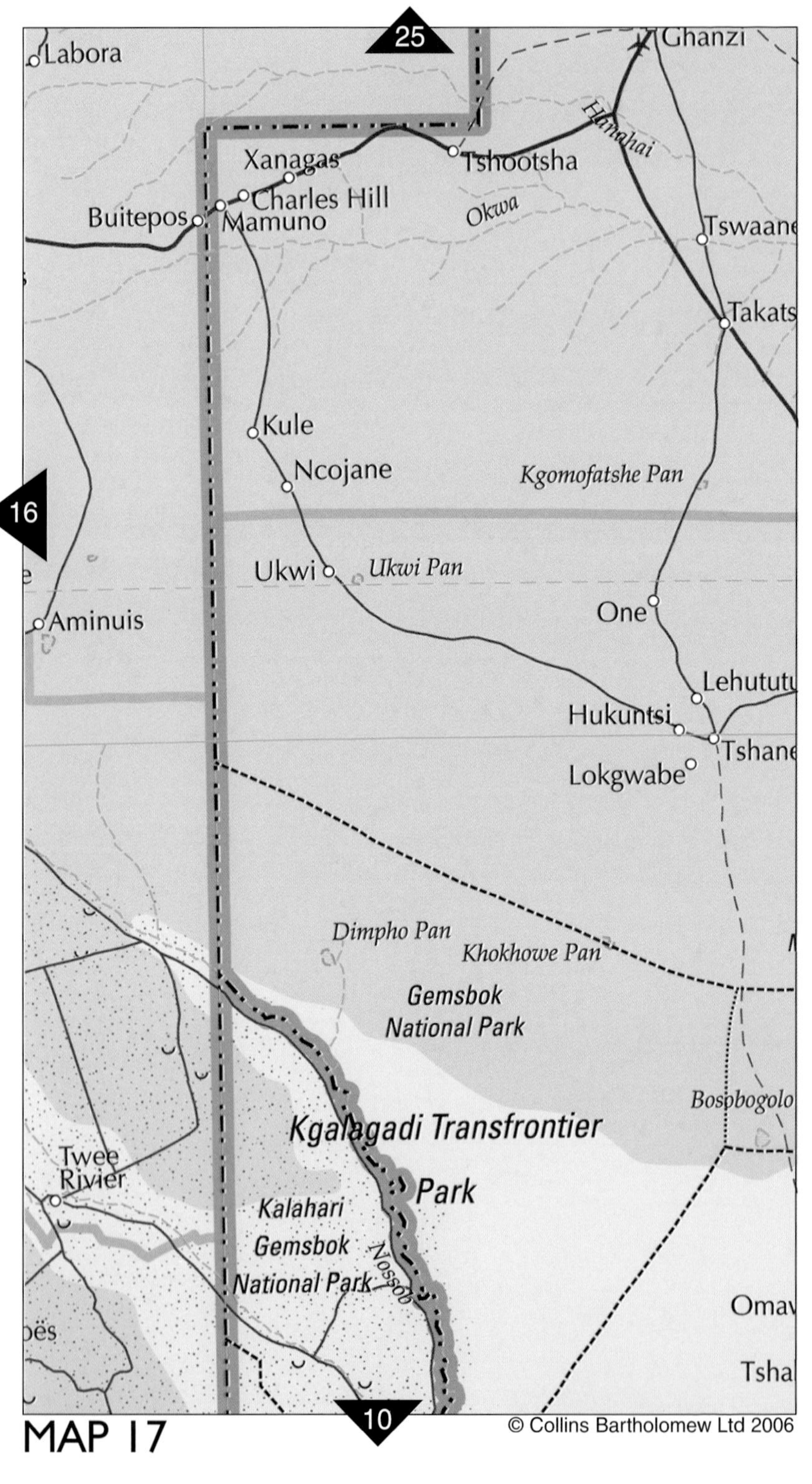
25
Labora
Ghanzi
Hanahai
Xanagas
Tshootsha
Charles Hill
Buitepos
Mamuno
Okwa
Tswaane
Takats
Kule
Ncojane
Kgomofatshe Pan
16
Ukwi
Ukwi Pan
One
Aminuis
Lehututu
Hukuntsi
Tshane
Lokgwabe
Dimpho Pan
Khokhowe Pan
Gemsbok
National Park
Bosobogolo
Kgalagadi Transfrontier
Park
Twee
Rivier
Kalahari
Gemsbok
National Park
Nossob
Omav
Tsha
10

MAP 17

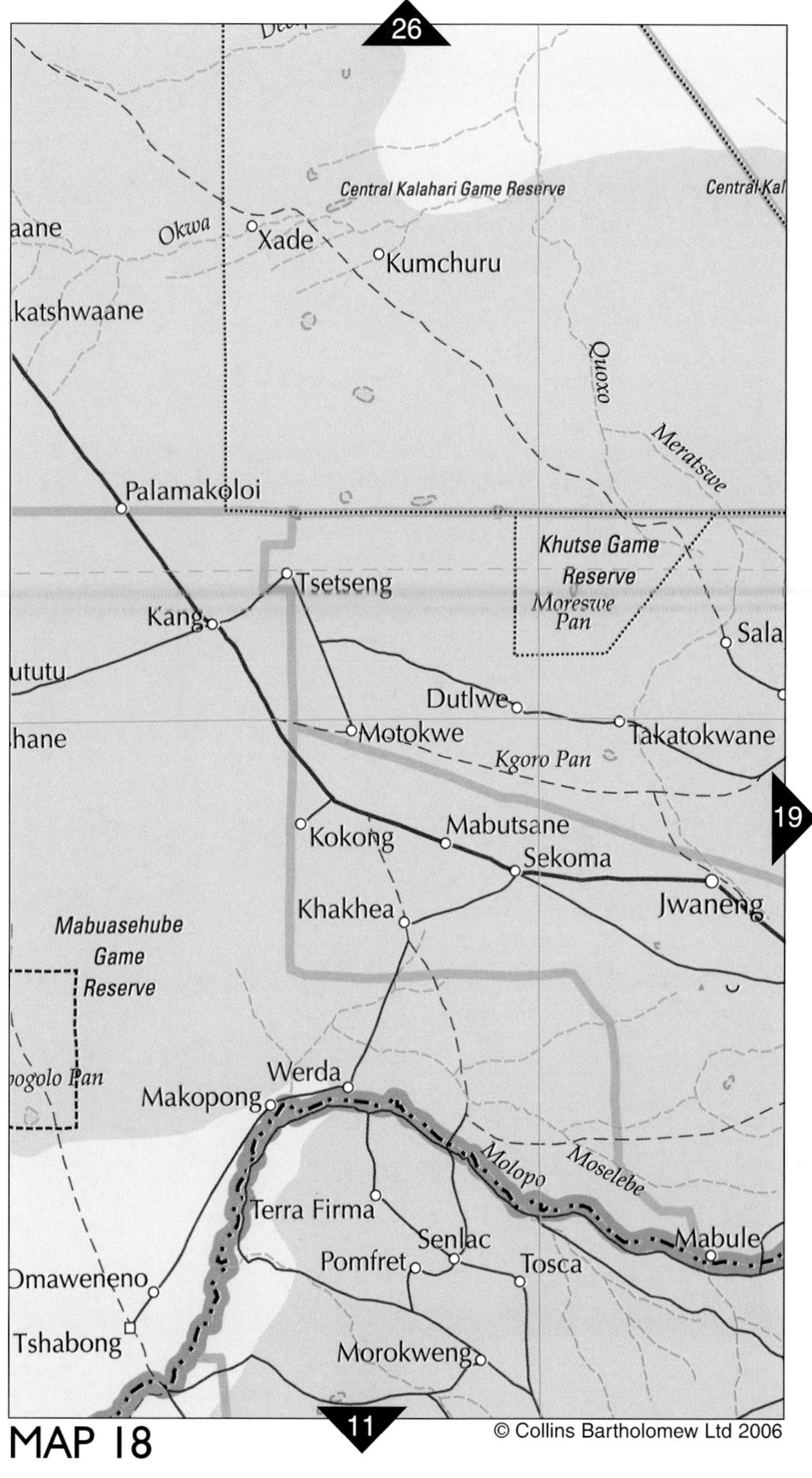
26
Central Kalahari Game Reserve
Central Kal
aane
Okwa
Xade
Kumchuru
katshwaane
Quoxo
Meratswe
Palamakoloi
Khutse Game Reserve
Moreswe Pan
Tsetseng
Kang
Sala
tutu
Dutlwe
hane
Motokwe
Takatokwane
Kgoro Pan
19
Kokong
Mabutsane
Sekoma
Jwaneng
Khakhea
Mabuasehube Game Reserve
pogolo Pan
Werda
Makopong
Molopo
Moselebe
Terra Firma
Mabule
Senlac
Pomfret
Tosca
Omaweneno
Tshabong
Morokweng
11

MAP 18

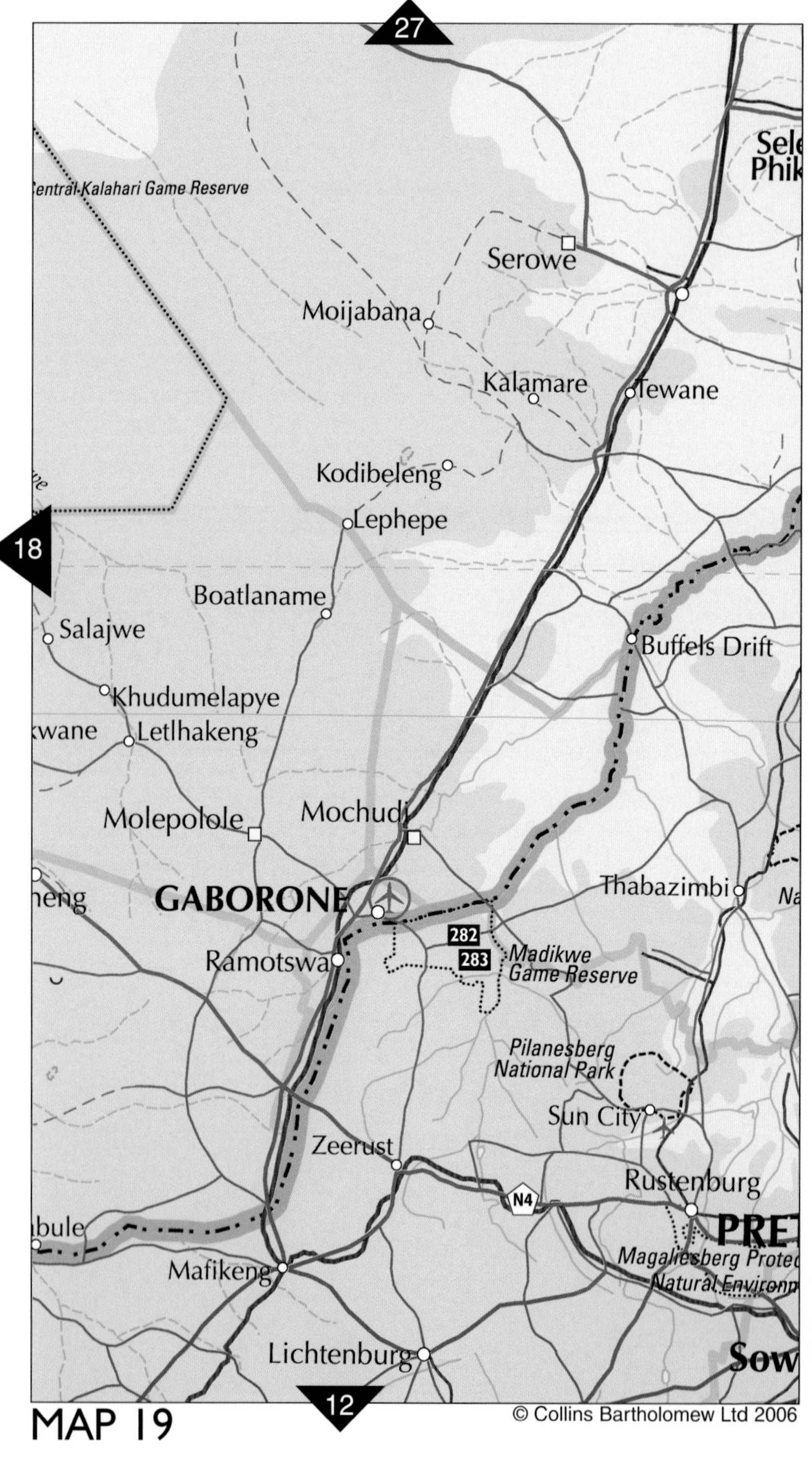
27
Serowe
Moijabana
Kalamare
Tewane
Kodibeleng
Lephepe
18
Boatlaname
Salajwe
Buffels Drift
Khudumelapye
Letlhakeng
Molepolole
Mochudi
GABORONE
Thabazimbi
Ramotswa
282
283
Madikwe Game Reserve
Pilanesberg National Park
Sun City
Zeerust
Rustenburg
N4
Mafikeng
Lichtenburg
12
Central Kalahari Game Reserve

MAP 19

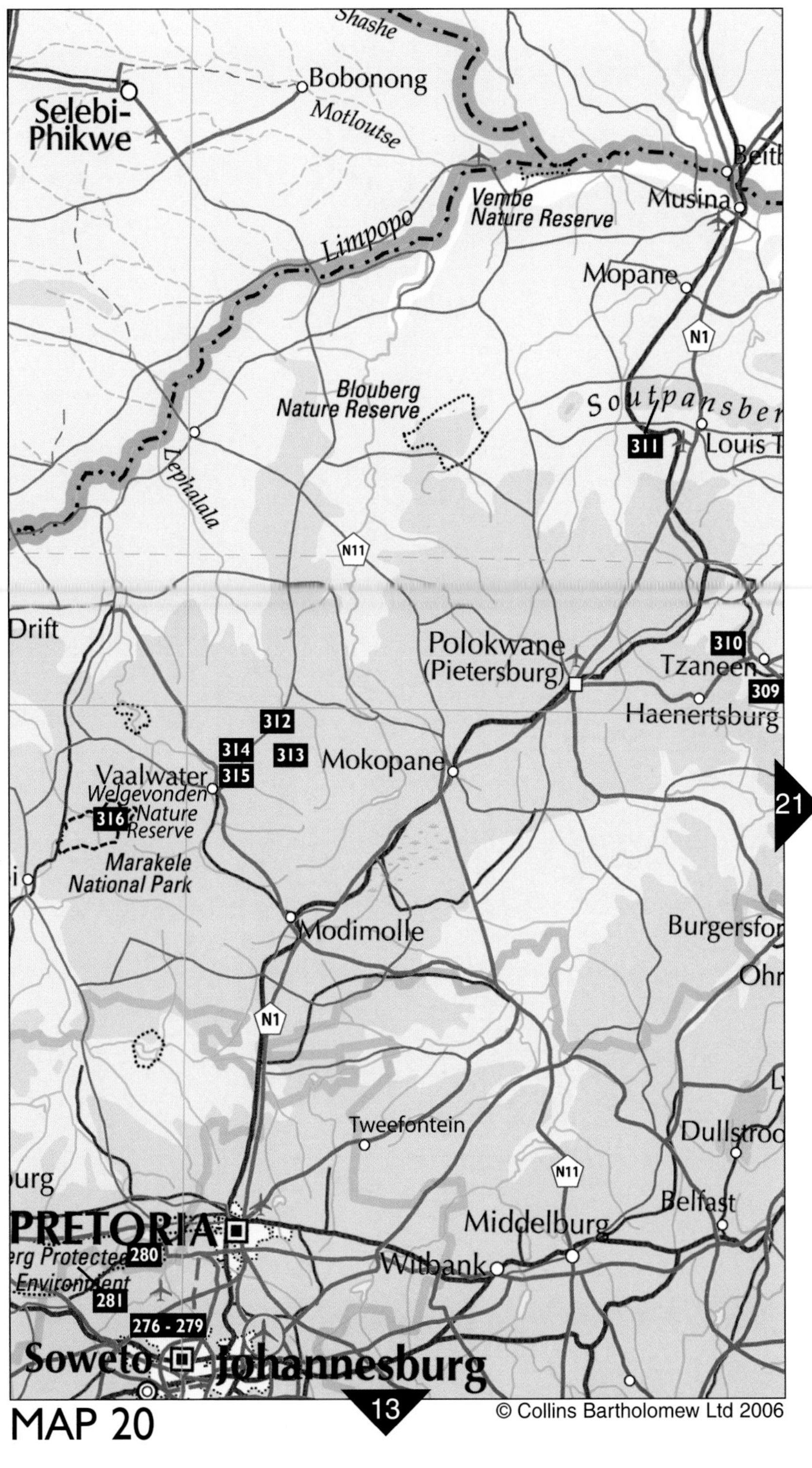
Shashe
Bobonong
Selebi-Phikwe
Motloutse
Beitb
Musina
Vembe Nature Reserve
Limpopo
Mopane
N1
Blouberg Nature Reserve
Soutpansber
Louis T
311
Lephalala
N11
Drift
Polokwane (Pietersburg)
310
Tzaneen
309
Haenertsburg
312
314
313
Mokopane
315
Vaalwater
Welgevonden Nature Reserve
316
21
Marakele National Park
Modimolle
Burgersfor
Ohr
N1
Tweefontein
Dullstroo
urg
N11
Belfast
PRETORIA
Middelburg
280
erg Protected Environment
Witbank
281
276 - 279
Soweto
Johannesburg
13

MAP 20

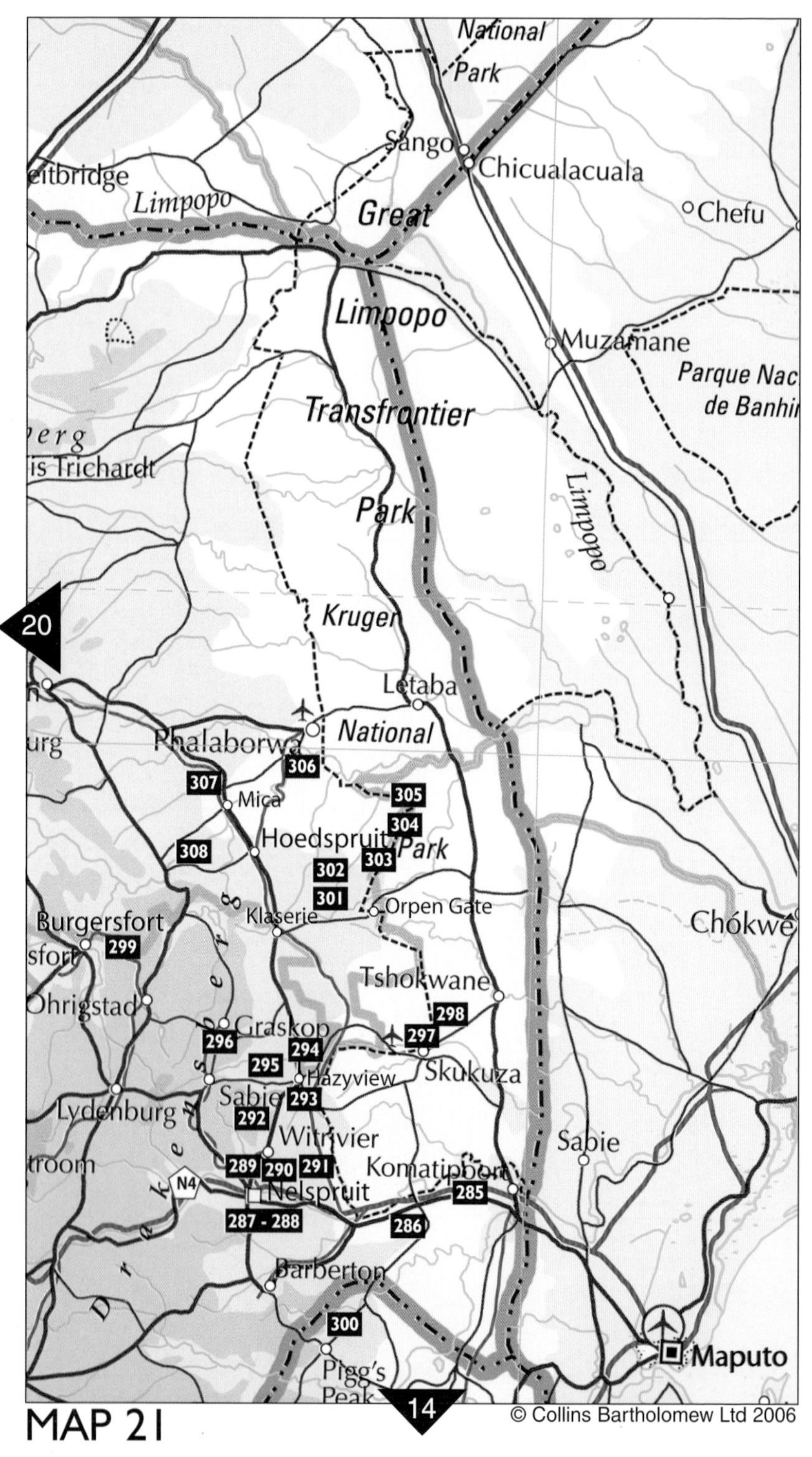
National
Park
Sango
Chicualacuala
eitbridge
Limpopo
Great
Chefu
Limpopo
Muzamane
Parque Nac
de Banhi
Transfrontier
erg
is Trichardt
Park
Limpopo
20
Kruger
Letaba
National
Phalaborwa
306
307
Mica
305
304
Hoedspruit
Park
308
303
302
301
Orpen Gate
Klaserie
Burgersfort
299
Chókwè
Tshokwane
Ohrigstad
298
Graskop
297
296
294
295
Hazyview
Skukuza
Sabie
Lydenburg
293
292
Witrivier
Sabie
289
290
291
Komatipoort
N4
Nelspruit
285
287 - 288
286
Barberton
300
Maputo
Pigg's
Peak
14

MAP 21

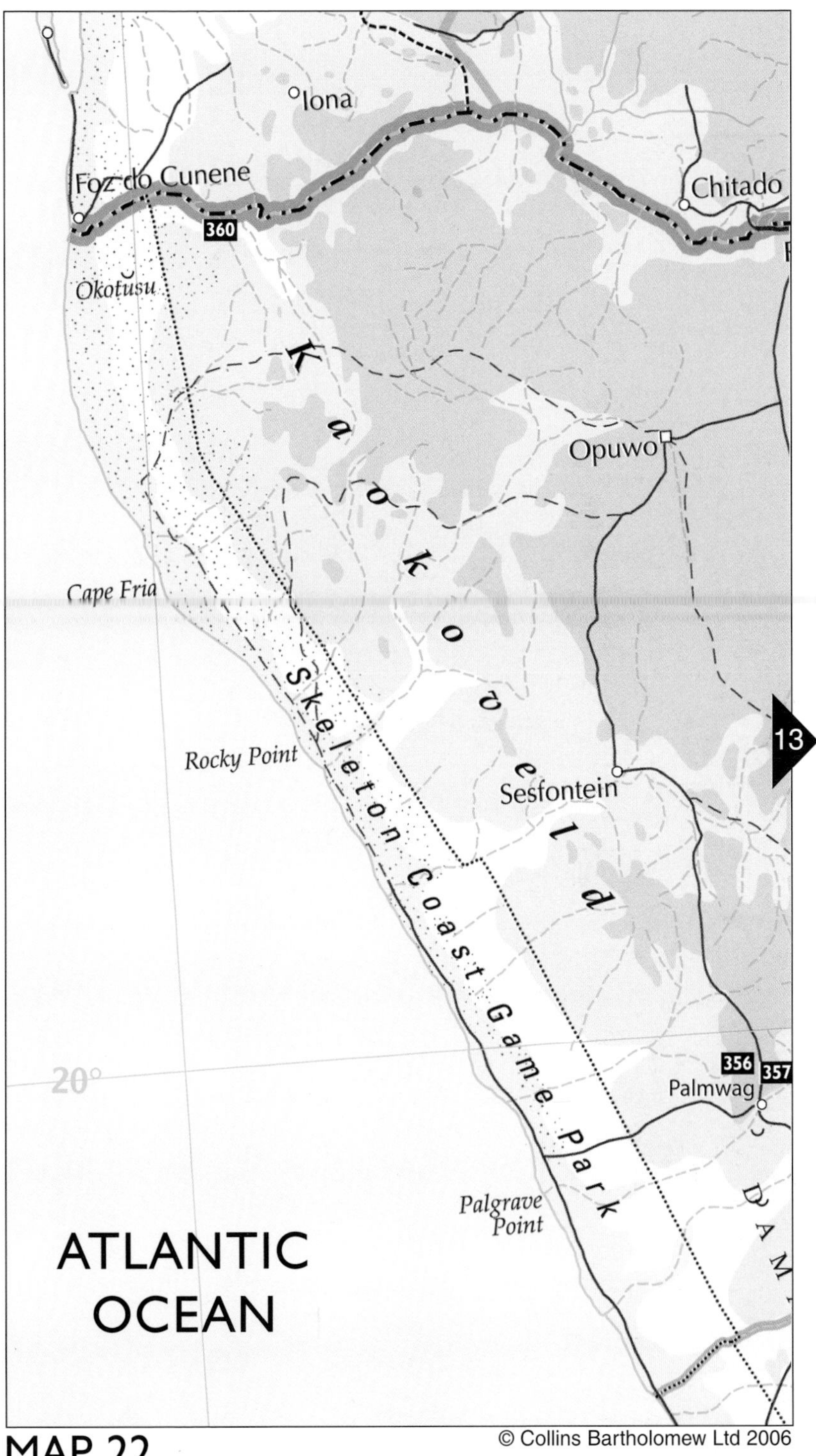

Iona
Foz do Cunene
360
Chitado
Okotusu
Kaokoveld
Opuwo
Cape Fria
Skeleton Coast Game Park
13
Rocky Point
Sesfontein
20°
356
357
Palmwag
Palgrave Point
ATLANTIC OCEAN

MAP 22

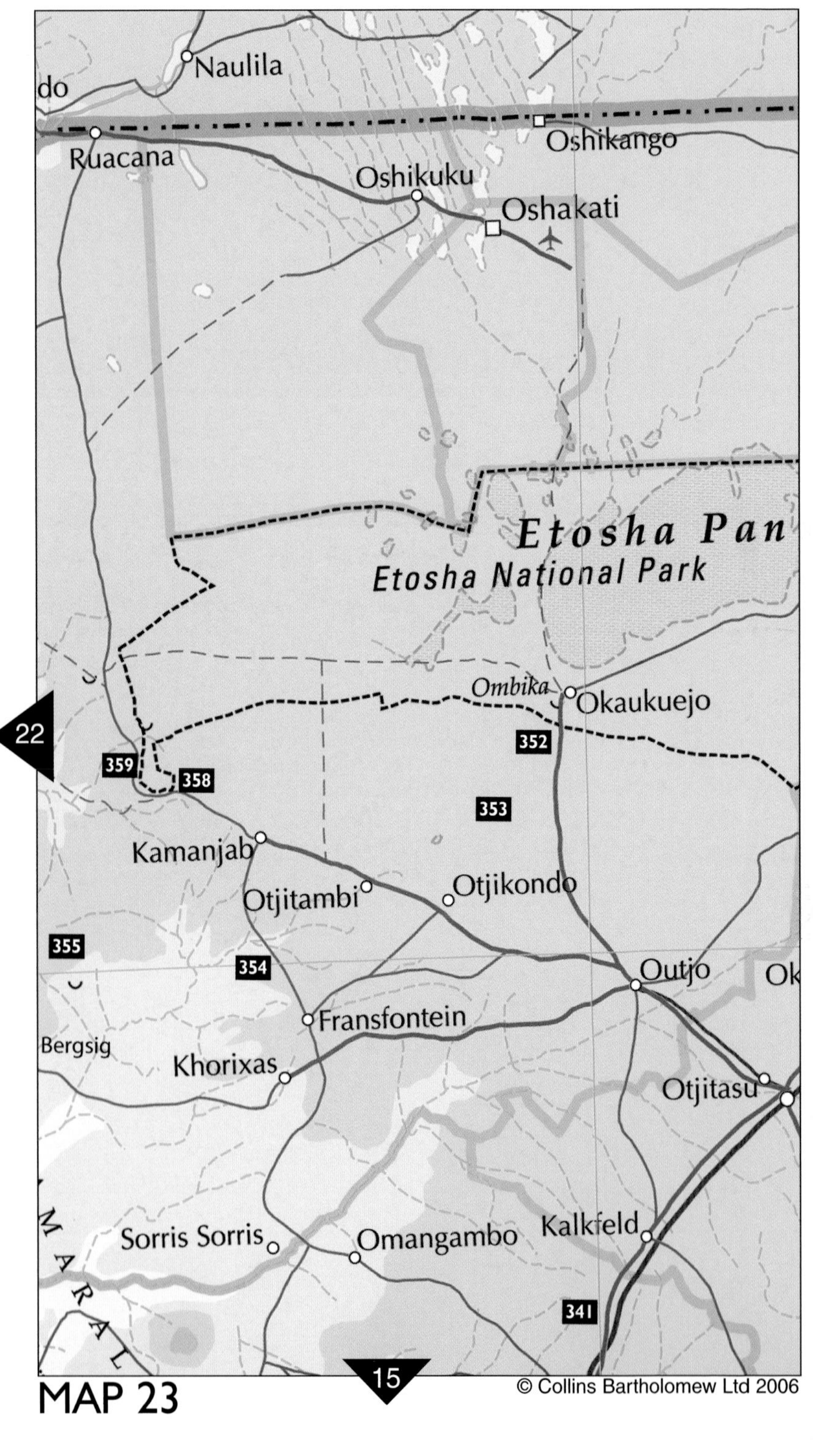
Naulila
do
Ruacana
Oshikango
Oshikuku
Oshakati
Etosha Pan
Etosha National Park
Ombika
Okaukuejo
22
352
359
358
353
Kamanjab
Otjitambi
Otjikondo
355
354
Outjo
Ok
Fransfontein
Bergsig
Khorixas
Otjitasu
Sorris Sorris
Omangambo
Kalkfeld
341
15

MAP 23

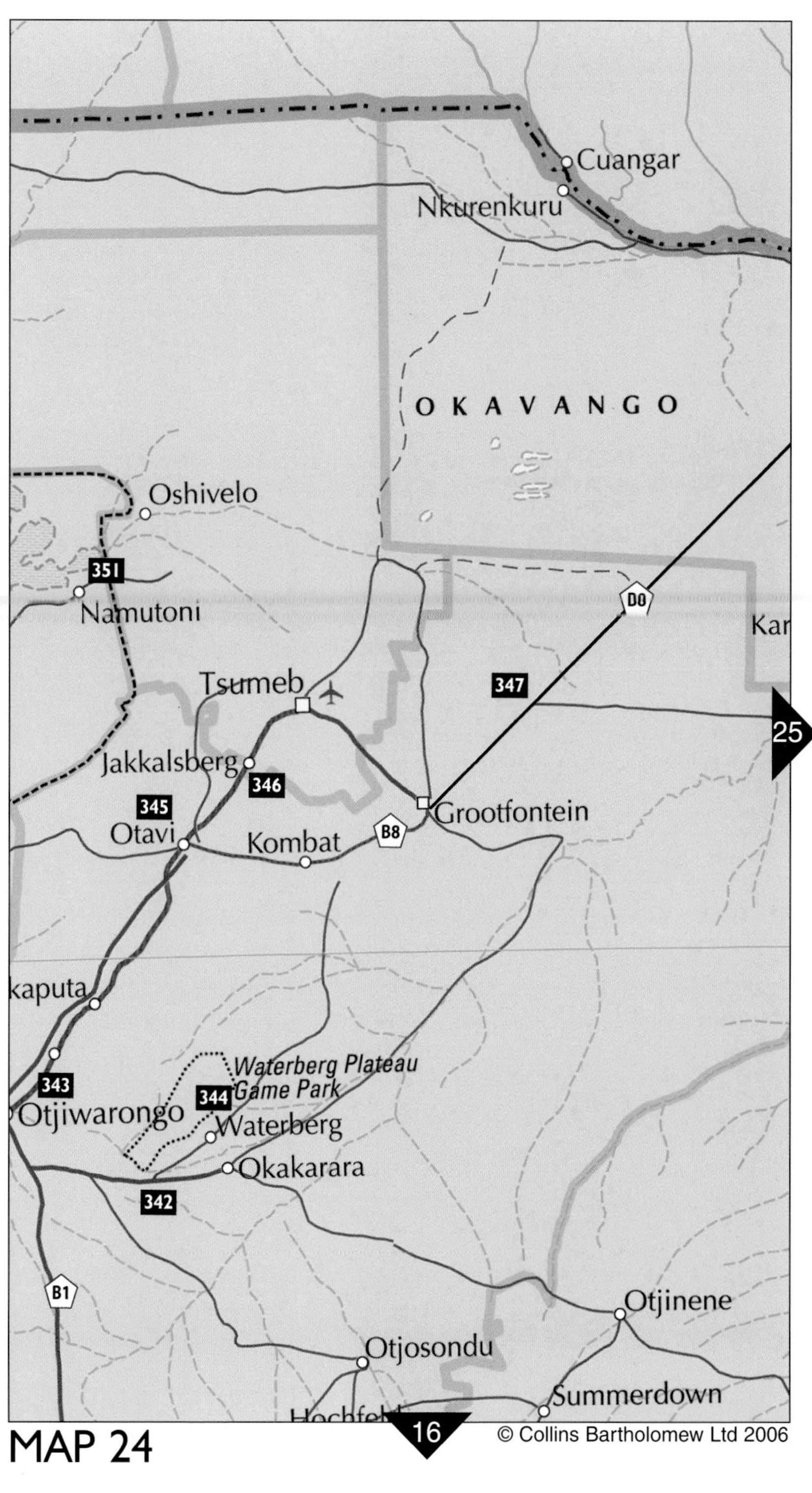

Cuangar
Nkurenkuru
OKAVANGO
Oshivelo
351
Namutoni
D0
Tsumeb
347
25
Jakkalsberg
346
345
Grootfontein
Otavi
Kombat
B8
343
Waterberg Plateau
Game Park
344
Otjiwarongo
Waterberg
Okakarara
342
B1
Otjinene
Otjosondu
Summerdown
16

MAP 24

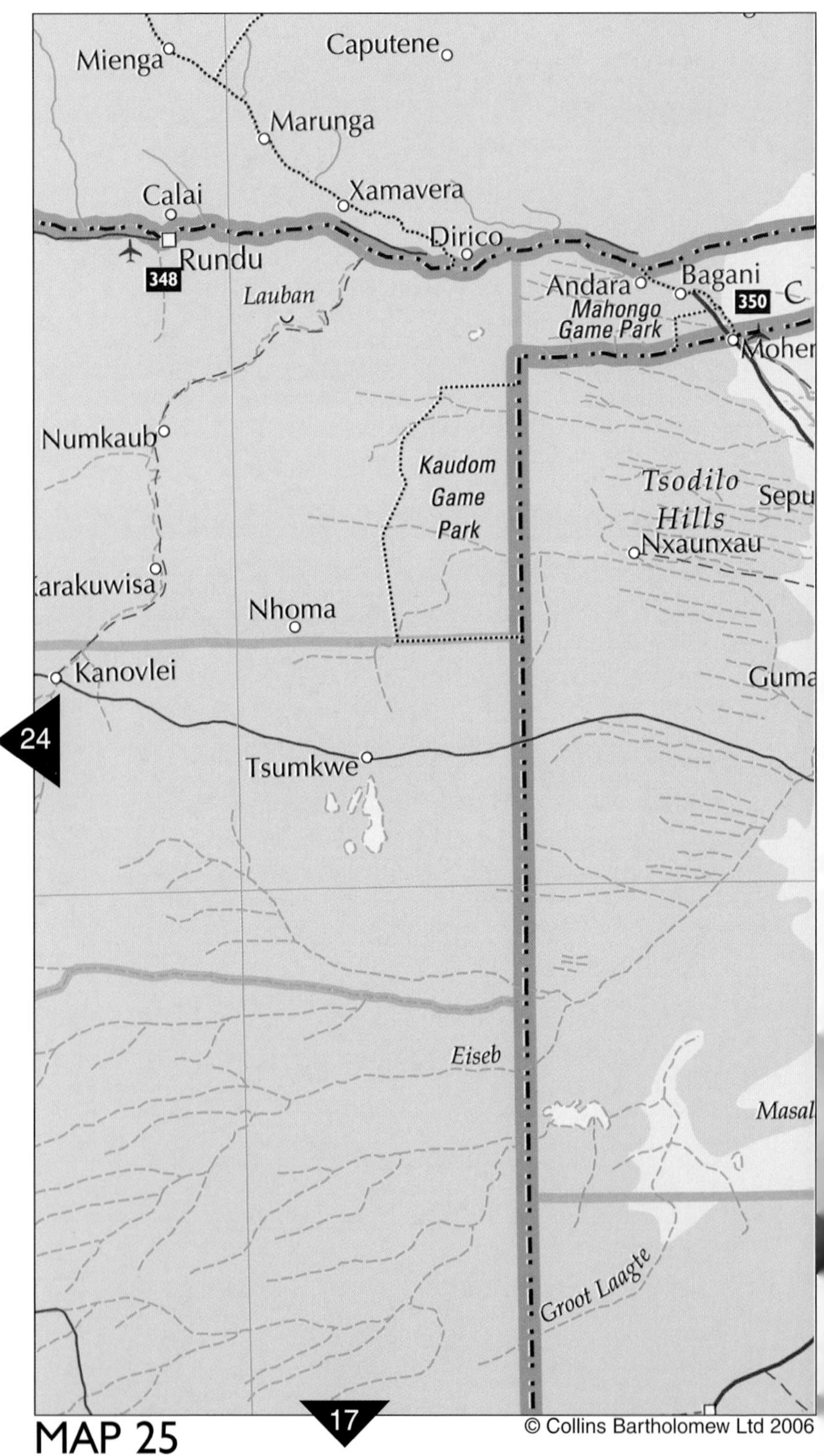
Mienga
Caputene
Marunga
Calai
Xamavera
Dirico
Rundu
348
Lauban
Andara
Bagani
350
Mahongo
Game Park
Numkaub
Kaudom
Game
Park
Tsodilo
Hills
Nxaunxau
Nhoma
Kanovlei
24
Tsumkwe
Eiseb
Groot Laagte
17

MAP 25

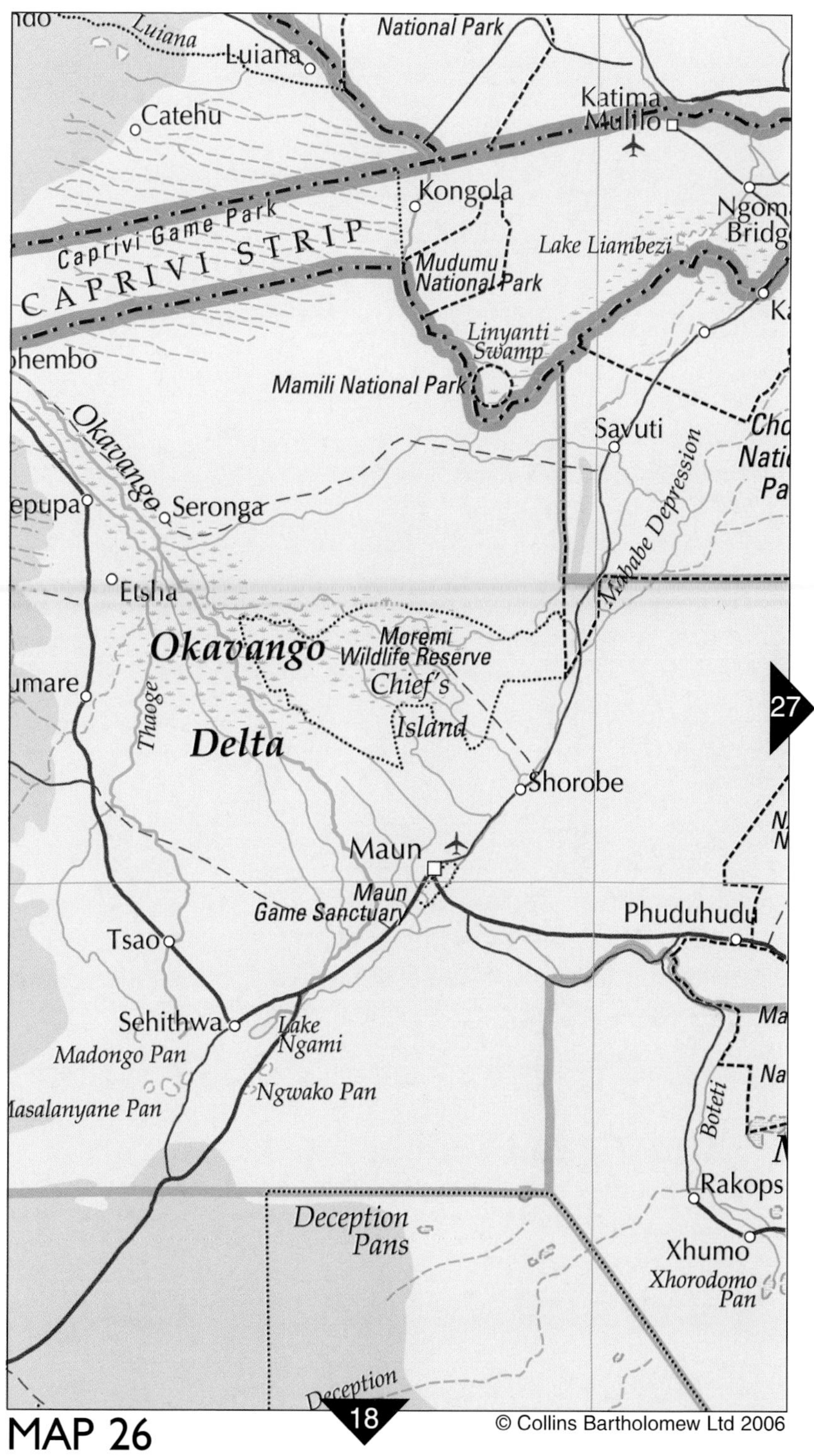

National Park
Luiana
Luiana
Catehu
Katima Mulilo
Kongola
Caprivi Game Park
CAPRIVI STRIP
Lake Liambezi
Mudumu National Park
Linyanti Swamp
Mamili National Park
Okavango
Savuti
Seronga
Mbabe Depression
Etsha
Moremi Wildlife Reserve
Okavango
Chief's Island
Thaoge
Delta
Shorobe
Maun
Maun Game Sanctuary
Phuduhudu
Tsao
Sehithwa
Lake Ngami
Madongo Pan
Ngwako Pan
Boteti
Rakops
Deception Pans
Xhumo
Xhorodomo Pan
Deception
27
18

MAP 26

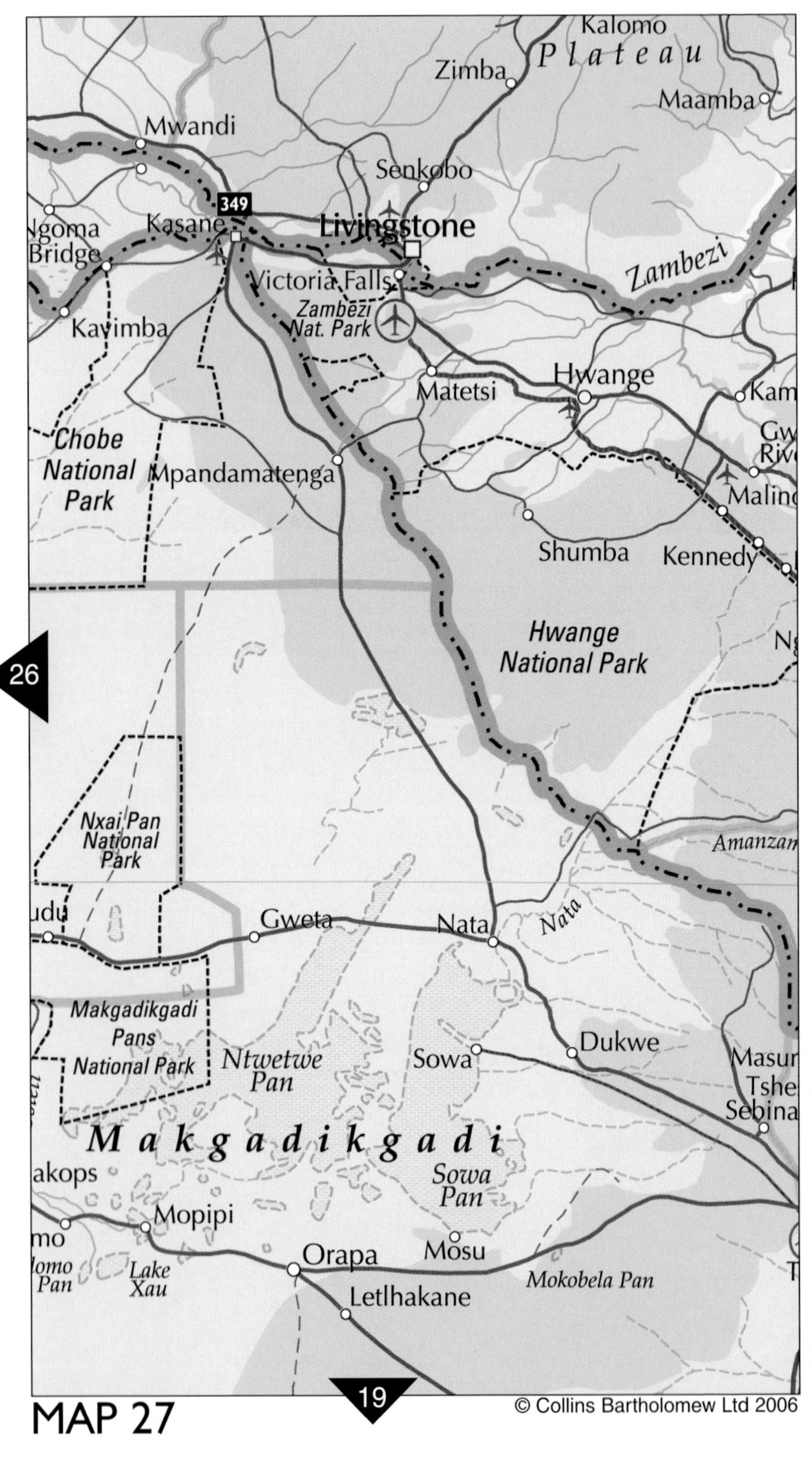
Kalomo
Plateau
Zimba
Maamba
Mwandi
Senkobo
349
Ngoma
Bridge
Kasane
Livingstone
Zambezi
Victoria Falls
Zambezi
Nat. Park
Kavimba
Matetsi
Hwange
Chobe
National
Park
Mpandamatenga
Shumba
Kennedy
Hwange
National Park
26
Nxai Pan
National
Park
Amanzam
Gweta
Nata
Nata
Makgadikgadi
Pans
National Park
Ntwetwe
Pan
Sowa
Dukwe
Makgadikgadi
akops
Sowa
Pan
Mopipi
Orapa
Mosu
Lake
Xau
Mokobela Pan
Letlhakane
19

MAP 27

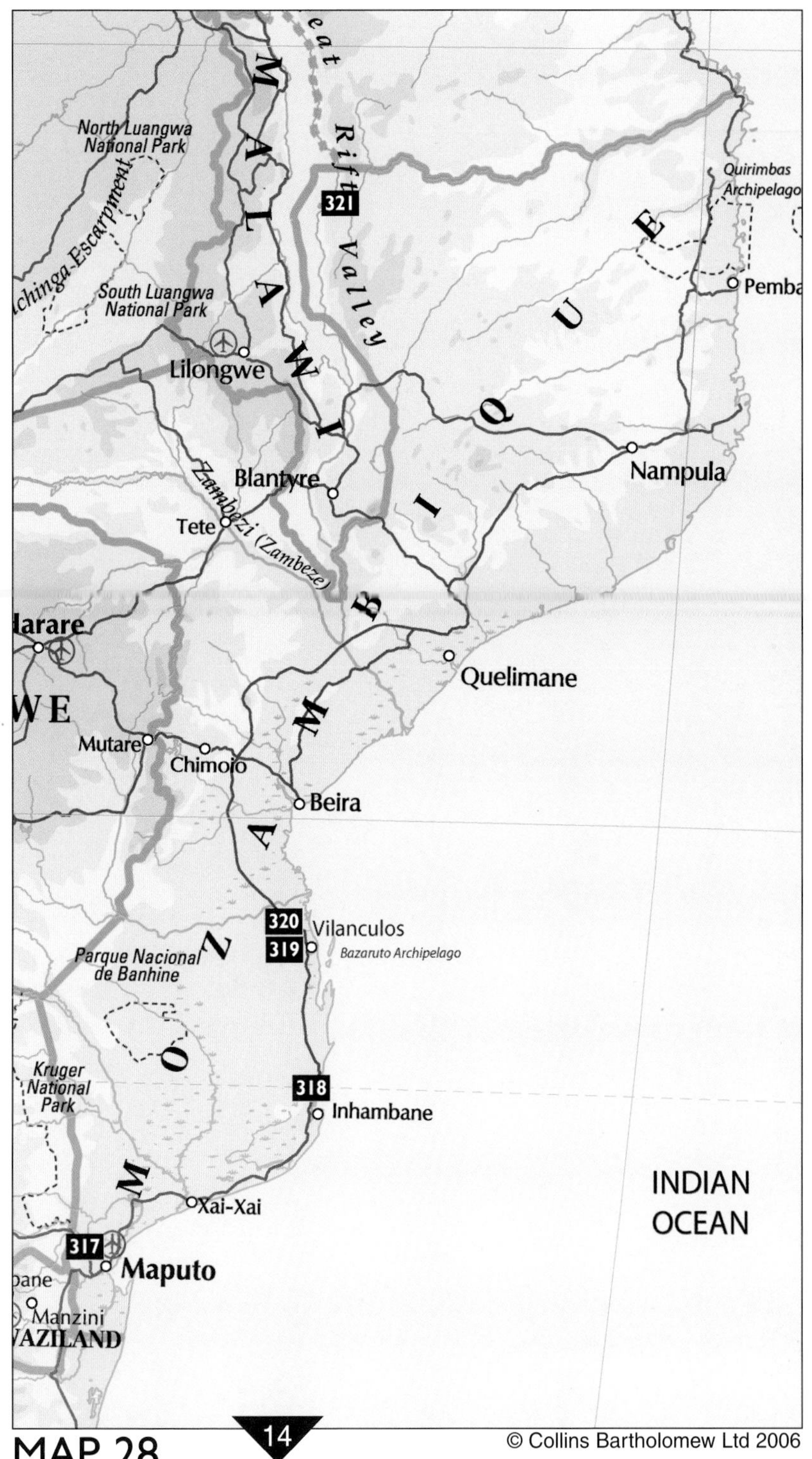
North Luangwa
National Park
Muchinga Escarpment
South Luangwa
National Park
Lilongwe
Blantyre
Tete
Zambezi (Zambeze)
Harare
Mutare
Chimoio
Beira
Quelimane
Nampula
Pemba
Quirimbas
Archipelago
Great Rift Valley
MALAWI
MOZAMBIQUE
321
320
319
318
317
Vilanculos
Bazaruto Archipelago
Parque Nacional
de Banhine
Kruger
National
Park
Inhambane
Xai-Xai
Maputo
Manzini
SWAZILAND
INDIAN
OCEAN

14

Western Cape

Duart

Jean & Jimmy Weight
3 Kleintuin Road, Simon's Town 7975
Tel: 021-794-4531 or 021-786-1328 Fax: 021-794-4531
Email: info@duart.co.za Web: www.duart.co.za
Cell: 083-255-1884

Being at Duart is like living in a Calvin Klein ad: white-washed wooden decking, swing swaying from a tree in the sheltered garden, luminous waves crashing on the beach and white horses galloping ashore from a lighthouse in the aquamarine distance. Well on the route to Cape Point, and just a stone's throw from Cape Town's be-penguined beaches (Penguin HQ is just next door), this is a place of Pimms-o'clock-cricket-on-the-lawn-style summer revelry. However, it also provides a great escape, a place to switch off the phone and devour that book you've been meaning to read. Shortly after arriving, I found myself ensconced among geraniums in the perilously comfy alcove on the wide verandah, where I happily lazed the afternoon away chatting with Jean and Jimmy over tea and buttered fruit loaf. The second oldest house of its kind in Simon's Town, Duart bears witness to each of the five generations that have enjoyed it. All inside is original and uniquely charming, from the hand-blasted sash-window panes to its collection of antiques and paintings on the walls. There's heaps of space too, with an elegant dining room and proper homely kitchen, the perfect venue for quiet Sunday night suppers. On my way out I passed Jimmy and their two black pooches who had succumbed at last to the 'fatal' corner and gone off for a zizz.

Rooms: 4: all twins, 3 shared bathrooms and showers.
Price: R1,800 - R2,400 per night for whole unit.
Meals: Self-catering.
Directions: Take M3 south towards Muizenberg and on to Simon's Town. Go past the naval base, then turn left into Seaforth Road. Go down the hill, past the car park and turn right into Kleintuin Rd.

Water's Edge

Anne Browne and Patricia Martin

7 Kleintuin Rd, Simon's Town, 7975
Tel: Contact Rachel Browne on 011-487-1458 or 083-483 8218
Email: blueseas@bucksmail.com or pauline@bluseaholidays.co.za or rachel@pix.co.za Web: www.weholiday.co.za
Cell: Contact Pauline Batt on 021-786-3847 or 072-403-2805

If you've never lain awake and listened to the noise of whales breathing not ten metres from your very bed, then you should come to Water's Edge during the season (August to November). The Browne family retreat (and GG hot spot) is a dreamy far-away place, so relaxed and in such a beautiful location that you may have to pinch yourself as a reality check. There is a big proper kitchen and cavernous games room. Downstairs the seaside rooms are the best. But my favourite place of all has to be the open-fronted stoep. A table on one side and a sofa on the other channel the eyes out to sea. Locals make use of the beach during the school holidays, but always go home in the evening. Otherwise it's all yours. On both ends of the crescent of sand, huge smooth boulders are perfect for rock hopping, fishing, reading and watching for sea mammals. Adults and children alike will spend hours poking around in rock pools, barbecueing on the beach, building sand castles and watching the sun set. Kids can also go off finding fairies in the garden or making dens under up-turned dinghies. There really are no other places like this in Cape Town and it is a treat to be able to stay here. *Deck chairs and beach towels provided. Open fire and braai. Lodge phone number: 021-786-1958.*

Rooms: 1 self-catering house with 4 bedrooms: 2 doubles & 2 twins with shared bathroom & shower room, plus 1 day bed and a games room. 8 people max. Serviced once a week.
Price: Peak season: R2,400 per day. High season: R2,000 per day. Low season R1,650 per day. Min stay 1 week. To secure booking 25% of total rent at time of booking.
Meals: Restaurants nearby. Catering can be organised. Full kitchen.
Directions: Take M3 south towards Muizenberg & in Simon's Town pass naval base. Seaforth Rd signed to your left. Down hill & pass car park, turn R into Kleintuin Rd & follow wall to end. No. 7 beachside.

Map Number: 3

Boulders Beach Lodge

Frans Hollenbach
4 Boulders Place, Boulders Beach, Simon's Town 7995
Tel: 021-786-1758
Fax: 021-786-1825
Email: boulders@iafrica.com
Web: www.bouldersbeach.co.za

I screeched to a halt at the sight of three penguins sitting unperturbed on a garden wall. I excitedly snapped shots, delighted at their tame nature and vanity poses, until some passing tourists suggested that I save my film and look around the corner. Here on the beach front, with Boulders Beach Lodge on one side and the ocean on the other, was an entire colony of plumed p-p-p-penguins, some in their natural habitat on the boulders and sandy beach, and others, wherefore I know not, waddling along the streets. In the limited time I was here I ate wonderfully fresh king prawns at the in-house restaurant and sipped complimentary cream liqueur in my enormous bath. Bedrooms all have wrought-iron beds and are decorated with wooden carved sculptures of microscopic sea life. But time spent in your room will be limited by the multitude of activities on your doorstep: safe bathing from the penguin beach, kayaking in False Bay, beach walks with views of the distant Hottentots Holland mountain range, mountain hikes above Simon's Town, mountain biking, practising your golf swing at the next-door golf course, sailing at the yacht club, fishing, scuba diving and whale-watching. Phew. I suggest you stay at least three nights to take full advantage of this superb location. *There is also a quirky Curious Penguin Shop where to buy essential penguin paraphernalia below the restaurant terrace.*

Rooms: 14: 9 doubles, 2 twins, 1 triple, all with en-suite bath and shower or bath with shower overhead. 2 suites for 6; 1 double, 2 single beds, double sofa-bed and kitchen.
Price: From R395 pp sharing. Singles R450. Suites R1,500.
Meals: A choice of breakfasts is included. In-house restaurant for lunch and dinner.
Directions: Emailed or faxed.

Blue Marlin Apartments

Hamish and Alison Currie
Runciman Drive, Simon's Town
Tel: 021-794-1536 or 021-715-2498
Email: backtoafrica@iafrica.com
Cell: 082 469 2740

The main and not insignificant attraction of these two apartments in Simon's Town are their large verandahs, wide enough and protected enough to braai supper on. And what a spot to while away an evening, high above town, looking down over the boats moored below, the submarine and aqua-dynamic corvettes of the South African navy like action toys down there in the harbour. And then the arcing expanse of False Bay and the distant Hottentots Holland. It is a view that will not easily be ignored. The flats themselves are based on open-plan kitchens and sitting areas extending out into the balcony, bright and modern with the kitchens well equipped and TV's all cabled up. The tables are wooden, the floors matting-carpeted, with tall thin animal sculptures adding a spot of vertical African appeal here and there. All the bedrooms have lovely views but those at the front clearly take the gold. Hamish is a water-sports expert so if you want some advice or help organising sailing charters, fishing or diving trips then just ask. Fresh flowers and a few breakfast things to get you started are provided for your arrival. Simon's Town is a great choice, by the way. We lived just around the bay in St. James and thoroughly enjoyed the area and all it has to offer.

Rooms: 2 apartments: one 2-bed (1 x double and 1 x twin); one 3-bed (2 x double and 1 x twin); both with bath and shower rooms.
Price: R350 pp sharing. Max R1,400 per day. One weekly service included. R100 per day for the flat to be serviced more often (this is up to you).
Meals: Basic first-morning breakfast materials, bottle of wine and fresh flowers for your arrival. Full kitchens.
Directions: Ask when booking.

Avian Leisure

Marie-Louise and Patrick Cardwell
88 Dorries Drive, Simon's Town 7995
Tel: 021-786-1414 Fax: 021-786-1414
Email: avianleisure@netpoint.co.za Web: www.simonstown.com/accom/avian or www.avianleisure.com (tours) Cell: 083-272-2455

The Cardwells have two smashing self-catering apartments under their Simon's Town home, but what we really liked was that they offer so very much more than that. Patrick is a naturalist and there is nothing he doesn't know about his surroundings – and that's the whole of South Africa, not just Simon's Town. Whether it's a bird-watching tour from the Zimbabwe border to the Garden Route coastline, or a detailed search for Northern Cape lizards, he's your man. But no need to go cantering off just yet, when there's so much right on your door step. High above Simon's Town proper, both flats have a wonderful position, gazing out across False Bay past penguins and whales (in season) to the distant Overberg mountains. Your own mountain starts just across the road. It's a two-hour walk to the top of the 678m (roughly) Swartkop peak. We didn't have time to test the theory, but Marie-Louise assures us the view from up there is even better. I don't doubt it. Both apartments are tiled throughout with massive airy bedrooms. Downstairs the glass wall slides back to give you a private wooden verandah overlooking the fynbos garden below. Upstairs, one wall of the vast lounge is taken up by a mini-library, the shelves bulging with National Geographics – one guest had his nose buried in a bird book, ticking off his sightings before the next expedition. *The Cardwells also run winery tours via six 4-star estates, all different settings and grape varieties. Towels, chairs etc provided for beach.*

Rooms: 2 apartments, one with 1 twin/king and 1 twin sharing separate bath and shower, the other with twin/king and a shower. Serviced twice a week.
Price: R210 - R285 pp sharing. Singles supplement on request.
Meals: Continental breakfast basket by arrangement R45 pp. Full kitchen in lower apartment, kitchenette only in Watsonia. Weber for braais on the deck or full BBQ facility upstairs.
Directions: M3 from CT to Muizenberg, then Main Road through Fish Hoek to Simon's Town. Continue for 2km past golf course on L. Immediately after Oatlands Holiday Accomm turn R into Dorries Drive. House is 1km uphill on the R.

Map Number: 3

Rob Roy

Urszula Perry
14 Hope St, Simon's Town 7975
Tel: 021-786-1280 Fax: 021-786-2225
Email: info@robroy-guesthouse.co.za Web: www.robroy-guesthouse.co.za
Cell. 083-308-8943

Urszula is one of the lucky few that has had the pleasure of entertaining the whole GG team in one sitting. Not that this felt by any means a crowd, for Rob Roy certainly is roomy. Built in 1850, this charming Victorian cottage sits in the old part of 'navy-to-the-core' Simon's Town, quietly surveying the action in the harbour below. Although this is still a proper B&B - Urszula lives on the other side of the courtyard and comes down each morning to cook you breakfast - you are not cooped up in your room and you do not have to share any facilities. Instead you are given the whole cottage, complete with kitchen, dining area, two bathrooms, sitting room, and your own courtyard and private garden to boot. If this place were a breakfast egg it would definitely be served sunny-side up. Bright colours, fresh flowers, and yellowwood furniture and floors seemingly smile throughout. In the middle of the generous living room is a two-sided fireplace that billows double rations of cosiness on those stormy coastal nights. The Victorian-style bedroom is delightful too; with its wrought-iron bed, cotton-fresh linen and super-plump pillows I did all I had to not to jump in. My favourite place though, is the delicate, fragranced garden, cunningly wound around the back of the house, entered through a jasmine arch and shaded by lemon trees and a venerable fig.

Rooms: 1 unit with 1 double, with en-suite bath, and an extra day bed and separate shower room.
Price: R275 - R350. Singles +50%.
Meals: Full breakfast included. Typically croissants from Olympia Café, fruit platter, yoghurt muesli, crumpets etc. Cooked breakfasts on request too.
Directions: Ask when booking.

Moonglow Guest House

Gillian O'Leary
7 Bennett Close, Cairnside, Glencairn 7975
Tel: 021-786-5902 Fax: 021-786-5903
Email: seaview@moonglow.co.za Web: www.moonglow.co.za
Cell: 082-565-6568

"We've been here four and a half years now but I still get goose-bumps every time I see the moon hanging over it," Gillian confides in me as we stare out over the smooth expanse of False Bay. I challenge you to find a better view of the bay than this one and unsurprisingly most of the rooms at Moonglow take full advantage - even the ones that don't still get their own private seating areas round at the front. With Matty the dog dancing around my feet, and her friend Jess staring lovingly at the succulent blueberry muffin that was supplied with my tea, I could have happily stayed for an eternity ensconced on the sofa of the bar-lounge… but an ever-enthusiastic Gillian was keen to show me more and I had a job to do. Throughout this house you'll find original artworks everywhere, including a stunning leopard print and four-foot-high figurines honed from solid granite. If it catches Gillian's eye she's got to have it. Vibrant oil paintings add a splash of colour to creamy rooms, all drenched in sunlight from large picture windows or glass doors. Beds and tables have been individually designed, and a multitude of mohair blankets and the finest quality linens have had Gillian's hand-embroiderers busy detailing them with intricate dragonflies and bumblebees "... just so the colours match". Moonglow shines.

Rooms: 6: 2 queens and 2 doubles all with shower only; 2 twins with bath and shower over.
Price: R275 - R375 pp sharing. Single on request.
Meals: Full breakfast included. Lots of restaurants nearby.
Directions: Map on website, directions can be emailed on booking.

Map Number: 3

Blue Yonder

Sally and Bruce Elliott
14 Hillside Rd, Fish Hoek 7975
Tel: 021-782-0500 Fax: 021-782-0500
Email: info@blueyondercape.co.za Web: www.blueyondercape.co.za
Cell: 082 441 9589

For those of you on the self-catering trail this is a must. A three-storey house converted into flats, Blue Yonder is a luxury ocean liner of a place. When Sally opened the door to an invading GG team the sun was blasting through the wall-to-wall windows. She was keen to show me around but I spent the first ten minutes standing out on the enormous silver-railed balcony, transfixed by the view. From all three apartments here you can watch the full arc of the sun, rising over a glittering False Bay, and finally sinking behind the red-tiled roofs of the Fish Hoek bungalows below. Excellent for whale-watching. Once the trance wears off (which it won't) head inside and polish off your complimentary drinks or make the most of the stainless steel and cream kitchens, complete with all mod cons (including my personal favourite: the dishwasher). Sally grew up in this house but after a huge conversion job the Rhodesian teak floors are the only reminder of her family home. Now, gloriously indulgent queen-sized beds look out on the bay and cool, beige armchairs are just waiting to be lounged in. Once you summon the energy for a dip in the ocean, your own private steps lead down to the beach, just a stone's throw away. My advice? Bring the whole family, light up a braai on the balcony and settle in for at least a month. *5 mins to food shops. All apartments have braais.*

Rooms: 3 self-catering apartments: "Upper" 1 queen with en-suite shower & 1 twin with en-suite bath & shower; Middle: 1 queen en-s b & sh, 2 twins en-s b & sh; Lower: 1 queen en-s sh only. Serviced every week day.
Price: R175 - R300 pp sharing.
Meals: In fridge on arrival: fruit juice, wine, tea, coffee, milk, sugar. Full kitchen.
Directions: Head to Muizenberg from Cape Town, continue south along main road through Fish Hoek. At roundabout at the end of F.H. main rd turn L towards Simon's Town. 1 km further take 1st R at traffic lights up Hillside Rd. Blue Yonder about 300m up on the R.

Map Number: 3

Dunvegan Lodge

Sylvia and Peter McLeod
106 Clovelly Rd, Clovelly, Fish Hoek 7975
Tel: 021-782-2958 Fax: 021-782-2958
Email: dunvegan@iafrica.com Web: www.dunvegan.co.za
Cell: 082-938-0380

For golf enthusiasts, Dunvegan Lodge, the McLeod highland retreat on the slopes of Clovelly Mountain, could hardly be better placed. It overlooks the Clovelly Country Club and I could see the twinge of longing in Sylvia's eye as we stood on one of the many wooden decks that enjoy bird's eye views over the 18-hole course to the white beaches that frame the peninsula. A keen fisherman, Peter was busy rounding up novices and enthusiasts alike for a crayfishing expedition in False Bay as they emerged for breakfast on the deep verandah at the top of this labrynthine house. No doubt a successful day on the ocean waves will end with a crayfish braai and heroic stories being traded in the small, tiled bar before descending the stairs to bed (it's an upside-down house). All of the rooms are different, some within the main home, each with a private patio or verandah, others hidden within the stepped, landscaped garden that borders the nature reserve. Rock steps wind their way to the different levels of the lush, overflowing garden and the pool has uninterrupted views of the Fish Hoek Valley. Venture a little further and you'll find a jacuzzi where you can watch the sun set over the Atlantic Ocean or simply rest those aching golf shoulders. *Bedrooms have underfloor heating, electric blankets and safes. Towelling gowns provided. All rooms have TV's.*

Rooms: 6: 3 suites (queen or twin), lounge & kitchenette; 1 x 2-bed suite (1 queen & 1 single), lounge & kitchenette; 1 twin with kitchenette; 1 queen. All rooms en-suite bath +/or shower. Shampoo provided in bathrooms. Serviced daily.
Price: R220 - R360 pp sharing. Singles on request. The whole lodge can be rented as a unit - price on request.
Meals: Full breakfast on request. Excellent restaurants nearby. Kitchens well-equipped with decent sized fridges & mini-stoves (with oven). Food shops very close by. Braais with all units.
Directions: Follow M4 through Muizenburg, St James & Kalk Bay. Turn R at traffic lights after Kalk Bay harbour traffic lights into Clovelly Road.

Map Number: 3

Hattons Hout Bay

Liz Davis
2 Harold Close, Oakhurst Estate, Hout Bay 7806
Tel: 021-790-0848 Fax: 021-790-3050
Email: liz@hattons.co.za Web: www.hattons.co.za
Cell: 082-760-2624

Nature has run its course at Hattons since the last edition: the vine arbour has gone, leaving Liz an uninterrupted mountain view, and her son Connor is a wee bairn no more. The approach, however, remains perfectly unassuming. Only once you're inside do the building's true dimensions reveal themselves, a great surprise with breezy open spaces and a cavernous sitting room with pole beams and steepling thatched roof. Doors open on both sides, one leading to the pool, the other out to the view over the back of Table Mountain and their own garden. This is immaculately laid out with paths that wind past tropical blooms, riotous colours against white-washed walls… and where the rooms, named after plants – acacia, lavender, mimosa, kumassi – are kept. Not so much rooms as little cottages, with their own doors to the garden and fully-equipped kitchenettes. The most popular has an unusual gallery bedroom, which looks down on its own sitting room from a great height. Liz is dedicated to her guests, and she'll welcome you in with wine, OJ or coffee. Nearby, enjoy a sunset concert at Kirstenbosch, and listen carefully when she is spilling the beans about the best spots on the coast; or stroll down to Acorns restaurant for lunch or dinner (the food is amazing!); or pick up some local produce and wine from the Oakhurst Farmstall deli and sit outside your room with a chilled bottle of Chardonnay and a ripe brie for a sundowner.

Rooms: 6: 3 apartments (self-catering or B&B) with en-s shower & bath; 1 B&B double en-s shower; 1 B&B king en-s shower and bath; 1 B&B family suite 1 double & 1 twin room, both en-s shower.
Price: R250 – R350 pp sharing. Singles R350 – R450. Less R40 if you don't have breakfast.
Meals: Self-catering possible. Breakfast served buffet-style on either terrace or in the main lounge.
Directions: Emailed or faxed on booking.

Buchan Estate

Fiona and Pieter van Aswegen
Welbevind Way, Hout Bay 7806
Tel: 021-791-2100 Fax: 021-791-2101
Email: info@buchanestate.com Web: www.buchanestate.com
Cell: 082-560-8165

Rolling down the drive under towering cedars, past the whitewashed stables and a football-friendly paddock I had a finger-tingling feeling that this was just the place for us. Fiona and Pieter were wrestling with renovations when my GG predecessors first visited. Twenty-four months down the track, construction is complete (including the kids' jungle gym in the lunging ring) and their riverside farm is bubbling with life. "A Gentleman's Equestrian Estate" was how it was advertised when they moved in, but these days it's a family home complete with daughter (a chattering baby Mara), son, dogs (the soppiest doberman I've ever met) and tortoises (as yet unnamed). Fiona is a Scot and these two 30-somethings gave up the corporate life and the vile weather of Edinburgh to head south – about 6,500 miles south - in a Land Rover. Their three cottages have a classic African feel, "but not over the top," shivers Pieter. Roofs are thatched, beams dark and ceilings surprisingly high. Romantics will love the four-poster bed and enormous oval bath. Self-catering is the general idea, but Fiona is happy to supply a hamper stuffed with breakfast goodies to your cottage door in the morning. And if you really are loth to fend for yourself, she can rustle up a Cape-Malay curry or some local fish to whack in the oven for supper. What more can you ask?

Rooms: 3 cottages: 1 king with bath and shower and mini-kitchen; 1 queen with bath and shower and full kitchen; 1 two-bedroom cottage with king and king/twin beds and a shared shower and full kitchen.
Price: R295 – R495 pp sharing.
Meals: Breakfast on request for R35. Dinner can also be provided.
Directions: From Cape Town turn R off M3 onto Rhodes Drive, signed to Hout Bay. Follow signs for World of Birds into Valley Rd. Opposite the bird sanctuary turn R into Welbevind Way. Buchan Estate is the last property on the left.

Amblewood Guest House

June and Trevor Kruger
43 Skaife St, Hout Bay 7806
Tel: 021-790-1570 Fax: 021-790-1571
Email: info@amblewood.co.za Web: www.amblewood.co.za
Cell: 082 881 5430

After negotiating the Amblewood driveway, I was rewarded by Trevor who fixed me a G&T, and amid heavy beams and family antiques we chatted away until the rains came (which I'm afraid they do on occasion, even in the Cape). Guests wearing borrowed woollies and waterproofs returned and Trevor raced out with a brolly for June. This softly-spoken duo love doing what they do. They share an eye for detail and an enthusiasm that will leave you right at home. I browsed the library and admired the beach, bay and mountains from my balcony, which I shared with two turtle-doves. Friday is braai day, but that night we headed to a steakhouse, where everybody knew the Krugers. I enjoyed my stay so much that I think they wondered whether I was doing a job at all. But I wasn't alone - as I left, wise-looking guests were extending their stay. For those on a return visit and with an interest in photography, you can now allow Trevor, an experienced photographer, to help you polish your snapping skills. He organises 5-day tours taking you to the most interesting locations as well as offering helpful tips and advice so you may remember your stay always. There are also two new rooms to try, including a self-contained suite with a bedroom looking out into the surrounding hills.

Rooms: 6: all doubles with en-suite bath or shower.
Price: R225 – R550 pp sharing. Singles rate R360 – R525.
Meals: Full cooked breakfast included.
Directions: Faxed or emailed on booking.

Frogg's Leap

Jôke and Stewart Glauser
15 Baviaanskloof Rd, Hout Bay 7806
Tel: 021-790-2590 Fax: 021-790-2590
Email: info@froggsleap.co.za Web: www.froggsleap.co.za
Cell: 082-493-4403

The huge Frogg's Leap verandah, with its impressive views of the Hout Bay mountains and se seems to be the focal point of life here. At breakfast the house springs to life with Jôke (pronounced *yokie*) and Stewart engaging in easy banter with all who emerge, and chiding guests for sitting at the long wooden table inside when the parasol-shaded tables outside are so enticing Then, in the evening, with the sea breeze swinging the hammocks and a sundowner in you hand, it is not hard to get to grips with being lazy and on holiday. I can't remember a place where guests made themselves so at home. Jôke and Stewart used to run charter boats in the Wes Indies and Frogg's Leap has a breezy Caribbean feel with many open French doors and windows Bedrooms are cool ensembles of natural materials: painted floors, seagrass matting, palms, natura stone in bathrooms, lazy wicker chairs, reed ceilings, thick cotton percale linen and old wooden furniture. Hout Bay itself is a fishing harbour enclosed by mountains and is within minutes c beaches and hiking trails. Jôke and Stewart keep a 26-ft catamaran there and, when the spiri moves them and weather permits, will take guests cray-fishing, or whale-watching when whale are in town. This is a place that has been consistently recommended both before and since the first edition and it is a continued pleasure to recommend it myself. *Guest phone 021-790-6260.*

Rooms: 6: 5 doubles/twins and 1 double, all with en-suite bathrooms; 2 with shower, 4 with bath and shower. Plus extra single room.
Price: R300 - R400 pp sharing. Singles on request.
Meals: Full breakfast included and served until 10am There are 20 restaurants nearby for other meals.
Directions: A map will be faxed to you on confirmation of booking.

Makuti Lodge

Doreen and Peter Wright
Farriers Way, Tarragona Estate, Hout Bay 7806
Tel: 021-790-1414 Fax: 021-790-1414
Email: doreen@makutilodge.co.za Web: www.makutilodge.co.za
Cell: 083-457-5231

Forget Kirstenbosch, head for Makuti Lodge! (Well, almost....) Gardeners will find plenty of common ground with Peter and Doreen. Even if you do exhaust the riches of their stunning garden (you'll have to stay quite a while to achieve this), then you can just walk out of the driveway and find yourself at the foot of Myburg Peak. It's not that the grounds of Makuti Lodge are especially large; but they are just so full. From the patios, the lawns, the flower beds and the 'forest' area, to the hidden bark paths that twist between the cottages, you could spend hours wandering around contemplating life (or joining in a game of pétanque, if you've the stomach for it). Play your cards right and you may be invited to a wine-tasting session in the stone depths of the cellar among the animal carvings and hanging swords. Here you can sample vinous treats from all over the southern hemisphere under the guidance of Peter and Doreen, who modestly admit to amateur enthusiast status only. The cottages themselves are quaint (Peter is responsible for construction, Doreen for the finishing touches) with local art on the walls and wood-burning fires whose black iron flumes rise up through the bedrooms upstairs, providing heating for them too. And I haven't even mentioned the dogs, the pool, the hot tub or the breakfasts.

Rooms: 4 cottages: 1 x 1-bed cottages; 2 x 2-bed with 2 bathrooms; 1 x 3-bed with 2 bathrooms.
Price: R250 - R350 pp sharing. Or in winter: R400 - R1,000 per cottage; summer: R500 - R1,500 per cottage.
Meals: Full or Continental breakfast an extra R40 - R50 pp.
Directions: M63 to Hout Bay. Turn R at Disa River Rd, L at end. First R into Garron Ave. Then R into Connemara Drive. Then L into Hunter's Way. R into Farrier's Way. Makuti on R.

Paddington's at Jongamanzi

Di and Don Lilford
3 Lindevista Lane, Hout Bay
7800
Tel: 021-790-8703
Fax: 021-790-8703
Email: dlilford@new.co.za
Web: www.paddington.co.za
Cell: 083-259-6025

Standing in Di's garden, I sighed with relaxed satisfaction, gazing across a valley and beach bathed in late-afternoon sunshine. Well away from the hustle and bustle of Cape Town proper, Hout Bay runs at a pace of its own, and Paddington's and the Lilfords are right in step. After years on their valley-floor farm, they have moved up onto the hillside accompanied by a gaggle of visiting guinea fowl (impatiently tapping on the French doors for their tea when I arrived), Rollo the dog and their steady stream of guests. There's a relaxed feel of country living here and while the building itself may be new and square, it's full of old prints, family furniture and well-trodden rugs. Visitors have the run of the tiled ground floor, with both bedrooms just two yawns and a stagger from breakfast, tacked onto the drawing room and kitchen. One room gets the morning sun, the other the afternoon rays and both are blessed with gigantic beds. If you feel up to it, Don and Di will point you in the direction of the best golf courses and the beach, while for the lethargic loungers among you there's pétanque on the gravel patch or a book on the verandah. Oh choices, choices....

Rooms: 2 king/twins, 1 with bath, 1 with shower.
Price: R275 pp. Singles R350.
Meals: Continental breakfast included.
Directions: Faxed or emailed on request.

The King's Place

Kim and Ian King
Valley Rd, Hout Bay 7806
Tel: 021-790-4000 Fax: 021-790-4000
Email: kim@plant-people.co.za Web: www.thekingsplace.com
Cell: 082-773-8831

Even as I trundled down the drive I could see that Kim and Ian, with a helping hand from Mother Nature, have crafted a truly special place. Whether you're knocking up on the floodlit tennis court, somersaulting skywards on the trampoline, or simply lazing by the pool, the views over Hout Bay and the Constantiaberg remain imperturbably lovely. An ever-smiling Kim greeted me in wellies and a bodywarmer, fresh from tending to the animals (I counted dogs, horses, chickens and Chinese geese, but am sure plenty more are lurking within the eight acres). Strolling through the landscaped garden (Ian is a horticulturalist) we came to the expansive, single-storey 'Valley House': light, airy and well able to sleep Von Trapp-sized families if required. It's in the open-plan kitchen, dining and living area that the heart of the King's Place beats. The maple and granite kitchen has chopping space for a whole troupe of cooks, and they'll all fit around the huge dining table too, strategically placed in front of the full-length, full-view windows. If you've exhausted all the activities on offer or have simply exhausted yourself, the lounge provides a sanctuary of cushioned, wicker armchairs that face a warming hearth in winter, or look out through glass doors to the pool terrace in summer. *They can sleep 2 - 20 people.*

Rooms: 2 self-contained units: 1st: 4 x double & 1 x 4-bed (2 with en-s bath/sh, 2 separate bath & sh rooms); 2nd: 1 double with en-s b/sh & 1 twin with sep' bath/sh. Units can be connected.
Price: R150 - R350 pp per day.
Meals: Self-catering, Continental breakfast available at R20 – R40 pp. Basics provided in fridge.
Directions: Main Road into Hout Bay from Constantia. Right into Disa River Road. Left into Valley Road. Go past World of Birds on the right and The King's Place is 150m on the left.

Dreamhouse

Ivanka Beyer
53 Mount Rhodes Drive, Hout Bay 7806
Tel: 021-790-1773 Fax: 021-790-4864
Email: dreamhouse@yebo.co.za Web: www.dreamhouse.de
Cell: 082-547-7328

You cannot fail to be inspired by Dreamhouse and its mountainous harbour-view setting. The staggered garden contains many intimate leafy places that envelope both you and the landscape in the foliage. This is an artist's oasis and, if the mood takes you, Ivanka will dish out brushes, watercolours, canvas and frame so you can paint your own memories and take them home. The house and rooms reflect your host's own creative flair in colour, texture and line, with sweeping-armed suede sofas (it's always handy when your other half deals in furniture), a heavy wooden-beamed fireplace and high ceilings. The rooms are all different and named after their predominant colour, my favourite being the red luxury suite at the heart of the house where I imagined star-gazing from bed or rocking in the balcony-bound hammock for two. I was intrigued by hand-made mirrors, draped sarongs from Pakistan and the abundance of shells that adorn the daily-different table décor. "Everything has its own story," according to Ivanka. Devoted to her guests, she applies attention to detail and impeccable yet unobtrusive service at all times. Whether it's a picnic basket you need, a cocktail by the saltwater pool or directions for a sunrise walk up Little Lion's Head she'll be there. Also trained in reiki, aromatherapy, reflexology and various massages there are a multitude of blissful experiences available at her hands. As we used to say at university (for some reason), "live the dream!"

Rooms: 5: 3 doubles with en-suite shower and 2 twin/kings with en-suite shower & bath and kitchenette.
Price: R380 - R570 pp sharing. Singles on request.
Meals: Full breakfast included. Dinner and light lunches on request (preferably with 24 hours notice as only fresh produce used).
Directions: Emailed or faxed on request.

River Lodge

Michelle and Stephan Froelicher
Boskykloof Rd, Hout Bay 7806
Tel: 021-790-1236 Fax: 021-790-1236
Email: riverlodge@mweb.co.za
Cell: 083-444-2408

You might well want to stage an open-air production of A Midsummer Night's Dream down on the wooden decks at River Lodge. The house is sequestered in an indigenous forest where great rocks emerge from the earth and a busy stream runs down the mountain and disappears into the trees below the house. At night the setting is particularly enticing as spotlights have been set among the trees and you can sit out and have a braai on the spreading lake of wooden decking that encompasses whole trees and a heated swimming pool too. There is even a rather charming dassie family that live among the rocks here and who come out during the day. The house itself has an open-plan design with vaulted ceiling, big windows and huge verandahs, and is way more luxurious than it needs to be! Decadently large leather sofas, heated towel rails, antique English furnishings, under-floor heating, an amazing kitchen.... Whether you pass your time swinging in the hammock lulled by the sounds of silence, investigating the nearby rock pools or sizzling yourself in the sauna, it will be hard not to lose yourself here. Don't panic if you lose your children, by the way, for, within a safe-yet-pleasantly-removed distance, they have another (tree) house, trampoline, play area and the Froelichers' own boys (6 and 10 and counting) to keep themselves occupied and up to mischief.

Rooms: 1 self-contained lodge: 1 queen with en-suite jacuzzi-bath; 1 twin with en-suite shower; 1 double futon en-suite bath. Serviced each week day. Laundry R100 a load includes ironing.
Price: R1,050 - R1,750 a day for the lodge.
Meals: First breakfast materials and a complimentary bottle of wine in the fridge. Sparkling wine for honeymooners. Full kitchen includes dishwasher and state-of-art cooking range.
Directions: Ask when booking and they will email directions.

The Tarragon

Mark and Julia Fleming

21 Hunters Way, Tarragona, Hout Bay 7806
Tel: 021-791-4155 Fax: 021-791-4156
Email: info@thetarragon.com Web: www.thetarragon.com
Cell: 076-191-7755

These globe-trotting Brits have retired their backpacks and settled at the opposite, luxury end c the accommodation world. Seduced by South Africa's charm and sunshine Mark and Juli permanently un-packed, kids and all, building a new life and some very stylish self-catering cottage on the wooded southern slopes of Hout Bay's leafy valley. When I arrived a fruitless effort to fin a pen sent Mark dashing for a replacement and I was able to enjoy a purple moment inspired b the towering evergreens and the incredible stillness. A koi pond plinked occasionally with frogs o fish exploring the sun-freckled surface. Other visitors to the Fleming's subtly-crafted garden includ peacocks, Egyptian geese, cormorants, butterflies and dragonflies. From the pool-side sun loungers and braai area your eye will be drawn across the lawn and rocky peaks before sweeping like the garden, into an area of dense wood. All units have private outdoor areas dappled by vine wound frames. Marble-topped kitchens are fully kitted out with everything from top-of-the-rang toasters to dishwashers, and laundering is available with the lady who does the daily servicing Living areas, bedrooms and bathrooms are kept simple with clean-cut lines and contrasting tones quality white linens gleam against dark leather headboards, fresh-cut sunflowers pose upo polished tables and square silver-tapped sinks rest against natural slate or travertine tiling. Th Tarragon offers a finely-tuned mix of character and luxury.

Rooms: 5 fully-contained self-catering units: 2 x 3-bedroom units, 1 x 2-bedroom unit and 2 x 1-bedroom units. All with full kitchen, living area and en-suite bathrooms.
Price: R700 - R2,000 per night. Rates vary depending on length of stay, time of year and numbe of people.
Meals: Fully self-catering.
Directions: Faxed or emailed on request.

Ocean View House

Dominyc Pollitt
33 Victoria Rd, Bakoven 8005
Tel: 021-438-1982 Fax: 021-438-2287
Email: oceanv@mweb.co.za Web: www.oceanview-house.com

There's no end to Ocean View's eccentric delights with its Russian marble and award-winning gardens. Everyone has either a balcony or a terrace with fabulous views of both the sea and the garden. It is a hotel, I suppose, but such a personal one. The unobtrusive style endures, so too the humour noted in our last edition. The zebra room is kitsch-but-fun, though sadly the two-ton wooden elephant that wallowed in the water fantasia garden, amongst 200-year-old milkwood trees, got worms and was removed. Of course there's a great pool and how many hotels run an honesty bar? To cap it all, Ocean View has its own nature reserve, a tropical garden that ushers an idyllic river from the mountains to the sea. They have placed tables and sun-loungers on the grassy river banks, a sort of exotic *Wind in the Willows* scenario with rocks, ferns, trees, tropical birds and butterflies. If you ever feel like leaving Ocean View, Camps Bay beach is a stroll away with its string of outdoor restaurants and zesty atmosphere. It's a good place to watch trendy Capetonians-at-play. Tired out long before they were, I walked back to the hotel. The nightwatchman was expecting me and escorted me to my room, which was also expecting me, tomorrow's weather report by my bed.

Rooms: 14: 7 suites (1 Presidential, 1 Milkwood, 4 Royal, 1 Garden); 5 Luxury Rooms (all sea-facing) & 2 Pool Deck rooms. 13 have shower, 1 Royal has bath & sh.
Price: R400 – R1,300 pp sharing. Singles rate available off-season. Prices may change from Oct 2006.
Meals: Full breakfast is included and served until 10.00 am.
Directions: On the coast road a mile out of Camps Bay towards Hout Bay.

Cramond House Camps Bay

Gail Voigt
Cramond Rd, Camps Bay 8040
Tel: 083-457-1947 Fax: 083-118-457-1947
Email: gailvoigt@mweb.co.za
Cell: 083-457-1947

Easily stylish enough to keep the smart crowd calm, Cramond House is yet as walk-in-and-make-yourself-at-home as you'll find anywhere. Set high up, dandled on the knees of the Twelve Apostles, wall-to-wall windows along the ocean-facing front look down over Camps Bay's palm-fringed crescent of white sand. The glorious view is unavoidable, from the bedrooms, from the pool, from the wide sundeck. Will you get out of the house at all, I wonder! This is a dreamy place, the epitome of understated easy living, big on simplicity, space and light and small on clutter. My suite was huge and super-swish, with a cavernous walk-in wardrobe, deep spa and a sundeck… but all the rooms are special, particularly the fabulous new queen-bedded suite. There is a sandpit, a pool, a stunning garden, a family of tortoises…. Delicious things to eat and drink spill from the fridge, the bar and cupboards. Gail will come to settle you in and introduce you to the permanent house staff (Gerald, Jan, Beauty and Miriam). Here's part of an email from her that sets the scene rather well: *My husband is a very keen hiker and would gladly take visitors on hikes… we are so close to so much in CT. Walt, my son takes folk on wine routes and sightseeing. We love people and I am from the Eastern Cape originally where one's life is.... people!* Luxury at Cramond House is only half the story.

Rooms: 4: 1 queen with en-suite spa bath & shower; 1 twin en-s bath & shower; 1 double en-s sh'r & adjacent area with sleeper couch; 1 queen en-s bath & sh'r plus kitchenette. Cot, high chair etc available.

Price: For the whole house: May – July per night R2,200. Dec - Jan R4,400. All other times R3,300. Discounts for stays longer than 10 days. For requests relating to number of guests, ask Gail. Free ADSL Wireless internet access.

Meals: By arrangement.

Directions: Directions forwarded on reservation or complimentary airport transfers can be arranged with hired vehicles delivered to Cramond House.

The Bay Atlantic Guest House

David Mercer & Jennifer, Bernie and David Smith
3 Berkley Rd, Camps Bay 8005
Tel: 021-438-4341/2 Fax: 021-438-4340
Email: seaview@iafrica.com Web: www.thebayatlantic.com
Cell: 082-321-6175 or 082-777-8007

  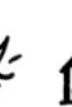

For someone who insists he "tries not to work there" David's father Bernie seems to be nonetheless a very comforting and integral part of the set-up at The Bay Atlantic Guest House (the rest of the line-up consists of Jennifer Smith, David "Surf" Smith and David "Beach" Mercer). After making a flustered apology for my dodgy old driving trainers (I had forgotten to change into my 'inspecting' shoes!), I was placed immediately at my ease by Bernie who nodded towards his own slippered feet and smiled a collaborator's smile. It seems comfort is the primary concern in this guest house where bedrooms provide you with everything you could possibly need, including TV, phones, mini-fridge, crisp white linens, towels and dressing-gowns. If the pool's too cold, hop into the solar-warmed jacuzzi. And if that gets too hot Bernie will cool it down for you (although he still insists he doesn't work there). This may be a coastal Cape Town property, but prepare yourself for sightings of the 'big 5' within. It's a sofa safari (a genuine kudu leather sofa at that) of life-size black-and-white portraits of rhinos, elephants and lions, a cheetah fireguard… and then there's real-life Jessie the jovial dog. To make the most of your last day 'the departure room' will house your baggage and allow you to shower off the remnants of a sandy stint on the beach. It's all there for your convenience, so borrow a book from the fireplace, grab a drink from the bar and settle down by the pool.

Rooms: 6: 3 doubles, 2 king/twins and 1 twin; 1 with en-suite jacuzzi bath and shower, 2 with en-suite bath and shower and 3 with en-suite shower.
Price: R250 - R750 pp sharing. Singles R375 - R1,100.
Meals: Full breakfast included.
Directions: Emailed or faxed on request.

Ambiente Guest House

Marion Baden and Peter Forsthöuel
58 Hely Hutchinson Ave, Camps Bay 8005
Tel: 021-438-4060 Fax: 021-438-4060
Email: info@ambiente-guesthouse.com Web: www.ambiente-guesthouse.com Cell: 072-460-1953

Marion and Peter's affair with Ambiente Guest House began with a holiday. An initial joke to buy from the previous owners became a reality that ended in signatures on more than one dotted line when they not only bought the place, but also were married here. Four years later and they're still going strong. So what does Ambiente have to sustain such marital harmony? A base of sturdy functionality is hidden beneath a layer of exciting features and continual surprises. Original native masks, chairs and colour schemes are fused with a Mediterranean feel to produce an effect of African-themed modernity. Choose from beds suspended by chains or with wavy topless posts. Immerse yourself in the big luxurious bathrooms where showers are powerful, sinks are exciting (trust me, sinks can be exciting, you'll see) and baths cry out for a glass of champagne. Amidst these mirror-filled havens things aren't always what they seem. Is that an African spear disguised as a towel rail? A boulder in the shower? This place has playful passion. It has the drama of half the mountain in the breakfast room, the shock of sand beneath your feet in the loo. If that's not enough to keep you amused, the views of mountain and ocean will make you gawp, the pool and garden will refresh and the paintings, if you look long and hard enough, will make you blush.

Rooms: 4: 3 king suites, all with en-suite bath and shower; and 1 double room with en-suite bath/shower.
Price: R405 - R650 pp sharing. Airport transfers R300 per transfer, one way.
Meals: Full breakfast included. BBQs possible by arrangement.
Directions: Take the N1 or N2 to Cape Town and follow signs to Cableway/Camps Bay. Remain on M62, Camps Bay Drive, with the 12 Apostles to your left and Camps Bay down to your right. Turn Left into Ravensteyn Ave then first right into Hely Hutchinson Ave. Ambiente is number 58.

Sundowner Guest House

Cherry Kohla and Michael Crowden
41 Geneva Drive, Camps Bay 8005
Tel: 021-438-2622 Fax: 021-438-2633
Email: stay@sundowner-guesthouse.com
Web: www.sundowner-guesthouse.com Cell: 083-690 5683

The Crowden Kholas insist on superlative quality and at Sundowner Guesthouse the freshly-ground coffee is even praised by Italians. It is Cherry's hobby to gather authentic ingredients and transform them into a specifically tailored, innovative feast. As she spoke of locally-sourced seasonal fruits, cold meats and cheeses, home-made preserves, croissants, muesli and crispy-baked loaves, I wished I had coincided my visit with breakfast. This Anglo-Austrian duo have built up a remarkable knowledge of their locality which they enthusiastically share with guests (I also gleaned my fair share of advice). Cherry's unique flair, originating in her design background, permeates throughout the guest-house where a wholesome base of whites, creams and dark chocolate browns are spiced up with flashes of tangy oranges and lime greens. In the Penthouse Suite strips of window frame sections of Table Mountain, which appear to hang like pictures on the wall, a peepshow of the Camps Bay view. Vibrant décor, quiet reading corners and a quirky, cube-seated TV area gather to form a living space accommodating of every holiday pursuit; or you could just take it easy by the pool. I pitched up for a grapetizer at Michael's watering-hole, but there are far heftier drinks on offer for those not driving and wishing to toast the sunset. A fantastic place that will keep everyone happy.

Rooms: 4: 3 double bedrooms with en-suite bath and shower and 1 king-size bedroom suite with en-suite bath and shower.
Price: R350 - R800 pp sharing. Singles + 50%.
Meals: Full breakfast included and light meals available on request.
Directions: Faxed or emailed on request.

Map Number: 3

Villa 54

David and Michelle O'Brien
54 Hely Hutchinson Avenue, Camps Bay 8005
Tel: 021-790-2665 Fax: 021-790-2665
Email: info@Villa54.co.za Web: www.Villa54.co.za
Cell: 072-296-9696

It just so happened that I managed to coincide my visit to Villa 54 with their opening launch party. Cradling a glass of champagne (and suspended strawberry), we watched a fiery sun slip smoothly from the sky and I for one was charmed. Michelle breezed elegantly through the two-storey affair pointing out some of the most outstanding features: an unusual octagonal pool, a mahogany-tabled dining room, luxurious sandy stone bathrooms, a fully-equipped kitchen with protected braai area (just in case those summer winds are whipping out back) and various living areas suited to different pursuits. The main lounge, also octagonal in shape, seems to mimic the contours of Lion's Head, which Villa 54 looks onto. Here the onus is placed on cheery conversation spurred by drinks from the honesty cabinet and sweeping sea views. DSTV viewing is saved for another less sociable room. I chatted with an excited Paul who had been putting Villa 54 through its paces and was certainly enjoying the Jacuzzi bath and downstairs bachelor flat, a unit in itself with open-plan kitchen, living room and its own sauna. Young Jamie managed to cajole me into reading her a story putting my baby-sitting skills to the test in the children's bedroom, a tri-single bed arrangement with bright kid-friendly paintings and fun feel. It was a real experience to see this self-catering villa come alive in company, a great spot for groups of family and friends.

Rooms: 4-bed self-catering house: 1 queen en-suite Jacuzzi & sep' shower, 1 queen, 1 kids room with 3 singles and 1 downstairs bachelor flat wit queen & en-suite shower. All beds extra-length.
Price: Rates per day & dependent on season, number of people and length of stay: R600 - R3,900.
Meals: Possible to arrange breakfast with resident house-keeper (& ironing and babysitting) at extra cost.
Directions: Take N2 towards Cape Town & take De Waal Drive. Follow signs for Cable Station. Continue on Orange St (past Mt. Nelson Hotel) & turn L at T-jct into Buitengracht to top of hill. Follow Kloof Nek Rd into Camps Bay Drive. Take 1st L into Prima & 1st L into Hely Hutchinson, past Pletteklip & Villa 54 is on your R.

Map Number: 3

Camps Bay Beach Villa

Simon and Helena Kneel
6 Strathmore Rd, Camps Bay 8005
Tel: 021-438-3416 Fax: 021-438-3416
Email: info@capeportfolios.com Web: www.capeportfolios.com
Cell: 072 238 4757

Left to my own devices in this sophisticated house, I kicked off my shoes and padded bare-foot on cool tiles straight to the balcony. Spreading arrow-like from the corner, the heated pool, shimmering with scintillas of sunlight, directed my gaze over Camps Bay beach to the formidable Twelve Apostles. Here the sea has a unique sparkle, a spread of amethyst protected by its mountain allies. Feeling inquisitive as I looked up at the bedroom balconies, faintly nautical in their sail-like sweep, I turned my attention back to the house. This time I paused to note the dramatic pillars, slick edges and contrasting wave of the ceiling. An elegant steel and glass dining table was softened by a quirky fynbos-flower arrangement, one of the many thoughtful touches left by Simon and the Cape Portfolios team. Cutting through the lanky-furnitured bar, I entered the black marble-topped kitchen. Yet more goodies surprised me here; a huge fruit platter, muffins, crisps and a fridge stocked with fruit-juice, cheese and grapes. This is not your usual managed self-catering operation. Although the property comes complete with independence, Simon, Helena and their team will ensure you have everything you need or could want organised. Fridges can be pre-stocked, taxis, car hire, chefs or caterers booked, baby-sitters or nannies arranged, activities and eateries highlighted. With big sofas to slouch upon and restful beds, immaculate style comes as comfy as your favourite jumper.

Rooms: 5-bedroom self-catering house: 1 king with en-suite bath and shower, 1 queen with en-suite shower, 2 queens with shared bath/shower and 1 twin with en-suite shower. There is also a basic double outside with en-suite shower.
Price: Winter rates R3,000 per day, summer rates R4,000 - R8,000. Prices flexible dependent on season, size of group & length of stay. Min 1-week stay. Includes daily servicing Mon - Fri.
Meals: Fully self-catering. Fridge can be stocked by prior arrangement and chef or caterer can be organised for all other meals at extra cost.
Directions: Faxed or emailed on confirmation of booking.

Huijs Haerlem

Johan du Preez and Kees Burgers
25 Main Drive, Sea Point 8005
Tel: 021-434-6434 Fax: 021-439-2506
Email: haerlem@iafrica.com Web: www.huijshaerlem.co.za

Don't even try and pronounce it! Imagine, it used to be called 't Huijs Haerlem, so small thanks for small mercies! But what a great place: a secret garden, perched high on the hill above Sea Point, enclosed behind walls and gates, abloom with tropical flowers in beds and earthenware pots, with suntrap lawns, a pool (salt-water, solar-heated) and views over Table Bay. The verandah frame is snaked about with a vine and small trees provide the shade. Johan and Kees have a lovely caring approach to their guests and look after you royally. There's no formal reception area, the bar is based on honesty, all their fine Dutch and South African antiques are not hidden away for fear of breakage. In fact both of them suffer from magpie-itis and walls and surfaces teem with eye-arresting objects: a tailor's mannequin, cabinet-making tools, old linen presses. Of course breakfast is enormous with fresh breads, rolls and croissants, fruits, cheeses, cold meats and the full cooked bonanza. This is Johan's domain, a chance for him to banter with guests and make a few suggestions. All the bedrooms are different, but all have their advantage, some with private terraces, some great views, one a four-poster. Whichever room you are in you will feel part of the whole.

Rooms: 8: 5 twins and 3 doubles; all en-suite, 2 with separate bath and shower, the rest with shower over bath.
Price: R390 – R600 pp sharing. Singles plus 25%.
Meals: Full breakfast included.
Directions: Faxed or emailed on booking.

The Villa Rosa

Lynn Stacey
277 High Level Rd, Sea Point 8005
Tel: 021-434-2768 Fax: 021-434-3526
Email: villaros@mweb.co.za Web: www.villa-rosa.com
Cell: 082-785-3238

How I managed to drive straight past the Villa Rosa I'll never know. With dramatic red- and white-tinged walls the villa is hardly a shrinking violet. But I did anyway... I wandered up the front path through mingled scents of wild jasmine, chives and roses and was met at the stained-glass door by Lynn, who emits the same bright warmth as her villa walls. As we chatted over juice in the kitchen we were interrupted by Buttons, a newly-adopted and very vocal cat - a happy addition to the family. The villa continues its rosy persona within. Soft rose pinks are set off with hints of contrasting greens and dark wooden furniture. Most rooms are lit by enormous bay windows and intricate chandeliers, each one unique in its delicate hanging flowers, gems and metalwork. I soon discovered that Lynn had had a chandelier 'binge' at some point. And that chandeliers were just one of many such undeniable urges; the 'bathroom binge' resulted in a complete bathroom overhaul producing the fresh stone-floored en-suite beauties now in place. The metal leaf-chairs in one room (literally chairs that look like giant leaves) were "so wacky we just bought them" says Lynn. The art binge is ongoing and the walls continue to fill up with local talent. Looking at Buttons, I wondered if Lynn would ever consider an 'adoption binge'. If so I'll be volunteering myself as the next eligible stray.

Rooms: 8: all doubles, 4 with en-suite bath and shower, 4 with en-suite shower. Possibility of joining two rooms to form a family suite. 1 self-catering unit.
Price: R250 - R400. Singles R350 - R550.
Meals: Full breakfast included.
Directions: Emailed or faxed on request. Also on Villa Rosa web site.

Cheviot Place Guest House

James and Brooke Irving

18 Cheviot Place, Green Point 8005
Tel: 021-439-3741 Fax: 021-439-9095
Email: cheviot@netactive.co.za Web: www.cheviotplace.co.za
Cell: 082-467-3660

Cheviot Place is something fresh for the Cape Town accommodation scene. This was apparent to me from the moment James opened the front door, dressed in Hawaiian shirt (sunny) and trainers (trendy), Jamie Cullum (jazzy) wafting out behind him. When he moved in a couple of years ago, this venerable, early 20th-century house, with its high ceilings, pillars and arches, was in desperate need of renovation. So new wooden floors, natural hemp-style rugs and black metal light fittings now set off the original marble fireplaces. Cheviot Place has been transformed into a contemporary home while retaining the best of its Victorian heritage. And, first and foremost, a home it is. There was nothing on display to suggest that James and Brooke actually run a guest house (apart from the guest bedrooms, of course) so any visitor here would feel like an old friend come to stay. James was even sure he recognised me from somewhere. The self-catering unit below the main house is surely the ultimate in 21st-century living, reminding me of the troglodyte homes carved out of the rocks deep in the Sahara. Apart from the bed there is no free-standing furniture: everything has been sculptured from the stone. Original? Yes. Cool? In both senses of the word.

Rooms: 4: 3 queens (1 with en-suite bath and shower, 1 with en-suite bath & shower-head & 1 with en-suite shower); 1 twin with en-suite shower. Self-catering suite also available with 1 queen.
Price: R250 - R400 pp sharing. R285 - R500 for singles.
Meals: Full breakfast is included. Picnics provided on request for R35 - R150. Braai on request for R55 - R100.
Directions: Ask when booking.

Cedric's Lodges

Jutta Frensch and
Inge Niklaus
90 Waterkant Street and 39 Dixon Street, Green Point
"De Waterkant" 8001
Tel: 021-425-7635
Fax: 021-425-7635
Email: info@cedricslodge.com
Web: www.cedricslodge.com
Cell: 083-327-3203 or 083-326-4438

Once Cape Muslim slave-quarters, De Waterkant's brightly-coloured, cobbled hill-side streets are amongst the most cosmopolitan in Cape Town, full of fashion labels, interior design showrooms, art galleries and trendy bars. The city's heart beats fast here and Inge and her architect sister Jutta have their fingers on the pulse. They metamorphosed a 17th-century slave-house into Cedric's, a washed-grey, contemporary town house. Downstairs is given over to an open-plan living space with steel-and-chrome kitchen, sleek dining table and grey suede sofas arranged around a concrete fireplace. There's glass, polished floorboards and colourful prints throughout and, upstairs, beds have dark headboards and chinoiserie fabrics. My room also had Indian chairs, slate bath and balcony, a blissful spot in the thrall of Table Mountain for this cold-blooded European to bake. Inge and Jutta will take you up there or up Signal Hill for champagne as the sun dissolves into the Atlantic. They'll just as likely drag you off to a concert or they might invite you to join them for lunch with friends in the Cape Flats. Inge edits the village rag and is an inspirational source of what's hot in the Mother City. Spend a lazy breakfast in one of the corner cafés and meander round this forward-looking historic area and you'll be hooked. As the Eagles (almost) said: "You can check out any time you like, but you can never (really) leave." *5 minutes' walk to Convention Center. Also now opened Cedric's Country Lodge in Greyton with 3 double rooms.*

Rooms: 8 (2 x 4): all doubles with en-suite bath or shower.
Price: R800 – R1,100 per room. The whole house can be let from R3,200 – R4,400 per night.
Meals: Rate includes vouchers for breakfast at next-door cafés or in-house. Cape Town's most fashionable restaurant on the doorstep.
Directions: For directions see the Cedric's Lodge web site.

Launic House

Nicolette Longden and Lauren Zarges
10 Romney Rd, Green Point
Tel: 021-434-4851 Fax: 021-434-0913
Email: stay@launichouse.co.za Web: www.launichouse.co.za
Cell: 084-207-7888 or 084-207-7722

Strings of pebbles clacking gently against the wall welcomed me to Launic House and I soon discovered that this sort of eye-catching, even ear-catching, creative quirk is the norm here. The original Victorian building (is 1903 still Victorian?) had fallen into disrepair, all the more enticing a purchase for Nicky and Lauren, who salvaged some beautiful old fireplaces and wooden floorboards for the new incarnation. They also unearthed a lot of other stuff to which they have mostly assigned a new role: shutters have become head-boards, antique newspapers found in the attic have become wallpaper (read the news from 1904 in the downstairs loo) and many other materials have been worked by Nicky into zany and colourful bits of artwork. Otherwise the original house has been almost completely overhauled, with rich earth-browns and creams on walls, brisk whites in bed linen and sofa covers, and using natural materials such as wicker and wood to create a solid, natural, modern, well-made feel. The stone bowl-sinks and heavy-walled showers only add to the effect. Breakfast in summer takes place outside by the plunge pool, with a view of the bay and Robben Island across local rooftops. Check out the enormous avocado tree too, its aged branches drooping from the weight of huge fruits. Nicolette and Lauren are definitely in the right job… and it took a while after I left before I stopped expecting ordinary objects to thrill the eye.

Rooms: 6 double rooms.
Price: R250 - R375. Singles +50%.
Meals: Traditional South African BBQ available on request.
Directions: Emailed or faxed on request.

Cape Heritage Hotel

Nick Garsten
90 Bree Street, 8001
Tel: 021-424-4646 Fax: 021-424-4949
Email: info@capeheritage.co.za Web: www.capeheritage.co.za

Wham-bam in the city centre, on the fringe of Cape Town's historic Bo-Kaap area, the small, intimate and innovative Cape Heritage Hotel has a delightfully informal, sociable guest house feel. Central to the breakfast room is a communal table bordered by large grapefruit and pomegranate paintings and cocoon-like lampshades hanging over the coffee bar. Architects and archaeologists have played their roles in the reconstruction of the building which dates back to 1771. I admired the black-and-white photos and line drawings in the hallways depicting the building's history, amongst other old photos of Cape Town. Throughout the building patches of murals and exposed walls have been left untouched to showcase the original architecture and workmanship. High-beamed ceilings and burnished wooden floors line the rooms, and each of the bedrooms has been individually styled with antiques: sleigh beds or four-posters and rooms in Malay, African, Zulu and Japanese style. I particularly liked the Pakhuis (pack house) historic room. A major attraction is the choice of restaurants on your doostep and, come evening, in the courtyard there is a thriving atmosphere, even live music... and, as it happens, the oldest known living grapevine in South Africa. Heritage Square also houses a virtual museum of the oldest operational blacksmith in SA, a health club and a resident masseuse.

Rooms: 15: 2 suites, 6 luxury and 7 standard, all with en-suite bath and shower.
Price: Seasonal. Standard R480 - R610, Luxury R520 – R720, Suites R780 - R1,000 pp sharing. Single supplement + 50%.
Meals: Breakfast included. Other restaurants on site.
Directions: From airport take N2, turn off at Strand St exit. At 8th set of lights turn left into Bree St. At 2nd set of lights hotel is on your right.

Cape Cadogan

Liesl Briedenhann
5 Upper Union Street, Cape Town 8001
Tel: 021-480-8080 Fax: 021-480-8090
Email: reservations@capecadogan.com Web: www.capecadogan.com

Gorgeously discreet - that's how I'm going to describe the Cape Cadogan, if only to save my blushes because I actually walked right past it three times before I eventually found it (and yes it is that building with the words 'Cape Cadogan' above the door). The façade is not just a façade. This boutique hotel really is as opulent as its exterior suggests. Long white drapes flutter in the breeze as they run down the pillars of this stately Georgian and Victorian national monument, while behind heavy wooden doors there is a hushed harmony of pale cream colours, decadently thick fabrics, and an eclectic mix of contemporary and antique furniture. The high-ceilinged bedrooms are bathed in light, and boast quite the biggest (limestone) bathrooms I've ever seen. I must admit I felt slightly guilty as I stood dripping water onto the sea-grass carpet (Cape Town isn't so lush and green without reason), but it provided a taste of what this place is famed for... its service. In the time it took to say, "I thought it only rained like this in England", Liesl's team had sprung into action and my soaking brolly was whisked away to dry, a towel produced to mop up the excess, a seat offered next to the roaring fire, and a pot of coffee conjured up from nowhere... see I told you it was good. 'Guests are our privilege' is the mantra here, but let me tell you, the privilege was all mine.

Rooms: 12: all twins or doubles with en-suite bathrooms.
Price: R900 - R1,700 per room per night.
Meals: Full breakfast included. Mr Delivery service available at other times, or plenty of local restaurants within walking distance.
Directions: On website, or can be faxed/emailed on request.

The Village Lodge Portfolio

Richard Gush and Tobin Shackleford
49 Napier Street, De Waterkant 8001
Tel: 021-421-1106 Fax: 021-421-8488
Email: reservations@thevillagelodge.com Web: www.thevillagelodge.com
Cell: 072 457 4387

Now here is something a little bit different, the chance to have your own home (albeit only for the period of your stay), right in the centre of one of Cape Town's trendiest neighbourhoods. The Village Lodge Portfolio is a constantly evolving array of brightly-painted former slave cottages (some dating from the 18th century) and more modern, but sympathetically styled, homes in the National Preservation site that is De Waterkant Village. Each is individually owned, but all are run on a day-to-day basis by Richard Gush and his team. Only the best are selected, which means you're assured of high-quality fixtures, fittings and furnishings. All have standardised luxury linen, plates, knives, forks etc, in fact everything you could ever want or need to make your stay here a pleasure. The concept is all about choice (which, trust me, will be no easy thing). First you'll have to choose between traditional and contemporary, but then you'll need to choose your exact cottage. There are too many to go through them all, but of the ones I saw I witnessed roof decks galore, exposed wooden floors, luxury leathers sofas, private gardens, swap-system bookshelves, rain-head showers, flat-screen TVs, real fires, amazing views, total privacy, plunge pools... the list goes on (see, I said it wouldn't be an easy choice). "People come here to buy into a lifestyle", gushed Richard Gush, and the good news is, it's an absolute bargain to boot!

Rooms: 12 cottages, with one, two or three bedrooms (queen, king & twin), all main bedrooms with en-suite bathrooms and showers. 8 cottages have aircon. Online bookings and availability.
Price: R850 - R1,500 per night per cottage.
Meals: All meals can be provided on request.
Directions: Web site map and instructions.

Dunkley House

Sharon Scudamore
3b Gordon St, Gardens 8001
Tel: 021-462-7650 Fax: 021-462-7649
Email: reservations@dunkleyhouse.com Web: www.dunkleyhouse.com

Dunkley House is so cunningly hidden in the city centre that, despite dozens of visits to Cape Town, you might never have found it without our help. So pats on backs all round. Tucked into a quiet street in central Gardens this compact boutique hotel is a mosaic-floored, chic-Mediterranean-villa of a place. Chic maybe, but delightfully relaxed with it. Manager Sara supplied me with home-made biscuits as we chatted on a massive, caramel leather sofa that I had to struggle out of when I stood up. This really is a place you are encouraged to feel at home in, no small feat for a hotel, however small and 'boutique'. You want to lounge under palms by the pool?… lounge; you want to help Eunice in the kitchen?… go for it. She's a fantastic cook and aside from endless breakfast delights (don't miss the fluffy omelettes), she has been known to rustle up a feast for those who want to eat in of an evening. The long dining table is neatly arranged next to a pot-bellied wood-burner for winter nights and framed by black-and-white prints of Dar es Salaam. Plus, the bedrooms are just a stagger away, bay-windowed, whitest linen on beds and flashes of colour in the cushions. For something on the quirky side, the retro mezzanine apartment upstairs - perfect for family stays - is decorated in blacks, whites and reds. This place really is a hidden gem worth digging for.

Rooms: 6: 2 kings, 3 queens, 1 with bath all others with shower only. One apartment with 1 double and 1 twin sharing shower.
Price: From R350 – R495 pp sharing. Singles R550 – R800. Apartment R1,150 per night.
Meals: Full breakfast included. Other meals by arrangement.
Directions: Faxed or emailed on booking, also on website.

Acorn House

Bernd Schlieper and Beate Lietz
1 Montrose Avenue, Oranjezicht 8001
Tel: 021-461-1782 Fax: 021-461-1768
Email: welcome@acornhouse.co.za Web: www.acornhouse.co.za

Bernd and Beate can barely contain the happiness they derive from Acorn House, and their enthusiasm rubs off quickly on all but the stoniest of their visitors. I was a pushover. The listed building, designed by busy Sir Herbert Baker in 1904, sits on the sunny, sea-facing slopes of Table Mountain with tip-top views to Table Bay. The house is typical Sir Herbert, timber colonnade, broad verandah et al, and there is an immaculate garden with black-slate swimming pool and a sun-lounging lawn, cleanly demarcated by agapanthus and lavender bushes. Breakfast, often served by the pool, is a no-holds-barred display of meats, cheeses, eggs and freshly-squeezed fruit juices; "probably the second-best breakfast in Cape Town" is Beate's carefully-worded claim! Upstairs, in your wood-floored bedroom you will find notes of welcome or farewell, chocolates and sprigs of lavender. Wine-lovers are also well served: Bernd is pazzo for the stuff, and regularly visits local vineyards to ensure that his house wines are up-to-the-moment (just for his guests' benefit, of course). Having lived in South Africa for five years now, Bernd and Beate are still awash with excitement about their surroundings. A stay in Acorn House will leave you feeling much the same.

Rooms: 8: 1 king, 3 twins and 3 doubles all with en-suite bath; 1 family suite with twin.
Price: R420 - R520 pp sharing. Singles R400 - R700. Family suite as double R840 - R1,040 + R200 for up to 2 kids.
Meals: Full breakfast included.
Directions: See website or ask for fax.

Four Rosmead

David Shorrock
4 Rosmead Avenue, Oranjezicht 8001
Tel: 021-480-3810 Fax: 021-423-0044
Email: info@fourrosmead.com Web: www.fourrosmead.com
Cell: 082-900-3461

From "the back end of a bus" to the frontage of a French country house, Four Rosmead has undergone an impressive facelift since David got his hands on it. When I first visited, some two years ago now, the last licks of paint were drying and pictures being straightened ready for their first guests, but even then I could tell it had élan and panache! It's a familiar story: David's a thoroughly affable ex-investment banker with a passion for art and all things French, who fled a hectic Jo'burg life for a change of gear in the Cape (no one ever seems to change career to go into the financial world!). And what a spot to pick… the house and its position are magnificent. Four Rosmead is a provincial monument, built in 1903, but restyled with a thoroughly modern feel. The rooms are all wonderfully light and airy thanks to chalky-toned walls and high, pitched ceilings. Cushions and oils add the colour (all the art in the house is South African and for sale) and from enormous windows (particularly in the showers) the views are great, whether looking through ancient oaks to Lion's Head, or peeking over rooftops to the City Bowl and ocean. But why spend your time inside when you can mooch by the pool or amble crunchily along the gravel paths of the Mediterranean garden soothed by the scent of lavender and the rustle of bay trees, oranges and olives? There is also a 'pamper room' offering massage, reflexology and aromatherapy. *WIFI.*

Rooms: 8: 1 cottage suite with 1 queen with shower over bath & outdoor shower; 3 twin/kings, 1 with bath & shower, 2 with shower only; 4 queens, 1 with bath & shower, 3 with shower only.
Price: R525 – R1,100 pp sharing. Singles +50%.
Meals: Full breakfast included. Snack lunches can be ordered in. Other meals on request.
Directions: Faxed or emailed on booking, also available on website.

Lézard Bleu Guest House

Chris and Niki Neumann
30 Upper Orange St, Oranjezicht 8001
Tel: 021-461-4601 Fax: 021-461-4657
Email: welcome@lezardbleu.co.za Web: www.lezardbleu.co.za
Cell: 072-234-4448

It's going to be hard to book the tree-house, particularly when word gets round, but you have got to try! Surely the most wonderful bedroom in Cape Town. The trunks of two giant palm trees spear through a wooden deck at vertiginous heights and a tiny balcony is in among the topmost fronds and spikes. Lézard Bleu was just about the best guest house in Cape Town anyway, so this latest extravagant addition represents one great big cherry on a mouthwatering cake. Niki is an actress and Chris is a chef, although he has hung up his hat now… no, don't even ask! They are still young and humorous and the house remains sleek and modern with solid maplewood bedframes, white pure cotton, sandy shades and tones, bright splashes of local and modern art on the walls. Breakfast is the best beanfeast in Cape Town (and that's the opinion of other guest house owners). The Blue Lizard snakes pleasingly from area to area, each room with its own doors out to a patio and to the large pool, where deck loungers take it easy on a surrounding timber deck. There are real fires in winter, an honesty bar, free ADSL internet access - mere details, but typical. Individual, creative, very comfortable, but most importantly this is somewhere really natural and friendly.

Rooms: 7: 1 family room; 5 doubles/twins; 4 with en/s bath and shower; 1 with en/s shr; 1 tree-house double en/s b and shr.
Price: R425 – R630 pp sharing. Single rate +50%.
Meals: Full (enormous!) breakfast included and served till 10.30 am.
Directions: Ask for directions when booking.

Redbourne Hilldrop

Jonny and Sharon Levin
12 Roseberry Avenue, Oranjezicht 8001
Tel: 021-461-1394 Fax: 021-465-1006
Email: info@redbourne.co.za Web: www.redbourne.co.za

One of the happiest and most humorous guest houses in Cape Town, so it always seems to me. Many of Jonny and Sharon's guests refuse to stay elsewhere and gifts arrive daily from overseas… well almost. One day you may be surprised to find yourself packing up toys for their kids. It's a small, intimate place and you are spoiled: free-standing baths, fluffy duvets, big white pillows, unflowery good taste in mirrors and wood floors, magazines, African artefacts, great showers. One room has a spiral staircase down to its bathroom. You eat breakfast at a diner-style bar stretched along a wall of pretty windows with incredible city views. Guests are treated as far as possible as friends and each time I visit I notice the easy rapport that Jonny and Sharon have generated with them – probably overnight. The wall-enclosed pool has now been up and running for a couple of years, complete with a mini-waterfall spanning the length of it and Table Mountain looming above. A perfect finishing touch. *WIFI.*

Rooms: 4: 2 doubles and 1 twin; 2 with en/s bath and shower, 1 with en/s sh. And 1 family room with sunroom (pictured above).
Price: R325 - R450 pp sharing. Singles on request.
Meals: Full breakfast included. Dinners by prior arrangement. Restaurants nearby.
Directions: Ask when booking.

1 on Queens

Ursul Neidherdt & Lisa Williams
I Queens Rd, Tamboerskloof 8001
Tel: 021-422-0004 Fax: 021-422-0027
Email: golfpart@iafrica.com Web: www.1onqueens.co.za

You know, we can always make a plan', beamed Ursula again, this time referring to food arrangements for guests. Open-hearted, relaxed and tirelessly flexible are the qualities that mark 1 on Queens out as a uniquely Capetonian institution, where nothing is too much trouble. An easy stroll into town, Queen's sits up on a hill peacefully removed from the bustle below and guarded over by the lion's rump of Signal Hill. Lisa and Ursula have done a terrific job in transforming the house from its former shockingly dilapidated state into the terracotta Tuscan-style villa it is today. The marble-topped kitchen, its bowls over-spilling with fruit, takes pride of place in an 'afro-chic' living area. Next to this is the large, social dining table, laden with sunflowers in full bloom, where guests congregate to taste Queens' famous fruit platters at breakfast. Positioned around the big fireplace, dark leather sofas make the ideal spot for pre-dinner drinks amongst wise-looking African masks and animal-print cushions. Bedrooms are all decorated in subtle sandy colours with proper wine racks ('none of those silly miniatures here') and surfaces aplenty in the porcelain bathrooms. I particularly liked the sandstone-tiled family cottage that felt rather like a luxurious desert cave. Outside, a purpling jacaranda and 400-year-old olive tree provide the shade to chill by and soak up the vibe.

Rooms: 8: 5 kings & 3 twins, all en-suite with full bathrooms except one with shower only. 1 cottage with a king-size bed and a sleeper couch.
Price: R295 - R1,200 pp sharing.
Meals: Full breakfast included. Sandwiches can be provided during the day for additional cost while guests have use of Mr Delivery service.
Directions: On website. Can be emailed or faxed at time of booking.

An African Villa

Jimmy van Tonder and Louis Nel

19 Carstens St, Tamboerskloof 8001
Tel: 021-423-2162 Fax: 021-423-2274
Email: villa@capetowncity.co.za Web: www.capetowncity.co.za/villa
Cell: 082-920-5508

Louis ditched the interior design world to focus his full creative zeal on this magnificent house – or rather houses – and when I pitched up he was hard at work, pen in mouth, bent over plans for the next step. Not content with just five fabulous rooms at nearby Liberty Lodge, he and Jimmy are converting three entire houses into a den of "African Zen". The structure may be classically Victorian, but the décor is anything but with bold, tribal colours offsetting black-painted floorboards and neutral carpets. Jimmy gave me the grand tour – trailed as ever by dachshunds Zip and Button – pointing out Louis' designer eye in every detail, from the lacquered ostrich eggs and porcupine quills (please don't pinch them, he pleads) to the hanging Zulu spears and African wedding hats. The bathrooms are compact but perfectly formed, the bedrooms are wonderfully roomy, and when you finally and reluctantly slide from between the percale cotton sheets, breakfast is a communal affair in the large airy kitchen or out on the terrace. This house is a haven, a cool retreat and while others may be sweating their way up Table Mountain just minutes away, you can be thumbing through a book in the shade of an orange tree or cooling off in the plunge pool. Go on… treat yourself. *Library and Internet available to all guests. Also 3 lovely self-catering units, Mountain Magic Garden Suites, all with mountain views in a garden setting: R550 for 2.*

Rooms: 12 king/twins: 5 Superior with bath & shower; 5 Classic, 3 with shower, 2 with bath & shower; 2 Standard (street-facing without air-con). Liberty Lodge: 3 Traditional guest rooms with shower, 1 with bath & sh'r; 1 Budget Room (a little smaller) with shower.
Price: R350 - R550 pp sharing. Singles on request.
Meals: Full breakfast included.
Directions: From central Cape Town follow signs to the Cableway. At the bottom of Kloofnek Rd double back and turn left into Carstens St. Look for the second block on the left with a yellowwood tree outside.

Bayview B&B

Christine Matti
10 De Hoop Avenue, Tamboerskloof 8001
Tel: 021-424-2033 Fax: 021-424-2705
Email: baychris@iafrica.com Web: www.baychris.com
Cell: 082-414-2052

Christine's partner Corinne had her arm in a sling when we met. She'd torn a tendon pulling a cork out of a bottle – an unfortunate accident, but a large tick in the "commitment to the cause" category for GG candidates. These two are passionate about their wine and, well, passionate about just about everything. When not buzzing around the house, Swiss-born Christine is usually out cranking up Cape Town kilometres on her racing bike or working on her annoyingly low golf handicap. She arrived in South Africa a wide-eyed whippersnapper some twenty years ago, and has never quite got around to leaving. Her home is an airy haven of healthy living. White-washed walls, floor-to-ceiling tinted windows and tiled floors make this a perfect mountain-side retreat from the city centre's summer heat. Breakfasts are an Alpine feast of German breads, selected cheeses and cold meats and guests are encouraged to help themselves to a bottomless bowl of fresh fruit. Take a dip in the pool, head off for a massage at any number of nearby wellness centres, read a book on your decking balcony, and - once you've done all that - lie back on the sofa and gaze at a perfectly-framed Table Mountain through the sitting room skylight. My only disappointment? I didn't have time to stay the night. *WIFI.*

Rooms: 4: 2 queens, 1 with en-suite shower and bath, 1 with en-suite shower; 1 double with en/s shower, 1 twin with en-suite shower.
Price: R200 - R480 pp sharing.
Meals: Healthy breakfasts included. Cooked breakfast on request.
Directions: Follow signs from the city centre to the Cableway. From Kloofnek Rd turn R into St. Michael's Rd and then third L into Varsity St. At the T-junction turn R into De Hoop Avenue and Bayview is the second on the right.

Hillcrest Manor

Gerda and Gerhard Swanepoel
18 Brownlow Rd, Tamboerskloof 8001
Tel: 021-423-7459
Fax: 021-426-1260
Email: hilcres@mweb.co.za
Web: www.hillcrestmanor.co.za
Cell: 082-700-5760

Step inside my fantasy world for a moment: the real politik of real estate doesn't exist and you can choose anywhere in Cape Town to build your new home. You'd probably end up precisely where I am now. Sadly, you're a hundred years too late and Gerda and Gerhard already live here. Happily, however, they've opened their home to guests and you'll be assured a warm welcome. Situated at the foot of Lion's Head in a leafy hillside suburb, their Victorian town house looms above the street and faces the most stunning view of Cape Town. From pool, balcony or bed you can see all the detail of the city and waterfront and Table Mountain's acclaimed acclivity clearly. This elegant house, its tall windows and wooden shutters set atop an elevated blue-stone foundation, is where Gerhard grew up. Nowadays the whitewashed steps lead up past a sunny lawn, patio and pool to a sitting room with original pressed-metal ceiling and a bright breakfast room, where the local artwork is for sale. Upstairs the bedrooms are designed to give respite from the long hot summer. Floors are a mix of polished timber and seagrass, beds are pine, furniture wicker. Ceiling-fans loll lazily and curtains billow in the breeze. One bedroom is pure C.S.Lewis, though here the wardrobe leads not to Narnia, but to your own claw-foot bath.

Rooms: 7: all doubles with en-suite shower, one with bath too.
Price: R260 – R400 pp sharing. Single supplement R100.
Meals: Full breakfast included. Meals for groups by prior arrangement. 3-course dinner R45, wine not included.
Directions: Faxed or emailed on booking.

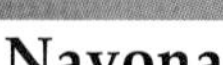

Navona

Elle Jahnig
Unit 25, Park Road Place, 11 Park Road, Tamboerskloof 8001
Tel: 021-794-0945 Fax: 021-794-0945
Email: info@navona.co.za Web: www.navona.co.za
Cell: 082-082-7051

Slap, bang in the middle of town, this cosy studio loft apartment is perfect for young couples looking for a taste of city life. Tucked away just off Kloof Street, Navona offers great privacy and calm with an enviable full-frame view of Table Mountain. Elle is passionate about interiors and this space is a showcase for her eclectic tastes. Vying for your attention are sparkling Hollywood mirrors, a Louis XIV armchair, framed photos on the wall, a giant marble chess table, modern lighting that are artworks in themselves and flower-pots of cascading palms. Upstairs, the main bedroom is a thoroughly romantic cocoon, replete with candles, mohair blankets and a pretty roof garden to appreciate from your bed. On the landing floor there is a double bed for extra bodies and a big storage cupboard. Elle is herself the mother of an inquisitive little lady, so the apartment is safe for young children; and for the larger ones there's a 'DSTV/internet/DVD multiplex corner'. Not that there should be any need to sit indoors, with all Cape Town has to offer quite literally on your doorstep. Step outside into an array of chic eateries, fashionable bars and mingle with the in-crowd... though of course you do have a wonderfully-equipped modern kitchen at your disposal too! Even if you can't be bothered to cook, I'll bet you make your way through the Belgian chocolates and biscotti when you return home after hours.

Rooms: 2: 1 double bedroom and 1 double bed on open-plan landing.
Price: R500 - R900 for whole apartment dependent on season. Maximum 4 people.
Meals: Self-catering. Daily servicing can be arranged at a reasonable daily rate.
Directions: Emailed or faxed on booking. Also available on web site.

Map Number: 3

Trevoyan Guest House

Philip Lamb and Max Bowyer
12 Gilmour Hill Rd, Tamboerskloof 8001
Tel: 021-424-4407 Fax: 021-423-0556
Email: trevoyan@iafrica.com Web: www.trevoyan.co.za

Max and Phil visited in 2001 and didn't even get past the brick terrace and the front step before they had decided to buy Trevoyan. Bit rash you might think? Not once you've seen it. There's something cool and sequestered about the place that cossets you from the noise and heat of the surrounding city. It faces Table Mountain and from seats set out on the long brick terrace you can see those forbidding cliffs through the branches of the massive oak that lords it over both house and garden. It's an under-canopy kingdom, complete with glamorous swimming pool, a perfect lawn bordered by leafy perimeter hedge and a recently added eight-seat jacuzzi, a spiral staircase and rooftop sun deck. The main building was built for entertaining military types visiting the Cape in the early 1900s. Rooms are indulgent now, furnished in soft pashmina tones - mint, cadmium yellow and sailor's blue - with many extras like big TVs, cream sofas, mini-bars and safes. The main bedroom is the most indulgent of all, with its enormous double shower, and state-o'-art entertainment system. Take breakfast on the back arched terrace in summer or the sunny dining room in winter. Max and Phil share a warm sense of humour and are natural hosts.

Rooms: 7: 2 kings and 2 queens all with en-suite bath and shower. 1 king with twin showers only. 2 twins with en/s bath and shower.

Price: R650 – R800 double occupancy. Singles R450 – R600. Garden Suites R750 – R1,000.

Meals: Full breakfast included. Restaurants 5 minutes' walk.

Directions: From city centre take Buitengracht Rd towards Table Mountain until it becomes Kloof Nek Rd. Take 2nd right into Gilmour Hill Rd. 100 metres on right before stop sign.

Cotswold House

Jenneke Pybus (Manager) & Nick and Bettina Wiesmann

6 Cotswold Drive, Milnerton 7435
Tel: 021-551-3637 Fax: 021-552-4228
Email: cotswold@mweb.co.za Web: www.cotswoldguesthouse.com
Cell. 083-306-1061

You arrive at this house as a guest and leave as a friend, with a hug," Jenneke joyfully informs me. Two cups of tea and some raucous giggles later I could see how this might happen. Jenneke is just one of those people you naturally open up to. On more than one occasion she has sat up into the wee hours with a heart-broken or over-worked soul providing tissues and hot chocolate when required. She knows when you want company and when you don't (guiding you in the direction of a hot bath and some chill-out time when you don't). This mother Yen (a nickname coined by some recent guests) is not clucky or fussy, she is just a warming presence, a bit like, well, your mum I suppose! Here anything is possible: hen night drinks by the pool (the whole wide expanse of it; as pools go in the city this is one to be proud of), golfing missions (yup, there's a links golf course just across the way), kite/wind-surfing (you're right next to the wind-whipped sea and lagoon) and even one-to-one counselling. Then there's the Cape Dutch-style house and garden (the latter is a work in progress, but it's green and getting there). From the vine-topped patio Table Mountain dominates the view, and from the upstairs rooms Robben Island begins to creep in as well. Fresh, comfortable and exceedingly clean you will awake feeling as bright as your backdrop and ready for a big Cotswold breakfast.

Rooms: 6: all twin/king; 4 with en-suite bath and shower, 1 with en-suite shower only and 1 with a full private bathroom.
Price: R350-R540 pp sharing. Singles on request.
Meals: Full breakfast included. It is possible to organise lunches and other meals for larger groups.
Directions: Emailed or faxed on request. Directions are also available on the website.

Medindi Manor

Geoffrey Bowman, Leshira Mosaka and Mamalema Molepo
4 Thicket Road, Rosebank 7700 Tel: 021-686-3563 Fax: 021-686-3565
Email: manor@medindi.co.za Web: www.medindi.co.za
Cell: 082-658-9955

Medindi is a secluded Edwardian manor of grand dimensions, banded by ground and first-floor verandas with a garden and swimming pool tucked away behind tall hedges and bushes. Some of the rooms have their own doors out onto the stoep and the main building has been renovated with panache and a sensitive feel for the period. Although well-stocked with bar fridges, telephones, TVs etc, Medindi avoids like the plague any h(ot)ellish homogeneity in its décor and design. The Oregon pine floors, bay windows, intricate ceilings and marble fireplaces are original and there are unique, antique touches everywhere, such as Edwardian designs for stately marble and slate floors. Bathrooms have free-standing baths, Victorian "plate" showerheads, brass fittings and a small antique cabinet has been found for each. There is modernity too, in bright wall colours (yellows and blues), and splashes of modern art – from the turn of one century to the turn of the next. Music is an important ingredient for Geoffrey, Medindi's owner, and classical music and a bit of jazz wafts through reception. A freewheeling, relaxed and youthful place. Geoffrey, Leshira and Mamalema share the day-to-day management of Medindi and six new rooms have been created from a converted outbuilding – the smaller rooms are cheaper.

Rooms: 13: 7 in the manor house: 6 dbles & 1 twin, 4 with en-s bath + shower, 3 with en-s shower; 3 garden rooms & 3 large garden suites in converted outbuilding, all en-s shower; 2 self-c cottages.
Price: R345 - R545 pp sharing. Singles R495 - R895.
Meals: Buffet Breakfast included. Full cooked breakfast extra R35. Many restaurants nearby for dinner or take-out.
Directions: See map on web site or phone ahead.

3 Pear Lane

Vo Pollard
Newlands Village, Newlands 7700
Tel: 021-689-1184 Fax: 021-689-1184
Email: pollards@iafrica.com Web: www.pearlane.co.za
Cell: 002-926-3000

At the foot of Devil's Peak mountain, deep within the lush greenery of Newlands and within one decently hooked six from the cricket ground, there lies a distinctly English garden idyll. The hugest oak I've seen marks the spot and the place in question is Vo's picture-perfect pad. A food stylist by trade, it's good to see that she employs her craft after-hours too. Everything here is just as you'd like it; the huge sash windows breathe beams of light into the rooms, the king-sized bed is dressed up in the best percale linen and embroidered cotton throws and the bathroom comes with storage space aplenty, two big stone basins and a mighty-looking, pebble-floored shower. With its French wrought-iron table, silk-cushioned chairs and vase of delicate daisies, the view out to the garden could be straight from one of Vo's shoots; home-baked scones, strawberry jam and clotted cream, naturally, would be the scene's edible accompaniment. There's a nice collection of guide-books and yes, foodie mags for you to devour, perhaps whilst lounging by the salt-water pool. Lavender, moonflowers, roses and azaleas, to name but a few, adorn the patio and lawn. Manicured but never overdone, sniffable but not overwhelming, this is exactly the way gardens... well, dainty English ones anyway... should be. Should you want to stretch your legs, Newlands Forest, my favourite Cape Town walking haunt, is right next-door.

Rooms: 1 cottage with king/twin bed and en-suite shower and well-equipped kitchen.
Price: R300 - R350 pp sharing. Singles on request.
Meals: By prior arrangement, menu on request.
Directions: Take M3 from Cape Town towards Muizenberg. Take the Newlands feed-off and then turn right into Newlands Avenue. Go over one set of lights, then turn first left into Palmboom Rd. Pear Lane is half-way down on the right.

Little Spotte

Zaria Dagnall

5 Cavendish Close, Cavendish St, Claremont 7700
Tel: 021-762-4593 Fax: c/o Mr C Dagnall 021-595-1173
Email: zaria@mweb.co.za
Cell: 082-374-3399

With all the shopping, dining, coffee-drinking and general urban whirl of Claremont excitedly clattering about it, Little Spotte is a time capsule of stillness and calm. A narrow path leads between designery shops to this delightful Victorian bungalow. There is no doubt of its Englishness once past the bird-of-paradise flowers in the front garden. The owners keep it a living space, in case they themselves want to come down from Jo'burg to use it. Thus you are blessed with antiques, yellowwood and oak furniture, and an astoundingly well-equipped kitchen. The cottage is self-catering, but Zaria is a very hands-on manager who will see you settled, make sure flowers, chocolates and a few breakfast commodities are arrayed for your arrival... and she is also a dynamic source of recommendation to lesser-known wineries, walks in Cape Town, local coffee-houses and restaurants. The cottage itself is far bigger than you might expect at the front door, with a central courtyard with table and green parasol, completely secure from the noise of the city and opened onto from the main bedroom and the dining area. Mod cons include TV/video with DSTV and a fully-equipped laundry and your local food shop is no less than Woolworths (M&S equivalent if you're a Brit and getting confused). A lovely pied-à-terre bang in the middle of one of Cape Town's most lively restaurant districts. *Very central for all city sight-seeing spots.*

Rooms: 1 cottage with 2 bedrooms: 1 twin with en-suite shower; 1 double with en-suite shower.
Price: Minimum stay 2 nights at maximum rate of R800: otherwise R550 in low season for the cottage. In high season R650 for 2 people, R720 for 3 and R840 for 4. Discounts for longer stays.
Meals: Fully self-catering, although Zaria will put a few things in for your first night.
Directions: Faxed or emailed when booking.

Dendron

Shaun and Jill McMahon
21 Ou Wingerd Pad, Upper Constantia 7806
Tel: 021-794-6010 Fax: 021-794-2532
Email: stay@dendron.co.za Web: www.dendron.co.za
Cell: 082-1911-617 or 082-296-0691

(Quite) A few years ago, Shaun bought a Land Rover in Taunton (UK) and drove it here. Hardly odd when you see the place, now replete with relaxed family atmosphere, collie dogs and cricket pegs (or whatever they're called) on the front lawn. You get all the benefits of living the South African good life by default here. Green-fingered Jill genuinely loves having guests and her enthusiasm for life is evident in everything. The cottages are private in leafy, jasmine-scented gardens and have fully-equipped kitchens stocked with basics, a braai and stunning views to the mountains on the right and False Bay in the distance. Two cottages have terracotta-tiled or wooden floors and beds with Indian cotton throws - perfect for families. The other two are newly-renovated cottages with kilims, safari prints and plump sofas. All are fully serviced. Evening pool-side views at sunset and moonrise, helped along by wine from over-the-hedge Groot Constantia vineyard, will make you want to throw away the car keys and stay (which is exactly what Shaun did when he first clapped eyes on the place). When you are hungry, Jill will send you off there through the back gate and across the vineyards to the Simons restaurant for dinner. Return by torch- and moonlight. Dendron (GK=tree) is a small slice of heaven. Don't stay too long, jealousy will take root!

Rooms: 4: 2 cottages with 1 double and 1 twin with bath and shower; 2 cottages with twin, 1 with bath & shower, 1 with shower only. Serviced daily Mon - Sat.
Price: From R300 pp sharing. Singles on request.
Meals: Breakfast for first morning provided and afterwards if requested at R30 pp.
Directions: Fax on request.

The Bishops' Court

Paul and Bernadette Le Roux
18 Hillwood Avenue, Bishopscourt 7708
Tel: 021-797-6710 Fax: 021-797-0309
Email: paul@thebishopscourt.com Web: www.thebishopscourt.com
Cell: 082-550-4533

Paul turned his back on an accounting career to become a guide and establish this fantastic place to stay and when I arrived he was briefing an English family who had taken over the whole place. "... Gigi will drive you into town for supper... yes, of course I can do a braai for 14, no problem...". Etc. He'll take you on tours galore, to the winelands, down the Cape Peninsula or on visits to housekeeper Connie's home in the township. For the moment this lot were going nowhere. The boys were hurling themselves into the pool and hunting for tennis racquets to test out a tree-shaded court at the foot of the long sloping garden. Their parents sat on a shaded terrace, soaking up *the best* Table Mountain view I have yet to stumble across. From this spot, a green carpet of tree canopy unrolls directly from two-storey house to hillside, with Kirstenbosch botanical gardens planted somewhere in the middle. The rooms (each one roughly the size of my entire flat) all have that view and my favourite had a mosaicked outdoor jacuzzi and shower. Wood-panelled ceilings and book-shelves give the dining/living room a relaxed beachy feel and, though there's no sand, bare feet at breakfast are more than welcome. "Barefoot luxury" - a perfect two-word description of The Bishops' Court. Well, it's good enough for the (Sir Steve) Redgrave's anyway, who were staying when I last passed by.

Rooms: 5 king/twins, 3 with en-suite bath, 2 with en-suite shower.
Price: R550 – R1,375 pp sharing (depending on the season). Singles plus 50%. Entire villa R9,300 a day in summer, R5,500 in winter.
Meals: Full breakfast and all drinks included. Now a full-time chef is in residence, so gourmet eating is available each night.
Directions: From airport take N2 towards Cape Town then M3 towards Muizenberg. On M3 go through 4 traffic lights then turn R to Bishopscourt on Upper Torquay Ave. Turn L at end then first R into Hillwood Ave. Property is about 200m down on R.

Montrose Palms

Jenny and Leon Jacobs
7 Montrose Terrace, Bishopscourt-Constantia
Tel: 021-762-3212 Fax: 021-762-3864
Email: info@montrosepalms.co.za Web: www.montrosepalms.co.za
Cell: 083 448 4545

The electric gates at Montrose Palms do more than merely let you in and out. They transport you to somewhere palm-fringed and water-bound in the South Pacific... somewhere serene and luxurious... somewhere like Bali. The lofty position, plummeting hillside and giant (transplanted!) date palms encouraged me to peer down into the foliage expecting to see rice terraces stepping down the mountain. In fact, wearing the Constantiaberg as a stiff high collar, Montrose Palms gazes long, high and handsome out to False Bay and the Muizenberg Mountains. Naturally, all the rooms have private terraces, which get their fair share. This house is frankly spoilt and has its every whim indulged! Smooth surfaces, satisfyingly solid fittings, sleek taps and handles, underfloor heating, and floor-to-ceiling glass doors that lead out onto the fabulous terraces; percale linen, TVs, drinks cabinet, great bathrooms, of course, and so much space. The house is surrounded by refreshing rectangles of water. Mottled-orange koi carp swim - as if they know why - in stone pools that run beneath the house itself; and the long decking-encased swimming pool with its little bridge of sighs (under which you can swim laps) and Balinese lanterns is irresistible at the other end of the house. Here you will no doubt find a day or two of your holiday plans slipping by unrealised.

Rooms: 8: 2 suites (kings) and 6 standard rooms (queens); 6 have en-suite bath and separate shower; 2 have shower only.
Price: R365 - R1,000. Single rates in low and mid-season only. Full room rates for the rest of the year.
Meals: Self-catering possible with frozen meals on request (typically R40 a meal). Full-blown dinners by prior arrangement: up to R200 p.p.
Directions: From CT take M3 towards Muizenberg, turn R at Hout Bay/Kirstenbosch turning on to M63. Follow for 1 km past Kirstenbosch. At T-jct turn R into Rhodes Drive. 1st L into Klaassens Rd. Then 2nd R into Montrose Ave. Turn R into Montrose Terrace.

Dalmeny Guest House

Pam Hewitt
3 Archie St, Kenilworth 7008
Tel: 011-788-9774 Fax: 011-788-3763
Email: pammy@global.co.za Web: www.dalmeny.co.za
Cell: 083-357-1115

Early for my appointment, Sannie (appropriately pronounced 'sunny'), much-loved housekeeper and busy-bee, sat me down in the drawing room with a pot of rooibos and some home-baked almond shortbread. And there, in quiet refinement, I whiled away a half-hour, leafing through a well-thumbed book on feng shui between sips and nibbles. I could more than happily have extended my stay and waited all afternoon, a feeling common amongst guests, many of whom return to Dalmeny year after year to relax in its peacefully elegant surroundings and be looked after by Sannie, lauded by guests as a darling, a star, a dream and even a national treasure. The house belonged to Pam's late mother, who collected all the antiques, mahogany dining furniture old Persian rugs, gilded mirrors and fine china. Amongst these goodies are homely Liberty-print sofas and squishy armchairs all basking in the sunshine that jumps through the tall, shuttered sash windows onto the pale green carpet and creamy walls inside. The bedrooms are tasteful affairs decorated with fresh lavender. There is also a cosy DSTV/DVD room to hide out in, stacked with magazines and books. Out in the intimate garden, sweet-smelling jasmine on the walls and purple-flowering chives in pots put on a good show around the pool. Well-situated for the racecourse, golf courses, Kirstenbosch and shopping centres, this place really feels like home and I guarantee that you will be spoiled rotten.

Rooms: 2: 1 king with en-suite bath & shower, 1 twin with separate bath.
Price: R350 - R400 pp sharing. R1,500 per night for whole house.
Meals: Full breakfast included. Other meals by prior arrangement with Sannie, from simple suppers to dinner parties. Priced according to menu. Kitchen can be used to self-cater.
Directions: Emailed or faxed on booking.

Klein Bosheuwel and Southdown

Nicki and Tim Scarborough
51a Klaassens Rd, Constantia 7800
Tel: 021-762-2323
Fax: 021-762-2323
Email: kleinbosheuwel@iafrica.com
Web: www.kleinbosheuwel.co.za

Who needs Kirstenbosch? Nicki has manipulated the paths and lawns of her own garden (which is pretty well an extension of the Botanical Gardens anyway - less than a minute's walk away) so that the views are not dished out in one vulgar dollop! Instead you are subtly led into them, with glimpses through mature trees (flowering gums, yellowwoods and camellias) and lush flower-beds. And finally your stroll leads you down to umbrellas on a ridge with Table Mountain and the Constantiaberg laid out magnificently before you and the sea distantly below. "Keep it plain" is Nicki's motto, so the upstairs bedrooms are simply white and all naturally endowed with garden views. The salt-water swimming pool is hidden deep in the garden and Klein Bosheuwel is the sort of place where you could just hang out for a few days. I was introduced to one English guest who had clearly no intention of going anywhere that day - the cat that got the cream! Or you can stay next-door at Southdown. With a small-scale Lost Gardens of Heligan on her hands, Nicki peeled back the jungle to find pathways, walls and, best of all, enormous stone-paved circles just in the right spot between the house and pool. Today the house is filled with surprises: zebra skins, porcupine-quill lamps, onyx lamp stands, a whole stuffed eagle, a wildebeest's head, a piano, two tortoises, deep carpets and couches, marble bathrooms and terraces off most rooms.

Rooms: 8: 1 twin en/s bath; 2 queens with en/s bath and separate shower; 1 queen en/s large bath; 1 king with corner bath & separate shower; 1 twin and 1 king with en-suite bath and shower. 1 self-catering cottage (2 bedrooms, 2 bathrooms, open-plan kitchen and lounge area).
Price: R435 - R545 pp sharing. Singles R650.
Meals: Full breakfast included.
Directions: Fax or web site.

Kaapse Draai

Annelie Posthumus
19 Glen Avenue, Constantia 7806
Tel: 021-794-6291 Fax: 021-794-6291
Email: info@kaapsedraaibb.co.za Web: www.kaapsedraaibb.co.za
Cell: 082-923-9869

Annelie has been charming Greenwood Guide travellers since the very first edition and should be in the running for some sort of award for B&B brilliance. Relaxed, simple and beautiful seems to be the rule here. Her daughter is an interior designer and their talents combine to make the house a peaceful temple to uncluttered Cape Cod-style living. Neutral furnishings and white cottons are frisked up with pretty floral bolsters and country checks. Sunny window-seats are perfect for reading guide-books on the area and there are posies of fresh flowers in each room. I was lucky enough to stay with Annelie and once installed in my room, she invited me down for a soup later. She is a prolific gardener and you can walk (perhaps with Annelie's dogs) from the tropical greenery of Kaapse Draai, with its mountain stream, huge ferns and palms, into lovely Bel-Ombre meadow and the forest next door. From there it is a three-hour walk to the Table Mountain cable station. Porcupines come into the garden at night from the mountain (they love arum lilies apparently) and there are many birds too, including the noisy (and palindromic) hadedah. A grand old willow tree is what you'll park your car under. Delicious breakfasts are taken outside in the sunshine whenever possible. All I can say is – do. *Wine estates and Constantia shopping village nearby.*

Rooms: 3: 1 double and 2 twins with en-suite shower.
Price: R310 pp sharing. Singles R375.
Meals: Full breakfast included. Annelie sometimes cooks if the mood is upon her. But do not expect this....
Directions: Ask for fax or email when booking.

Constantia Stables

Lola and Rick Bartlett
8 Chantecler Lane, off Willow Rd, Constantia 7806
Tel: 021-794-3653 Fax: 021-794-3653
Email: tstables@mweb.co.za Web: www.capestay.co.za/constantiastables
Cell: 082-569-4135

I loved The Constantia Stables and would be as happy as a pig in clover to be among Lola and Rick's regular visitors. Not only is it a stunning spot of shaded indigenous gardens and beautifully renovated stable buildings (ask for the hayloft room!), but there's a genuine family feel to the place that is immediately relaxing. The Bartlett children are actors and their photos are plastered across the drawing room and bar. This is the heart of the Stables, a congenial snug of heavy armchairs, low beams and earth-red walls where guests are encouraged to tap into a well-stocked bar. I liked the breakfast room too with its red-brick fireplace. My mouth watered as Lola reeled off her gargantuan breakfast menu: fresh fruit salad with home-grown guava, quince and peaches, hams, salamis, a giant cheese board, yoghurts, cereals and croissants and that's before you even think about cooked delights. She and Rick have done a fantastic job converting the original stables into bedrooms with old, olive green stable doors opening onto an ivy-fringed courtyard. The garden suite overlooks the pool and, like Lily's cottage, seamlessly blends into the mass of plants that spread out beneath two enormous plane trees. And once you're suitably chilled there's a whole bunch of vineyards and restaurants to explore just next door.

Rooms: 6: 1 king with bath, 1 queen with bath and shower, 1 queen with shower, 1 twin with shower, also cottage with 1 queen, 1 twin, 2 showers and kitchenette.
Price: From R375 pp sharing. Singles on request.
Meals: Full breakfast included.
Directions: Follow M3 towards Muizenberg. Take Ladies Mile off-ramp. Turn L at traffic lights onto Ladies Mile and L at next lights onto Spaanschemat River Rd. Keep L at fork then turn L into Willow Rd and L into Chantecler Lane. The Stables is at the end on L.

Cape Witogie

Rosemary and Bob Child
9 Van Zyl Rd, Kreupelbosch, Constantia 7945
Tel: 021-712-9935 Fax: 021-712-9935
Email: capewitogie@netactive.co.za Web: www.capestay.co.za/capewitogie
Cell: 082-537-6059 or 082-537-6059

Billy, a desperately friendly Staffordshire bull terrier, is public relations officer at Cape Witogie and this is probably the only B&B with a dog that gets his own mail. His owners Rosemary and Bob are equally friendly and when I visited Rosemary was frantically shifting beds post-renovations. The latest addition to their red-bricked home is an airy conservatory/sitting room, which now adjoins one of the two bedrooms. Both rooms are whitewashed, tile-floored self-catering units that open on to a compact garden full of ferns and firs, lavender pots, lemon trees and citrus-smelling verbena. Hot-plates, a small oven and microwaves give ample scope for knocking up your own meals, though Rosemary enjoys making occasional breakfasts and bakes bread for those who'd rather not bake their own. I'd recommend coming with some pals and taking both rooms as a base from which to explore the Cape Town area. From the City Bowl and beaches to Table Mountain, the botanical gardens and nearby winelands there is just so much to do in the Cape that a full week with Bob and Rosemary flies by in the blink of an eye. These are great people (with great dogs), running a great value get-away.

Rooms: 2 units: both consist of 1 twin room (1 extra single bed can be added to each if required) with en-suite showers and small kitchens.
Price: R200 - R240 pp sharing. Single supplement R50.
Meals: Breakfast on request R65.
Directions: Faxed or emailed on booking.

Map Number: 3

Vygeboom Manor

Callie & Luli Hamman
14 Valmar Rd, Valmary Park, Durbanville 7550
Tel: 021-975-6020 Fax: 021-976-5029
Email: vygeboom@gtrade.co.za Web: www.vygeboom.co.za
Cell: 083 270 4021

Vygeboom is a destination in itself. Callie is a prosthodontist and microlight pilot, Luli an artist and these disparate talents merge seamlessly to create a fantastic guest house experience in Cape Town's northern suburbs. Durbanville is an ideal location for visitors, with easy access to the bright lights and beaches of Cape Town, but also on established wine routes (including the ruling triumvirate of Paarl, Stellenbosch and Franschhoek). New this year is a cellar deep within, where wine tasting will give you the chance to get a flavour of the area. Prisoners of the game of golf will also find themselves embarrassed for choice. But this assumes, of course, that you feel like going anywhere. Luli has based the themes of each amazing room on her own gigantic and wonderful murals, doffing the cap to Rubens, Matisse, Manet etc. Comfort, however, does not play second fiddle to artistic whimsy - beds are huge, bathrooms luxurious. Add to this charming hosts (Callie does his dentistry next door), spectacular views to the distant wall of the Hottentots Holland Mountains, a vast sitting room with three-quarter size snooker table, a covered 'inside-outside' braai area and a large pool in the garden. Vygeboom remains a real find and outstanding value. *Callie can organise microlight trips for guests - an exciting way to go whale-spotting in season. Free access to health club/gym.*

Rooms: 5: 1 double, 4 twins; 3 with en-suite bath, 2 with en-suite shower.
Price: R350 - R450 pp sharing. Ask about specials for families and groups.
Meals: Full breakfast included and barbeque dinners by arrangement.
Directions: Junction 23 N1, R302 north for 5km. Turn right into Valmar Rd.

Harbour View B&B

Marlene and Koot de Kock

8 Arum Crescent, Yzerfontein 7351
Tel: 022-451-2615 Fax: 022-451-2615
Email: info@harbourviewbb.co.za Web: www.harbourviewbb.co.za
Cell: 082-770-3885

Entering the living room at Harbour View I was greeted with a wolf whistle! "Oh don't worry, that's just Simon," Marlene explained soothingly. Feeling a mite unsure of myself, I scanned the room to discover (with some relief) that Simon was the African Grey parrot chuckling merrily to himself in the corner. Although usually besotted with Marlene (I don't blame him - she's great), Simon's whistling could also have been aimed at Harbour View's legendary position. Protruding out alongside the harbour the sea seems to fill every window in the house. The north-facing aspect means a continual influx of sunlight that brightens the fresh blues or oatmeal hues in each bedroom. "You can whale-watch from any bed in the house," Marlene tells me proudly and, as she is a keen birder, that's not the only watching to be had. Personally I'd be content just gazing out all day at the boats as they come and go. Breakfast is a different event every day, the table decoration as changeable as the seascape it looks out on. I wondered if the ever-growing collection of wooden cats, an ongoing fad started and continued by guests, would ever make a table-top debut. "We grow crayfish in the garden," Marlene nodded and I followed her gaze. The 'lawn' at Harbour View is blue and white-crested and, if you want to pick some crayfish you just take your fishing net down to the pier. *Crayfish permits available at the local post office. Wind- and kite-surfing available in the area.*

Rooms: 6: 2 suites with own lounge area kitchenette and en-suite shower and 4 doubles, all with en-suite shower and shared lounge & kitchenette facility.
Price: R295 - R340 pp sharing for standard rooms. R355 - R420 pp sharing for suites. Single supplement R200 - R250.
Meals: Full breakfast included. Kitchenette facilities in rooms for limited self-catering.
Directions: On the R27 heading North from Cape Town take the left signed Yzerfontein. When you arrive in the village follow the brown 'Harbour View' signs to front door.

Langebaan Beach House

Claire Green
44 Beach Road, Entrance in Jacoba St, Langebaan 7357
Tel: 022-772-2625 Fax: 022-772-1432
Email: lbh@intekom.co.za Web: www.langebaanbeachhouse.com

This very popular, friendly B&B was once Claire's family's seaside retreat in the days when Langebaan was a small fishing village. It has grown since then, but still has a nice holiday feel. The house is Claire's home, complete with two typically upbeat labradors (and two cats), and set right on the lagoon. The garden goes directly down to sand and water. The original part is over 100 years old, while the rest has gradually been added as the family expanded - most of it is now for guests. Two of the bright bedrooms are 'suites', with their own sitting rooms and views to the water. There is a big communal sitting area where Claire's collection of model boats lives and the garden has a plunge pool and sun-loungers. Breakfast is served in the glass-enclosed verandah, looking down to the beach. The sea is safe and swimmable, if a little chilly, and all water sports are allowed - swimming, motor- and wind-powered vessels, fishing and water-skiing (the Cape Sports Centre hires out water sports gear just up the beach). 250,000 migrating birds, including flamingos, live at the wilderness end of the lagoon and there are five restaurants within walking distance from the house. Claire herself is relaxed, warm-spirited and extremely knowledgeable about what's going on in her neck of the woods. Which is a lot.

Rooms: 4: 2 suites, each with sitting room; 1 double and 1 twin. All rooms have en-suite shower.
Price: Suites from R400 - R600 pp sharing. Other rooms from R300 - R400 pp sharing. Singles on request.
Meals: Full breakfast included. For other meals there are lots of great restaurants in Langebaan - 5 within walking distance.
Directions: Directions will be faxed or emailed when you book.

Kersefontein

Julian Melck
between Hopefield and Velddrif, Hopefield 7355
Tel: 022-783-0850 Fax: 022-783-0850
Email: info@kersefontein.co.za Web: www.kersefontein.co.za
Cell: 083-454-1025

Nothing has changed at Kersefontein since the last edition. Julian's convivial dinner parties are still a reason to book in on their own. And Julian himself remains a Renaissance man, described on his business card as 'Farmer, Pig-killer, Aviator and Advocate of the High Court of S.A.' He farms cows, sheep and horses on the surrounding fields, and wild boar appear deliciously at dinner. He also hires and pilots a six-seater plane and a flight round the Cape or along the coast is a must. He modestly leaves out his virtuosity as a pianist and organist and some of us trooped off one Sunday morning, braving a 40-minute sermon in Afrikaans, to hear him play toccatas by Bach, Giguot and Widor at the local church. When not eating, riding or flying, guests lounge on the pontoon, swim in the river or read books from Kersefontein's many libraries. Or they use the house as a base to visit the coast or the Swartland wineries, which are really taking off. The homestead is seventh generation and the rooms either Victorian or African in temperament, with antiques handed down by previous Melcks. You are fed like a king, but treated as a friend and I am always recommending people to go there.

Rooms: 5: 2 doubles, 2 twins and 1 separate 2 bedroom cottage.
Price: R370 - R470 pp sharing. No single supplements. Aircraft hire prices depend on the trip. Julian will also do fly/picnic trips out to various destinations.
Meals: Full breakfast included. Dinners by arrangement: R130 - R150 excluding wine.
Directions: From Cape Town take N7 off N1. Bypass Malmesbury, 5km later turn left towards Hopefield. After 50km bypass Hopefield, turn right signed Velddrif. After 16km farm signed on right just before grain silos. Cross bridge and gates on the left.

The Oystercatcher's Haven at Paternoster

Sandy Attrill
48 Sonkwasweg, Paternoster 7381
Tel: 022-752-2193 Fax: 022-752-2192
Email: info@oystercatchershaven.com Web:
www.oystercatchershaven.com Cell: 082-414-6705 or 083-267-7051

Sandy and Wayne, ex film and advertising people, do things in style and their guest house is a knock-out! The Cape Dutch house sits on the fringes of the Cape Columbine Nature Reserve, a spectacular, fynbos-covered, hand-shaped headland, bearing its lighthouse aloft like a nine-million-watt jewel. All along the coast and a mere 40 metres in front of the house knobbly fingers of grey and black granite merge into the sea and around the rocks there are secret white sandy coves where the dolphins come throughout the year. It is quite simply beautiful and I can assure you that the Oystercatcher is a haven by anyone's standards. Heave yourself out of that plunge-pool, off the rocks and away from the view (available from your bed) and head inside the house. The interior, with its white walls, untreated timbers and reed-and-pole ceilings, is intentionally blank-yet-rustic to showcase some exquisite pieces, such as a four-foot-high Angolan drum, some Malinese sinaba paintings (you'll have to come and see them if you don't know what they are), Persian rugs, art-deco couches, courtyards.... Just about everything is a hook for an eager eye. Beds and bedrooms too are bliss - trust me, I'm a professional.

Rooms: 3: 1 queen with en-suite bath and shower; 1 queen and 1 twin, both with en-suite showers. All rooms have private entrances.
Price: From R425 - R540 pp sharing. Singles on request (valid until September 2006).
Meals: Full breakfast included. Picnics from R75. Enquire about evening meals.
Directions: From Cape Town take the N1 and then the R27 north following signs to Vredenburg. Follow signs straight through Vredenburg to Paternoster (15km). At crossroads turn left and travel a full 1km towards the Columbine Reserve. Turn right into Sonkwas Rd, it is No. 48.

West Coast, Western Cape

Blue Dolphin

George Koning
12 Warrelklip St, Paternoster
7381
Tel: 022-752-2001
Fax: 0866-714-5109
Email:
bluedolphin@mweb.co.za
Web: www.bluedolphin.co.za

The Blue Dolphin concept is simple, natural and refreshing. Four very comfortable rooms, with views of the sea, a verandah with a day-bed for lying on and listening to the surf, a sandy beach that stretches from the house… and two great restaurants up the road for lunch and dinner. The house is open, wooden, breezy, with whites and blues dominating in tune with the beach and sea. All you have to do is lazily watch out for dolphins (and whales in season), kick sand along the strand, eat your breakfast, chat with George, read a book… chill those nerves, untie those muscles. Book early for the flower season (end of August/beginning of September). The dune fynbos blooms impressively and a rash of tiny brightly-coloured flowers emerge like magic from the very sand itself. George has kept the number of rooms down to just four so that he always has plenty of time for everyone. The bedrooms are well kitted-out with heated towel rails, satellite TV, mohair blankets, great beds and linen. Next door is the new Baby Dolphin, a self-catering option, but you can have breakfast at the Blue Dolphin. It has a giant fireplace, a wide sea-facing verandah and a track straight out to the beach. *Columbine Nature Reserve and the Fossil Museum are nearby.*

Rooms: 4: all doubles with en-suite shower.
Price: R300 pp sharing. Singles R400.
Meals: Full breakfast included. Excellent meals at Voorstrand and Ahoy Galley restaurants in Paternoster.
Directions: Take the N1 from Cape Town towards Paarl. Take the R27 leading to the West Coast and follow this road until the turn-off to Vredenburg. Follow signs straight thro' Vredenburg. Carry over the 4-way stop in Paternoster and follow signs to Blue Dolphin.

Map Number:

Oystercatcher Lodge

Luc and Sue Christen
1st Avenue, Shelley Point St, St Helena Bay
Tel: 022-742-1202 Fax: 022-742-1201
Email: info@oystercatcherlodge.co.za Web: www.oystercatcherlodge.co.za
Cell: 082-903-9668

You can't miss Oystercatcher Lodge. If you do, you'll end up in the sea. It's set right on the tip of Shelley Point, overlooking the full curve of Britannia Bay with its flocks of cormorants, pods of passing dolphins and wallowing whales (in season). Luc (smiley and Swiss) and Sue (home-grown, but equally smiley) are both from the hotel trade. After years doing a great job for other people deep in the Mpumalanga bushveld, they decided to work for themselves and made the move. Quite a change. Here on the West Coast the sea air has a salty freshness unlike anywhere else, the sun shines brilliantly on arcing white beaches and the crunching waves are a bottomless blue. A special spot indeed where the Christens' newly-built house juts out towards the ocean like the prow of a ship, a large pointy pool in its bows. Each of the six rooms, painted in calming sandy colours, looks across grassy dunes and beach to the sea. All have extra-large bathrooms. Breakfast feasts are served in the bar. If you're lucky Luc might summon some whales for you to view by blowing on his "kelperoo" (a whale horn made out of seaweed!) as you munch on the Christens' 'special Swiss recipe' bread. But for other meals you can head next-door to the family restaurant. It's seafood-oriented and the speciality is Shelley Point Platter... which sounds exciting!

Rooms: 6: 4 kings, 2 with bath and shower, 2 with shower only, 2 twins with shower only.
Price: R350 - R485 pp sharing sharing.
Meals: Full breakfast included. Other meals available at the restaurant next door (closed Sunday nights and Mondays).
Directions: From R27 heading north turn L to Vredenburg. At lights turn R to St. Helena Bay. Turn L 10km on to Stompneusbaai. 17km on turn L to Britannia Bay. 2km on turn R into white Golden Mile entrance. Turn R continue right through to Shelley Point. Oystercatcher is at the far end.

Villa Dauphine

David and Ann Dixon

166 Sandpiper Close, Golden Mile Bvd, Britannia Bay 7382
Tel: 022-742-1926 Fax: 086-634-0397
Email: dadixon@mweb.co.za Web: www.villadauphine.com
Cell: 083-409-3195

The focus of Villa Dauphine is placed entirely on the bay, whose broad crescent passes not twent yards from the stoep. Here you sit and peacefully beat out the rhythm of the waves. Two finnec backs breached some 30 metres from shore, my first ever sighting of wild dolphins. David anc Anne were unimpressed. The day before great schools of them had been leaping, frolicking doing crosswords and playing chess right in front of the house. You can take boat rides out tc cement the friendship and navigate the Berg River for bird-watching. The house is country cottage pretty, thatched and beamed with solid furniture, pots of fresh flowers, terracotta tiles, lots c whites and woods. Two atticky bedrooms are found up wooden steps, which lead from a flowery, sun-trapping, wind-breaking courtyard. The other is in the house itself. David used to be a vet and he and Anne are real bird enthusiasts. If you are too, they'll point you off to the Ber River (above 190 bird species) but everyone must visit the beautiful West Coast National Par nearby (250,000 migratory birds and a stunning turquoise lagoon). Golf courses and exceller restaurants nearby. Come here in spring and the countryside is carpeted in flowers. They appea out of nowhere and grow right down to the water line.

Rooms: 2 units: 1 suite with 2 double bedrooms with a shared bathroom (bath & shower); 1 twin with en-suite bath and shower.
Price: R250 - R325 pp sharing.
Meals: Full breakfast included.
Directions: From Cape Town take R27 to Vredenburg turn-off. Turn left to Vredenburg. At first lights, turn right to St Helena Bay. 10km to Stompneusbaai sign. Turn left. 17km turn left to Britannia Bay. 2km. Turn right at White Entrance to Golden Mile. Turn R & after 2nd speed bump turn left.

Ndedema Lodge

Johan and Wilma Jacobs
48 Park Street, Clanwilliam 8135
Tel: 027-482-1314 Fax: 027-482-1314
Email: ndedema@lantic.net
Cell. 083-456-2695

We have searched since GG's inception for a great place to stay in Clanwilliam and until now we have drawn a blank. A great shame as this town is the gateway to some fabulous Cederberg sandstone scenery. But at last Ndedema has been born! Wilma, very grounded and convivial, used to run the Department of Tourism at the City Council of Pretoria. Fuse this knowledge with her passion for fine art and antique-gathering abilities, and you are rewarded with a lodge both professionally run and piled high with character. Over a hundred years old, the house boasts thick sturdy walls and high ceilings that curtain-draped four-poster beds try their best to reach. Wilma and Johan promote the work of up-and-coming artists, exhibiting on walls, doors and propped up on chairs. When I was there a gallery of Cape Town University students' work had me wishing for enough money and suitcase space to cart them all home. Breakfast is usually served 'al fresco', dapple-shaded by vines and as beautifully presented as the many surrounding wall-hung masterpieces. The garden, a montage of fruit trees, flowers and heady scents, triggered an itch to explore, as did Ndedema's position at the end of Clanwilliam's oldest street. There is a distinct feeling of the farm and an openness to the bush, very rare qualities in a town house. Choose to embrace the spirited and festive community of Clanwilliam on your doorstep or leave it far behind as you enter the nearby wilderness searching for rock art or your own piece of solitude.

Rooms: 4: 2 kings with en-suite bath and shower, 1 suite with king/twin and double room with en-suite bath/shower and 1 garden cottage with 1 double and 1 twin room en-suite bath/shower.
Price: R300 - R450 pp sharing.
Meals: Full breakfast included. Dinner by arrangement for larger groups.
Directions: Take the N7 to Clanwillliam. Turn off into the village and right into Main Road. Continue until Main Road splits and follow Park Street to number 48.

Boschkloof and Oude Boord Cottages

Mariet and Doempie Smit
Boschkloof, Citrusdal 7340
Tel: 022-921-3533 Fax: 022-921-3533
Email: boschkloof@kingsley.co.za Web: www.boschkloof.com
Cell: 082-734-9467

We bumped along six or so sandy kilometres, past orchards of citrus trees and stumbled upon some sort of prelapsarian idyll! A private valley, cocooned in the Sneeuberg Conservancy, in the Cederberg foothills, flanked by sandstone mountains, its orange groves watered by a natural stream, the rocks and plants etched in hyper-real clarity by a setting sun. There are Bushman rock art sites, natural pools in the river to cool off in and hiking on mountain trails to be done from the house in the early morning and evening. We parked under an oak tree and were met by Mariet, her two small daughters and two large dogs. On return from a dip in the river we met Doempie and a glass of wine and were soon being treated to crayfish kebabs from the braai, seated under the oak with views up the kloof and a sensational tone to the air. Guests have a choice of staying in one of the original farmhouses (next door to the Smit's own original farmhouse) or in the newly-built, old-feel cottage hidden across the stream. Oude Boord (the new cottage) is beautifully set within the orange trees and, with only klipspringers as your early morning company, seclusion is complete. Although it is a self-catering arrangement the comparative proximity and openness of your hosts means you may as well be at a B&B, except with far more space and privacy. And the beds and baths? No time for detail - just trust me, they're spot on!

Rooms: 2 cottages each sleeping 6 with 1 double, 1 twin and double sofa-bed; all bedrooms have en/s bathrooms.
Price: R400 – R500 for 2 people. R100 for each extra person.
Meals: Fully-equipped kitchen - these are self-catering cottages. Mariet can provide breakfast materials for you by prior arrangement.
Directions: N7 to Citrusdal - turn into village, go left into Voortrekker Rd and right into Muller St (3rd turning on the right). Carry straight on. It becomes a dirt road. Follow it for 7km.

Petersfield Farm Cottages

Hedley Peter
Petersfield Guest Farm, Citrusdal 7340
Tel: 022-921-3316 Fax: 022-921-3316
Email: info@petersfieldfarm.co.za Web: www.petersfieldfarm.co.za
Cell: 083-626-3145

Hedley is an instantly likable and funny host and Petersfield his family farm (citrus and rooibos tea), the property ranging over the back of the mountain behind the main house, forming a huge private wilderness reserve. De Kom, an idyllic, simple-but-stylish stone cottage perched high in sandstone mountains will appeal to your inner romantic. This charming electricity-free cottage is lit by hurricane lamps and flares with gas for the stove, fridge and hot water. A private plunge pool with river stones at the bottom overlooks this secret valley with the Olifants River and purpling Cederberg peaks as a backdrop. And what a setting, guarded to the front by a citrus orchard, to the rear by craggy sandstone and looking deep and far from the stoep down the mountain. There is a secluded farm dam nearby (300 metres) to swim in or picnic by while watching nesting eagles. Or, 2km away, there is (electrified) Dassieklip cottage, a sweet wooden mountain cabin secreted in its own kloof and reached down an avenue of oaks. It too has a plunge pool to cool off in and other mod cons such as fridge, air-conditioning, TV and CD player. Bring your own food for both cottages, although breakfast materials for you to cook can be provided. *Wood is provided at no extra charge and pets are also welcome.*

Rooms: 2 cottages with 2 bedrooms each.
Price: Week-nights: R400 for 2 up to R600 for 5/6. Weekends, public holidays, flower season (15 Aug - 15 Sept): R450 for 2, up to R750 for 5/6. Prices are per night for whole cottage.
Meals: Self-catering, but breakfast materials provided in the fridge by prior arrangement.
Directions: From Cape Town 4km after Citrusdal on your left on the N7 travelling towards Clanwilliam.

Mount Ceder

André and Jaen Marais & Thomas and Rachelle Marriott-Dodington

Grootrivier Farm, Cederberg, Koue Bokkeveld 6836
Tel: 023-317-0848 Fax: 023-317-0543
Email: mountceder@lando.co.za Web: www.mountceder.co.za

Do not lose confidence as you rumble along the dirt roads that lead through the Koue Bokkeveld nature conservancy to this secluded valley - it's always a couple more turns. Finally you will arrive in the very heart of the Cederberg, dry sandstone mountains rising all around you in impressive dimensions. You will be given the key to your new home and drive off along half a kilometre of sand track to one of three fantastic rustic stone cottages. The river flows past the reeds and rock right by the cottages, clear, deep and wide all year round. You can swim and lie around drying on flat rocks. Birds love it here too. I imagine sitting out on that stoep, on those wooden chairs, looking at that view, beer or wine in hand… a piece of heaven as they say. You can either self-cater or you can eat at André and Jaen's restaurant back at the lodge. There are a few other cottages nearer the lodge, which are fine, but you must ask for the stone cottages, which are in a league of their own. A pristine slice of unspoiled nature, cherished by a very knowledgeable Marais family who will help with Bushman rock art, horse-riding and fauna and flora. Do not reach for your red pen by the way… that *is* how you spell ceder (in Afrikaans) and that is how you spell Jaen! *Serious hiking is available from here. Daughter Rachelle will happily take you horse-riding.*

Rooms: 3 river cottages with 3 bedrooms each.
Price: R880 – R1,450 per cottage per night self-catering (cottage sleeps 6).
Meals: Meals on request, breakfast R45, dinner R85 (extra for wine).
Directions: From Ceres follow signs to Prince Alfred's Hamlet/Op-die-Berg, up Gydo Pass past Op-die-Berg. First right signed Cederberge - follow tar for 17km then straight on on dirt road for another 34km into a green valley.

Villa Tarentaal

Christine and Mike Hunter
Tulbagh 6820
Tel: 023-230-0868 Fax: 023-230-0101
Email: mhunter@intekom.co.za

Known locally as 'Man of the Mountain', Mike's knowledge of the walking routes around the sleepy town of Tulbagh is surely unsurpassed. But his pride and joy, and the defining feature of Villa Tarentaal, is his garden. He has created lawns that would make the green-keepers of Augusta, well... green with envy, and a stroll around this sanctuary with the Man of the Mountain is a horticultural and ornithological education. Spidering their way up the mustard-coloured house are wisteria and grape vines, adding to the orgy of colour provided by the roses. As we sauntered past the tulbaghia, the liquid ambers and the strelitzias, Mike suddenly stopped in his tracks and pointed skyward: with its distinctive cry, a fish eagle swooped over our heads and soared off towards the Winterhoek Mountains that provide the backdrop to Villa Tarentaal. The terrace overlooks the pool and I sat sipping tea, as Mike and Christine plastered over some of the gaping holes in my knowledge about the natural world surrounding me. They claim to cater for the quiet traveller and where better to unwind than in a snug, well-equipped cottage overlooking garden, vineyard and mountain? *Christine also offers therapeutic massages and aromatherapy.*

Rooms: 2 cottages: one with 1 twin & 1 double, separate bath/shower room & fireplace; one with 1 double (with extra single on request) & sofa-bed in lounge, separate bath/shower room. Satellite TV in both cottages.
Price: R295 pp sharing B&B. R265 pp sharing self-catering. R350 singles.
Meals: Full breakfast included in B&B.
Directions: N1 from Cape Town to exit 47 Wellington/Franschhoek/Klapmuts turn-off, left onto R44 via Wellington. Follow for approx 1 hour to Tulbagh. Straight through town, 1.2km on left.

De Oude Herberg Guest House

Leslie and Jane Ingham
6 Church St, PO Box 285, Tulbagh 6820
Tel: 023-230-0260 Fax: 023-230-0260
Email: ingham@mweb.co.za Web: www.deoudeherberg.co.za
Cell: 072-241-4214

Leslie was a pilot in his former life and his last foray skywards saw him flying aid missions for the UN throughout Africa. Thankfully for a man who has lived with his head in the clouds, Jane's always been there to bring him back down to ground, and now she has brought him (luckily for us) to Tulbagh, to run a guest house. But this is not just any old Tulbagh guest house. Church Street is the town's - and indeed one of the Wineland's - most historic streets and De Oude Herberg is a jewel in the crown. Beautiful on the outside in a thatched roof and gable-fronted kind of way; venerably ancient on the inside in an everything-wobbles-when-you-walk-through-the-room kind of way. From the resplendent, flower-filled, basket-carrying bicycle, to the ribbon-tied towels in the rooms, and complimentary Church Street bookmarks by every bed, you know a lot of thought has gone into making this place special. I'd plump for the four-poster with access onto the verandah, but if you like your privacy, then go for one in the separate building out the back, which has its own access and small courtyard garden. But it will take a strong will not to be tempted back out for a drink and some lively chat at the bar. This is now part of Pielow's restaurant which adds some gourmet cooking to the scene.

Rooms: 4: 2 queens, 1 with additional small room attached to sleep child; and 2 twins. All have baths with shower over.
Price: R275 - R300 pp sharing. Singles + R100.
Meals: Full breakfast included. Lunch and dinner available in restaurant. A la carte menu.
Directions: On reaching Tulbagh turn L at the Shell garage into Church Street and R at the church. Next door to information centre.

Map Number: 4

Tulbagh Hotel

Diana and Ron Hamilton
22 van der Stel Street, Tulbagh
Tel: 023-230-0071 Fax: 023-230-1411
Email: tulbaghhotel@lando.co.za Web: www.tulbaghhotel.co.za

Hotels aren't normally the Greenwood thing, but then this isn't any normal hotel. Ron and Diana Hamilton worked for more than two years to return this landmark building to its former glory and what a job they have done. Not only does it ooze luxury from every orifice (five huge bedrooms with silk bed covers, exposed wood flooring, can't-reach-your-feet-to-the-floor-sized sofas) but it can also lay claim to being the first gastro-pub in all of South Africa. Called the Shamrock & Thistle - he's the Irish shamrock, she's the Scottish thistle, and the evidence is all about you - it serves up the kind of food that makes you feel all warm inside. "More style and less formality," Ron will tell you. That is if he is not busy delighting the crowds on the large verandah with his sweet-sounding saxophone. Like most people who keep something up from the age of 11 he's damn good at it. Diana will most likely be found (of her own volition!) in the kitchen. She does all the cooking herself and has even played host to royalty. And me? You will find me pleasantly whiling away the time staring at the walls (maps, photos, and scripts chart the influences on the Hamiltons' lives), in the company of grumpy Rex, snobby Tara and tearaway Tess, the resident canines… all of us waiting patiently to be fed. If the historical beauty wasn't reason enough to come to Tulbagh, the Tulbagh Hotel surely is now.

Rooms: 5: all kings, 3 with en-suite full bathrooms, 2 with en-suite bath (shower above).
Price: R450 - R650 pp sharing. Singles on request.
Meals: Full breakfast included. Restaurant on premises.
Directions: Property is in the centre of the village on the main road.

Map Number: 4

Groote Vallei

John and Fiona Acland

Off R46, PO Box 106, Tulbagh 6820
Tel: 023-230-0660 Fax: 023-230-0660
Email: johnfi@wol.co.za Web: www.tiscover.co.za/groote-vallei

Hot, dusty and flustered, I was greeted on arrival at Groote Vallei by a contrastingly fresh and enthusiastic Fiona, who took one look at me and sang, "Phew! I hope you've bought your swimming costume!" The Aclands have a stupendous swimming pool overlooked by mountains. And no, my swimmers were back in Cape Town! Groote Vallei, although troublesome in pronunciation, is divine in every other sense. The 110-year-old Cape Dutch farmhouse thrives amid mountains, rivers, olive groves and grape vines. The cooling surrounds of the newly-built self-catering cottage soon re-set my brain to 'function mode', which made a note of red terracotta tiling, fresh cotton sheets and a family fireplace for visits more wintry than mine. The other two smaller self-catering units, set alongside the house and sharing the same startling views as the pool, were equally well-equipped and spiced up with a bit of funky Tanzanian artwork. The intriguing Tinga Tinga paintings evolved from a creative fad using bright primary-coloured bicycle paints and continually remind Fiona and John of their time in Tanzania. Another great feature of the farm is John's mini-olive-oil factory and, as proud as Willy Wonker, he will cheerfully give you a guided tour. The finished product is fondly assembled for sale alongside jars of home-grown honey and comb in the (fully-stocked and licensed) country bar. I can endorse the honey and the oil and the big valley where they were sourced.

Rooms: 4: 3 self-catering cottages: 1 family unit with shared bath and shower rooms and 2 double units with en-suite bath/shower; also 1 double B&B room in the house.

Price: R250 - R300 pp sharing (breakfast included) R600 per night for family unit (breakfast not included).

Meals: Full breakfast included unless in family unit when breakfast is available for R50. Picnic baskets can also be organised.

Directions: Heading from Cape Town on N1 take Klapmuts/Wellington (R44) turn-off. Follow R44 for about 43km until almost at Tulbagh. Go straight over the crossroads marked Tulbagh left and Tulbaghweg right and farm is signed 1.2km on your right.

White Bridge Farm

Paul and Peppi Stanford
Wolseley 6830
Tel: 023-231-0705 Fax: 023-231-1836
Email: stanford@kingsley.co.za Web: www.whitebridge.co.za
Cell: 082-578-7881

Snow on the mountains, sun blazing down on the deck, water roaring through the river below... Mother Nature could not do a better job of showing off other people's wares if she tried (I wonder what they're paying her). White Bridge Farm is a working fruit farm, and if you come at the right time of the year (Nov-Aug), you can work on it too, or at least have a tour. Guests, Peppi tells me, are always amazed when they spot the citrus, pears and plums sporting labels of the well-known supermarket brands of home. But I have to say it would take more than a succulent satsuma to tear me away from one of the two log cabins (there is a more conventional larger cottage too). They really are about as rustic as rustic can be. Bamboos have been cut down to line the walls, trees have been felled to build the tables, even old drainpipes have been used as a bright idea for lighting! Nothing has gone to waste, and you won't want to waste your time here either. With walking, fishing, swimming and bird-watching this is a nature-lover's paradise. A family of otters liked it so much, they decided to stay at White Bridge, and you cannot get a better recommendation than that. Just 90 minutes from Cape Town, the perfect distance for a break from the city.

Rooms: 3 units: 2 log cabins with 1 double and 1 twin in loft space, shower only; 1 cottage with double and bunks, and a double futon in lounge, full bathroom.
Price: R450 - R550 per unit per night.
Meals: Meals can be arranged if requested. Restaurant and coffee shop less than 1km away.
Directions: At the junction of the R43 from Worcester and the R46 between Tulbagh and Ceres.

Bartholomeus Klip Farmhouse

Lesley Gillett
Elandsberg Farm, Hermon 7308
Tel: 022-448-1820 Fax: 022-448-1829
Email: bartholomeus@icon.co.za Web: www.parksgroup.co.za
Cell: 082-829-4131

Heavenly scenery cossets this Victorian homestead in its lush gardens and stands of oak and olive. The wall of the Elandsberg Mountains rises up from the game reserve, reflected in the dammed lake by the house. Here guests can have breakfast on the balcony of the boathouse before heading out for an excursion onto the wheat and sheep farm. You are also taken on late-afternoon game drives to see the zebra, a variety of Cape antelope, buffalo, quaggas (a fascinating experiment to reintroduce an extinct variety of zebra), eagles, flocks of blue crane... and the largest world population of the tiny, endangered geometric tortoises. But just to be out in such nature! The spring flowers are spectacular and there are more than 850 species of plant recorded on the property. Back at the homestead you can cool down in the curious, round, raised reservoir pool, sit in chairs on the stoep; or, if you have more energy, bike off into the reserve or go on guided walks in the mountains. Staff are very friendly, food is exceptional and a reason to stay on its own (and all included in the price). I recommend splashing out on at least two nights. A great place indeed and very popular so book ahead of yourself if possible. *Closed June – July and Christmas.*

Rooms: 6: 2 doubles and 3 twins, 4 with bath and shower, 1 with bath only. New self-catering cottage that sleeps 8 with 3 doubles and bunk beds.
Price: R900 - R1,450 pp sharing. Singles + 20%. Includes meals and game drives. R650 - R690 pp for self-catering cottage. 0 - 3 are free, 4 - 15 half price in cottage.
Meals: Coffee, rusks, brunch, high tea, snacks and sundowners and 4-course dinner included in price.
Directions: From CT take N1 towards Paarl. Exit 47, left at stop. Continue along turning left onto R44 signed Ceres. Follow for 30km. Past R46 junction signed Hermon, take next R signed Bo-Hermon. Gravel road for 2km. B.K. signed to L - 5km.

Oude Wellington Estate

Rolf and Vanessa Schumacher
Bainskloof Pass Rd, Wellington 7654
Tel: 021-873-2262 Fax: 088-021-873-4639
Email: info@kapwein.com Web: www.kapwein.com

There seems to be so much to catch the eye even as you rumble along the 800-metre paved and cobbled road to Oude Wellington: vineyards on both sides, ostentatious peacocks, geese and hadedas, pet ostriches peering over a fence. And that afternoon four pregnant alpacas that had just arrived all the way from Australia were to be added to the menagerie. Rolf and Vanessa are clearly the hospitable types (how else could ostriches find a home on a winery?). It took them two years to restore the whole estate to its former glory as a wine-grape farm. Four rustic double rooms are in the original farmhouse (built in 1790) with high, thatched ceilings, low pole beams, whitewashed walls and yet underfloor heating and air con; the other two are in the more modern main building (well, 1836!), along with the beautiful farm kitchen with old-fashioned pots, pans and irons, billiard room and bar, and a terrace overlooking the vineyards, where breakfast is served in the summer. There is a partly-shaded pool off to the side of the main house, a brandy still in the barn, and handily on the premises is a restaurant popular with the locals (always a good sign). Guests are also invited to watch wine-making taking place at the right time of year. "We farm and dine and love company," say Rolf and Vanessa in their brochure!

Rooms: 9: all doubles with en-suite Victorian baths.
Price: R250 pp sharing. R350 singles.
Meals: Full breakfast included. Restaurant on premises.
Directions: Turn into Church Street (Kerkstraat) in Wellington which becomes the Bainskloof Rd (R301/3). 2.5km out of Wellington on right-hand side follow brown signs to Oude Wellington.

Kleinfontein

Tim and Caroline Holdcroft
PO Box 578, Wellington 7654
Tel: 021-864-1202 Fax: 021-864-1202
Email: kleinfon@iafrica.com Web: www.kleinfontein.com
Cell: 072-108-5895

An evening leg-stretch with Tim proved the perfect antidote to a long and stressful day on the road. Guided by a labrador, an almost-labrador and a hairy, mobile sausage, we strolled past Jersey cows, through a shaded stream and between rows of sunlit vines. Kleinfontein is just an hour from Cape Town at the foot of the Bainskloof Pass and the Holdcrofts are delightful hosts. They'll eat with you, show you their farm and even have you out there clipping the vines or feeding the horses if you show willing (and riding them too if you're saddle-hardened). In fact there's enough to keep you busy here for days, from hiking in surrounding mountains and cellar tours galore, to the leisurely delights of a good book beneath magnificent oak trees, or a wallow in the pool in Caroline's fabulous garden. She is of Kenyan stock and Tim's British, but they spent years in Botswana and over a superb supper we washed down tales of Africa with home-grown cabernet sauvignon. Like me you'll stay in a roomy, restored wing of the thatched Cape Dutch farmhouse with poplar beams and reed ceilings. Like me you'll sleep like a baby. And, like me, you'll wake to breakfast on the verandah with fresh butter and milk, newly-laid eggs and honey straight from the beehive. Sound idyllic? Well, it is. *Closed June and July.*

Rooms: 2 suites, both with sitting room. 1 with en-suite bath and shower, 1 with en-suite bath with shower overhead.
Price: R1,000 - R1,200 pp sharing. Single supplement + 20%. Includes all meals, drinks and laundry.
Meals: Breakfast, tea/coffee tray, picnic lunch and 4-course dinner included in the price.
Directions: Directions are down dirt roads so map can be emailed or faxed.

Roggeland Country House

Gordon Minkley

Roggeland Rd, Dal Josaphat Valley, Paarl 7623
Tel: 021-868-2501 Fax: 021-868-2113
Email: rog@iafrica.com Web: www.roggeland.co.za

The highlight of a stay at Roggeland must be the food! All reports glow with praise: 8-12 different wines to taste pre-dinner, an opportunity to chat to other guests and Gordon himself; then four mouth-watering courses each with a different wine specially chosen to accompany it. Vegetarians will be particularly happy and meals and wines are never repeated during your stay. The house is an 18th-century Cape Dutch homestead with large, thick-walled rooms - sometimes huge - with a variety of original features: beam and reed ceilings, thatch, antique furniture. The dining room, for example, is in an old kitchen with its original grate and cooking implements. Some bedrooms are in the main house and some are separate from it, but none let the side down. Character abounds; floors slope, beams curve and attractive bright-coloured walls are often uneven with age; and there are always fresh flowers and home-made soaps in the rooms. Roggeland is family-run and the atmosphere is friendly and caring as a result. Farmland and mountains surround the property and the Minkleys will organise evening rides on horseback into the foothills. Great hospitality and very good value too. *Children by arrangement. Mountain biking and fishing.*

Rooms: 11: 6 twins, 4 doubles, 1 single. All with en/s bathrooms, 7 with baths and showers, 4 with baths and showers overhead.
Price: Seasonal R520 – R970 pp sharing. Single supplement in high season + 50%.
Meals: The highlight is a 4-course dinner with a different wine at each course and wine-tasting, all included in price. Full breakfast too. Lunches on request.
Directions: Approximately 60km from Cape Town, take exit 59 onto R301 towards Wellington. After 8km on R301 turn right at Roggeland sign. Follow sign onto gravel road for 1km.

Belair

Janet Plumbly
Suid Agter-Paarl Rd, Paarl 7624
Tel: 021-863-1504 Fax: 021-863-1602
Email: info@belair.co.za Web: www.belair.co.za
Cell: 082-572-7062

A straight 300-metre drive up two narrow strips of weathered red brick, past roaming gangs of guinea-fowl and rows of vines, takes you up to Belair, a beautiful guest house on its own farm beneath the round dome of Paarl Mountain. The view from the doorstep (and the garden and pool) across the valley towards Franschhoek and the Groot Drakenstein is spectacular… and it is rather lovely inside too. Steps lead up from a large threshing-circle style driveway into the hallway and open sitting room, which mixes antique furniture with comfy sofas and bookshelves bursting with swashbucklers. Behind is the bright breakfast conservatory, which looks onto a rose-filled garden. There are definitely green fingers at work here. Janet's light but stylish touch is in evidence everywhere at Belair, from the terraced gardens to the bedrooms themselves, each with its own distinct character. My favourite was the 'red' toile room at the end. From the house, it's a short walk up to the dam where birdlife abounds among the reeds (look out for buzzards when it all goes quiet), a great spot for a sundowner. For the more energetic, Paarl Mountain Nature Reserve is further up the hill, and there are lots of golf courses nearby. *Cape Town Waterfront is also only 35 minutes away and there are great restaurants in and about Paarl.*

Rooms: 5 doubles with en-suite bathrooms. 2 are twins joined together.
Price: R250 - R600 pp pn sharing. Single supplements not specified.
Meals: Full breakfast included.
Directions: On Suid-Agter Paarl Rd off R101 (next to Fairview Wine Estate).

Palmiet Valley

Frederick Uhlendorff
Palmiet Valley Estate, Sonstraal Rd, Klein Drakensberg, Paarl 7628
Tel: 021-862-7741 Fax: 021-862-6891
Email: info@palmiet.co.za Web: www.palmiet.co.za

Frederick has scoured not just this land but several in his relentless quest for fine things. There's hardly a nut or bolt in the place that isn't antique - even the loos, showers, free-standing baths and wooden wash-stands are Victorian, not to mention the aged safes and old-school slipper bed pans (that thankfully no-one ever uses!). But this is not a museum, despite the long history of the farm - Palmiet was one of the first to be established outside Cape Town in 1692. Guests come here for the luxury and the romance of the vineyards and mountains that stretch out and up from the old farm. One four-poster bed is positioned so that you can wake up and watch the sun rise over the mountains without moving your head. The beautiful gardens are interwoven with cobbled paths and peppered with numerous dreamy spots to sit. Herbs are harvested and transformed into fresh herbal teas or added to shady lunches by the pool. In summer candlelit dinners are held under the oaks and are as sumptuous as everything else, with top chefs employed to cook exclusively for residents. With so much character and reflection upon old-fashioned values, it's no wonder this place is a hot-spot for weddings. But you don't need to be married or coupled to enjoy it as I, a happy singleton, discovered.

Rooms: 12: 1 honeymoon suite en-suite bath/shower, 4 standard twins, 2 standard doubles & 2 single rooms (both with double beds), all with en-suite bath or shower. Also 3 self-catering cottages, 2 with bath & sep shower, 1 with double shower.
Price: Single rooms R795 or R950 for a couple. Standard R745 pp sharing. Honeymoon suite R945 pp sharing. Cottages R1,690 per night. 20% off in winter.
Meals: Full breakfast included. Lunches on request. 3-course set dinner R225.
Directions: Heading away from Cape Town on the N1 take exit 62a (Sonstraal Road), turn first left, straight over crossroads. Palmiet Valley is on left.

Map Number: 4

Paarl Rock Suites

Udo and Carmen Mettendorf

64 Main Street, Paarl 7646
Tel: 021-863-3192 Fax: 021-863-3192
Email: info@kapinfo.com Web: www.kapinfo.com

Based on the 'golden mile' of Paarl, ballooning-mad Udo and Carmen are pioneers in placing this "rough-diamond-of-the-Winelands-region" on the map. Golden mile basically means the 'old bit' of Paarl, a historic rush of Victorian houses, tree-lined with old oaks. The original house of Paarl Rock Suites dates back to 1860 when it featured as part of an old wine estate. Although split into various scattered sections now, you still get to look out over the Mattendorfs' rock garden and succulents onto regiments of vines beyond. Paarl Rock sits stately in the background, a massive granite feature thrown up by volcanic activity and asking to be biked to, walked around and explored; while the swimming pool in the foreground has been craftily crafted to reflect it. Udo and Carmen themselves are an open book of local knowledge. Originally from Germany, they came and explored as tourists gathering all the best inside information and wrapping it up with a big ballooning bow for their guests. You'll have to book fast if you want to bag a corner of the basket, however, as ballooning has seriously taken off (if you'll excuse the pun) since Udo and Carmen madly (some believed) introduced it a few years ago. I loved the luxury apartment, which caught my eye with leather sofas, spa bath and marble-topped kitchen, but all three qualify as the perfect base to negotiate all the Cape has to offer.

Rooms: 3 self-catering apartments: 2 with 1 double bedroom and 1 with 2 bedrooms, a double and a queen.
Price: R420 - R680 for the flat. Prefer a min of 3-night stay. ONLY OPEN OCTOBER TO MAY!
Meals: Fully self-catering, but many restaurants within easy walking distance.
Directions: On the N1 from Cape Town take exit 55 leading into Paarl Main Street. Follow until you reach no. 64 on your left, opposite number 113.

Natte Valleij

Charlene and Charles Milner
R44 betw' Stellenbosch and Paarl, PO Box 4, Klapmuts 7625
Tel: 021-875-5171 Fax: 021-875-5475
Email: milner@intekom.co.za Web: www.nattevalleij.co.za

Come and lose yourself in the depths of this wild and fecund garden - or do I mean jungle? Ancient trees such as the rare gingco (the oldest in South Africa, once thought extinct), several 200-year-old oaks and a wealth of growth besides keep the pool, 'moon gate' and old brandy stills secreted in their midst. Guests stay in the simple B&B room next to the main house, its verandah festooned with grandiflora, and eat a breakfast in this most lovely of Cape Dutch homesteads (pictured above), built in 1775. If the weather's fine then you eat out on the patio under its cooling roof of vine. Or you can take one of the cottages lost down garden paths. Vineyard Cottage (pictured below), with direct access to the swimming pool, is the oldest building on the property, its original 1714 reed ceilings still intact. While Cellar Cottage is the most recent addition at 'Nutty Valley', small, cute, rustic, perfect for couples. Come for great charm from house and hosts alike. Walks are in all directions up mountains and into surrounding vineyards. Or guests are welcome to enter the park (the entrance gate is just 50m from Vineyard Cottage) where at the last count 23 wildebeest, 25 eland, 24 springbok, 4 bontebok, 3 kudu, 2 oryx and 10 zebra (among others) can be seen. *Local bird-watching tours with Charles are a speciality. Well-positioned on the Stellenbosch and Paarl wine routes. Self-catering available in the cottages.*

Rooms: 3: 1 B&B room, double with en/s bath; 2 cottages (self-catering or B&B): Cellar Cottage sleeps 2 (plus 2 kids' beds); Vineyard Cottage sleeps 6 (3 bedrooms and 2 bathrooms).
Price: B&B R270 pp sharing. Rates for the cottages (i.e. NOT per person) per night depending on number of people and length of stay: R400 - R1,200.
Meals: Full breakfast included in B&B and an optional extra in cottages.
Directions: From Cape Town take N1 exit 47. Turn right onto R44. Farm 4km on left.

Auberge Rozendal

Tanya Esser
Jonkershoek Valley, Omega Road, Stellenbosch 7599
Tel: 021-809-2600 Fax: 021-809-2640
Email: rozendal@mweb.co.za Web: www.rozendal.co.za

Kurt, Tanya's father, swears by his home-made vinegar apéritif. This concoction of ten-year-old matured vinegar infused with lavender, coco, carob, wild olives, seaweed and chillies is said to aid digestion and blood circulation. Apparently some guests love it, although I confess that I winced when swallowing. But then Tanya started to laugh when my stomach rumbled afterwards – the digestive catalyst obviously does the trick! Here on the organic bio-dynamic wine farm their philosophy is health and well-being and the proof is in the eating. With a focus on organic food, delicacies such as abalone, crayfish and free-range duck breast are not to be missed. Meals are served either on the verandah under the vines or in the dining room with its gallery of canvases by world-famous local artists such as Paul Emsley (Tate exhibitor), Cecil Skotnes and Larry Scully. From their 26 hectares, the Ammann family harvest fruits and vegetables, collect eggs from the chickens and milk from their Jersey cows and guests can even participate in the trampling of the grapes in February/March. Separated from the main house, the purpose-built rooms fronted with olive trees and rose bushes have terraces with magnificent views that stretch over vineyards to either Table Mountain or the Botmaskop mountains. If the fresh air and natural environment do not provide you with enough feel-good endorphins, there is a massage therapist who visits on request. *Restaurant closed June – September.*

Rooms: 16: 9 queens, 7 twins, all with en-suite bath with shower overhead.
Price: R472.50 pp sharing. Singles R590.
Meals: R60 for breakfast. 4-course evening menu R150, 3 courses for R130. Lunch also available.
Directions: From Cape Town take N2, then take exit 33 to Stellenbosch on R310. Turn R at T-jct. After station turn left onto Adam Tas Rd. At second traffic light turn R onto Merriman Rd. At roundabout look out for L'Auberge Rozendal sign. After 2km turn left into Omega St. "A.Rozendal" signposted at top of Omega St.

Map Number: 4

The Beautiful South Guest House

Lars and Emily Feldscher
4 Hospital St, Stellenbosch 7600
Tel: 021-883-8171
Email: enjoy@thebeautifulsouth.de Web: www.thebeautifulsouth.de
Cell: 072-545-3072

The genial answer-phone message informs you that Lars and Emily are 'probably out buying lovely things for your breakfast'. They probably are too! This is a special meal at The Beautiful South, with a promise of something different every morning, always home-baked bread, muffins, scones, tomato-mozzarella toast and such specials as 'Fruity Djibuti' from the buffet bar. Not wanting to miss out on their own handiwork, the Feldschers (minus the most recently-arrived family member, clues to whose existence can be spied throughout the house) join their guests at the feasting table. It is here that excursions into the winelands and the surrounding hills are plotted and restaurants are suggested for the evening. The house is quaintly thatched and whitewashed, with wooden windows and the surrounding garden with its mature trees and large pool is directly accessible from each of the bedrooms. While outside is all rustic cottage, inside the emphasis is on style, modernity and function: clean lines, natural materials, modern fittings in bathrooms and high-quality orthopedic beds. A waist-high wall is all that separates the oval, free-standing bath from the sleeping area in the Desert Rose room with its sandstone-tiled floor; while the Sunset Room, with its lime-washed floor and walls, boasts a private wooden terrace. Although new to the guesthouse game, hosting comes only too naturally to Lars and Emily.

Rooms: 6: 2 twins, 4 doubles. 5 have en-suite bath or shower, 1 has private shower room opposite.
Price: R195 - R375.
Meals: Breakfast included with new 'special' every morning.
Directions: From N1 or N2 take turn-off marked to Stellenbosch. On entering Stellenbosch turn into Merriman Street. After white pedestrian bridge turn 2nd left into Bosman. Take 1st right into Soete Weide. Next left into Hospital Street.

Malans Guest House

Laetitia Malan
4 Keerom St, Stellenbosch
7600
Tel: 021-887-8859
Fax: 021-887-9909
Email: malansgh@gmail.com
Web: www.malansgh.de
Cell: 083-664-1517

Laetitia has uniquely and beautifully decorated each of her guest rooms with antique furniture, kilims on beds, fresh flowers and even proper home-found shower caps in the bathrooms! (Ladies with long hair will know what I'm taking about.) She also collects Voortrekker wedding dresses that date back to the 1860s, while her other lace collections are displayed under glass-covered breakfast tables. And what a breakfast room: antique Chinese vases and vessels, exotic orchids, furniture inlaid with mother-of-pearl, 'grandparent' clocks, newly-painted frescoes and a flower-imprinted Chinese screen. Laetitia admitted that she may have lived in China in a previous life. She also collects porridges (!) after a fashion: try maltabela porridge (a traditional black-corn variety), maize or oatmeal at breakfast. And if you're not a porridge fan (no reason why you should be), there are plenty of mueslis, fresh fruits, bacon, eggs and all. Laetitia and her daughter treated me to their home-made chocolate cake and my first-ever rooibos tea, and sitting on the verandah in the sunshine I felt serene. A rare quote from one of our other hosts in this book: "I have stayed there myself and I often send guests on to her. Incredible value for money and an experience in its own right. A very interesting owner, with staff who know the art of hospitality and the most beautiful antiques." This all turns out to be pretty exact. *Nearby: cycling, horse-riding, golfing, fly-fishing and wine-tasting.*

Rooms: 5: 1 queen and 1 double with en-suite showers; 3 twins with en/s bath and shower.
Price: R275 - R350 pp sharing. Singles R350 - R450.
Meals: Full breakfast included. Restaurants aplenty nearby.
Directions: From Cape Town take N2, then R310 to Stellenbosch. Drive into town, at railway turn right into Dorp St. After right-hand bend turn left up The Avenue, first left to Neethling St and first left again into Keerom St.

Summerwood Guest House

Christian and Ann Baret
28 Jonkershoek Rd, Stellenbosch 7600
Tel: 021-887-4112 Fax: 086-600-0374
Email: summerwood@mweb.co.za Web: www.summerwood.co.za
Cell: 072-633-9341

You notice the huge stinkwood tree first, then the swimming pool (a proper one for swimming in). The smooth, well-tended lawns of the garden seem to beckon the guests, who convene round tables on the terrace in the evening or take a few hours out from wine and history to brave the sun by day. The house itself was built in 1904 by an Italian architect – light and airy, with pretty 'Italian' windows. All the bedrooms are furnished with a summery feel (lots of yellows) and uncluttered, allowing for much clean wall and floor space. The 'room at the top' has panoramic views of garden and mountain. Having seen Ann in action, it is clear that she revels in the relaxed and friendly atmosphere at Summerwood, a far cry from her old life in bustling Johannesburg. She takes the greatest care that all guests are properly orientated by suggesting local excursions and booking you into the best restaurants in town. Some of the best are a short walk away, as is the Jonkershoek Nature Reserve and its mountain trails. And obviously Summerwood is an ideal base for the Stellenbosch wineries.*Stellenbosch is only twenty minutes from Cape Town International Airport. Closed in June.*

Rooms: 9: 5 king-size doubles, 4 twins. All have en-suite bathrooms with baths and showers.
Price: R440 – R725 pp sharing. Singles R650 – R1,000.
Meals: Full breakfast included and served until 9.30 am. Restaurants nearby.
Directions: Exit 33 from N2, L to Stellenbosch R310. At T-jct turn R for 2.5km. 2nd lights turn R up Dorp St to pancake roundabout. L into Meul St, next roundabout R into Plein St, becomes Van Riebeeck St. Keep L at fork, house on R.

Glenconner

Emma Finnemore
Jonkershoek Valley, PO Box 6124, Stellenbosch 7612
Tel: 021-886-5120 Fax: 021-886-5120
Email: glenconner@icon.co.za Web: www.winelands.co.za/glenconner
Cell: 082-354-3510

Looking up at the imposing mountains, which rise on both sides of the property, and surrounded by lush vegetation - including all that wild strelitzia and agapanthus - it's almost impossible to believe that you're just six kilometres from Stellenbosch. Such a spectacular location. Sit with a glass of wine on whichever stoep belongs to you for the night and watch the lowering sun paint the mountains a deep pink. You don't need to do any more than this to lift the spirits by many notches. There are three private-terraced, light-filled, simple country-furnished sleeping locations to choose from: the homestead with its four-poster bed, Victorian bath and English country feel; the newly-renovated Oak Cottage, with its cosy fireplace, pale blue beams and terracotta tiles, and a beautiful patio enclave that crouches beneath a looming mountain and gazes upon Emma's indigenous garden; and lastly the Studio, also a separate cottage with an open-plan bedroom, quaint stripy sitting areas, charming little kitchen and second bedroom (with the best in-bed view of the lot). A round, spring-water-fed swimming pool sits directly in front of the homestead and a tan-coloured river is a little further away for paddling, picnics and otter-sighting. And horses graze peacefully on the luminous green grass in the paddocks. If all this is not enough for you, the Jonkershoek Nature Reserve is just down the road with some of the best hiking in SA, from 2-hour to 2-day walks.

Rooms: 3: 2 self-catering cottages: the Studio has double, twin & shared bathroom; Oak Cottage has double, twin & single room with shared bathroom & shared shower in out-house); 1 double room in the Homestead.
Price: The homestead B&B, R395 pp sharing. Self-catering cottages are from R275 pp. Under 12's half-price, under 4's free. Discounts for stays of 5 nights or longer.
Meals: Continental breakfasts included in B&B or R50 for self-caterers. 5 minutes' drive into Stellenbosch with restaurants aplenty.
Directions: From CT, N2 to Stellenbosch, follow signs to Jonkershoek Nature Reserve. 4km from Stellenbosch turn right and cross over bridge on right just after entrance to Neil Ellis vineyard.

Map Number: 4

Caledon Villa

Johan and Ode Krige
7 Neethling Street, Stellenbosch 7600
Tel: 021-883-8912 Fax: 021-883-8912
Email: info@caledonvilla.co.za Web: www.caledonvilla.co.za

Charmingly Victorian, Caledon Villa sits pretty as a picture in leafy Stellenbosch, its elegant wrap-around verandah adorned with pillars, eaves and vines. Yet, once you step inside, the villa is African through and through. As you'll see (quite literally, in the portraits on the walls of the previous seven) Johan and Ode are the eighth generation of the Krige family and the house is stocked to the brim with Cape Dutch antiques, paintings and family heirlooms. Many of the bedrooms have original wooden floors, Victorian dressers and chaises-longues, and one even has a handsome four-poster dating all the way back to 1860 (if beds could talk...). Not that you'll be staying in your room for long however, as soon you'll be in town with your Johan-penned map brushing up your historical knowledge. And there's an awful lot of history in Stellenbosch, itself the second oldest town in South Africa and, being descendents of the founding fathers, there is nothing this pair don't know about it. As with each item in his house, Johan is more than happy to wax lyrical about the town and its people through the years - often entertaining guests with his humerous (and informative) tales at breakfast. And if all that culture gets your grey matter in a whirl, you can always lounge by the shaded pool in the garden, watched over by the stunning aspect of the town's church spire.

Rooms: 15: 12 doubles or twins. 3 family units. All have en-suite bath and/or shower.
Price: R345 - R380 pp sharing. Singles R450 - R520.
Meals: Full breakfast included. For other meals, 15 restaurants within 10 mins' walk.
Directions: Directions will be sent when you book.

Camberley Cottage

John and Gael Nel

Camberley Wine Estate, Helshoogte Pass, Stellenbosch 7612
Tel: 021-885-1176 Fax: 021-885-1822
Email: john@camberley.co.za Web: www.camberley.co.za
Cell: 082-690-4975

Gazing down the splendid Franschhoek Valley, all chequered with fruit farms and vineyards, Camberley occupies the kind of spot we all dream of making our own. This is exactly what Johnny and Gaël did 14 years ago when they bought this former fruit farm. Heaps of pips and barrels of grape juice later, Camberley is now a small family-run vineyard producing some of the Cape's best reds and Johnny a highly-acclaimed wine-maker well-used to plum accolades (such as the Double Veritas award) being lobbed his way. An immensely likeable lot, the Nels are more than happy for you to pull up your sleeves and get busy in the picking and barrelling processes. The cottage itself sits in the thick of the vines, which screech to a halt at the rose-filled garden's edge. Although recently built, its rather sophisticated country air feels authentically matured, the floor-to-ceiling sash windows and Oregon pine floors taken from a former Cape Dutch-style bank in town. Although it has a very well-equipped kitchen and dining area, there are several top restaurants literally minutes from home, so, happily, washing-up is unlikely to feature in this holiday equation. This low-key, homely winery is the perfect point from which to explore the Winelands and Johnny helpfully has listed all his favourite places for you. Festooned with bubbles, the plunge pool makes a fantastic sunset spot for when you're well and truly corked.

Rooms: 1 king/twin, en-suite shower and bath.
Price: R350 - R450 pp B&B, R300 - R400 pp self-catering. Singles on request.
Meals: Full breakfast included in B&B prices.
Directions: From Cape Town, take N2 and turn off at Baden Powell Dr/R310 to Stellenbosch. Continue on R310 through town, about 8 mins out of S'bosch, Camberley is signed on right, opposite Le Pommier restaurant.

Babylons Toren

Margie Louw
Klapmuts - Simondium Rd, Simondium 7670
Tel: 021-863-3494 Fax: 021-863-1804
Email: babylon@mweb.co.za Web: www.babylonstoren.co.za
Cell: 082 331 3310

Babylons Toren (the Tower of Babylon) is named after the koppie or rocky hill by the house, thought to resemble a ziggurat by earlier (much earlier – the house was built in about 1700) romantics with a bit of imagination. The property is all that you could hope for from a working Cape Dutch farm. There are the old gabled house, the surrounding outbuildings and vineyards, the backdrop of mountains, the sporadic sound of tractors, dogs… and Margie has opened up one of the courtyard outbuildings – these were once dairy, butchery, bakery – and created a rustic, but very stylish cottage for guests next to the old hen house that is now used for wine-tasting. The ceiling of the cottage is of pole beams and cut reeds (the width of the house was apparently dependent on the length of the wagon that carried these beams), walls are thick and whitewashed, and the main bedroom itself is of grand dimensions with high ceilings and a decorative mosquito net over twin beds. You can self-cater or Margie will supply all you need for a healthy breakfast in your fridge each day. The large pool in the garden is as much yours as your hosts'. In fact a major reason why Margie has guests at all is to share what Babylons Toren has to offer with new people.*27-hole golf course nearby. Horse-riding easily arranged.*

Rooms: 1 cottage with 2 double rooms sharing 1 bathroom with bath. Self-catering or B&B. One-group booking only.
Price: R220 - R280 pp sharing B&B. Single supplement. Self-catering R400 - R800 for cottage (sleeps 4), depending on numbers and length of stay.
Meals: Fridge restocked each day for breakfast. For other meals self-catering or restaurants aplenty in the area.
Directions: From Cape Town take the N1 exit 47 onto R44 towards Stellenbosch. Turn left signed Simondium/Franschhoek. Follow road for 6km. Babylons Toren is on your right in vineyards.

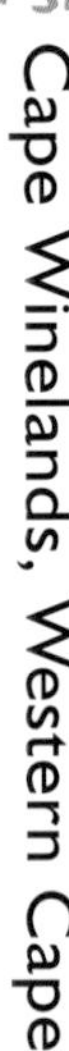

Lekkerwijn

Wendy Pickstone
Groot Drakenstein , Franschhoek Road, near Boschendal 7680
Tel: 021-874-1122 Fax: 021-874-1465
Email: lekkerwijn@new.co.za Web: www.lekkerwijn.com

Lekkerwijn (pronounced Lekkervain) is a 1790s Cape Dutch homestead with a grand Edwardian extension designed by Sir Herbert Baker. You would probably have to pay to look round if Wendy didn't live there. It positively creaks with family history. You can tell when one family have lived in a grand house for generations - all the furniture, fittings and decoration look so at home. This is not some country house hotel nor some converted annexe. You share the house fully with Wendy, whose family have lived here since the late 19th century - unless of course you would prefer the privacy of Coach House Cottage. My strongest impressions are of the central courtyard with its gallery and cloister, the yellowwood floors and beams and the towering palms planted by Wendy's grandfather, the informal taste of the nursery bedroom, a wonderful breakfast... and Wendy herself, who is full of character and together with her management team, so caring of her guests.

Rooms: 5: all either double or twin, all en-suite. 2 self-catering cottages for couples either alone or with children.
Price: R290 (winter rates) - R620 (summer rates) pp sharing. Singles on request. Discounts for stays of 3 nights or longer.
Meals: Full breakfast included for B&B. You can self-cater in Coach House cottage and breakfast in the courtyard is an optional extra.
Directions: On R45 at intersection with R310 from Stellenbosch (after passing Boschendal), alongside the Alllée Bleue entrance walls.

Cathbert Country Inn

Ann and Robert Morley

Franschhoek Rd, Simondium, Franschhoek 7620
Tel: 021-874-1366 Fax: 021-874-3918
Email: info@cathbert.co.za Web: www.cathbert.co.za
Cell: 082-414 0601

Ann and Robert have a complete set of correct attitudes, as far as we are concerned: they have purposefully kept Cathbert's small (only eight rooms), "so we get to know our guests"; it's smart without going over the top and yet totally relaxed; and the food is a major focus. Bedrooms have views over a reservoir, farmland, vineyards, and the Simonsberg Mountains loom behind the house. Guests can walk up Kanonkop from Cathbert, a hill from which they used to signal to ships out at sea. You sleep in chalets with open-plan bed/sitting rooms and are refreshingly simple in style (and well-equipped with towelling bathrobes and other welcome luxuries). Each chalet has its little front garden where you might be honoured with a haughty visit from one of the resident peacocks, whose home this really is. Ann spends her day between reception and the kitchen where she is *maestro*- (set) menus are based on what she finds freshest around her. Her food is truly delicious, beautifully presented (only to residents) - 'modern' without being outré - and a real pull for Cathbert's burgeoning fan club. Robert, meanwhile, acts as (and *is*!) the charming and knowledgeable sommelier and host.

Rooms: 8 suites: 2 standard, 4 luxury, 2 executive. All with en-suite bath and shower. All king-size/twin beds. All air-conditioned.
Price: R500 - R750 pp sharing. Single supplement +50%.
Meals: Full breakfast included. Set menu 4-course dinner (except on Sundays).
Directions: From CT take N1, take exit 47, turn right at end of ramp, over 4-way stop, left at next road towards Franschhoek. Pass Backsberg Wine Estate. At the stop just before railway crossing turn right onto private tar road. Follow for 2.5km.

Résidence Klein Oliphants Hoek

Ingrid and Camil Haas
14 Akademie St, Franschhoek 7690
Tel: 021-876-2566 Fax: 021-876-2566
Email: info@kleinoliphantshoek.co.za Web: www.kleinoliphantshoek.co.za

Sometimes it all comes together so satisfyingly! Ingrid and Camil opened their first restaurant in a Dutch windmill, at the venerable age of 23, then worked their way across Europe – Turkey, France, Belgium - before moving out to South Africa in 2000 and falling in love (at first sight) with Klein Oliphants Hoek. The building has been reincarnated many times in its hundred and some years, built by an English missionary as a chapel in 1888 and at other times a school and a theatre. I'd only been at the guest house a very brief while before I knew instinctively that no single aspect of the place was going to let the side down. The centrepiece inside is the chapel hall itself, with its high-vaulted ceiling, fireplace and original beams, now the guest sitting room; but there are the bedrooms, the scented garden, the verandah and salt-water pool, the views. The highlight, perhaps, are Camil's evening meals which are now served at the "Bouillabaisse" restaurant located on the main road (a 5-min stroll into town). Here guests can experience 'front-cooking' which means the kitchen is based in the restaurant and guests watch the chefs at work while they enjoy culinary seafood taster dishes and wines and champagne by the glass. All in all, a real treat. *Closed in June.*

Rooms: 8: 4 doubles & 4 twins/doubles, all with en-suite showers and baths; 1 is a sundeck room with jacuzzi and full body-massage shower (no bath), while 2 have private pools.
Price: R300 - R900 pp sharing. Single supplement.
Meals: Full breakfast included. Evening supper platters daily. 9-course dinner extravaganza for R295 at their new seafood restaurant "Bouillabaisse" on Mon, Wed, Fri & Sat. Open daily for lunch.
Directions: Akademie St is parallel to the main road in Franschhoek (Huguenot St), two streets up the hill.

Les Chambres

Bill and Sandy Stemp
3 Berg Street, Franschhoek 7690
Tel: 021-876-3136 Fax: 021-876-2798
Email: gg@leschambres.co.za Web: www.leschambres.co.za
Cell: 083 263 1926

So much to take in even as I ambled up one of many garden paths towards the house: the palm tree, reputed to be the tallest tree in the village, the herb garden boiling over with basil, rocket and tomatoes - that stone bench would be the perfect spot to make some progress with a paperback, I noted. Venturing further, I found Chinese poplars, gardenias and numerous shrubs and bark-strewn flowerbeds. And finally the house, a verandah-fronted Victorian gem, with Bill, Sandy and Archie (a cat) and Frank (another cat) forming a reassuring welcoming committee. Refreshed with a cool drink, I was shown through to the breakfasting patio where goldfish waft prettily about in a stone pond and French doors provide easy access to the continental-style buffet: fresh fruits and cereals, home-made granola and bread. Cooked options might include poached eggs on English muffins, or "Eggs Benedict", or scrambled eggs with smoked salmon-trout. Ze bedrooms of ze title are furnished in a mix of the antique and the contemporary with mahogany dressing tables and wicker bedheads; while the bathrooms have travertine tiles, roll-top Victorian baths and separate showers. Some rooms are carpeted, others display the original wood flooring, complemented by a fireplace and Persian rugs. Private courtyards are available to two rooms, red-tiled with whitewashed walls and an overhanging orange tree. There is much to enjoy cloistered behind these gates. Not least the heated swimming pool.

Rooms: 4: all king-size extra-length doubles or 2 twins, and all en-suite bath and shower. All rooms should be air-conditioned too by the time this goes to print.
Price: R340 - R495 pp sharing. R495 - R725 singles.
Meals: Full breakfast included.
Directions: From R45 drive through village of Franschhoek and turn left into Berg Street just before monument.

Clementine Cottage

Malcolm Buchanan

L'Avenir Farm, PO Box 333, Green Valley Rd, Franschhoek 7690
Tel: 021-876-3690 Fax: 021-876-3528
Email: lavenir@iafrica.com Web: www.clementinecottage.co.za
Cell: 082-320-2179

Running late with my mobile battery dead, I was touched to find Jef waiting expectantly for me just beyond the low-lying bridge that marks the entrance to L'Avenir Farm. He kindly guided me through the orchards of plums and clementines to meet Malcolm, who runs this 21-hectare, family-owned, working fruit farm. Jef, by the way, is a boerboel, as loyal to Malcolm as Robin is to Batman. In retrospect, my timing was perfect: the sun was setting behind the mountains that frame the Franschhoek Valley and from the stoep of Clementine Cottage, looking out over the pool and the vineyard beyond, the sky was stained a deep red. The only sounds I could hear, as I enjoyed a most welcome cold beer with Malcolm and his folks, were the frogs croaking contentedly in the dam that forms the centrepiece of the farm. If you find the pool too confining, a few lengths of this dam should satisfy any Tarzanesque impulses you may harbour. Being only 3km from the village I was able to enjoy a fine meal at the legendary Topsi's, before returning to the biggest bed I've ever had the pleasure of sleeping in. Recently refurbished in the original farm cottage style, Clementine Cottage has everything you could desire from pool, braaing area and satellite TV to large, stylish en-suite bedrooms.

Rooms: 1 cottage: 1 double with en-suite bath and shower and 1 twin with en-suite bath and shower.
Price: Oct - Apr R450 pp sharing. May - Sept R350 pp sharing.

Meals: Self-catering, but numerous restaurants nearby.
Directions: From Franschhoek Main Road driving towards Franschhoek Monument turn R. Drive for about 2km. Turn L up Green Valley Rd (Clementine Cottage signed). Turn L up first gravel road (Clem' Cottage signed again). Drive over white bridge onto L'Avenir, thro' orchards, pass shed on L, Cottage 150m further on your R.

Akademie Street Guesthouses

Katherine and Arthur McWilliam Smith
5 Akademie Street, Franschhoek 7690
Tel: 021-876-3027 Fax: 021-876-3293
Email: katherine@aka.co.za Web: www.aka.co.za
Cell: 082-655-5308

The parade of flowers and stepping-stones through citrus trees, fig trees, rose bushes and bougainvillaea made an otherwise rather thundersome day (ooh and the gale that was blowing!) much brighter. The airy cottages, which sit detached within the flower arrangements, open out onto private stoeps, gardens and even swimming pools. Vreugde, meaning 'joy', is a garden suite for two that has a neat kitchenette in an alcove and a sofa on the terrace. Oortuiging is a restored 1860s cottage for three that retains the old Cape style with antiques throughout. And Gelatenheid is a luxurious villa with, again, a private swimming pool and a wide wrap-around balcony. At the end of the balcony, suitably screened by tree-tops, is an outdoor, repro Victorian bathtub in which you can soak while gazing out at the mountain views… then wrap up in a towel from the heated bath rail. Inside, an expansive open-plan studio is home for just two people (though there's space enough for a four-bed house), with high wooden ceilings, Venetian blinds and French doors… a decadent holiday home. As full as a full breakfast can be (including boerewors - a type of SA sausage if you really didn't know) is served under the vines at the homestead. Katherine and Arthur - he was formerly Mayor of Franschhoek and they are both sooo nice - are easy smilers and happy to help with any day-tripping tips.

Rooms: 3 cottages: Vreugde: twin or king on request, en/s bath + shower; Oortuiging: 1 king + 1 double, both en/s bath + shower; Gelatenheid: 1 king + en/s bath + shower.
Price: R275 - R1,050 pp.
Meals: Full breakfast included.
Directions: From Cape Town take N1 then R45. Akademie St is parallel to main road in Franschhoek, two streets up the hill.

The Garden House

Barry and Annette Phillips

29 De Wet St, Franschhoek 7690
Tel: 021-876-3155 Fax: 021-876-4271
Email: info@thegardenhouse.co.za Web: www.thegardenhouse.co.za
Cell: 083-340-3439

As soon as I met Barry who runs the local newspaper (The Franschhoek Tatler) and Annette, who rescues and re-homes cats, a small inner voice instinctively told me, "Ah, this is somewhere I feel at home!" Annette and Barry have fully immersed themselves in village life since their impulsive holiday decision to leave London in '01 and buy their Cape Victorian house. Their enthusiasm is palpable. And, quite frankly, why shouldn't it be? From the restaurants and wineries we saw when we went out in Barry's "Maigret"-style 1951 Citroen, I could see why Franschhoek claims to be the food and wine capital of the Western Cape! And the Garden House, originally called Belle Vue, with views across the valley to the mountains beyond and an abundant garden, well deserves both names. Guests stay in the air-conditioned and stylishly decorated cottage with its original wood-beamed bedroom and large bathroom with underfloor heating. In summer guests can also stay in a pretty guest room in the main house where the lovely double bed, being Victorian, is "only suitable for very friendly couples". Come morning, Barry took me on a rigorous ride on a mountain bike – he keeps two for guests – while Annette prepared a smoked trout breakfast for our return. Village folk talk and I had already heard on the other side of the valley about Annette's local trout treat. Lovely, down–to-earth people. *Large swimming pool, along with nearby fishing, horse riding, hiking and tennis. Annette will also arrange day trips.*

Rooms: 2: Cottage Room: 1 queen with en-suite bath and shower; Main House Room: 1 standard double with en-suite bath and shower overhead.
Price: Cottage Room: R325 (winter - with a light breakfast served in the room) - R450 (summer) pp sharing. Main House Room R325 (summer only).
Meals: Breakfast included plus complimentary drinks in room and sundowners.
Directions: N1, then R45, then, as you come into Franschhoek, turn left into de Wet St just before the canon and go up the hill. The Garden House is on your right.

Plum Tree Cottage

Liz & John Atkins
Excelsior Road, Franschhoek 7690
Tel: 021-876-2244 Fax: 021-876-2398
Email: plumtree@kleindauphine.co.za Web: www.kleindauphine.co.za

The setting could not be more perfect. A sanctum of blooming plum-blossom, vineyards and oak trees spatter dappled shadows as they rock gently in the breeze, while magnificent mountains rise steeply from the Franschhoek valley. The Plum Tree Cottage balcony is the perfect spot to soak up all this serenity. Having run B&Bs for many a year, Liz and John know exactly what people want and with this newly-built cottage they deliver it in spades. Entirely self-contained (it even has its own separate orchard-lined driveway), it allows you the space to do your own thing. This may be in the elegantly-paved courtyard, cooling off in the invigorating plunge pool, or popping out to the restaurants and wineries in Franschhoek, itself just pip-spitting distance away. The interior is a calming refuge in blues and whites, much like the roses and lavender outside. With each room sharing the magnificent view, you won't know where to put yourself.... I'd choose the corner bath and peek through the oaks at the Arab horse stud behind. By now, Liz will be busy clothing its clotted-cream-coloured walls with wisteria, roses and any other creepers she has creeping around for when she runs out of space in the garden, 'I just send the plants up the walls'. Perfectly tranquil and delightfully quaint... a proper English-style country cottage.

Rooms: 1 queen with en-suite bath and shower. Mezzanine floor accessed by Swedish ladder (so sensibly-made its almost impossible to fall off) can sleep two children (over the age of 12).
Price: R300 pp sharing. For additions (up to 2) R100 pp. Singles R600.
Meals: (Strictly!) self-catering.
Directions: Drive through Franschhoek and turn right at the monument. After 1.3km turn left into Klein Dauphine, then follow separate drive to the right for Plum Tree Cottage.

Longfield

Pieter and Nini Bairnsfather Cloete
Eikendal Rd, off R44, Somerset West/Stellenbosch 7130
Tel: 021-855-4224 Fax: 021-855-4224
Email: ninicloete@longfield.co.za Web: www.longfield.co.za

Perched on the foothills of the dramatic Helderberg mountains, Longfield occupies a truly sensational vantage that drifts across the Winelands and over to the very tip of False Bay at Cape Point. Dreamy by day and by night (when Cape Town's lights put on their glitzy show), there are now three cottages from which to enjoy the view. All are fresh, breezy and decorated in a relaxed country-house style and many of the furnishings are rare, early-Cape family heirlooms. Comfy beds are made up with the highest quality hand-embroidered linen and there are spoiling lotions in the pretty bathrooms and plenty of up-to-date mags, coffee-table books on SA wine, flora and fauna etc, and African objets d'art in the cosy living areas. When I dropped by 'The Stables', a handsome cottage beautifully renovated from (you guessed it) the stables. Each has its private patio or lawn, and fridges and cupboards are re-stocked each day with breakfast materials for you to help yourself to. It is self-catering but you'll enjoy chatting with Nini and Pieter who live on the mountain with you. Formerly wine-farmers themselves, they can arrange exclusive garden and wine tours and will happily point you in the right direction for good restaurants and golf courses, all invariably within easy striking distance. A wonderfully secluded spot and ideally placed for many of the Cape's attractions.

Rooms: 3 cottages: 2 with twin beds, bath and separate shower. 1 with kingsize bed.
Price: R250 - R500 pp sharing. Single supplement by arrangement.
Meals: Breakfast included.
Directions: From CT take N2 past the airport, take exit 43 Broadway Bvd. Left at lights. From the next lights 6.3km exactly, then right into Eikendal Rd. Follow up gravel road, jink left onto tarmac and follow to top and Longfield House.

Map Number: 4

La Sandra House

Chris Olsen and Isobel Kilmister
2 La Sandra Close, Cnr. Adam Tas Street., Somerset West 7137
Tel: 021-852-9453 Fax: 021-852-9453
Email: iksb@mweb.co.za Web: www.lasandrahouse.co.za
Cell: 082 924 7472 or 072 238 8678

New kids on the block Chris and Isobel come fresh from Jo'burg, and are bursting with enthusiasm for their new hosting career. As keen to explore the area as you are, they have already stockpiled a great store of knowledge on local delights. Somerset West is a perfect springboard for the Winelands estates, coastal exploration, golf courses, Cape Town and mountains (to name but a few). La Sandra, however, is enchanting enough in itself. Previously owned by an artist, the property has retained and flaunts much inventive zeal. I was seduced by the garden where immaculate carved rings of hedges pose symmetrically and glistening iceberg roses model amidst a lilac sea of convolvulus. Overlooking the whole show is a view-devoted folly complete with intriguing chandelier and cooling star-painted roof (other artist-left tokens), which Chris and Isobel have very cleverly converted into a mini-gym. "Watch this!" cried Chris as he waved from the end of a newly-finished swimming pool and I laughed as a waterfall of pool-water sprung into action. My favourite of the rooms had to be 'The Studio', a conversion from the artist's original creative zone that now houses not only a large bedroom, chic marble-tiled bathroom and fully-equipped kitchen, but also an aura of inspiration. If only I had made the time to join Chris and Isobel for a lunch of crusty bread, cheese and wine in the sunshine.

Rooms: 3: 1 queen with en-suite bath and shower and kitchen, 1 twin with en-suite shower and kitchen and 1 double with en-suite shower.
Price: R390 pp sharing bed and breakfast. R350 pp sharing self-catering.
Meals: Full breakfast included in bed and breakfast price.
Directions: From Cape Town (or airport) take the N2 to R44 (Broadway turn off, Somerset West). Turn left into Broadway, right into Main, left into Dummer, right into Aberdeen then left into Adam Tas. Entrance to La Sandra is on the corner of Adam Tas and La Sandra Close. Directions also emailed or faxed on request.

Map Number: 4

Helderview Homestead Suites

Carl and Sibylle Linkmann

16 Prunus St, Somerset West 7130
Tel: 021-855-1297 Fax: 021-855-1297
Email: linkmann@mweb.co.za Web: www.linkmann.com
Cell: 072-424-1360

As nice timing would have it, I rolled through the gates of Helderview just as an impressive tea was being unleashed on the terrace. I enjoyed many biscuits and much cake, whilst gazing down to False Bay and the Hottentots Holland Mountains… and getting caught up in Carl's enthusiasm for this dramatic 19th-century house. A self-confessed anglophile, he has collected together period furniture on what must have been several grand tours around the Commonwealth: dressing tables, hefty drinks cabinets, throne-like armchairs around an open fire in the cigar lounge (where Carl holds court), swallow-you-whole brown leather sofas in each of the enormous suites. The three largest are 90 square metres! Commonwealth is a suggestion not an order and there's plenty from elsewhere too, such as the Italian polished granite tiles that lead to the Buffalo suite, and a heavy-looking wooden sculpture from Malawi that guards the bar. Helderview may be lavishly furnished, but these are not laurels upon which Carl has rested. This is a place where you will be pampered. Fancy watching the latest DVD? It's waiting for you in your room. Want to catch up on the news from home? Carl will find your newspaper of choice. Carl's quest for a home fit for a connoisseur naturally includes a sophisticated wine list. Even if you have no idea what you are looking at, or what you're drinking, I think you will find a way to settle in.

Rooms: 7 suites: 5 with 1 bedroom and 1 shower room; 1 with 2 bedrooms and 1 bathroom and 1 shower room; 1 with 2 bedrooms and 1 shower room.
Price: R500 - R850 pp sharing. Single supplement + 50%.
Meals: Full breakfast included. Light menu available at additional cost.
Directions: Airport transfer included and can arrange car hire. For those not coming from Cape Town International, directions can be emailed or faxed.

Manor on the Bay

Hanél and Schalk van Reenen
117 Beach Rd, Gordon's Bay 7140
Tel: 021-856-3260 Fax: 021-856-3261
Email: manorotb@mweb.co.za Web: www.manoronthebay.co.za
Cell: 082-896-5790

Hanél and Schalk van Reenen are a young couple, and their enthusiasm for the job is palpable. They have poured great vats of time and energy into restoring their property. First it was moving an impressive tonnage of earth to create a raised garden at the front below a long terrace; and now it is the addition of six new rooms and even a beauty salon. This is a great place to watch sunsets over False Bay or even whales in spring, and the view is conveniently framed by two large palms. An old English sheepdog completes the very friendly reception committee. Beach Road, you won't need telling, is just next to the sea, and a hop, skip and a dive takes you across the road and into the water. If you don't fancy the walk however, there's also a pool out the back. Of the twelve rooms, four of the new units have self-catering facilities. But if you are feeling like being spoilt, then you can still opt for the breakfast, which is either healthy (in Hanel's case eaten after an early run on the beach - you don't have to join her, but you can) or hearty, and is served in the bright dining room or on the terrace outside.

Rooms: 12: 11 doubles and 1 family room with 2 queens. All with en-suite shower and/or bath.
Price: R400 - R600 pp sharing. Singles on request.
Meals: Full breakfast included.
Directions: From Strand on the R44, take Beach Rd turning just before BP garage. From N2 take Sir Lowry's Pass to Gordon's Bay and cross over on to van der Bijl St, down to Beach Rd and L.

Fraai Uitzicht 1798

Axel Spanholtz and Mario Motti

Historic Wine and Guest Farm with Restaurant, Klaas Voogds East (Oos), Between Robertson and Montagu on Route 62 6705
Tel: 023-626-6156
Fax: 023-626-5265
Email: info@fraaiuitzicht.com
Web: www.fraaiuitzicht.com

Fraai Uitzicht' means 'beautiful view' in Dutch - no idle promise as it turns out. The 17th-century wine and guest farm is four kilometres up a gravel road in a cul-de-sac valley ringed by vertiginous mountains. People come from far and wide for the well-known restaurant and the seven-course *dégustation* menu is basically irresistible. Matched with local wine, it features trout salad, springbok carpaccio, beef fillet with brandy sauce and decadent Dream of Africa chocolate cake. Shall we just say I left with more than one spare tyre in the car. You could also be entertained by a Xhosa choir who give performances every other Wednesday night. Where to sleep is not an easy decision as you are spoilt for choice. A few cottages take it easy in the garden, each comfortable and pretty with impressionistic oils and views of the mountains, while others offer you masses of character with metre-thick walls and timber interiors; my favourite was the loft bedroom in the eaves. Or opt for one of the garden suites with their own entrances and balconies. Make sure you take a peek at the wine cellar - guests have first option on the (uniquely) hand-made merlot. I can't count the number of recommendations we had pointing us to Axel and Mario's door. *Restaurant closed June & July. Limited menu available for guests.*

Rooms: 8: 4 cottages, 2 with 2 bedrooms (1 x queen & 1 x twin), 2 with 1 bedroom (queen & extra sleeper couch); 4 suites, 2 with king, 2 with queen, all en/s shower.
Price: Cottages are R700 pp. Suites are R420 pp.
Meals: Continental breakfast included. R30 extra for English. Lunch and dinner available on premises.
Directions: On R60 between Robertson & Ashton. Approximately 5km from Ashton and 12km from Robertson, Klaas Voogds East turn-off, 4km on gravel road, turn-off to left.

Overberg, Western Cape

Paul Cluver Guest House

The Cluver Family

Grabouw 7160
Tel: 021-844-0605 Fax: 021-844-0150
Email: info@cluver.co.za Web: www.cluver.com

I trundled through vineyards and more vineyards, fruit trees (apples, pears and plums), past grazing springbok, eland, tame ostriches, horses, cows, blue crane (twelve of them), past the Reebok river, a large oak tree and finally I arrived at the Cluver family's early eighteenth-century house, mule stable and school. What an estate! All 2,000 hectares of it! And the Cluvers set their substantial - and one assumes very time-consuming - wine and fruit production to one side in order to accommodate, welcome and feed their guests. Inge, one of Dr Cluver's daughters, introduced me to part of their family history: a Grégoire on the wall depicts the house and its outbuildings from before Inge's grandmother's time and antiques passed down through generations of Cluvers are plentiful. The buildings have been totally renovated with clay-tiled floors and there are such things as electric blankets, heating and a lounge with satellite TV and videos. There are three rooms in the homestead and the other two are the converted cottages (the mule stable with its fireplace is especially popular in winter). *The Cluvers are soon to be part of a unique bio-diversity wine route in the region, the first of its kind. The Paul Cluver Amphitheatre season runs from November to March. Closed in June.*

Rooms: 5: 3 twin rooms and 2 doubles. All en-suite showers.
Price: R340 - R400 pp sharing.
Meals: Full breakfast included. Gourmet cuisine every other weekend May - September.
Directions: From Cape Town take N2, past Somerset West, over Sir Lowry's Pass. You will see the Orchard farm store on the left and the Paul Cluver Wine Estate sign follows shortly on the left (about 20km from Somerset West).

Wildekrans Country House

Alison Green and Barry Gould
Houw Hoek Valley, Elgin 7180
Tel: 028-284-9827 Fax: 028-284-9624
Email: info@wildekrans.co.za Web: www.wildekrans.co.za

From the tufts of moss poking out between the old flagstones of the front path I knew that this was my sort of place. The 1811 homestead is raised above its garden and looks down on lawns, abundant roses, pear orchards, the large swimming pool and old oak trees. The scene is magnificent with the 'wild cliffs' ('wildekrans') of the berg setting the property's limits, rising from a meadow at the back of the garden. Take a stroll beside landscaped watercourses and lily ponds that neighbour the orchards, and you will encounter wonderful, some might think surreal, sculptures that have been positioned with much thought, and I think argument, where they now stand. They add a touch of the unexpected to this magical garden. Finally a rickety bridge - that inspires little in the way of confidence, but is quite safe – crosses a stream and you find yourself at the foot of the steep, forested mountain. A path leads straight up or you can cross a neighbour's land in search of gentler gradients. The bedrooms are charming, each with a four-poster bed, originally parental gifts to Alison and her many sisters, and views out to the garden. There is a large pool, a contemporary art collection and the Wildekrans winery nearby.

Rooms: 4: 3 four-poster doubles in the homestead all with en-suite bath (1 has a shower too and 1 has a private study); and 1 self-catering cottage.
Price: B&B: R325 - R380 pp sharing. Singles R420. Self-catering: R225 - R340 pp sharing.
Meals: Full breakfast included. Dinner from a one-course simple supper R85 to three courses R135. All meals are self-served.
Directions: On N2 from Cape Town for 1 hour approx, past Grabouw and 12km further turn L signed Houw Hoek Inn. Or: half an hour from Caledon on N2, at top of Houw Hoek Pass, turn R signed Houw Hoek Inn. Through Houw Hoek gate posts, follow road round to left. Farm on right.

Wonderlings B&B

Jenny Stark and Koos Smith
Camp Rd, Rooi Els, Pringle Bay
Tel: 028-273-8961 Fax: 028-273-8955
Email: wonderlings@iafrica.com Web: www.wonderlingsbandb.com
Cell: 082-896-8152

Wedged between khaki fynbos-clad mountains and the sea, Wonderlings B&B holds its own against the elements. As I was led into the lounge, a moody landscape, one of many pieces of original art, caught my eye with its dramatic colour; "it's unpredictable, beautiful and in control of all of us," Jenny said with excitement, referring to the incredible surrounding terrain. Located within the Kogelberg Nature Reserve, yet only a brief car journey from Pringle Bay (and an even briefer walk to Rooi Els village), you are perched here on the fringes of the wild. Nature roams freely, its most boisterous representatives being the baboons, who earn the flight of a red flag when they are in town. Jenny and Koos are from Jo'burg and have turned their questing minds from medical research (amongst other brain-engaging pursuits) onto sustaining the complex biosphere of their new home. The balconies at Wonderlings are pole-position from which to enjoy the views and it's an absolute bonus to have basket-bound breakfast brought to your suite. Yoghurt, muesli and muffins are all scrumptiously home-made and are one of many discreet personal touches that strike a balance with the independence generated by self-catering facilities and a separate sweeping-staircase entrance. Here the sea is not just for swimming - make sure you're first in line for one of Koos' 'catch-and-cook-your-own-crayfish' canoeing trips.

Rooms: 2: 1 suite with king/twin, lounge area, kitchen and en-suite bath/shower; 1 suite with double, kitchenette and en-suite shower.
Price: R275 - R350 B&B. R210 - R275 self-catering. Single supplement R50.
Meals: Full breakfast included in B&B price R45 if self-catering. During the season (Apr - Dec), Koos will take you in his boat to catch crayfish for dinner.
Directions: From N2 east towards Somerset West take R44 'Kleinmond/Gordon's Bay' turn-off. Continue on R44 coastal road for about 21km until you reach Rooi Els estuary. 500m beyond the bridge, as you go around bend turn left onto dirt road and Wonderlings is signed on right.

Barnacle B&B

Jenny Berrisford
573 Anne Rd, Pringle Bay 7196
Tel: 028-273-8343 Fax: 028-273-8343
Email: barnacle@maxitec.co.za Web: www.barnacle.co.za
Cell: 082-925-7500

Come and explore Jenny's seaside idyll. Several natural environments collide right outside her cottage. From the deck at the back – with views all the way to Cape Point – you walk down rickety (but safe!) steps to her lawny enclaves in the marsh reeds where narrow paths lead you to the river and beach. The sea is a hundred yards of the whitest, finest sand to your left; beyond the river fynbos and milkwood 'forest' climb the mountain, a nature reserve. You don't have to be a kid to love this. There are otters in the river, baboons on the mountain, estuarine and fynbos birds aplenty… and Jenny is a horticultural expert in one of the world's most amazing natural gardens. Rooms are simple, rustic and country cosy, one with a Victorian slipper bath, another with a solid brass bed and the whole place is super relaxed… a hidden gem. *Both flats have fully-equipped kitchenettes for self-catering. Jenny has canoes and paddle skis to take out on the river. This area has been proclaimed a world biosphere reserve.*

Rooms: 2: 1 outside annexe double with en-suite shower, small sunroom and kitchenette; 1 double with en-suite 'slipper' bath and kitchenette.
Price: R250 - R350 pp sharing. Singles R300 - R350.
Meals: Full breakfast included. Restaurants in Pringle Bay.
Directions: From Cape Town along N2 turn towards Gordon's Bay before Sir Lowry's Pass - follow coast road for 30km to Pringle Bay turn - follow signs down dirt roads.

Wild Olive Guest House

Gloria and Peter Langer

227 Hangklip and Bell Rds, Pringle Bay 7196 Tel: 028-273-8750
Fax: 028-273-8752 Email: g-langer@mweb.co.za
Web: www.wild-olive.de or www.wild-olive.co.za Cell: 082-442-5544

After restauranteering for 27 years, Peter decided to dedicate his love of cooking to his B&B guests in the white sandy-mouthed bay of Pringle. Food is certainly the *spécialité de la maison*. I couldn't believe my luck when I noticed the certificate in the kitchen declaring him a top-ten SA chef of 1999. While preparing the freshly-caught yellow-tail he informed me that in the summer, when the bay is calm, he takes guests out in his engine-powered dinghy (rubber duck to South Africans). The guests catch the crayfish and Peter cooks it for supper. The breakfasts eaten on the sundeck (with ocean view... and whale view too between July and November) boast fresh, home-baked breads, pancakes, croissants, fruit, muesli, yoghurt and the full 'English' breakfast. I almost popped. The bedrooms have private terraces and baboon-proof window locks. I scanned the mountainside for primate life in my (private and enclosed) open-air washroom. I can imagine that when it is sunny it must be so lovely to have your skin sun-kissed while showering. I had blustery weather, but still wanted to test it out (hot water – phew). There is an inside option too, of course. All the bedrooms have this novelty and the twin/king has an up-a-ladder bed for couples with a child (8+). Gloria and Peter are very attentive and professional hosts. *They have also recently installed a natural rock swimming pool surrounded by trees.*

Rooms: 3: 2 queens, 1 with en-s bath with shower overhead & 'al-fresco' shower, 1 with en-s shower & 'al-fresco' shr & separate loo; 1 twin/king with loft, en-suite shower and 'al-fresco' shower.
Price: R250 - R350 pp sharing. Singles on request.
Meals: Full breakfast included. 3-course evening dinner prepared by Peter.
Directions: From Cape Town on N2, turn towards Gordon's Bay, follow coast road for 30km to Pringle Bay turn – follow signs.

556 Clarence Road

Bernd Schlieper & Beate Lietz

Pringle Bay 7196
Tel: 021-461-1782 Fax: 021-461-1768
Email: welcome@acornhouse.co.za Web: www.acornhouse.co.za

Welcome to baboon country!" Bernd bellowed as I approached the house. "Rule number one: baboons are only interested in food," he informed me as I hastily and surreptitiously wolfed down a rogue Maltezer that was lingering in my back pocket. Indeed, one of the joys of this (fully baboon-proofed) property is that there are no fences to separate the house from the expanse of wild fynbos that encircles the property and clambers to the mountaintop behind. The house itself is set back from the village, but is still just 5 minutes' walk away. Inside, the strong features of the face-brick walls and terracotta tiles are cleverly juxtaposed with light, modern touches… halogen lights, crisp, white linen, soft carpets and plenty of big windows. An enchantingly rustic, slatted terrace stretches the length of the house and I rather fancied myself sipping sundowners from it whilst enjoying the sunset over False Bay and Table Mountain in the distance. This is definitely a place that nature-lovers will relish. The Kogelburg Biosphere Reserve is right next-door. Pringle Bay itself is a very safe, tranquil and (as yet) a well-kept secret far removed from the hustle and bustle of the big smoke (Cape Town is just 1hr away), making this house an ideal base from which to explore the region. As an ongoing project, Bernd can hardly contain his excitement over new plans for the place... watch this space.

Rooms: One house with 3 bedrooms: 1 twin with en-suite jacuzzi, indoor and outdoor showers, 1 king and 1 twin with shared bath/shower.
Price: R1,200 - R1,500 per night.
Meals: Fully self-catering. Decent restaurants very nearby. Fully-equipped kitchen and a traditional Old Dover stove by the fireplace.
Directions: Emailed or faxed on request.

Buçaco Sud

Jean Da Cruz
2609 Clarence Drive, Betty's Bay 7141
Tel: 028-272-9750 or 028-272-9628 Fax: 028-272-9750
Email: bucaco@hermanus.co.za Web: www.bucacosud.co.za
Cell: 083-514-1015

Everything in this beautiful place has been designed and built by Jean, including the house itself, which sits halfway up a mountain in South Africa's first Biosphere Reserve, a nature lover's paradise with tranquil lakes, stunning beaches, the Harold Porter Botanic Gardens and a penguin colony. Buçaco Sud was once Jean's castle in Spain (or Portugal I should say), now a flight of personal fancy come true. The upstairs sitting room has windows on both sides, and light streams through to mountain views in one direction and sea views in the other. Guest bedrooms are eye-catching, full of startling colours, flowers and eclectic 'stuff' collected by Jean or donated by friends. They all look down over the sea, except 'Shangri-La' at the back - perhaps my favourite - where you can walk straight out through French doors onto the Kogelberg mountain. Local artists' work (for sale) adds even more colour to the vibrant decor. It's not a place for TVs and mobile phones. Genuine care, a sense of humour and enthusiastic hospitality in a house where every detail is home-spun. *Arabella Golf Estate is about 18km away.*

Rooms: 5: 3 doubles and 2 twins ; 4 with en-suite shower, 1 with en-suite bath.
Price: R220 - R295 pp sharing. Singles on request.
Meals: Full breakfast included. Variety of restaurants in the area.
Directions: Follow R44 from Gordon's Bay along coast for 30km, house signed to left in Betty's Bay, 1 hour from Cape Town. Directions emailed or faxed on booking.

96 Beach Road

Annelie and Johan Posthumus

Kleinmond 7195
Tel: 021-794-6291 Fax: 021-794-6291
Email: info@kaapsedraaibb.co.za Web: www.kaapsedraaibb.co.za

When the family bought "the beach house" in 1954, the milk was delivered by bike. Kleinmond still feels like a sleepy little town, but it's hardly surprising that more have fled here since. The house is but a kite-tail's length from the sea, the blue Atlantic stretching forth beyond a strip of fynbos. You can choose to watch the whales passing by (from August to December) from two spots, the sea-side verandah or the upstairs bedroom. The latter runs from one side of the house to the other under a vaulted ceiling and ocean-side the walls stop and the glass starts, forming a small square sitting room jutting out towards the blue. Here there is a soft couch and a rocking chair, perfect for siestas, sunsets (and of course whale-watching). Downstairs is equally adorable. It feels a bit like a Nantucket Island house: white, light, airy and adorned with simple understated beach furnishings. Interior designers, *nota bene*! It is totally self-catering here, but walk a kilometre west and you'll find some untouristy cafés in the old harbour; a three-minute drive east will take you past a decent restaurant and miles of white, sandy, blue-flag beaches, perfect for kids, flying kites, swimming and walking. There is a rock pool about 50 yards from the house, and apart from that all the swimming takes place at the beach and lagoon, walking distance 15 mins. Kleinmond is near the Arabella Golf Estate, the Kogelberg Biosphere with its myriad fynbos species, the wild horses of the Bot River Estuary and Hermanus, but avoids its touristy-ness.

Rooms: 1 unit with 2 rooms: 1 double with en-suite shower, 1 twin with bath. Fully-equipped kitchen with dishwasher and washing-machine. Heating. Open-plan kitchen/dining/living area. Serviced once a week but more frequently on request.
Price: Max 4 persons. Minimum R600 per night or R1,000 if 4 persons. Min 2-night stay.
Meals: Starter pack provided with cereals, butter, milk etc. Braai areas with firewood provided.
Directions: In Kleinmond town face east. Drive through 3 stop signs and turn towards the sea on 6th Avenue. Keep going to the sea then turn left and No 96 is the penultimate house from the corner.

Beaumont Wine Estate

Jayne and Raoul Beaumont
Compagnes Drift Farm, PO Box 3, Bot River 7185
Tel: 028-284-9194 (office), 028-284-9370 (home)
Fax: 028-284-9733 Email: beauwine@netactive.co.za
Web: www.beaumont.co.za Cell: 083-9906-319

Jayne's guests stay in the charming buildings of an 18th-century former mill house and wagon shed, today snug with wood-burning heaters, but left as far as comfortably possible as they were, with original fireplaces in kitchens and hand-hewn, yellowwood beamed ceilings. Outside, you can sit around an old mill stone and admire the antediluvian water wheel, while the willow-shaded jetty on the farm lake offers one of the Western Cape's prettiest settings for sundowners and wheatland views. While meandering through the flower-filled garden I realised that there is no real need to move from the farm, despite being only half an hour from Hermanus. While Jayne and her family busy themselves producing their annual 150,000-odd bottles of wine, you can swim in the informal swimming pool – being the lake - under the weeping willows where the weaver-birds make their nests or you can roam about on their land – they own half a mountain! You can even put the idea of cooking on the backburner and instead arrange to have home-cooked meals delivered to you. The Beaumonts make a pinotage for London wine merchants Berry Bros and Rudd's own label and you can wine-taste in the cellar flanked by an old wine press. The estate is soon to be part of an exciting bio-diversity wine route which will include tours, tastings, hiking and mountain-bike trails. Also, to find horses and horse-riding you only have to trot down the road. The setting is beautiful - well worth spending several nights here.

Rooms: 2 self-catering cottages. Mill House has 2 bedrooms (plus 2 extra can sleep in living room); Pepper Tree has 1 double (again 2 extras possible).
Price: R190 - R350 pp sharing. Extra people R80 pp. Call for high season rates.
Meals: Self-catering breakfast and home-cooked meals by arrangement. All meals are self-served.
Directions: From N2 take exit 92, sign-posted to Bot River. Follow signs to Bot River and Beaumont Wine Estate is signed off to the right-hand side. Map can be faxed.

Schulphoek Seafront Guesthouse

Petro and Mannes van Zyl

44 Marine Drive, Sandbaai, Greater Hermanus 7200
Tel: 028-316-2626
Fax: 028-316-2627
Email: schulphoek@hermanus.co.za Web: www.schulphoek.co.za

Waves roll into the bay, five foot high when I visited, and crash against rocks right in front of Schulphoek Seafront Guesthouse. The sitting room has one of the most exciting sea views you could hope for and, naturally, whales steal into Schulphoek Bay during the season for private viewings. The best room, Scallop - I don't think there is any doubt, despite the extremely high overall standard! - is upstairs, the whole seaward wall an expanse of window with a sliding glass door and parapet. The smells of the sea are powerful. The other rooms, although without sea views, have solid, hand-crafted oak or mahogany beds and spectacular bathrooms with double sinks, double showers and spa-baths... I mean, you will not find better *anywhere*. Not many places in this area feel the need to provide in-house dinners but your hosts are not taking chances on outside eateries. Guests who want to guarantee themselves delicious food stay in (4-course *menu du jour* herbs, salad and veg picked straight from their vegetable garden) and eat at one long table, on chairs made from vintage wine vats. You can choose from an exhaustive cellar of the finest South African wines. Schulphoek is an intimate, state-of-the-art seaside lodge, but still the sort of place where guests socialise with each other, drinks are on an honesty system and meals are all eaten together. *Closed in May.*

Rooms: 7 suites: superior, luxury and standard, all with luxurious en-suite bathrooms. Also 1 family suite.
Price: R499 - R1,150 pp sharing. Singles supplement +50%. Seasonal and discounted rates for longer stays. Whole guest house on request.
Meals: Professional kitchen with chef. Dinner: 4-course menu du jour. Lunch: on request. Wine cellar with 7,000 SA wines. Full breakfast included in tariff. First night dinner complimentary.
Directions: Take R43 towards Hermanus. At Engen petrol station by traffic lights (signed Sandbaai) turn right. At 2nd 'stop' turn left into 3rd Street. Continue to next stop and turn left. Marked by flags – entrance off Piet Retief Crescent.

Swallow's Loft

Lesley Hanson-Moore
19 Glenfruin Meadows, Hemel-en-arde, Hermanus 7200
Tel: 028-316-4001 Fax: 028-316-4002
Email: swallowsloft@futurenet.co.za Web: www.swallowsloft.co.za
Cell: 082-777-5562

".... Sam, speechlessly cross, woke me one night as the darn porcupines were turfing out my cymbidiums!" Lesley lamented, recounting another heroic deed carried out by the sprightlier of her English springer spaniels. You'd be hard-pressed to find the space to fit any more personality into this place although space is something you most definitely get a lot of. Not only is there a rather grand courtyard with pool at your disposal, but you also get not one, not two, but three private, beautifully manicured and floodlit gardens. Among these is the resplendently elegant rose-garden, onto which the master bedroom's French windows open out. Step inside and you'll also find in here that everything is just so... and frankly I wouldn't have expected anything less from Lesley. The bedrooms are bright, refreshingly uncluttered and fitted out with plenty of storage cupboards. A cheery bunch of newly-cut sunflowers beamed me into the cavernous living area and kitchen. With a cosy fireplace at one end, kitchen hearth at the other, generous dining table and colourful artwork on the walls, the atmosphere is genuinely warm and homely. Don't forget to venture beyond the back garden into the wilderness beyond. It's just a quick stroll away, and is where you'll discover mountains, a river, lily-ponds, tortoises, meer-cats, Egyptian geese... and the aforementioned porcupines.

Rooms: 1 cottage let to one group at a time: 1 king with en-suite bath/shower and 2 doubles which share a bath/shower.
Price: R300 - R400 pp sharing and single.
Meals: Breakfast of guests' choice included. Picnic baskets available on request.
Directions: Detailed map on the website.

Villa Blu

Riana & Tino Delle Donne

234 8th Street, Voëlklip, Hermanus 7200
Tel: 028-314-1056 Fax: 028-314-1123
Email: info@villablu.co.za Web: www.villablu.co.za
Cell: 082-4436-340

This place does a strange thing to you. Whilst Tino was preparing my coffee (the best I've had in SA, but then he is Italian), my head began to whirl with happy memories of holidays past where faces are golden, living is easy and time passes idly by. Just another guesthouse, this is certainly not. Built around an open courtyard that tinkles, trickles and crashes with the sounds of wind chimes, fountains and waves, Villa Blu inspires within you an invigorating lightness of heart. Be it the beach-time photographs, colourful paintings (some are Riana's own), antique Indonesian furnishings, shells scattered around or the blue-tinted hue, everything feels fresh, homely and so very, very relaxed. With pale-washed Oregon pine furnishings and floors, huge mirror-walls in the bathrooms and doors opening onto private patios, every room is as light and airy as the rest of the house. Head up to the roof terrace for stunning views onto the blue-flag 'Grotto' beach just ahead or the green velvet-swathed mountains which loom large behind. Regrettably, as mine was only a quick visit, I didn't get to swing carefree in the garden's hammock, doze by the pool or try Tino's wonderful cooking (he is clearly as passionate about food as he is about the guesthouse). But I didn't just want to stay here anyway... I wanted to live here. Oh, bring on those lazy, hazy days of summer.

Rooms: 5: 3 queens, 2 with en-suite bath/shower and 1 with en-suite shower; 2 king/twins with en-suite bath/shower.
Price: R350 - R450 pp sharing. Singles supplement 50%.
Meals: Full breakfast included. Culinary weekends offered in winter months.
Directions: From N2, take R43 into Hermanus. Drive through the town, staying on Main Road as you cross the roundabout. Turn right into 13th Avenue and then right into 8th Street. It's the 3rd house on the right.

Pebble Beach Guest House

Mike Munro and Kirsty-Lee Wortmann
8 Fernkloof Drive, Hermanus Heights 7200
Tel: 028-313-2517 Fax: 088-028-313-2517
Email: info@pebblebeachguesthouse.com Web:
www.pebblebeachguesthouse.com Cell. 004-019-6149 or 072-128-1751

Mike and Kirsty-Lee have taken their 12 years of working in game lodges and traded them for whales and golfing here at Pebble Beach. When we dropped by for the last edition, the paint dry was barely on the wall-to-wall French windows and high vaulted ceilings of this entirely homespun guest house. A year on and many contented guests have now congregated for evening drinks on its colonial-style, wrap-around balcony to contemplate remarkable views down the tree-lined 16th fairway of Hermanus Golf Course… and to pass derisive comment on the golf swings on show. This can be enjoyably achieved with equal smugness on colder days in the Rocky Lounge with its open fire. Others will eschew golf criticism altogether and settle down by the swimming pool among the olive trees. The house, with its Indo-African furnishings draws on Mike and Kirsty-Lee's experience in the African bush and abroad. Natural materials have been used wherever possible, with sunset-slate flooring, stone baths, wooden mirrors and the harmonious result is restful on both eye and spirit. For non-golfers, the front door opens onto the Hermanus Mountains, complete with nature trails through the fynbos, and both beaches and village are close by. Both Mike and Kirsty-Lee are happiest outdoors, and will guide you if time permits along the hiking trails, organise shark diving, mountain-biking, golf etc. Pebble Beach has so much to offer both the action man and the poolside potterer.

Rooms: 6: 3 twins, 2 with en-suite bath and shower, 1 with en-suite shower; 3 doubles, 1 with en-suite bath and shower, 2 with en-suite shower.

Price: R380 - R520 pp sharing. Singles + 50%. Children under 5 stay free.

Meals: Full breakfast included. Trained chef Kirsty-Lee will prepare evening meals and seafood barbeques on request, not included.

Directions: From N2 take R43 to Hermanus. Go all the way through village and left at Shell garage. Hug the golf course and turn first right before the school. House is 2nd after the bend.

Map Number: 4

Mosselberg on Grotto Beach Guest House

Nato Barnard

253a Tenth Street, Voelklip, Hermanus 7200
Tel: 028-314-0055 Fax: 028-314-0102
Email: bookings@mosselberg.co.za Web: www.mosselberg.co.za
Cell: 072-259-9245

An empty plot of land on the only Blue Flag beach in the Western Cape and possibly the best views in Hermanus? This called for something special. A world-renowned architect was duly called in to do this magnificent spot some justice… and he has duly created a masterpiece. The sheer size and magnificence of Mosselberg is only manifest once the gargantuan front door has swung open. The courtyard is dominated by an elongated swimming pool, constantly supplied by a gushing torrent of water from three ducts poking through the wall. Wooden decking around the pool provides access to the rooms, the upstairs ones reached by climbing steep, narrow, castle-like private staircases. Dwarfed by the size of my room, I spent five minutes searching for the light switch, and a further ten hunting down the bathroom. All the bedrooms have balconies with great views of the bay, huge beds, underfloor heating and are dominated by glass. So too the open-plan lounge-breakfast area with windows stretching from ceiling to floor and a mechanism for sliding the entire wall back into the brickwork to create a three-sided room overlooking the deep wooden verandah. From here a stroll through the natural fynbos garden leads down to the white sands of Grotto Beach or onto the cliff path and some great whale-watching spots. Breakfast here is a special meal and provokes many an admiring comment. And Nato is a caring host to boot.

Rooms: 5: 4 king/twins and 1 king all with en-suite bath and shower.
Price: R650 - R950 pp sharing. Singles on request. Up to 50% discount in winter months.
Meals: Full breakfast included. Access to full kitchen facilities to self-cater for all other meals.
Directions: Faxed or emailed on request.

Hartford Cottage

Gys & Wendy Hofmeyr
3, 3rd Ave, Voelklip, Hermanus 7200
Tel: 028-314-0102 Fax: 028-314-0667
Email: gyswendyhof@telkomsa.net
Cell: 082-879-773

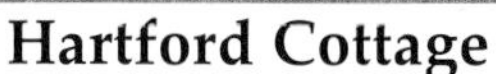

If you were asked to paint a picture of your perfect country cottage, I suggest it might look a bit like Hartford; white walls, soaring chimney and a perfectly pitched thatched roof, all enveloped by a large, tranquil, lawned garden. As I sat under the welcoming shade of the umbrella next to Grecian urns choked with flowers and humming with buzzing bees, Wendy told me - and I didn't register much surprise - that complete strangers have knocked on the door begging to stay here, even though originally they only built the cottage for the family. Hiding away from the hurlyburly of Hermanus in a seaside suburb, Hartford is enviably positioned, with mountain walks five minutes in one direction, beach, sea and whales a minute or two in the opposite. Gys is a stickler for detail and a lover of wood and thatch. Door surrounds and light switches were rescued and resurrected from a condemned house in town, while an original yellowwood door hanging on huge hinges is his pride and joy. Don't think Wendy hasn't been busy too. Her eye for interior designs led to the stunning black slate fire hearth, bathroom sink surrounds and kitchen worktops. The open-plan A-frame roof makes it cool and spacious, while the whitewashed walls and an abundance of Cape antique furniture, means it retains all of its delightfully cosy cottage charm.

Rooms: 1 cottage with 1 double room, full en-suite & 1 twin bedroom with sep' bathroom. Also a large attic bed/sitter with 3 beds for children. Cottage not available between 20th Dec & 15th Jan each year.
Price: 2 people sharing whole cottage: R900 plus R100 per extra (May - Aug inclusive). R1,200 plus R200 a head per extra (Sept - April inc'). Min 3-night stay. Children under 12 free.
Meals: Cottage fully self-catering, including breakfast provisions for your first morning.
Directions: 4km from Hermanus in direction of Stanford, take 3rd exit off roundabout into 10th Street (seafront road), past CEM motors & continue for about 300m. 3rd Ave on R, then thatched house immediately on R. Map faxed on booking.

Map Number: 4

Bellavista Country Place

Georges and Sonja Schwegler

R43 between Gansbaai and Stanford, Stanford 7210
Tel: 028-341-0178 Fax: 028-341-0179
Email: bellavista@hermanus.co.za Web: www.bella.co.za

High on a sweeping slope with panoramic views down to the Atlantic and fynbos ad infinitum (300 hectares to be precise), Georges and Sonja are blissfully ensconced in their dream South African home. So happy, in fact, that they converted the old tumbledown farm buildings, a mere stroll from the homestead, into a set of three luxurious suites for Swiss relatives and friends to come and stay. Fortunately a change of heart (and a slight miscalculation - it's a long story) expanded this idea somewhat. So now you too can enjoy basking in the rim-flow swimming pool as the wilderness of the Walker Bay Reserve stretches out below you to the coast. This is the kind of place that encourages the laziest part of you to take control. Good news therefore that Georges has now added a restaurant to save you the effort of having to bother to travel into town to eat. Good food complements the equally good views, and the floor-to-ceiling windows allow the sun to flood over the round tables, while the glass doors slide back to reveal a pillared Romanesque stoep, where breakfast is served from the buffet table. Georges couldn't help wondering whether the two main suites were too big for a guesthouse with their large Italian-tiled bathrooms, huge sitting rooms and private patios. I don't envisage too many complaints, Georges!

Rooms: 4: 2 double suites, one with shower only, one with bath with shower over; 1 junior double suite with shower only; 1 cottage with 1 en-suite double, and twin with separate shower room.
Price: R600 - R900 pp sharing. Singles on request.
Meals: Full breakfast included. Fully licensed restaurant on site.
Directions: From Hermanus follow R43 to Stanford. Continue for 8km. Follow signs to Bellavista on the left. From the Garden Route take the R326 after Riviersonderend. At Stanford turn left. Continue for 8km. Follow signs, Bellavista is on your left.

Map Number: 4

Fair Hill Private Nature Reserve

Val and Tim Deverson

R43 between Stanford and Gansbay,Stanford 7210
Tel: 028-341-0230 Fax: 028-341-0230
Email: fairhill@yebo.co.za Web: www.fairhill.co.za
Cell: 082-788-2086

A gate in the middle of nowhere, then a sandy track which leads into the fynbos, arriving finally at Val and Tim's single-story guest house. I guarantee that you will be stunned by the quality of natural silence that envelops you as you step from your car. I think you can hear the fynbos growing! Just walk out in any direction and encounter the eland who, Jeeves-like, only materialise when you aren't looking. We stayed here for a weekend break from Cape Town (two hours max) and completely refilled our energy tanks. Walks are lovely down through Fair Hill's fynbos to the beach, which is hard to get to any other way and will most likely be deserted. Those with more momentum can walk all the way to Hermanus and, if she can, Val will pick you up there. Or you can sunbathe by the pool, protected from the wind in the lea of a natural cave. Big rooms are all blessed with verandahs whence to commune with the wilderness. To top it off, the Deversons themselves couldn't be nicer and delicious dinners are part of the (*incredibly* good value) package - with a choice at every course. Fair Hill is an authentic, uplifting and special experience. We recommend you stay for a minimum of two nights.

Rooms: 4 doubles with en-suite bath and shower attachment.
Price: B&B R330 - R370 pp sharing. Dinner B&B R440 - R480.
Meals: All dinners included with choice for each course.
Directions: From Hermanus follow R43 to Stanford. Continue past for 8.7km. Electric gates on right. From the Garden Route take R326 after Riviersonderend. At Stanford turn left, continue for 8.7km, electric gates on the right.

Blue Gum Country Lodge

Nic and Nicole Dupper
PO Box 899, Stanford 7210
Tel: 028-341-0116
Fax: 028-341-0135
Email: reservations@bluegum.co.za
Web: www.bluegum.co.za
Cell: 082-564-5663

After a day spent rattling my bones on dirt roads, my eventual arrival at Blue Gum, bathing in the lengthening shadows of the Klein River Mountains, was an immeasurable pleasure. There is a very long list of things you can get up to here… but after such a tiring day, I'm afraid I was grateful not to have time. I had to give myself over instead to some lounging around and some terrifically good food. Blue Gum is not half good at this. Around the crackling fire in the main lounge, other guests had had the same idea, sprawled in deep sofas, chatting jovially and sipping apéritifs, waiting for their à la carte dinner, whose enticing aromas could almost be seen emanating from the kitchen. Disappointment was not on the menu: succulent steaks melted in mouths and Nic ensured our wine glasses were kept pleasingly full. Back in my Lion Room I sampled the cheese and sherry that had appeared from nowhere on my private terrace, before dismantling the mountain of pillows and collapsing into a long, satisfying sleep. As morning broke over the vines, weaver birds busied themselves by the dam and guests prepared for the day ahead, some clutching tennis racquets or mountain bikes and some bearing towels for a day to be passed lazing by the newly enlarged pool. Others motored off to explore the majesty of the surrounding Overberg: whales, curios and art in Stanford and horse-riding, birding and fishing galore. So… good food, a beautiful setting, R&R and tons to do – not a bad definition of 'holiday'.

Rooms: 10: 5 queens, all with en-suite bath and shower. In manor house; 4 twins, 1 king, all bath and shower except one which is double shower.
Price: Seasonal. R525 - R1280 pp sharing. Single supplement + 50%.
Meals: Full breakfast included. Light lunches, 4-course evening dinner (R160 – R180).
Directions: From CT take N2, then R43 turn-off to Hermanus. Drive through Hermanus on R43, following signs to Stanford. At Stanford turn left onto R326 for 6.7km, then left onto dirt track for 4km.

Cliff Lodge

Gill O'Sullivan and Gideon Shapiro

6 Cliff St,De Kelders 7220
Tel: 028-384-0983 Fax: 028-384-0228
Email: stay@clifflodge.co.za Web: www.clifflodge.co.za
Cell: 082-380-1676

This is the closest land-based whale-watching you could possibly find. I could see the whites of their eyes (I was only shooting with a camera!) and the callosities on their heads. It was as though Gill and Gideon had paid them (in plankton) to put on a special show for me; blowing, breaching, spyhopping, lob-tailing. I applauded delicately from the royal box. The viewing from my room and from the breakfast conservatory-balcony was don't-turn-your-eyes-away-for-a-minute magnetic. But the fun wasn't just in the looking. As soon as I walked through the door, Gideon, formally a dive-master, whisked me down to the ocean for a swim through the cave (bring shoes you can swim in for the rocks) and Gill kindly booked me a whale-, sea-lion- and penguin-watching boat trip for the following morning. For the 'help-danger' adrenaline rush, there is also the shark-cage diving. The guest house décor is classy and modern and there are whale-spotting terraces for those rooms on the side of the house. The luxurious new penthouse suite has a huge balcony and glass-fronted living room for whale-gazing in true style. On the cliff edge is also a small swimming pool. Gill and Gideon are wonderfully hospitable hosts and really look after their guests. After the best breakfast you could possibly have - not only because of the food but also the panorama - indulge in an aromatherapy massage from Gill, nature reserve walks in front of the house and the nearby flower-farm. Cliff Lodge rocks.

Rooms: 4: 1 twin/king with bath and shower, 1 queen bed with bath & shower overhead, 1 twin/king with bath and shower overhead & 1 luxury suite with king bed, separate living room, bath & shower.

Price: R450 - R1,200 pp sharing. Single supplement +50%.

Meals: Full breakfast included.

Directions: N2, then R43 through Hermanus. Past Stanford towards Gansbaai. Turn right at first De Kelders turn-off, then right into De Villiers Rd, left into Kayser Rd and right into Cliff St.

Map Number: 4

Whalesong Lodge

Stanley and Lainy Carpenter
83 Cliff St, De Kelders 7220
Tel: 028-384-1865 Fax: 088-028-384-1865
Email: stanley@whalesonglodge.co.za Web: www.whalesonglodge.co.za
Cell: 082-883-5793

Am I a rain god, I sometimes wonder in my less humble moments? Here was another fabulous ocean view obscured by a veil of heavy rain. There were whales out there somewhere! Stanley and Lainy used to run the Pontac Hotel in Paarl, but I suspect they always hankered after a nice small place where they could give their guests more love and attention, cook for manageable numbers… and be themselves. Whalesong Lodge, with just five rooms, is it. All the bedrooms have sea views, of course, either from a panoramic window or a small, private balcony, and under-floor-heated bathrooms are separated from the sleeping areas by shoulder-high walls. All is slick and modern. Many cookbooks and a well-ordered, well-stocked kitchen loudly trumpet Stanley's culinary expertise. So will he be cooking for his happy hordes? The eyes narrow. "Only if I'm feeling inspired," comes the reply, through a suppressed smile, "but we're quite happy to have guests cook for us". In fact it is true! You are encouraged to help with preparation if you want… much great seafood fresh from Walker Bay and delicious desserts made by Lainy. But Stanley does not want to HAVE to cook every night so ask when you book. Breakfast ("from 8 till late") is fresh and all-encompassing, with homemade preserves and jams (Lainy's), local cheeses, seasonal fresh fruit, muesli, yoghurt as well as all the eggs and bacon and stuff. Oh yes, and great coffee.

Rooms: 5: 2 twins, 3 doubles, all en-suite bath and shower.
Price: R420 - R800 pp sharing.
Meals: Full breakfast included.
Directions: From N2 take R43 through Hermanus and Stanford. Take first right signed to De Kelders and follow down to the sea. Turn right into Cliff Street. Third house on right.

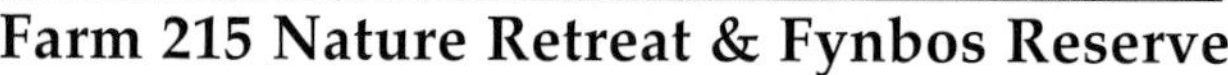

Farm 215 Nature Retreat & Fynbos Reserve

Maarten Groos
Hartebeeskloof, Baardskeerersbos, Overstrand Municipality
Tel: 028-388-0920
Email: farm215@telkomsa.net Web: www.farm215.co.za
Cell: 082-097-1655

Are you sure you don't want any chocolate cake? It's the best you'll ever taste…" I looked down at my expanding waistline then back to Natasha offering the plate of dark delight and faltered… boy was it good! Farm 215 perches neatly among the fynbos of this private nature reserve and, although there were parts still in the construction stage when I visited, it was already inspired and all will be in readiness by the time this book comes out. The individual cottages, angled to look rosy-faced into the sunset onto sea and mountains, squat above the 45 different species of protea that contribute to the vast and wild garden. Yellow lichen, a sign of air purity, paints the rock faces of this self-sufficient solar-powered retreat. Maarten led me around existing and planned boardwalks speaking with eager animation of plans in progress. A wide sweep of arms detailed where the bar, fireplace and fish-tank will enliven the restaurant. A splayed hand indicated where Henki (the chef), in the act of producing incredible food, steering clear of frivolous gourmet towers, will be seen and not heard through a future-built window. The established farmhouse rooms sporting black-framed historic photographs and slate-finished bathrooms left a thoroughly reassuring impression of things to come. With the chlorine-free 25m-lap pool, 20km of hiking trails radiating from the door or your cottage, an astonishing number of birds, and horses ready to be ridden on site there is every opportunity to earn yourself a slice of heaven.

Rooms: 6: 3 cottages all with kings, lounge area & en-suite bath & shower; 2 double rooms in main house, en-suite bath & shower; 1 cottage 500m from villa, self-catering or B&B, master bedroom (en-s bath & sep' shower) & 2 smaller bedrooms.
Price: R650 - R750 pp sharing for rooms in house. Cottages from R550 - R850 pp sharing. Enquire about singles. R100 pp less in winter.
Meals: Full breakfast included. On-site restaurant for lunch and 3-course dinner. Picnic baskets available.
Directions: Take N2 East from Cape Town. At Bot River turn to Hermanus (R43). After Franskraal L into dirt road signed Elim. Follow road approx 10km. Gates to Farm 215 are on L after lake & vineyards.

Map Number: 4

Klein Paradijs Country House

Susanne and Michael Fuchs
Pearly Beach, Gansbaai 7220
Tel: 028-381-9760 Fax: 028-381-9803
Email: kleinparadijs@lando.co.za Web: www.kleinparadijs.co.za

Paradise would be a proud boast, so perhaps Little Paradise is a more defensible claim. But you can see why the name stuck: nature on the one hand, man-made environment on the other, and all rounded off by delicious cooking and green fingers. I'll elaborate. The property stretches up a mountain covered in indigenous fynbos vegetation and nearer the house there is a reed-edged dam with weaver birds, an old camphor tree in the courtyard and an amazing garden whose swimming pool acts as a moat to a tiny island of plant life. Inside, high open spaces are punctuated with lovely things: bright paintings, vases of proteas and pincushions, a stinkwood grandfather clock for example. A-shaped rooms have soaring thatched roofs, dormer windows, beams, window-seats, balconies and the curtained-off bathrooms are truly luxurious. The Fuchs are Swiss and have brought many talents with them. Susanne was a translator and speaks English, German and French, while Michael is a chef – they open a small but excellent restaurant in the evenings. *Large dam with canoe and rowboat available on the property. Whale-watching possible nearby from June – November.*

Rooms: 5: 2 twins and 3 doubles all with en-suite bathrooms; 2 with bath and shower, 3 with showers.
Price: R500 - R800 pp sharing. Single supplement +50%.
Meals: Full breakfast included. Light meals and dinner by arrangement. The restaurant is fully licensed.
Directions: From Hermanus take the R43 through Stanford and Gansbaai. Go left at Pearly Beach crossing, then 1st left again. The house is on the right.

Roosje van de Kaap

Nick and Ilzebet Oosthuizen
5 Drostdy St, Swellendam 6740
Tel: 028-514-3001 Fax: 028-514-3001
Email: roosje@dorea.co.za Web: www.roosjevandekaap.co.za
Cell: 082 380 4086

Nick, a lawyer, chef, dad and food-magazine editor (his dog can ride a skateboard...), wants people to come here for food, space and good living. And you'll get it, at "nearly ridiculous" prices. I mean, where else can you get mussels for R30, a bottle of exceptional Springfield Sauvignon Blanc Special for R100 and listen to a live jazz band while you enjoy them! The candlelit restaurant, named by *Eat Out* magazine as one of the ten best restaurants in the Garden Route, is charming and encourages intimacy, with guests often ending up chatting to each other across the tables. It's not open for lunch though. Some rooms at the lodge face the pool, some are bonsai Cape Dutch cottages that face the mountain and next-door's sheep. The Honeymoon suite is all about the view and has a huge four-poster. They vary in feel and size, but all are adorable with bunches of wild flowers everywhere you look. Guests can bask like reptiles in the garden or pool on those hot Swellendam summer days. Nick also has a secret track to a ravine where you can swim below a waterfall. He'll pack you a picnic.

Rooms: 10: 4 doubles, 5 twins and 1 family room, all with en-suite shower, except 1 king with bath.
Price: R250 - R320 pp sharing. Singles on request.
Meals: Full breakfast included. The restaurant is open from Tuesday till Sunday evening, but not for lunch.
Directions: From Cape Town, take the 4th exit off the N2 to Swellendam. (Count the turn-off to Swellendam industrial area as the first.) After turning off, take the first street left. From the east, after turning off the N2, it's the first street on the left.

Rothman Manor

Andreas and Franziska Gobel
268 Voortrek St, Swellendam 6740
Tel: 028-514-2771 Fax: 028-514-3966
Email: guesthouse@rothmanmanor.co.za Web: www.rothmanmanor.co.za

With lily-littered dam, salt-water pool and cobbled courtyard Rothman Manor boasts grounds of park-like calibre. The original Cape Dutch house and venerable oak tree (whose shady canopy acts as a parasol for your breakfast table) both date back to 1834, yet fresh, clipped interiors (born of Andreas and Franziska's combined flair for design) shift matters decisively into the present. With pale-blue or cream-hued walls and cloud-white curtain-swept beds, heavenly rooms are earthed by wooden flooring and black-framed artwork. "I wish we could move in here," says Franziska referring to the voluminous attic suite with its kitchenette, dining table and choice of balconies. Bathrooms sport chequered tiles and African-themed titbits seem to hang suspended in cubby-holes, unique reminders of the grounds and its outdoor inhabitants. Here, in wine-dominated Swellendam, I was bowled over with sightings of zebra, sprightly springbok and a couple of ostriches, all residents of the Gobel's eco-reserve. Learning by lazy example from our long-limbed feathered friends I was tempted to bag a lounger near the deck-bound Jacuzzi where you can keep an eye on any animal action. Each generous room has its own view-treated patio for outdoors delight or spoil yourself indoors with a therapeutic, individually-tailored massage. With easy access to numerous nature reserves, wine farms and Bontebok National Park, Rothman Manor is its own destination and a gateway to others.

Rooms: 6: 3 kings and 3 twins, 4 with full baths, 2 with shower only.
Price: R320 - R750 pp sharing. Single on request.
Meals: Full breakfast included.
Directions: Turn off N2 onto R60, and then turn R into Swellendam. Rothman Manor on R.

Map Number: 2

Eenuurkop

Tersia and Jeremy Purén
PO Box 63, Swellendam 6740
Tel: 028-514-1447
Email: eenuurkop@webmail.co.za Web: www.eenuurkop.mrinfo.co.za
Cell: 082 956 9161

Don't let your inability to pronounce the name stop you from calling up and booking in here. Not to do so would be an error. These two self-catering cottages, found at the foot of the Langeberg Mountains, were built or converted entirely by your hosts. "It is more fun to create something from nothing," says Tersia, pointing out that the floor in the smaller Misty Point is made from the tiles of an old church roof (you can still see the holes where the nails held them in place). While it may be ideal for honeymooners, I can see it being the cause of some mild marital disharmony too - there might be a power struggle over who sleeps on the side of the bed with its own half-moon window for an eye-opening view of the mountains. (To pacify the loser Jeremy put in a high-level square window near the roof, which perfectly frames the top of the mountain when your head is on the crisp cotton pillow.) Even the larger family cottage has design aplenty. I loved for example the outside sofa-seating on top of the wood store. The wood is for the braai. One thing they have not felt the need to recreate though are the views. You will find no pictures on the walls here, which might distract you from the changing ones outside the windows. Absolutely breathtaking - there is no other way to describe it. A truly magical find!

Rooms: 2 cottages: Eenuurkop: 2 doubles and 1 family room with 2 bunks and 1 full bathroom; Misty Point: 1 double with en-suite bath and shower.
Price: Misty Point R400 for cottage. Eenuurkop price depending on number of people: R500 - R700 for the cottage.
Meals: Breakfast basket on request for late arrivals.
Directions: From Swellendam, 4km along R60. Past cheese shop on R60, about 40 metres more, sign for Eenuurkop 1.2km along gravel track.

Kliphoogte

Herman and Marita Linde
Swellendam 6740
Tel: 028-514-2534 Fax: 028-514-2680
Email: kliphoogte@telkomsa.net
Cell: 084-581-4464

Three kilometres of dusty track bring you to Kliphoogte, one of South Africa's most charming farm B&B's. Herman, absurdly cheerful for a man who gets up at 4:30am, runs a fruit and dairy farm on the banks of the Leeurivier.... while his mother Marita looks after the guest house. Herman represents the fifth generation of Lindes to work the property and will take guests on walks around the farm, or leave them in the company of the boisterous weaver-birds to swim at the small lake. At meal times Marita takes charge and cooks typical South African dinners. Herman will probably then take you in his 4x4 up a nearby hill to look at the stars. The main bedroom is a sweet, blue affair with sturdy old Afrikaner furniture, family photos and rugs made by the farm workers. The other is more functional (though it does have a four-poster bed), but this is not a place where you'll want to spend long in bed; there is too much going on outside. To sit on the Kliphoogte stoep, listening to cicadas, and looking out over the small, lush valley is to know contentment indeed.

Rooms: 2: both doubles; 1 with en-suite shower, 1 with separate bathroom.
Price: R320. Singles R350.
Meals: Dinner by request and will be 3 - 5 courses. Marita will ask you what you want when you book. Lunches and picnics available too. Ask about prices.
Directions: Turn off N2 onto R60 (Swellendam turn-off). After 10km, Kliphoogte (blue sign) is on your left. Then 3km more on gravel road.

Jan Harmsgat Country House

Brin and Judi Rebstein
Swellendam 6740
Tel: 023-616-3407 or 023-616-3311 Fax: 023-616-3201
Email: brinreb@iafrica.com Web: www.jhghouse.com

A true country house, Jan Harmsgat is a breath of fresh air in an often-chintzy genre. Judi (a producer in the film industry) and Brin rescued it from tumbledown oblivion in 1989. They swept out the old rotted beams, mould, even pigs, and set about pouring a cellar-full of TLC into it. It is a beautiful place. The above photo does not lie but what it doesn't show is that the restaurant and its increasingly famous staff are starting to catch the food-media's eye... or that your hosts are so gracious. Past resident Hermanus Steyn proclaimed the Independent Republic of Swellendam in 1795 and farmed wine here originally, but I doubt he dined on butterfish bobotie stacks with coriander. Perhaps he did! His 25-metre barn-cellar (now the dining room, complete with grand piano) today looks out of a glass wall. Guests are housed in old slave quarters whose large rooms and great comfort might make you forget the history of the place. However, sympathetic renovation means that windows in the clay walls have not been enlarged, and the wonky lintels, wooden shutters and vast beams all play their part in preserving the original character here. Mine was high up in the apex of the thatch, had a free-standing Victorian bath, gilded chairs and come morning I had a colour-me-happy moment when I opened my shutters and was drenched in a sweet citron-scented breeze gusting across from the orchard. Bliss.

Rooms: 5: 1 double with shower & 1 twin with en/s bath; 1 dbl & 1 twin, with Victorian baths in room & en-suite loo. 1 double luxury room with full bathroom.
Price: R450 - R750. Luxury room R850.
Meals: Full breakfast included. Lunch by arrangement only. The restaurant is open for dinner to the public (reservations essential). Four-course set menu R190 pp.
Directions: From Cape Town on N1 to Worcester turn right into R60 (Robertson) at Worcester. Carry on thro' Robertson and Ashton. Turn R after Ashton and stay on R60. House on left after 21km. From Cape Town on N2 to Swellendam turn into R60. Carry on 24.5km after Swellendam towards Ashton, house on right.

Bloomestate

Maarten and Carla van der Ven
276 Voortrekker Street, Swellendam 6740
Tel: 028-514-2984 Fax: 028-514-3822
Email: info@bloomestate.com Web: www.bloomestate.com

When I read my notes and saw there were 'Earth, Wind and Fire' themed rooms at Bloomestate, I was half expecting to see mirror balls and gargantuan flares devoted to the '70s "super group". Thankfully the rooms are about as far from the 'decade that taste forgot' as it is possible to get. Bloomestate is impossibly cool, the kind of place where you might expect to see supermodels and film stars. You will feel like one too, lounging by the pool with its one striking blue wall perfectly framing the mountains beyond. When Maarten and Carla decided to leave Holland and move to South Africa they scoured the land to find a property that was just right. From the moment they popped their heads through the elegant black gates of Bloomestate, they knew their search was over. The house is the quintessence of modern living and overflows with originality. The seven enormous garden rooms are identical in size and furnishings, with chunky beds looking through French windows to the pool. Each is coded by season or element, with one brightly painted wall, matching cushions and a spray-painted canvas. "Spring" is a vibrant green, "Summer" a sun-burnt orange, and the honeymooners' "Fire" a passionate red. This is a place that naturally inspires and delights.

Rooms: 7: 4 kings and 3 twins, all with bath and shower.
Price: R420 (May-Sept) - R575 (Oct-Apr). Singles plus 50%.
Meals: Full breakfast included. Other meals on request.
Directions: From CT and N2 take Swellendam West exit (R60) towards Ashton. At the crossroads turn right and Bloomestate is first on the right.

Augusta de Mist Country House

Madeleine and Rob Harrisson
3 Human St, Swellendam 6740
Tel: 028-514-2425 Fax: 028-514-2057
Email: info@augustademist.co.za Web: www.augustademist.co.za
Cell: 082 775 0834

Cool, contemporary decor meets rustic heritage architecture at Augusta de Mist, each setting the other off to great advantage. And Madeleine and Rob are grandmaster hosts at this most laid-back of guest houses. Since our last visit two new luxury garden cottages have sprouted in the garden with white-linened, king-sized beds, spa baths and walk-in showers. Under reed-and-pole ceilings you'll find fireplaces, large indigo sofas or chairs and organza curtains billowing in the breeze. The main house is a unique Cape Dutch national monument, dated from 1802. Rob does up old tools and farm implements in his workshop, so all round the house you'll find intriguing wagon boxes, shutters, hinges, doors and once-cherished peasant furniture that has been tailored and restored under his furnace and bellows. The rose nursery garden is a peaceful haven with red-brick paths winding up the hill through banks of lavender towards the swimming pool with its swanky canvas brolly and loungers… and then off to the right over a stream. All the indigenous trees and shrubs mean an abundance of birds. This year Madeleine and Rob have introduced a great new supper option which will only be available in high season... soups, cheeses, tapas, a dessert and a good wine, that sort of thing. The idea is to keep it informal with the emphasis on atmosphere with lots of candlelight on the patio, verandah and dining room.

Rooms: 8: 3 kings with bath and/or shower; 1 queen, 1 double and 2 twins with en-suite bath & shower; 1 double with adjoining single and en/s bath & shower.
Price: R300 – R700 pp sharing. Singles on request.
Meals: Full breakfast included. From Oct-Apr cheese and wine or set meals are available in evening at additional cost.
Directions: From Cape Town thro' village centre, past white church on left. As road bends to R, carry on straight for 20 metres. Then L into Human Str. From Garden Route down hill, past Drostdy Museum, over bridge, take R leg of triangle, then L, then R into Human Str.

Map Number: 2

Honeywood Farm

John and Miranda Moodie

Between Swellendam and Heidelberg, Heidelberg 6665
Tel: 028-722-1823 Fax: 028-722-1823
Email: john@honeywoodfarm.co.za Web: www.honeywoodfarm.co.za
Cell: 083-270-4035

Attention all botanists, ornithologists, dendrologists, zoologists and, well, pretty much any kind of "–ist"... Honeywood is the place for you. Part conservation area, it's an open, free place, bang next-door to the bird-watching mountain paradise of the Grootvadersbosch Nature Reserve. John is a bee farmer and an expert on everything from olive-back shrikes to yellowwoods and tree frogs. He'll point out the highlights on the five-kilometre trip to the wind-swept and wistfully romantic Hunters Cottage. A truly wild spot, this little bothy is tossed in a sea of green hills, lit only by hurricane lamps and warmed by an open fire. Down in the valley, the track winds past thick forest to the Bush Camp. Incorporating parts of the original homestead site, it feels like a wooden hay-barn with a cinematic element, since a quarter of the blackwood walls slide out of sight so you can observe the scenery. It has an enormous fireplace, old couches, chunky beds and you only need to BYO sleeping-bag and sustenance. For those who prefer their creature comforts there's the more conventional farm cottage near the main house and Miranda, who trained as a cook in Italy, can provide all meals on request. This Moodie clan hasn't moved house since 1817 and, frankly, after a few days at Honeywood, you'll understand exactly why. *Children under 12 half price. Farm may also be hired out as a wedding venue.*

Rooms: 7 self-contained cottages, each with 2 or 3 bedrooms, some with en/s bathrooms. Oakvale sleeps 6 – 8. 1 booking per cottage (sleeps 10).
Price: R200 – R250 pp sharing.
Meals: Full breakfast R40 pp. Lunch platters R55 for two sharing. Dinners R80 pp for 3 courses including wine. All meals must be pre-booked.
Directions: From Cape Town on N2 take the first road to Suurbraak (R324) after Swellendam and continue straight (you will pass the turn to Tradouws Pass) until you arrive at a dirt road. Carry on straight until you start seeing signs for Honeywood.

Grootvadersbosch Farm

Michele Moodie
Heidelberg 6665
Tel: 028-722-2044 Fax: 028-722-2044
Email: info@grootvadersbosch.co.za Web: www.grootvadersbosch.co.za
Cell: 082 412 5991

Deep in the Overberg vales, this Jersey dairy farm was the first stop-off for the ancestral Moodie clan on their way from Orkney way back in 1818. Soon they spread far and wide (my visit coincided with that of a Kiwi Moodie for example), but a lucky few stayed on. And now, the fifth generation, Keith and Michelle, want to share their very special farm with you. Exclusively yours, you'll feel right at home in the rambling country house, where guests are just as likely to be found curled up on the sofa by the blazing kitchen hearth as out checking fodder and feeding calves in the late afternoon. The rooms are delightfully rustic, my favourite being bottle-green with a yellowwood floor and ceiling and four-poster bed. Another room has its own spinning wheel (if you feel the urge, spinner Michelle will show you how) and a cavernous bathroom up in the eaves under the thatch (a free-standing Victorian slipper bath making this quite the romantic spot). Wholesome dinners are enjoyed each night with the family by candlelight taking you back to 1740 when the house was first built. Particularly popular with weaver-birds (one of the 170 varieties of birds on the farm), are the nest-drooped trees beside which farm-fresh eggs can be devoured for breakfast. You may even catch Michelle here testing her skills re-weaving a fallen nest.

Rooms: 3: 1 queen with full en-suite bathroom; 2 twins, both with en-suite baths. The unit will only be let as one.
Price: R450 pp sharing, dinner B&B.
Meals: Full breakfast and 2-course evening meal with the family included in the price.
Directions: From Cape Town take the N2. Turn L onto R324 and drive through Suurbraak (don't take the turning to Barrydale), continue along R322 towards Heidelberg onto gravel road (only 2km). Farm signed on left.

Skeiding Guest Farm

Neels and Anné-Lize Uys
Route N2, Heidelberg 6665
Tel: 028-722-1891 Fax: 028-722-2223
Email: skeiding@sdm.dorea.co.za Web: www.skeiding.co.za
Cell: 082-451-4965

Neels and Anné-Lize are fantastically energetic – you need to be to run a farm, a young family and a guest house in the same lifetime. You are welcome to become involved in the workings of the farm as far as possible. This could mean watching the 1500 ostriches being fed in the morning, but there are also indigenous beef cattle, and some sheep, two dogs called Asterix and Jessie… and a couple of young children too. The farm is on high, open, rolling terrain, but it is only a short drive into surprising, Garden Route-style forest and the beautiful Grootvadersbosch Nature Reserve for day hikes. The area is a birder's paradise too with 17 endemic species and they have counted at least 50 species on the farm itself. Alternatively, you can head down over South Africa's only working ferry to the De Hoop Nature Reserve or go to Witsand (35km) for the whales (June to November) and boat rides. It's an outdoorsy sort of place and bedrooms have all you need; private patios, strong showers, ostrich-skin slippers and three have their own sitting rooms. Out in the garden you'll find the largest hammock I've ever seen and a pool, both with great views onto the surrounding hills and beyond. Guests eat at the family dining table, wholesome farm fare like ostrich fillet, bobotie, pumpkin fritters etc. A friendly family farm and an education for city slickers. *Professionally run horse rides can be arranged.*

Rooms: 4: all doubles/twins; 1 with en-suite bath and shower; 2 with en-suite shower; 1 with wheelchair-friendly en-suite shower.
Price: R250 - R400 pp sharing. No singles supplement.
Meals: R80 for 2 courses pp. R100 for 3 courses pp. Price excludes wine.
Directions: From Swellendam take N2 towards Mossel Bay. 45km after Swellendam (12km before Heidelberg) farm signed to left. Follow 2km then signed left again. 3 more km then signed left again. House on hill.

Waterkloof Guesthouse

Hannes and Christine Uys

Witsand
Tel: 028-722-1811
Fax: 028-722-1811
Email: info@waterkloofguesthouse.co.za
Web: www.waterkloofguesthouse.co.za
Cell: 083-270-2348

Ever played chicken with an ostrich? Now's your chance. Admittedly I had the protection of a bull-barred pick-up truck but it was exciting stuff, rattling around the farm collecting still-warm eggs for the incubator and doing our best to avoid overly ruffling their fathers' feathers. Waterkloof is an ostrich farm through and through and there is nothing that Hannes (only the seventh generation of the Uys family to work this land!) doesn't know about these feisty fowl. They use the leather for bags, the eggs for breakfast, the eggshells for lampshades and the meat for supper. The only thing you can't do with an Uys ostrich is ride it – there are horses for that, and Hannes and Christine's daughters will happily take you out on a tour. Sunk into rolling fields of barley and wheat, this is a hard-working farm but a great place to take it easy. Cool, luxurious bedrooms open onto the garden and fountain, wild fig trees shade benches built for reading on and the pool area has its own kitchen for help-yourself Sunday lunches. And if you feel like a change of scenery (and wildlife) Witsand is the place to see migrating whales. Back at the house Hannes patiently answered my babble of questions as we sank into ostrich-leather-covered armchairs and tucked into Christine's cheesecake - no ostrich in that, I take it.

Rooms: 4: 2 doubles and 1 twin all with bath, 1 twin with shower.
Price: R250 - R400 pp sharing.
Meals: Full breakfast included. Dinner on request.
Directions: From the CT and the N2 turn R onto R324 after Swellendam 32 to the farm. From Mossel Bay take R322 to Witsand. At the crossroads turn R. Farm is on the L after 17 km.

River Magic

Bosky and Paul Andrew

Reservations: 35 Pear Lane Constantia, Cape Town, 7806, Physical address: Vermaaklikheid, Nr Riversdale Tel: 021-794-6294 or 028-713-2930
Fax: 028-713-2930 or 021-794-6294 Email: rivermagic@zsd.co.za
Web: www.vermaaklikheid.co.za Cell: 082-732-3003

Welcome to the centre of the universe," said Paul, as our tubby little rowing boat sliced through the early morning mist, its oars stirring the clear cola-coloured water and groaning in their rollocks. We bumped gently against the jetty and then hopped out onto a dew-damp riverbank, the best and, for that matter, only way to arrive at River Magic's 'Glory Be'. Silence. I fumbled for an appropriate superlative. What a spot... what a find. Two low, stone-built, thatched cottages, buried in the folds of brush-carpeted, ancient sand dunes and, without doubt, the most enchanting place I had yet encountered. I longed to return with a gang of pals, threading our way between the banks of Spanish reed, ferrying supplies across the river, fishing for grunter from the jetty (or canoes) and sharing beers and a braai around the huge outdoor table on the even more enormous shaded veranda. Inside, the cottages are comfortably (not extravagantly) kitted-out with wooden furniture and all kitchen essentials. There are beds for as many as you can muster, some secluded, others tucked into tents or in sociable four-man rooms. On a hot tip, I wheeled mine outside to sleep under the stars where I lay heaped in a duvet, inventing constellations, listening to hadedahs in the blue gums and scribbling notes by torchlight. Sound alright?

Rooms: 2 cottages: Glory Be sleeps 12 in 5 bedrooms (3 en-suite); Back Track sleeps 6 (2 twins en/s shr, 1 tented hut).
Price: From R130 – R150 pp sharing. Min R350 per cottage per night. Min R500 - R800 over long weekends and R800 - R1,000 over Christmas hols.
Meals: Self-catering, bring your own wood, towels and torches. Seafood restaurant nearby.
Directions: From Cape Town take N2. 3km before Heidelberg turn R at signs marked "Port Beauford; Witsand". 6km down tar road, turn L at dirt road signed Vermaaklikheid. After 14km turn L at T-jct, cross Duivenshok River over causeway. Follow signs to Vermaaklikheid & then to River Magic.

Map Number: 2

De Doornkraal Historic Country House

Jacolette Olivier
8 Long Street, Riversdale 6670
Tel: 028-713-3838 Fax: 028-713-3050
Email: dedoornkraal@mweb.co.za Web: www.dedoornkraal.com
Cell: 082 958 0622

If the hectic pace of today's world leaves you feeling out of breath, or even slightly nauseous, I couldn't think of a more suitable antidote than a stay at De Doornkraal. Formerly a doctor's surgery (operations can still legally be performed on the premises!), this Cape Dutch beauty dates back to 1746 and is the oldest building in Riversdale. Listen very carefully and you can almost hear the history echo through the walls; at the very least you can certainly see it. After a painstaking restoration, the original yellowwood floors and ceilings, blackwood furnishings and the stunning rosewood front door are now revealed in all their former glory. Understatedly elegant rooms have simple, neutral-coloured upholstery so as not to upstage the beautiful woodwork throughout. Original paintings add splashes of colour, the work of a well-known artist who previously lived here. They also share a fine drawing room with honesty bar, the ideal place for an after-dinner nightcap. Across the road are two comfortable and airy cottages set by a large willow-shaded pond in a fruit-filled garden that rolls on into the paddocks beyond. Honeymooners can contentedly picnic under the oaks here, while children could acquaint themselves with the aquatic and farm animal neighbours. Happily, I sat listening to the fountain murmur in the tea garden, lost to the outside world; its only reminder hoots from the thrice-daily steam-train that runs through an otherwise sleepy town.

Rooms: 6: 3 rooms in main house (2 queens & 1 twin/king, all en-suite free-standing baths & shower). Also 2 cottages: Cedar Cottage (1 queen, lounge & en-suite shower); Willow Cottage (1 queen room with en-s bath & shower, 1 twin with en-s shower, lounge & kitchenette).
Price: R350 - R750 pp sharing. Singles supplement +50%.
Meals: Full breakfast included. Restaurant and tea garden on the premises open breakfast, lunch and dinner.
Directions: N2 from Cape Town to Riversdale, L into town, follow signboards. Turn L just before you leave town into Long Street. 100m on LHS.

Riversong Farm

Piers Sibson
Waterblom Street, Stilbaai
Tel: 021-465-4078 Fax: 021-465-4078
Email: pierss@mweb.co.za Web: www.riversongfarm.co.za
Cell: 082-374-8274

Rustic, down-to-earth and outdoorsy. If these words jump out at you, then this is a truly great find. Sheltered by reeds and milkwood trees on the banks of the Goukou River, Riversong Farm is the ideal spot to relax, get outside and experience nature's simple pleasures. In fact it would be shameful not to spend at least most of the time by, in or on the river or off exploring the farm's kloofs, dams and bushman paintings as it stretches back into the fynbos backlands beyond (also ripe for investigation). Not that the indoors is not for enjoying as well. The four wooden chalets are comfortable, unfussy and cosy affairs. Whilst 'Jordan' would be especially snug for a romantic getaway, the gargantuan 'Zambezi' could easily manage two families and then some. Each has a well-equipped kitchen, wood-burning stove and verandah from which you can follow the river as it idles its way down to the Indian Ocean. Braais in the chalets and on the lawn by the reed-lined deck provide ample opportunity to cook up the day's catch. Also living on this working farm are Simon and Manuela, both very knowledgeable about the area's wildlife, particularly the abundant bird life. Barely had I stepped out of the car before I had seen two eagles! So, with all this on hand and surfing, golf, 4x4 trails and horse-riding nearby, I promise there won't be a dull moment. *Home-grown organic vegetables and meat available.*

Rooms: 4 chalets: Zambezi sleeps 8 (2 doubles plus extra bunk beds, en-suite showers); Thames sleeps 4 (1 double plus extra bunk bed, separate bathroom); Orange sleeps 4 (1 dble, 2 singles, en-suite shower); Jordan sleeps 2 (1 queen with sep' bathroom).
Price: R400 - R1,000 for one whole chalet. Special rates for booking the whole farm.
Meals: Fully self-catering. Restaurant next-door serves breakfasts and lunches. Fishing permits are available from the post office.
Directions: Take Stillbaai turning off N2, 12km after Riversdale. Once in town, turn right over the bridge, then immediately right into Waterblom Street. Farm clearly signposted about 12km upriver.

Otters Spring River Lodge

Sue Byrne
Waterblom Street, PO Box 676, Stilbaai 6674
Tel: 028-754-3112 Fax: 028-754-3112
Email: suebyrne@webmail.co.za Web: www.ottersspring.co.za
Cell: 082 775 5053

I heard Sue before I saw her. Her laughter is often heard echoing around the house, emblematic of a thoroughly jolly place, equally suited to family fun as to lazy, pampered getaways. Otter's Spring is plugged into the hillside above the Goukou River and surrounded by 90 hectares of paddock, riverbank and dam to let the kids loose on while you sink into a good book, the pool or both. Rooms, each with a basic but brightly-coloured bathroom, are hidden under the thatched roof or tucked into the hillside. I slept blissfully in the charming and slightly more secluded room that sits on the edge of the clumpy meadow mowed by podgy sheep which tumbles down to the river. Sooner or later, you'll be down there too, hurling yourself in from the bobbing pontoon, or (probably not 'and') looking out for the elusive otters. You're welcome to fish too, though to date no one has ever caught anything substantial in size. Back up at the house the chickens provide the eggs, the goose chases the dog, Sue chases the chickens and prepares the delicious evening meals (sometimes at the same time!)...and you? Your job is to lie back in a hammock or to treat yourself to a massage (available on-site). Water-skiing and wake-boarding are available further down-river and Stillbaai has excellent surf.

Rooms: 6: 1 twin and 3 doubles, all with bath and/or shower; 1 family suite with 2 doubles, separate toilet and shared bathroom.
Price: R275 - R440 pp sharing.
Meals: Full breakfast included. Dinners on request.
Directions: From N2 take the Stilbaii turning between Riversdale and Albertinia. Arriving in town, cross the bridge and turn immediately right into Waterbloom St. Otters Spring is 13km upriver on the right.

Sandpiper Cottages

Fred Orban
Boggoms Bay 6500
Tel: 044-699-1204 Fax: 044-699-1204
Email: forban@mweb.co.za Web: www.sandpiper.co.za
Cell: 082-550-4788

This secretive beachside spot is creeping shyly onto the map with Sandpiper's budding cluster of thatched white-walled fishermen's cottages. Fred, a developer by trade, started building with his children in mind but, like swallows, they have flown to Europe, leaving you to take up residence instead. My favourite was Fred's most recent project, the honeymoon cottage, to be christened 'Sea Mist' when it is complete. Here a tender haze emanates from the affectionately planned and implemented interiors. Red clay tile floors are ornamented with yellowwood and Oregon pine furniture, while a sleeper-wood worktop and recycled timber staircase showcase Sandpiper's originality and your host's particular love of trees. An extraordinary hearth gathers you with fire-warmed fingers into its seated inglenook and a three-roomed bathroom flaunts its own lounge. Hugely roomy yet indisputably cosy, the varied cottages combine an atmosphere of the past with luxuries of today. Fred himself is a truly lovely chap and, although the cottages are fully self-catered, he can sort you out with a 'real Boggoms breakfast' and even dinner as well. You will certainly need the energy if you want to make the most of the superb Fred-built sports centre or hike the dazzling, Fred-established Oystercatcher Trail. Untamed fynbos encourages bees, buck, rabbits and birds to gather in the garden; the vegetation extends from your cottage to the beach where sand and rock scuffle with the sea, vying for attention with the distant Outeniqua Mountains.

Rooms: 6 cottages: 2 with 2 beds, and 4 with 3 beds. All have multiple bathrooms.
Price: R290 - R635pp sharing. Singles on request. Minimum 2-night stay.
Meals: Meals on request. Full or continental can be delivered to your door for R60. Evening meals R100.
Directions: 34km along N2 from Albertinia in direction of Mossel Bay, turn R at Boggams Bay junction. Continue for 11km before turning L into village. More detailed directions can be emailed on booking.

85 Hill Street

Lesley Peju
Mossel Bay 6500
Tel: 044-690-7333 Fax: 086-684-9550
Email: lesley@pixie.co.za Web: www.85hillstreet.co.za
Cell. 082-924-9063

After a Steve McQueen-esque drive up what I can only guess is Mossel Mountain, I arrived at 85 Hill Street to meet Jean who was frantically busying the builders, and a laid-back Lesley who was simply taking it all in her stride; "he's Swiss, he's a perfectionist", laughed the lass from Sheffield. Although still a few months from completion when I came to visit, I could instantly see why the couple had fallen in love with this house. The view is pick-your-jaw-up-off-the-floor amazing, gazing over roof-tops and across the entire expanse of Mossel Bay. Everything about the apartment is designed with the view in mind too, with great glass doors in the ocean-matching blue bedroom, a choice of two lounges, "… one to watch TV in and one to watch the scenery in," and a colossal verandah. Oh, and not to forget a number of prized nautical possessions courtesy of Jean who appears to be yet another landlocked Swiss mesmerised by the sea. Despite the fact it was little more than a shell when I was here (although a mighty marble-topped kitchen to make even Delia green with envy had just been fitted), I'm going to stick my neck on the line and say this place will be perfect. Why am I so confident? Well, Swiss-trained chef Jean and Forte-taught Lesley have oodles of experience and their previous endeavours have gained them hordes of loyal disciples. This newest incarnation promises to be no different. So join the pilgrimage now to 85 Hill Street.

Rooms: 2: 1 queen unit with separate lounge/kitchen and full en-suite bathroom; and 1 twin room with en-suite shower room.
Price: From R200 - R450 pp.
Meals: Ingredients of a health breakfast provided in fridge. Other meals on request.
Directions: Take 1st exit into Mossel Bay, then Marsh St exit off that. Turn R at lights. At next lights turn R into Kerk St. Take 3rd street on left into Hill Street. Continue over 2 stop signs and the property is on left.

Map Number: 2

Botlierskop Private Game Reserve

The Neethling and Wiggett Families

PO Box 565, Little Brak River 6503
Tel: 044-696-6055 Fax: 044-696-6272
Email: info@botlierskop.co.za Web: www.botlierskop.co.za
Cell: 083-628-1105

The Garden Route is best known for its scenery and sea life, so the last thing I expected to see as I navigated the back roads was a rhino. But there it was, chewing the cud like a contented cow. Botlierskop is a private game reserve that brings the big five south. It's not as wild as its northern counterparts (the lions are in a sanctuary) but it's a magical place to stay, set in 2,400 hectares of grassy plains and forested sandstone hills. The park is open to day visitors but it's skillfully co-ordinated to ensure your paths never cross. Two of the highlights are Sam and Totsi, orphaned elephants trained not only in giving rides, but also as actors. Did you see Far of Place? Or Elephant Boy? Trust me, they were great! Elephant back rides and elephant picnics are a big pull at Botlierskop. Overnighters are appointed their own private guide and I had Hentie, an animal almanac and rock art aficionado. A short quad-bike ride from the cavernous hilltop restaurant, he ushered me into a dinghy and we drifted off down the wooded, Moordkuil river to the guest tents. More of a marquee than a tent, each is set on its own patch of decking with steps leading to a floating jetty (a great spot to fish from). It's luxury with a capital 'L' and inside; deep armchairs, a writing desk and a room-for-two bath accompany the mosquito-netted four-poster. One tip though, zip it closed when you leave - the vervet monkeys have a penchant for coffee and cookies. *Helicopter scenic flights R350pp for 3 passengers, R450pp for 2 for 15-min flight (weather permitting).*

Rooms: 12: 7 kings and 5 twin luxury tents all with en-suite bath.
Price: R1,290 - R1,990 pp sharing. Rates include game drive, activities and all meals. Drinks are extra.
Meals: Fully catered.
Directions: From Mossel Bay and CT on N2 take Little Brak River exit (401). Heading inland turn R to Sorgfontein. Continue 4km and after causeway turn R for 4km along gravel road to Botlierskop.

Malvern Manor

Sandra and Michael Cook
Nr Fancourt, Blanco, George 6530
Tel: 044-870-8788 Fax: 044-870-8790
Email: malvernmanor@msn.com Web: www.malvernmanor.co.za
Cell: 084-867-6470

If you are having any difficulty understanding why the area is called the Garden Route, well, have a trundle up Michael and Sandra's drive. Much more colourful and vibrant than anything visible from the public thoroughfares. I drove past cows and dams onto a redbrick road overflowing with thick tangles of foliage that hide Malvern from view - and all this perfectly framed by the imposing Outeniqua Mountains. Here is another English couple who fell in love with South Africa, upped sticks and bought their country idyll. Both of farming stock, this 21-hectare dairy farm was perfect. But despite being just a hop, skip and a jump from George, it was no easy task converting the Manor House, the keep at the heart of the farm, into a guest house; just ask Michael about the basin palaver. But it's all come together so nicely. My room opened onto the garden through French doors, and lavish Greek-style pillars pick out the bath – the perfect place to unwind after a round of golf at Fancourt (recent host of the President's Cup). For non-golfers, two dams offer blue gill and big-mouth bass fishing or else there's endless scope for pre-breakfast walks. Play your cards right on your return and Michael might don his apron and prepare his speciality 'chocaccino'. Delightful people in an enchanting setting.

Rooms: 3: 1 queen, 1 twin or king, 1 double with single bed. All have en-suite bath and shower.
Price: R350 - R650 pp sharing. Singles on request.
Meals: Full breakfast included. Restaurants nearby and deliveries can be arranged.
Directions: From N2 take George airport exit onto R404 and follow signs to Oudtshoorn for approximately 8km. After Fancourt Golfing Estate, sign to Malvern Manor on left. Follow signs.

Fairview Historic Homestead

Philda Benkenstein
36 Stander St, George 6530
Tel: 044-874-7781 Fax: 044-874-7999
Email: benkenstein@mweb.co.za
Cell: 082-226-9466

This picturesque, listed Victorian house on the eastern edge of George is an intriguing place to stay. With its high ceilings and abundant Victoriana, Fairview has the feel of an old English rectory, although the vivid colours owe more to African than Anglican themes. All the bedrooms are a treat: the two on the ground floor still have their original 1880s floorboards, beams and fireplaces; the Orange Room, complete with dashing white trim, bathes in afternoon sunlight; while the Yellow Room soaks up the morning. The sitting room has the same high ceilings and wooden floors, with shuttered sash windows and enormous linen press. The whole place has a happy family atmosphere, enhanced by the original home features, which have been retained wherever possible. Philda loves to host and have people in her beautiful home. She will cook too and if you do eat here, as the GG guests visiting were, then you'll enjoy mainly South African fare. Husband Desmond is a green-fingered doctor and the creative force in the glorious garden. There are fruit trees, an immaculate veggie patch, swathes of clivia and plans for much more.

Rooms: 2: both doubles with an extra bed. 1 has en-suite shower, 1 has en-suite bath.
Price: R280 - R320 pp sharing. Singles plus 40%.
Meals: Full breakfast included. Dinners by arrangement.
Directions: From CT on N2 take York Street turn off to George. Turn R at roundabout into Courtenay St. Over railway bridge and turn left into Second Street and turn L at stop sign into Stander St, house on right.

Acorn Guest House

Colin and Esther Horn

4 Kerk St, George 6529
Tel: 044-874-0474 Fax: 044-884-1753
Email: info@acornguesthouse.co.za Web: www.acornguesthouse.co.za
Cell: 083 539 7398

With birds chirping in the tree-lined street and church bells chiming (kerk is Afrikaans for church), I approached the pink, ivy-clad walls utterly unaware of the riches hidden within. Acorn Guest House is a veritable treasure trove and Esther was quick to explain: "where some people go to casinos, we go to auctions." Almost everything in this Edwardian house is second-hand and antique. Persian rugs are strewn over bare floorboards; battered wooden trunks are scattered throughout the bedrooms; mirrors and ornaments adorn the available wall space; every nook and cranny arrests the eye. The bedrooms are equally ornate, the master room boasting a large en-suite bathroom separated from the grand sleeping area by a gold-coloured curtain. Had I stayed a little longer (and deprived the Horns of even more of Esther's delicious home-baked cake) I could have joined Colin on a fishing trip… although not the leisurely pipe-and-picnic fishing I had envisaged. "If guests are able to swim 4km in the sea with a snorkel, they're welcome to join me," he proclaimed, re-emerging with his weapon of choice, a spear gun. If all this sounds a bit too James Bond for you, he also offers more serene tours of the estuary in his boat. Those with spoils to share come evening do so on the braai, whilst bargain hunters furiously jot down Esther's top tips.

Rooms: 7: 2 twins with en-suite bath and shower; 3 doubles with en-suite bath and shower; 1 family unit with en-suite shower; 1 double with en-suite shower.
Price: R275 - R395 pp sharing. Singles R400 - R500.
Meals: Full breakfast included. Picnic basket and dinner by arrangement. Self-catering facilities available.
Directions: Take York Street exit off N2 towards town. Go through town on York Street until the roundabout. Turn right (signed to Knysna) and Kerk Street is third turning on left. Second property on right.

Map Number: 5

Strawberry Hill Getaway

Di and Bill Turner

Old George-Knysna (Seven Passes) Road, Wilderness, George East 6539
Tel: 044-877-0055 Fax: 044-877-0055
Email: getaway@strawberryhill.co.za Web: www.strawberryhill.co.za

Bill and Di wouldn't swap this for all the animals in Africa. Their hill-marooned farm looks across to the mountains and, though shrouded in mist when I arrived, the view here has previously had guests applauding and trying to order prints! The garden plunges straight from the pool and lawns to two deep gorges and nothing spoils the unfettered vista. The area is home to afro-montane forest and over the years Di has identified 56 species of fern, while Bill has hacked his way through the bush to create numerous hiking tracks down to the deepest pools. He will happily be your guide - as he was for me - striding along, identifying the astonishingly diverse plant and bird life and pausing for well-earned breathers at stunning, log-bench lookouts. Di was away trekking through the Scottish highlands at the time, but when at home, she and Bill invite their guests to join them occasionally for wine and snacks on the verandah or beside the enormous log fire. The self-contained cottages are serviced daily and have their own gardens which happily cater for children with a playground and tree-house. A soft homey feel is created with pretty country furnishings and a sense of community prevails with the shared use of the Turner's pool. *Great hiking and well -situated for exploration of the Garden Route.*

Rooms: 2 self-catering cottages, both sleeping 6: 1 cottage with 3 x double bedrooms and 1 cottage with 2 x double bedrooms and a room with bunk beds. Shared bathrooms in each.
Price: Basic cost per unit: low season R400, high season R600, peak season R750, plus an additional R25 per head.
Meals: Breakfast baskets can be organised by prior arrangement.
Directions: From George: head towards Wilderness on Knysna Rd. L onto old George-Knysna road signed Nelson Mandela Uni (Pine Lodge on corner). Strawberry Hill after 7.5km on R. From Wilderness: up Heights Rd behind hotel. At T-Junc (3.5km) L towards George. Strawberry Hill is 3km on L.

The Waves

Liza and Iain Campbell
7 Beach Rd, Victoria Bay, George 6530
Tel: 044-889-0166 Fax: 044-889-0166
Email: thewaves@intekom.co.za Web:
www.gardenroute.co.za/vbay/waves/index.htm

Iain and Liza have an amazing photo from 1906 when The Waves was the only house on the beach, used as a holiday home by an Oudtshoorn farmer. It is not surprising a few others have since joined the club. The hamlet is closed to vehicles – only residents hold the key to the gate, so you can park your car securely at night. I'm no surfer, but the waves here are enticing, rolling up the perfect arc of the small bay at a height that is challenging, but not scary. Iain will arrange a wetsuit and surfboard or fins and a snorkel. Or if you like your activity less damp, there is horse-riding nearby, dolphin- and whale-watching in season and walks along the bay front. The house is right on the sea (see above) to which all three bedroom suites (each with its own lounge) look out, although you may spend more time on the verandah watching the waves roll in. They are hypnotic. Breakfast is served here in the sunshine and often goes on for hours. The Outeniqua Choo-Tjoe (yes, it's a steam train) runs through Victoria Bay twice a day. Both Iain and Liza are consummate hosts, love what they do and share a great sense of fun. Bay life could be addictive.
Fully no-smoking anywhere. Children over 12 only.

Rooms: 3: all doubles with extra beds, 1 with en-suite shower, 2 with en-suite bath and shower.
Price: R400 - R650 pp sharing. Singles R500 - R900.
Meals: Full breakfast included. Dinner can be ordered in and a table will be set for you.
Directions: From Mossel Bay on N2 past George exits where highways merge. 1km signed Victoria Bay to right - follow down hill 3km. Park and walk along beach road to collect the key for the gate.

Porcupine Pie Guest Lodge

John and Judy McIldowie
10 Mile Lane, Wilderness Heights 6560
Fax: 044-877-9900
Email: john@porcupinepie.co.za Web: www.porcupinepie.co.za
Cell: 083-447-6901

I'll be honest, when I visited Porcupine Lodge it was unfinished. But I am in no doubt whatever that it will become a flagship GG place once it is done (which it easily will be by the time this book is published). There was even something about Judy's home-made biscuits that told me all would be well! The lofty setting here is quite simply beautiful. Wilderness Nature Reserve unfurls before you, cupping a wedge of stunning blue sea between its foliage-fringed peaks. A rare commotion of birds, delighted to have found so unspoilt a spot themselves, provides possibly the best on-site birding around. You don't even need to leave the deck, just whip out a pair of bino's and watch. In the time it took me to munch just one of those biscuits, I had seen an eagle and two resident jackal buzzards. It was also enough time for a sudden breeze to whip up a handful of my paperwork and deposit it into the pool. Promptly rescued by John we continued our study of the plans for the three private free-standing units that he and Judy will share their awesome position with. Talk of view-saturated bathrooms with hand-painted basins, locally-crafted furniture, bars and the décor (which will include some of Judy's own artwork no doubt) had me aching to come back and see the finished result. You will be able to indulge in gourmet dinners, then spend the following day walking it off along the famous Kingfisher Trail.

Rooms: 3: all kings/twins with en-suite bath and shower.
Price: R450 - R550 pp sharing.
Meals: Full breakfast included. Light lunches and dinners also available. Dinner is a set 3-course gourmet affair.
Directions: From George follow N2 to Wilderness. Turn left into Wilderness Village, follow road past Protea Hotel to T-junction. Turn left and travel up Heights road for 3.8km. Do not turn off tar until you reach T-junction marked "Old George/Knysna Road". Turn right onto gravel road and after 1.6km turn right onto "Ten Mile Lane". Follow Porcupine Signs for 3.4km.

Whale's Way Ocean Retreat

Tim Ivison and Ali Drummond

858 6th Avenue, Wilderness 6560
Tel: 044-877-0482 Fax: 044-877-0436
Email: themagic@whalesway.co.za Web: www.whalesway.co.za
Cell. 076-113-6925

According to Tim and Ali this is "a place where magic happens." It certainly seemed like an optical illusion when Tim first showed me to my room, opening a door marked 'Ocean' onto a world of white. It was like entering the delicate vastness of a giant seashell, one that comes equipped with king-size bed and spa bath. Both ends of the room are more windows than walls and frame a different view, while the high white-beamed ceiling hovers gently above. You can lie, mesmerised by the wide expanse of sea, from the wide expanse of your bed or wallow in the jacuzzi admiring the mountainous backdrop of Wilderness Nature Reserve. Left to unpack I suppressed urges to cartwheel from one end of the room to the other (I calculated a good 10 would do it) opting for the more socially acceptable practice of playing my guitar (quietly - it's a classical). When I chose to rejoin reality, Tim proved himself a faultless host and conversation flowed freely into the night. Ali is qualified in Chi massage, a wonderful added bonus in situ. Unfortunately she was away when I visited and I missed out on one of Whale's Way's many heavenly experiences. Warmed by an evening's food, drink and chat I dived beneath waves of cotton and floated gently into sleep while promises of a sunrise bathe whispered soothingly from the sea.

Rooms: 5: 4 kings and 1 double; 4 with en-suite bath and shower and 1 with private bathroom (bath and shower).
Price: R300 - R1,000 pp sharing. Singles by arrangement.
Meals: Full breakfast included.
Directions: Travelling from George on the N2 towards Knysna, once in Wilderness, turn right at 2nd Caltex garage adjacent to the Wilderness Beach Hotel. Turn left at the roundabout and follow signs to Whale's Way.

Wilderness Manor

Johan and Marianne Nicol
397 Waterside Rd, Wilderness 6560
Tel: 044-877-0264 Fax: 044-877-0163
Email: wildman@mweb.co.za Web: www.manor.co.za

Marianne has a flair for interiors. You won't need one of the hundreds of books (African art and history, its wildlife and architecture, war memoirs, children's classics and psychology texts) that rub sleeves throughout the house to find this out. Overlooking the lagoon, the glass-encased sitting room is coir-carpeted with Afghan kilims, a low-slung ivory sofa and a pair of Morris chairs, given to the Governor of Gauteng. There's an old billiard table, too, somewhere under a pile of maps. African artefacts have been begged, borrowed or bought: Ndebele pipes and beads, bartered-for carvings and stones from the Cradle of Mankind. The bedrooms have similar horn-and-hide hues, all the luxurious trappings you could wish for, and room for Indonesian chairs and chests, chocolate leather sofas, slipper baths and dark canopied beds with reading lights. In the morning, linen tables were dressed with bone-handle cutlery and lilies in a square metal vase placed on an old country bench next to fruit and muesli. Your hosts are discreet and attentive, and after serving up a faultless (and greaseless) breakfast, will give you a map and bountiful beach-bag and set you off to explore your surrounds. Birdlife is rampant in the area and walks in the surrounding forests are a must. It is only a five-minute stroll along lagoon-side boardwalks to the beach, town and some good restaurants.

Rooms: 4: 2 kings with en-suite bath and shower; 2 twins, one with en/s bath and shower, one with shower only.
Price: R350 – R550 pp sharing. Single supplement plus 50% (100% in summer). Rates greatly reduced in winter.
Meals: Full breakfast included.
Directions: From George, follow N2 to Wilderness (beware of speed cameras on descent). Turn left into Wilderness Village and follow road to T-junction. Turn right along lagoon to Wilderness Manor on left.

Moontide Guest House

Maureen Mansfield
Southside Rd, Wilderness 6560
Tel: 044-877-0361 Fax: 044-877-0124
Email: moontide@intekom.co.za Web: www.moontide.co.za

It's a rare pleasure for us to stay somewhere on *holiday* and to experience it over a period of days. And Moontide was a palpable hit with all five of us. Its position is hard to beat, right on the banks of the lagoon, its wooden decks shaded by a 400-year-old milkwood tree. Here you can sit out for bountiful breakfasts or with an evening drink from your bar fridge, and watch giant kingfishers diving for fish – well, we saw one anyway. Birdlife is profuse on the lagoon. The long, white-sanded Wilderness beach is only a one-minute walk from the house, but you can also take a canoe straight from Moontide up the lagoon into the Touw River and then walk along forest trails to waterfalls to swim in fresh-water rock pools. Whatever we did it was a pleasure to return, play cards in a relaxed sitting room, or read in the cool of a bedroom. I was delighted with 'Milkwood' because I'm a sucker for dozing on a futon, in a loft, under thatched eaves, with river views by my head. But I would like to return and try them all. Since we descended *en masse*, Maureen has built herself a tree-top sanctuary. The deck, day-bed, even the free-standing bath, look out across thatched roofs to the river. Sportingly, she's decided it's too nice to keep for herself!

Rooms: 5: Moonriver Luxury Suite (king & 2 twins, bath & shower); Treetops (queen, bath & outside hot/cold shower); Milkwood (king or 2 singles & queen upstairs, bath & shower); Stone Cottage (twins & shower); The Boathouse (double & bath).
Price: R390 - R520. Single rates on request.
Meals: Full breakfast included.
Directions: From George on N2 ignore Wilderness turn-off. Cross Touw River bridge, first left signed Southside Rd. Moontide at the end of cul-de-sac.

Slanting Acres

Pam Ross
Bitou Road, Hoekwil, Wilderness 6538
Tel: 044-850-1195 Fax: 044-850-1195
Email: reservations@slantingacres.com Web: www.slantingacres.com
Cell: 082-907-2404

Horses were chewing, birds were roosting, ducks were swimming, cats were purring, chickens were foraging, and the guinea fowl... were just being guinea fowl. Animals are everywhere on Slanting Acres slanting seven and a half acres, plenty of room for everyone. The immaculate lawns sweep around this white-washed, wood-decked house, hoisted high on the Hoekwil hillside, with far-reaching views over Wilderness and into the wilderness of the deep-blue Indian Ocean. Equally blue is the figure-of-eight-shaped pool, where a waterfall is a constant cooling sight and sound. If lazing by the pool is not enough to occupy your mind, there is always the 18-hole putting green. Personally I would prefer to sink one in the nautically-themed bar inside. Iain is a ship's captain in the merchant navy, and he'll happily tell you all about his life at sea... that is if he is not actually at sea when you visit. Pictures of the various ships he's skippered fill the walls. Pam will keep you entertained in his absence. She's the driving force behind Slanting Acres. The bedrooms are small, but perfectly formed with white cotton sheets, pine wardrobes, and plenty of light. Homely comforts in a very friendly house.

Rooms: 3: 2 doubles and 1 twin, all with en-suite shower rooms.
Price: R300 - R385 pp sharing. Singles + 25%.
Meals: Full breakfast included. Lots of restaurants nearby.
Directions: From Cape Town take the N2 past George and 2km past Wilderness turn L to Hoekwil. Through lake and over railway, up hill and turn R at 1st brown B&B sign.

The Dune Guest Lodge

Gary and Melisa Grimes

31 Die Duin, Wilderness 6560
Tel: 044-877-0298
Fax: 044-877-0298
Email: info@thedune.co.za
Web: www.thedune.co.za
Cell: 083-941-1149

Gary Grimes is both consummate host and chief breakfast-maker at The Dune and when I pulled up (carefully avoiding parking in the space marked "for my girlfriend/wife") he and Melisa had just finished feeding the hordes with a man-stopping fry-up. "Anything you can do with eggs, I do it," he tells me. I made a note to arrive a little earlier next time. By most standards, he is greedily tall, but at 6'7" he insists he was pretty average among his basketball contemporaries and after years as a pro in Switzerland he dropped the ball in favour of a dishcloth, dinner plates and the wildness of Wilderness. If you're looking for a beach-house then you couldn't get much more beachy than this. As the name suggests it's smack-bang in the dunes and, to be numerically fastidious, exactly 85 wooden steps lead down to 7.5km of pristine sandy beach stretching away to both east and west. The whole place has a wonderfully soothing, seaside feel. Walls hung with seascape oils are whitewashed or sea-blue. Driftwood sculptures surround the fireplace and bedside sofas look south through wall-to-wall windows for round-the-clock whale-watching. Best of all though, wherever you are in the building, you can hear the surf heaving, sighing, thumping and crumping against the beach.

Rooms: 4: 2 doubles, 2 twins with 3/4 beds, all with en/s bath and shower.
Price: R350 – R700 pp sharing.
Meals: Full breakfast included.
Directions: From CT pass Wilderness on N2. Cross the Touw River and turn right into Die Duin 700m later. Take the right fork and The Dune is first on the left.

Forget-me-not Sedgefield-on-Sea

Mary and Derek Woolmington
4 Manila Crescent , Cola Beach, Sedgefield
Tel: 044-382-2916 Fax: 044-382-2916
Email: mary@forget-me-not.co.za Web: www.forget-me-not.co.za
Cell: 083-505-4225

Scatter thoughts and clothes to the breeze and plunge into Forget-me-not's north-facing pool. Found at the tail-end of a line of properties this Canadian-style house rises thatched head and log shoulders above the rest when it comes to first impressions. The interior is fresh and lively with rich, pine walls set off against sea-blues and whitewash-finished furniture. A fully-equipped kitchen and perfect BBQ verandah ensure that you have everything you need to cook up a family feast. David lives next door and services the chalet daily, providing a reassuring and 'happy to help' presence. Sedgefield beach is a mere 5-minute stroll away (don't forget your beach towel), but the rest of the world may as well not exist as you sit and contemplate the pristine swell of the dunes from the back deck. The back garden, which is a sea of fynbos, remains a natural wilderness - more peace, tranquility and birdlife for us. Come and forget everything at Forget-me-not Sedgefield-on-Sea. *5 minutes to Sedgefield where all amenities, a variety of restaurants and access to activities can be found. 20 minutes to Knysna.*

Rooms: 1 self-catering house that sleeps 6-8 comfortably. 1 double 3 twins and two bathrooms both with bath and shower. Fully-equipped kitchen.
Price: Seasonal: R700 per day in low season to R1,200 - R1,400 in high season (dependent on number of people).
Meals: Fully self-catered. Buffles Bay is worth a visit for breakfast.
Directions: Heading from George on the N2. Turn right at first traffic light in Sedgefield into Kingfisher Drive, straight over the roundabout and follow the Forget-me-not signs (more detailed directions on request).

Forget-me-not B&B

Mary and Derek Woolmington
21 Boekenhout St, Upper Old Place, Knysna 6570
Tel: 044-382-2916 Fax: 044-382-2916
Email: mary@forget-me-not.co.za Web: www.forget-me-not.co.za
Cell: 083 505 1225

Derek and Mary, a warm and down-to-earth English-Irish couple, embody all that we look for in hosts. Having built businesses and raised a family, they're starting out on their own again. Hence Forget-me-not (Self-catering and B&B, to give it its full title), with its sloping, slate roof, dormer windows and gravel drive. The house is edged with wisteria, primroses and forget-me-nots and other flowers Mary can't quite put a name to (and nor can I obviously) – she puts it down to "Outeniqua rust," a lethargic malaise blamed on easy living. Inside the sweep of a maranti staircase leads to two bedrooms. Iris has pine floorboards, leaning walls, blanket box and hanging space. There's a cushioned window-box from which to sit and stare. The rose room, more feminine in shades of pink with floral motifs, has Oregon pine furniture. An elongated bathroom harbours a bath tucked under the eaves. Everyone eats at the house (usually outside above the lawn and pool), even those in the self-contained flat, whose wooden deck faces the lagoon, Knysna Heads and the hills. All guests get use of the pool and the braai area and the house is within walking distance of the Waterfront and a short drive to the beaches. The long list of activities, both on water and inland, can be booked on your behalf by Derek and Mary.

Rooms: 3: 1 king and 1 queen both with en-suite bath and shower; 1 self contained apartment.
Price: R190 - R280 pp sharing. Singles on request.
Meals: Full cooked or Continental breakfast and variety of fruit and fruit/veg juice boosts. Plenty of local restaurants.
Directions: Head east out of Knysna and turn left onto Old Toll Rd, Upper Old Place. At T-junction turn right and take first left into Boekenhout St. Forget-me-not on right.

Narnia Farm Guest House

Richard and Stella Sohn
off Welbedacht Lane, Knysna 6570
Tel: 044-382-1334 Fax: 044-382-2881
Email: narnia@pixie.co.za Web: www.narnia.co.za
Cell: 083-325-2581

Narnia combines just about every element we search for in a place to stay. It's definately itself - the style (luxuriously ethnic, but never overdone) is so unusual and so genuine that you know it is the extension of real people, not some pretentious interior design job. Stella (graphic design graduate, potter, mother of two) is one of those people and Richard (lawyer, 'architect' and father of four) the other. Narnia is entirely their creation, a dream slotted round one or two key requirements: the house should have a deck with a clear view to the Knysna Heads; and there should be a big, open, friendly entrance hall. Otherwise the house has grown organically into some mad ship with wooden decks, gangways and staircases, swing chairs, heavenly colours of tropical brilliance ("In a previous life I must have been a Mexican," says Stella), a prize-winning garden, and smaller surprises everywhere. The decking-clad, black-painted pool (of swimming - as apposed to plunging - dimensions) shares the same long views in all directions as the fully-serviced self-catering cottages. Stella and Richard amaze me with their great energy and skill with people, despite holding down so many jobs. *Bushbuck are often spotted by the dam on the farm and visitors to the garden include porcupine, blue duiker, steenbuck, monkeys, bushpigs, lynx and 85 species of bird.*

Rooms: 3 units: 1 family suite with 1 double & 1 twin, both en-suite bathrooms (B&B basis). 2 self-catering cottages: 1 with double, en-suite bathroom & optional pull-out beds for kids; other cottage sleeps four; 1 double & 1 twin with shared bathroom.
Price: B&B: R325 - R500. Self-catering: R255 - R400. Seasonal rates & singles on request. Kids under 12 half-price. Under 3's free. South Africans & stays over 5 days, 10% discount.
Meals: Full breakfast is included for the B&B apartment. For self-catering full breakfast is R75 and continental is R50. Not available high season.
Directions: On N2 from George turn into Welbedacht Lane just before Knysna. Then follow signs to Narnia Farm Guest House.

Gallery Guest House

Lolly Hahn-Page

10 Hill St West, Knysna 6570
Tel: 044-382-2510 Fax: 044-382-5212
Email: gallery.guesthouse@pixie.co.za Web: www.galleryguesthouse.co.za
Cell: 083-309-3920

Lolly manages the happy trick of combining her work as an artist with running a friendly, laid-back guest house in a peaceful part of Knysna. She is a strong force for the promotion of arts and crafts in the town, itself a honeypot for those that can hold a pencil steady. Thus the "Gallery". Her own and local artists' paintings and sculptures dot the walls and cover the carpets in the guest house, one of the longest-running in Knysna. When she can, Lolly steals away to her private studio, handing the reins to the charismatic Miriam, grand-daughter of the King of Lesotho (!). The main room where breakfast etc happens is upstairs and the adjoining wooden deck has tremendous views out over the Knysna Heads, Leisure Isle and Pledge Park nature reserve. There is lots to do in town, what with sunset boat rides, the Outeniqua Choo-Tjoe, sea swimming, canoeing etc and Lolly is very knowledgeable. Best of all she has special private places – sunset spots, music venues, beaches, walks and restaurants – you will only find with her help. The bedrooms themselves are simple, showcasing more local artwork, but cater for all your needs. Choose Gallery Guest House for the irrepressible personality of both house and hostess. *Nine good restaurants within 2 mins.*

Rooms: 4: 2 twins and 2 doubles; 1 with private bath, 3 with en-suite bath or shower.
Price: From R230 pp sharing. Single rates on request.
Meals: Full breakfast included and served from 8 to 10 am.
Directions: From George take N2 to Knysna. At 2nd lights turn left into Grey St, then 2nd left into Hill St West, to end of cul-de-sac. Map on web site.

191 Nirvana

Madi Butler

Rheenendal Road, Knysna 6570
Tel: 044-386-0260 Fax: 044-386-0260
Email: rogue@cyberperk.co.za Web: www.roguesafaris.co.za
Cell: 072-209-2062

Who would have thought you could make a couple of self-catering cottages out of two water reservoirs? Evidently Madi Butler did. (First you have to empty out the water of course.) Her two circular, thatched properties now stand proudly on the top of the hill. The position, at the hub of outstanding panoramic views that stretch from the end of the Outeniqua Mountains, across Knysna Lagoon and into the surrounding forest, was just too good to waste. You won't quite know where to gaze first. Madi's brother Rolf runs Rogue Eco Safaris, which means that you have the option of fly-fishing, forest rambles, beach strolls and open Land Rover tours right on your doorstep. This is one self-catering place where you can be 100 per cent independent, yet still have the reassuring presence of a very friendly hostess just at the bottom of the hill. On top of all the added extras you require (Madi supplies beautiful white bed linen, towels, firewood and other tit-bits) a basket of home-grown herbs, veggies, honey and wine will find its way onto your doorstep each morning. The indoor fireplace doubles up as a braai area which - and this is my favourite part - becomes virtually outdoors when you 'roll up' the walls at the front of the cottage. What's that? Roll up the walls? I assure you it's possible, you'll just have to come and see for yourself.

Rooms: 2 self-catering units, both sleeping 4 in 2 double rooms with option of extra beds.
Price: Basic price for the cottage: R950 - R1,750 (for up to 4 people and children under 13). Add R150 per extra person.
Meals: Available by arrangement.
Directions: Heading to Knysna from George on the N2. Before you enter Knysna turn left into Rheenendal Road. Follow the road for 1.6 km and the entrance to 191 Nirvana is on your right.

Buffalo Hills Game Reserve and Lodges

Tony and Maria Kinahan

Plettenberg Bay 6600
Tel: 044-535-9739 Fax: 044-535-9480
Email: buffalohills@mweb.co.za Web: www.buffalohills.co.za
Cell. 082-771-9370

Fluttering its eyelashes in my direction, an inquisitive giraffe, intently cleaning its face with its tongue, stopped me in my tracks on the road. Fresh from the beach (Plett is a mere 15km away), I was taken aback to find myself so deep in the 'real' Africa of my imagination as I drove through the bushy reserve to the camp. Although more traditional accommodation is available, for a true outdoorsy experience the tented rooms here are a must. Replete with big proper beds, plump pillows and wooden furniture, tents have certainly come on a peg or two. These ones even boast their own spa baths and the shuffling and snorting of a herd of buffalo outside mine made bubbling away all the more memorable. As the sun began to set, I discovered there's nothing more pleasurable than to kick off the walking boots, hang up the binos and re-live the events of the day watching fire-flames dance in the sheltered boma. Here, Tony cooked up a hearty feast on the braai - being a reserve, local game is his speciality - whilst regaling us wide-eyed lot with heroic tales involving rhino scuffles and marauding buffalo. After supper, it was facial contortions all round as we sampled shots from the reserve's very own distillery - its liquors are sold in Harrods. I had a great time at Buffalo Hills and, above and beyond the tents and all the animals I think, this is down to the friendly way the place is run.

Rooms: 13: 8 tents, all twin/doubles with en-suite spa baths with shower over; 1 cottage with 2 doubles and separate full bathroom; 1 lodge with 4 en-suite rooms, 3 with shower only, 1 with full bathroom.
Price: R900 - R1,100 pp sharing. Ask for specials May-Sept. Game drive and guided walk included in price.
Meals: Full breakfast and dinner included. Lunch extra.
Directions: From Cape Town take N2, turn L 4km after Plettenberg Bay onto the R340. Turn L after 4km, then R after 1km onto Stofpad & follow signs.

Fynbos Ridge County House and Cottages

Sally and Paul Falla

Plettenberg Bay 6600
Tel: 044-532-7862 Fax: 044-532-7855
Email: fynbos.cottages@pixie.co.za Web: www.fynbosridge.co.za

Fynbos Ridge is a botanical paradise where eco-conscious Paul and Sally have made it their mission to remove all invasive alien vegetation. Painstakingly they have reinstated a wide variety of indigenous trees and shrubs and created a haven where Cape flora (fynbos) and fauna can flourish. There are birds here that you will only see in the fynbos. It is not just the environment that finds these green-fingered nature-lovers friendly… their guests kind of like them too. They will cushion your stay with super-down duvets, pure cotton sheets and a hearty breakfast in the light-filled, alfresco-esque dining room. If you're self-catering, choose from fully-equipped cottages in bright 'gazania' yellow, warm 'clivia' peach or refreshing 'aristea' blue, all inspired by indigenous flowers. This private nature reserve cries out to be walked in and Paul's collection of ornate walking sticks are displayed throughout the house as hints to get you on your feet. I, unfortunately, only made it as far as the ozone-purified swimming pool (no chemicals here - just a weird-sounding contraption). Follow the natural borders and discreet signposts to this oasis amongst the fynbos. This is the most awesome place to take a dip. Hidden within the depths of a private nature reserve and contemplating the meeting of the Outeniqua and Tsitsikamma mountains, you could easily spend the whole day here languishing with a book. Now where did I pack my swimming togs?

Rooms: 9: 6 rooms in the house: 4 luxury doubles, 1 superior luxury double and 1 self-catering studio, all with en-suite bath and shower; 3 self-catering cottages, all sleeping 4-5 with 1 bathroom & 1 shower-room.

Price: B&B R425 - R715 pp sharing. Self-catering R350 - R545 pp sharing (min. stay in the studio & cottage 2 nights).

Meals: Full breakfast included in B&B price or R65 for self-catering. Availability of other meals dependent on season.

Directions: 23km along N2 from Knysna heading towards Plettenberg Bay. Take L into 'Blue Hills Bird Farm.' Bear L where road forks to Fynbos Ridge.

Cornerway House

Dee and Robin Pelham-Reid
61 Longships Drive, Plettenberg Bay 6600
Tel: 044-533-3190 Fax: 044-533-3195
Email: cornerwayhouse@mweb.co.za Web: www.cornerwayhouse.co.za

Robin and Dee recently moved from my Wiltshire school-town (as it happens) to start Cornerway House, and fantastic hosts they make too. Although new to Plett, they've wasted no time in unearthing its treasure – Robin is active on the tourism board – and will ably point you off to the beach with sundowners or to the Robberg Peninsula walk, an exhilarating experience. After drinks in their English drawing room, we repaired for dinner, where wine flowed and conversation roamed. Dee uses what she can from the garden, herbs of course, but artichokes and strawberries too on the day I visited. When a professional cycling team came to stay they were so well fed they failed to win a single race (… not that professional then!). I retired to my room - wooden antiques, comfy bed and sash windows looking onto the garden – and at dawn joined Ocean Blue to spot whales, dolphins and sharks, returning to a proper breakfast, courtesy of Robin. Dee teaches art in the township and throughout the house there are colourful quirks, to wit the yellow-washed and lilac shutters of the house, the petunias bathing in a bath, a purple TV/sitting room with bright blue cushions and the pink and yellow mohair in the garden suite. I left Robin and Dee among the frangipani, gardenia and orange trees as I wrenched myself away.

Rooms: 5: 4 twins and 1 double; 2 with en-suite shower, 3 with en-suite shower and bath.
Price: R200 - R495. Singles plus 50%. Low season rates can be negotiated.
Meals: Full breakfast included. Lunch (salads & sandwiches) from 7; 3-course dinner from R150, includes pre-dinner drinks & bottle of wine per couple.
Directions: From N2 heading east, turn right into Plett. Continue to the circle and go straight over. Road descends to river and crosses it. Over circle, turn right onto Longships Dr. Continue down 0.9km to Cornerway House on right.

Bosavern

Vivienne and Gerald Dreyer
38 Cutty Sark Ave, Plettenberg Bay 6600
Tel: 044-533-1312 Fax: 044-533-0758
Email: info@bosavern.co.za Web: www.bosavern.co.za
Cell: 082-922-4721

The striking S-shaped waves of Bosavern's timbered ceiling mimic the sea and combine with minimalist white interiors and mirrors to strike a harmonious note with the blue ocean far below. Glass doors lead off the open-plan sitting room and onto the balcony where you can treat yourself on wicker chairs to a regal cliff-top view of the Robberg Peninsula and the white beaches of Plettenberg Bay. Powerful binoculars will pick out whales and schools of dolphins which are (can be!) plentiful in the clear water. The bedrooms downstairs have the same sliding doors that disappear smoothly into the wall and the sea breeze wafts in through a square gap of sky as if from a bright blue painting. The view from your room and private balcony is no less spectacular. Comfort is a priority, with goose-down duvets on enormous beds, fine cotton sheets, a welcoming bottle of Nederberg, gowns and slippers. Vivienne and Gerald are natural hosts, who provide great breakfasts and also picnic hampers for the beach or Robberg hikes, and mountain bikes and canoes for the madly active (a pool caters for loungers). They will also point you in the right direction for golf, and recommend a number of restaurants within easy walking distance.

Rooms: 5; 4 twins/doubles & 1 double; 3 with en-suite shower, 2 with en/s bath and shower. The 4 downstairs rooms and bathrooms all have heated towel rails and underfloor heating.
Price: R420 - R670 pp sharing. Singles + 50% out of season, 80% in season.
Meals: Full breakfast included and served from 8 – 9 am.
Directions: From Knysna take N2. Right at Shell garage into Plettenberg Bay. Turn 1st right into Cutty Sark Ave. Follow road round, then turn right again into cul-de-sac. House on left.

Beacon Lodge

Al and Clo Scheffer
57 Beacon Way, PO Box 1694, Plettenberg Bay 6600
Tel: 044-533-2614 Fax: 044-533-2614
Email: info@beaconlodge.co.za
Web: www.beaconlodge.co.za

This is a small (just two rooms), personal, friendly and involving B&B – and I mean B&B in the proper sense where you share the house with your hosts. (Both rooms have their own separate entrances, mind you, if you want to slip about more furtively.) The patio (for breakfasts, garden bird-watching or reading) has long views out to sea and it's only a short walk to the beach and the lagoon, presumably where you will want to spend at least some of your time. To this end Al and Clo have all beach necessities at the ready – umbrellas, towels and the like. The larger of the two rooms was my favourite (and also the more expensive) with sea views through a huge window and anti-glare solar blinds. There is seagrass on floors, plenty of immaculate seaside white in walls and towels and colour is added in the form of fresh flowers. The Scheffers take the greatest care of their guests. *Fridge facilities provided. Great restaurants within walking distance. Whales and dolphins in season. Closed mid-Dec - mid-Jan and either June or July. Enquire first!*

Rooms: 2: 1 twin and 1 double, both with en-suite bathrooms with showers.
Price: R175 - R350 pp sharing. Single rates on request.
Meals: Full breakfast included. There are good restaurants in town for other meals.
Directions: From Knysna take the N2. Take the second turn into Plett at the Engen 1-stop garage - the house is 600 metres on your left.

Southern Cross Beach House

Neill and Sue Ovenstone

1 Capricorn Lane, Solar Beach, Plettenberg Bay 6600
Tel: 044-533-3868 Fax: 044-533-3866
Email: info@southerncrossbeach.co.za
Web: www.southerncrossbeach.co.za Cell: 082-490-0876

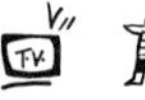    

...and relax. With this dreamy, whitewashed, wooden house at the quiet end of Robberg Beach's long arc, it is impossible not to. Plettenberg Bay is a lively town, with lots of restaurants and bars, but people really come here for the sea, and you would seriously struggle to get closer to it than at Southern Cross. During the Christmas holidays the beach is packed, but for the rest of the year there are more signs of life in the sea. Dolphins race by all year round, revelling in their position at the head of the food chain, with southern right whales often wallowing just in front of the house from June to November. The house itself is just up a wooden gangway from the beach. Wood predominates, with blues and white echoing the ocean. The brochure says 'plantation style', but I would plump for classic Massachussetts beach house. Wooden decking looks across the bay to the Tsitsikamma Mountains to the left and the Robberg Peninsula opposite, which is geologically identical to the Falklands, bizarrely... and a fantastic place to walk. Inside is the breakfast room and living room, and set around the garden on the ground floor (Sue and Neill live upstairs) are the five lovely rooms. Barefoot, laid-back luxury.

Rooms: 5: 1 double, 1 queen, 2 twins, 1 king. All have en-suite shower, 2 with baths as well.
Price: R375 - R650 pp sharing. Single supplement seasonal on request.
Meals: Full breakfast included. Kitchenette available for putting together salads and light meals.
Directions: From dolphin roundabout in main street descend the hill past Central Beach, over Piesang River bridge. Straight over the roundabout, past shops (kwikspar) to your left and take the first right into Longships Dr. 2km over 3 speed bumps turn left into Gris Nez Dr. Over stop street (Rothersands) turn left into Gemini St. Turn Right then left into Capricorn Lane.

29 San Gonzales Way

David and Monica Pickering
Plettenberg Bay 6600
Tel: 021-715-4577 Fax: 021-715-4577
Email: pickers@iafrica.com
Cell: 073-404-0577

This 4-bedroom, upside-down (I'll explain why in a minute) house is ideal for travelling groups seeking more independence. After picking up your keys in town (a short walk from the house) you feel as if you've won some kind of elaborate prize. Letting myself in through a dolphin-knockered door I was instantly impressed by a grand, sweeping staircase and vast entrance hall, the perfect dropping zone for sandy beach towels and inflatables. A massive antique carved wooden chest equipped with giant key, both heavy and ornate, gave the impression of important hidden treasures, the Holy Grail perhaps? Or maybe Pandora's box? Either way I wasn't going to open it (!). As I explored downstairs, a fair-sized lounge with fireplace, bright sofas, rustic corner unit, and books (lots of them), two garden-gazing bedrooms and a contrast of wooden and stone flooring all emitted charm and comfort. Yet it was only when I ventured upstairs that the most impressive aspect of 29 San Gonzales Street's many enticements revealed itself. The main living area, complete with fully-equipped, open-plan kitchen, is surrounded by windows. Quite right too considering the views, which span the length of Robberg beach to its peninsula. Your eyes will never tire of this town- and sea-scape, hence the upside-down arrangement; you may as well spend most of your time up there.

Rooms: 1 house with 4 bedrooms: 1 king with en-suite shower, 2 twins with shared bath and shower and 1 king with en-suite bath and shower.

Price: From R700 per night for 2 + R150 per extra person. R6,000 - R14,000 per week (dependent on season). Sleeps max 8 people. Min stay 5 nights. Refundable damage deposit payable.

Meals: Fully self-catering. If you fancy a rest from cooking Plett has restaurants to suit every taste and wallet.

Directions: Turn off N2 into Plett' at Shell Garage. At the dolphin roundabout turn right then left at the T-junction into San Gonzales St. 29 San Gonzales is the third house on the right.

Map Number: 5

Bitou River Lodge

Sue and Paul Scheepers
R340 Bitou Valley Road, Plettenberg Bay 6600
Tel: 044-535-9577 Fax: 044-535-9577
Email: info@bitou.co.za Web: www.bitou.co.za
Cell: 082-978-6164

For well-heeled South Africans "Plett" is *the* place to summer and its sophisticated buzz can border on the frenetic. Which is why Bitou River Lodge is such a find. Just east of town, it's close to Plett's glass-plated beach houses, bijou shops and restaurants, yet feels a million miles away. Paul and Sue wanted to make the most of the natural environment and have created a peaceful haven for nature lovers. The drive sweeps past a citrus orchard and horse paddock to the whitewashed lodge, which sits on five hectares of neat flower-filled gardens, with pool, chipping-green and river frontage. Behind pepper trees and honeysuckle, stable-style bedrooms have river-facing patios, where dazzling sunbirds congregate. The lime-washed, painted-pine rooms have slate-floored kitchenettes and bathrooms, and sliding doors keep them light-filled. Farmhouse feasts are served in the breakfast room, which adjoins a warm lounge where you can settle into birding books (there are 134 species in the area to tick off). Outside, the liquid-smooth lawn gathers all before it – boulders, benches and flowerbeds – as it slips silently toward the lily-leafed river. While away some time out here, watching busy weaver birds build upside-down nests and lazy ones sway in the reeds, while the ripple of canoe paddles, the splash of a kingfisher and whizz of a fly-reel provide a soothing summer soundtrack. *In season the bay hosts whales, dolphins and seals.*

Rooms: 5: 3 kings and 2 twins, all with en-suite bath and shower.
Price: R295 - R495 pp sharing. Singles on request.
Meals: Full farmhouse breakfast included. Plenty of restaurants in nearby Plett.
Directions: Head east from Plettenberg Bay on N2. Immediately after bridge, turn left onto the R340. Bitou River Lodge is signed on left, 4.2 km from the N2.

That Place

Jo and David Butler
The Crags 6602
Tel: 044-534-8886
Email: info@thatplace.co.za Web: www.thatplace.co.za
Cell: 082-578-1939

This is 'that place'... you know the one you talk about for years after you've been there. "Do you remember the time we went to South Africa and stayed in 'That Place' where we watched the elephants wandering through their paddock across the valley, where we hazily dreamt in the hand-crafted sauna. We braai'd and feasted for hours on the deck, the kids duck-diving and splashing in the waters of the private pool - do you remember?" Jo and David have created a memory-building, self-catering home. And that's just what it is - a home. It's not grand or pretentious, just comfortable and happy to have you. I was shown around by a very modest David who failed to mention that the great wooden table and chairs, the sauna and the three cheeky fish sculptures suspended on the wall (amongst other details) had sprung from his own gifted fingers. I met the dogs too, all six of them. Right from John Keats the Great Dane down to McGregor the feisty Jack Russell. Don't worry, these chaps live next door and won't bother you unless you want them to. But if you want them to...! "You named your dog after a poet?" I asked Jo. "David did," she replied, "he's very into his poetry." Sounds like the perfect man to me - unfortunately already taken by Jo who is equally wonderful.

Rooms: 3-bedroom self-catering cottage let as a whole: 1 king with en-suite bath and shower, 1 king/twin and 1 twin ideal for children.
Price: R600 for 2 people - R1,300 for 3 or more people.
Meals: It's possible to pre-order dishes from a company specialising in Continental cuisine by prior arrangement.
Directions: Travelling in the direction of Port Elizabeth on the N2, 20km east of Plettenberg Bay. At the 'Curiosity African Arts' shop, turn right off the N2 and follow the signs to 'That Place.'

Hog Hollow Country Lodge

Andy and Debbie Fermor

Askop Rd, The Crags 6602
Tel: 044-534-8879 Fax: 044-534-8879
Email: info@hog-hollow.com Web: www.hog-hollow.com
Cell: 082-411-6003

It was a little rude, but I said hello to no-one when I arrived at Hog Hollow and made a beeline straight for the view point, a tree-perforated deck that juts out over mile upon mile of tantalising, tumbling, Tsitsikamma forest. "Don't worry, everyone does that," said Jo, one of the bubbly team of local staff that make this place so special, the same Jo in fact from That Place. Back inside, I ran out of scribbling space listing intriguing oddities: the tobacco-leaf coffee-table, the mounted outboard engine, the sewing-machine lamp. I loved the irrepressible spontaneity of it all. Returning guests suggest a pool? Andy and Debbie make it a 15-metre one. Others want a sauna? That's just been finished too, along with three new forest cottages. They're hidden among the trees down snaking brick paths and their mezzanine lay-out make the view equally good from bed or bath. There's bags of space for kids too and with buckets, spades and bed-time stories they couldn't be better catered for. That leaves you free to join other guests for a communal supper, care of Big Joe. I thumbed through a menu of crayfish thermidor, rack of lamb and pesto-crushed line fish, praying a miracle flat battery might force me to cancel my other appointments and stay the night. No such luck.

Rooms: 15: 14 king/twins and 1 queen, all with bath and shower.
Price: R960 - R1,056 pp sharing.
Meals: Full breakfast included. 4-course dinner from R180 (or choice off menu) lunch also available.
Directions: 18km east of Plettenberg Bay, Hog Hollow is signed off to the right.

Lily Pond Country Lodge

Niels and Margret Hendriks

The Crags 6602
Tel: 044-534-8767 Fax: 044-534-8686
Email: info@lilypond.co.za Web: www.lilypond.co.za
Cell: 082-746-8782

From the moment I first saw Niels and Margret, dashing out to greet me with an umbrella, I was confident of a great stay despite the rain. Their lodge is a monument to mathematical modernity. Straight lines and strong angles prevail and sandy yellow or terracotta walls contrast strikingly with the surrounding greenery of Nature's Valley. And green it is! Lily Pond's lily ponds provide a lush home to a mesmerising array of flora and fauna, most noticeably the frogs, who serenaded me with their croaky chorus as I strolled beside the water and along winding, wooded paths. In summer, the ponds are a carpet of colour and balmy evenings are set aside for drinks and nibbles or even a candle-lit dinner on the miniature island, followed up by a many-coursed, mouth-watering meal in the newly-constructed (equally angular) restaurant. All the doors can be flung open into the sunshine, making you feel like you're dining al fresco. Margret is a supremely good cook - Niels her dashing waiter - and I was treated to mouth-watering springbok carpaccio and kingklip in Thai coconut and coriander sauce. Come breakfast-time and my reluctant departure, the rain was still hammering down, but it did nothing to spoil a cracking stay with a kind and charismatic couple who "never meant to run a guest house".

Rooms: 10: 4 doubles, 1 twin and 1 king/twin (4 with en-suite bath/shower, 2 with en-suite bath and separate shower); 3 luxury garden suites and 1 honeymoon suite, all 4 with en-suite bath and shower and additional outdoor showers.
Price: R400 - R725 pp sharing
Meals: Full breakfast included. Picnic lunch on request and on-site restaurant for dinner.
Directions: Off the N2. From CT take first exit to Nature's Valley. From Port Elizabeth take second exit after the toll. Then follow R102 for 3km and turn right at the sign.

Tarn Country House

Guy and Erica de la Motte

N2, The Crags 6602
Tel: 044-534-8806 Fax: 044-534-8835
Email: info@tarn.co.za Web: www.tarn.co.za

Ah, this is the life... 100 acres of bucolic bliss. Picture the scene if you will: frogs croaking contentedly, birds chirping merrily in the afternoon sun, and a smug inspector enjoying the top tea spot on the Garden Route. From the shade of a pine tree I overlooked the reservoir onto a forested valley and up to the Outeniqua Mountains stretching away into the hazy distance. My thoughts were only lightly disturbed by a lone guinea fowl clucking about in search of food and an ephemeral twinge of guilt as ruddy-faced guests returned from hikes through the foothills of the nearby Tsitsikamma Mountains in time for a fireside apéritif and a hearty dinner. But I quickly discovered that I'd also somehow earned a four-course Erica special. The restaurant enjoys the same views as my favoured tea spot, through the full-length French doors that flood the room with morning sunshine. Blissfully settled beside the ceramic wood-burning fire, I chomped my way through camembert-filled filo pastry parcels, a succulent fillet of beef with a mustard cream sauce, sorbet, rounded off with grilled plums, and all washed down with a local wine from Tarn's extensive collection. The sprawling, bungalowed building is surrounded by a brilliant moat of flowers, and as I slopped around in my over-sized tub, contemplating the king-size bed that awaited me, I realized that after only a few hours here I already felt revitalized and raring to go.

Rooms: 9: 6 doubles all with en-suite bath and shower; 2 twins both with en-suite bath and shower; 1 family room with shower.
Price: R385 - R869 pp sharing. + 50% single supplement.
Meals: Full breakfast included. Light lunch on request. Dinner at Erica's restaurant R170 for 4-course meal.
Directions: On N2, 15km east of Plettenberg Bay, sign to the left. Coming from PE direction, 19km from Toll Gate, sign to the right.

Tranquility Lodge

Judy Philips
130 St. Michaels Ave, The Crags 6602
Tel: 044-531-6663
Fax: 044-531-6879
Email: book@tranquilitylodge.co.za
Web: www.tranquilitylodge.co.za
Cell: 083-413-6091

Tranquility Lodge has been tucked into the forest and there it shyly waits to gather you into its leafy arms. A delicate stream trips happily over pebbles, weaving in and out of giant sweeping ferns and sings its way on into the forest. Branches peek through the deck and hold up tables from which you dine on a storm of flavours cooked up by the "pedantic-about-fresh-stuff" chef. Then there's the beach… ah yes, the beach. Beautiful pearlescent shells (the type you want to send home to your mum, or buy especially to arrange in bathrooms) peek out of 24-carat sand. It's all just a 50m (if that) stroll along a strip of decking. Forest one second, beach the next, a heady transition. Some weak-willed guests, egged on by a funky, enthusiastic Judy, will find themselves on the end of a bungy rope before they know it and plunging earthwards. There are many other activities if you have an appetite for the outdoors. You can go birding, fishing, trekking or picnicking and romancing. Purloin one of the lodge's double kayaks and take yourself off exploring the beautiful lagoon estuary. Maybe a spa and massage is more your bag? Alternatively you can just chill in the simple confines of your calm-inducing room and piece back together your nerves after dangling from a giant piece of elastic.

Rooms: 7: 4 doubles, 2 twins & 1 honeymoon suite; 2 with bath & shower, 4 with just shower & 1 with spa bath & double shower (honeymoon suite).
Price: R295 - R900 pp sharing. 3-night honeymoon package R2,995 (not valid 10 Dec - 15 Jan).
Meals: Full varied breakfast included. Lunch and dinner available by prior arrangement. Honeymoon package includes a packed lunch & dinners.
Directions: Travelling east on the N2 from Plettenberg Bay take the Nature's Valley turn-off right onto the R102. The road winds down the Groot River Pass. At the bottom of the pass turn right into the village of Nature's Valley and follow the signs to Tranquility Lodge.

Map Number: 5

Housemartin Lodge

Bill & Christina Martin
6 Kerk Street, De Rust
Tel: 044-241-2214
Fax: 044-241-2317
Email:
info@housemartin.co.za
Web: www.housemartin.co.za
Cell: 082-782-2087

Sometimes when it rains it pours. At other times there is just a splish-sploshingly giant deluge. Such was the occasion when I arrived at the gates of this old Victorian homestead and lodge and was welcomed in by Casey, the Martin's well-sodden yet clearly devoted-to-the-cause labrador. Though the heavens wept outside, inside there were nothing but smiles and laughter. Unmistakably the heart and soul of the guest lodge, the deep-red, high-beamed restaurant bustled with life. As I tucked into a hearty bobotie, jolly guests on the next table had the right idea, ordering a fresh round of Irish coffees. Bill and Christina, whose School of Food and Wine in Durban is world-renowned (my lunch was superb), bought the lodge 'on a whim' after falling for the charms of De Rust and the taste of village life it offered. And you can try a bite of it too. All rooms are similar affairs with original corregated roofs and Klein Victoria coloured windows decorating each private verandah. Inside, solid yellowwood floors and Oregon pine ceilings run throughout. Percale bed linen, mohair blankets and under-floor heating add a little luxury to the airy and tastefully decorated rooms. After a day spent exploring the dramatic Swartberg, collapse on your verandah, admire the abundant fruit garden, sample some local muscadet and then wait in anticipation for the culinary delights ahead.

Rooms: 12: all queen/twin with en-suite showers.
Price: R360 - R400. Singles on request.
Meals: Full breakfast included. Restaurant on site.
Directions: De Rust is just past Oudtshoorn on the N12 on route to Beaufort West, and is just 1hr from George. Guest Lodge is well sign-posted on main road through town.

Red Stone Hills

Petro and Hermanus Potgieter

Oudtshoorn 6620
Tel: 044-213-3783 Fax: 044-213-3291
Email: redstone@pixie.co.za Web: www.redstone.co.za

The humbling sense of the passage of time pervades this 3,000-hectare veld, whose desert colours swirl with Van Gogh vibrancy. The current Potgieters are the fifth generation to farm this land (ostrich, vineyards, cattle, fruit), but that lineage is put into perspective by the red stone hills. They date to the enon-conglomerate period, formed 65 million years ago when the earth twisted and a torrent of sanguine mud-stone settled and solidified; a few million years later, bushmen hid in the hills' stone pockets and painted wildlife; and in the 1790s Karoo cottages completed the picture. It's all been authenticated by erudite visitors: botanists, geologists and a chap from Roberts who identified 191 birds here, including eagles, black stork and five varieties of kingfisher. But you'll find Hermanus and Petro plenty knowledgeable themselves. We drove out along dusty tracks leading past the schoolhouse his father donated to the mixed community (which still congregates there), through babbling brooks to Chinese lanterns and blankets of fynbos and medicinal succulents. Hermanus will name them all. Petro says he lives in the past, whereas she's an artist facing the future. She's currently planning open-air opera for their natural stone auditorium. Also in the pipeline are geological, botanical and fossil tours. There are many ways to enjoy the scenery, cycling, hiking, riding, fishing… and ostrich-rich Oudtshoorn is minutes away. When you're tired out, your sleepy cottage, with original Oregon pine doors and floors and farm-made furniture, awaits.

Rooms: 5 cottages: all fully self-contained with one, two or three bedrooms and shared bathrooms.
Price: R190 – R290 pp self-catering. Singles on request.
Meals: Full breakfast R55, Continental breakfast R45. Formal dinners or informal semi-prepared braai-packs on request.
Directions: Red Stone is halfway between Calitzdorp & Oudtshoorn on R62. Head west from Oudtshoorn for 28km, then take Kruisrivier turn-off. Red Stone is 6km down this road. There is another well-signposted entrance between foot of Swartberg mountain and Cango Caves via Matjiesrivier.

Map Number: 2

The Retreat at Groenfontein

Marie and Grant Burton

PO Box 240, Calitzdorp 6660
Tel: 044-213-3880 Fax: 044-213-3880
Email: groenfon@iafrica.com Web: www.groenfontein.com

A tiny gravel road twists along the sides of this idyllic valley, beside the river that gives the Retreat its name, while abandoned Cape Dutch farm buildings line the route, which eventually leads to the Burtons' Victorian-colonial homestead. They ran a popular wilderness lodge in Namibia before trawling southern Africa for a new Eden, and it took years to find Groenfontein. It was worth the wait. The view from the verandah, where meals are served (and where I tucked into a bowl of Grant's excellent mutton broth), crosses a valley and climbs the Burtons' own mountain before joining the vast Swartberg Nature Reserve. What with hiking trails and mountain bikes, the opportunities for merry traipsing are limitless. If (when!) it gets hot, you can swim in river or pool, or collapse inside the gloriously cool house. The original marble fireplace and pine and yellowwood flooring remain, but much has been built by Grant himself. He designed the two slate-floor, reed-and-mud roof rooms (away from the house), with French-window views to the Swartberg. Airy bedrooms benefit from simple combinations of yellow, beige and cream. It is an incredible area to explore with kloofs, mountain wilderness, half-forgotten roads, with many animals to look out for. But, best of all, you come back to delicious dinners, welcoming hosts and a truly relaxed household. You'll want at least two nights. Pam and Colin Emmett, who also worked for the Burtons in Namibia, joined the team in January '05, enabling Marie and Grant to have their first holiday in 5 years!

Rooms: 6: 2 doubles & 2 twins (in house), 1 with en/s bath & shower, 3 with en/s shower; 2 king/twins, 1 with en/s bath & shower, 1 with en/s shower.
Price: R460 - R700 pp sharing for dinner and B&B. Singles plus R80.
Meals: Full breakfast & 3-course dinner (without wine) included. Light lunches and picnics from R35.
Directions: From Oudtshoorn take R62 towards Calitzdorp for 30km. Turn R onto dirt road signed Kruisrivier. After 17km keep L at fork as road gets narrower & follow for 10.7km until see sign for Burton's to your R. From Calitzdorp L at Groenfontein sign - 19km to house. Drive slowly.

Mymering Estate Guest House

Pam & Craig Miller
Dwarsrivier, Ladismith 6655
Tel: 028-551-1548 Fax: 028-551-1548
Email: mymering@mweb.co.za Web: www.mymeringestate.co.za

Following a sinuous trail of familiar, musky scents, my nose knew I was homing in on the Mymering Estate long before my eyes confirmed it. And what a picture I saw when they did. For in its sheltered valley swaying with poplar trees, were row upon row of lavender plants, stretching ahead like tightly-knit, violet braids. Presided over by the dramatically gashed mountain, the well-known Towerkop sentinel, this estate is home to Pam and Craig, who transformed this once wild valley into the working essential-oil farm it is today. Old hands at the hospitality game, they decided to combine their new-found calling with a bit of what they do best. Nearest to the main house is an old (dates back to 1930) country-style thatched cottage, now beautifully restored. With its vaulted ceiling, wooden floors, neutral colours, Dover stove and French windows opening onto olive groves, it is wonderfully light and open, yet retains its rustic, country feel. The two suites share a pool and large deck that hovers over the valley floor. These have a more modern feel, with mirrored headboards and swing-shutters separating off their rather opulent bathrooms. With aromatherapy massage under the oaks, the Springvale hike, the vineyard "meander", sundowners, gourmet dinners, as well as eco, fynbos and small game tours, it seems they have thought of absolutely everything to make your stay a memorable one.

Rooms: 4: 2 suites with 1 king/twin, both en-suite bath & shower & kitchenettes. Optional self-catering thatched cottage: 1 double & 1 twin (both with en-suite shower), living room & kitchen.
Price: R275 - R385 pp sharing. Singles supplement +30%.
Meals: Full breakfast included. Meals on request: lunch R75, dinner (3-course, fine dining) R140.
Directions: From Cape town on R62, Mymering Estate is signposted 13km before Ladismith. At T-jct when turn R watch for signs (left) as enter valley with vineyards. From Oudtshoorn, follow R thro' Ladismith, past white church, at T-jct turn L & after 9km, look for signs on R.

Map Number: 2

Rietfontein Guest Farm

Bernard and Lola Nicholls
33km from Ladismith and 45km from Barrydale on R62, Ladismith, Barrydale 6655 Tel: 028-551-2128 or 021-875-5960 Fax: 021-875-5965
Email: info@rietfontein.co.za Web: www.rietfontein.co.za
Cell: 082-400-1092

Boldly going where no man had gone before (I wilfully imagined), mission in hand and hands on the controls, I pressed on through the otherworldly veld that stretched before me, billowing dust masking the tracks behind me. And what a magical destination I discovered… a small, blossom-filled valley in the heart of Karoo country, a gloriously green oasis, teeming with life. Scattered within are five renovated farm cottages all connected by paths or footbridges that criss-cross their way through the pepper trees and reed bushes that divide them. Comfortable and unfussy, many of the beams inside and all of the sturdy furniture have been constructed using original train-track sleepers. Each cottage has its own flame-torch-lit verandah, outdoor braai and fire area. Do make sure you bring everything you'll need as this is pretty well off-the-beaten track stuff. Speaking of tracks, a network of mountain-biking, driving and hiking routes have been specially mapped out for you in the rugged Touwsberg Mountains all around. If that sounds rather exhausting you can just as easily spend your time within the sanctuary of the valley - a spot of pétanque perhaps, or how about a G&T at the fresh-water pool's very own thatched (BYO) bar? That's the daytime covered. As for the night, there's only one place to be… stargazing from the telescope mound into the extraordinarily dark heavens above.

Rooms: 5 cottages: 1 with open-plan room with 2 sets of bunk-beds & double bed with shared shower; 2 with double room, twin room, 2 sleeper couches & shared bathroom; 2 with double room, twin room & 1 sleeper couch, both with shared bathroom & 1 with extra shared outdoor sh'r.
Price: R525 - R630 per night per cottage. For 3 people or fewer R160 - R190 pp sharing.
Meals: Fully self-catering, though basics provided for first morning.
Directions: Signposted off R62, 32km from Ladismith and in the other direction 45km from Barrydale, another 10km from Main Rd.

Merwenstein Fruit and Wine Farm

Hugo and Heidi van der Merwe

8km from Bonnievale on Swellendam Road, PO Box 305, Bonnievale 6730
Tel: 023-616-2806 Fax: 023-616-2806
Email: merwenstein@lando.co.za Web: www.merwenstein.co.za
Cell: 082-377-6638 (Heidi) or 082-922-4846 (Hugo)

The van de Merwes are simply the kindest people you will ever meet. After scoffing a plate-full of Heidi's koeksisters on arrival, Hugo took me for a stroll around their beautiful fruit and wine farm. It was a stunning springtime evening, rows of peach trees were in full blossom and the air vibrated with the hum of busily pollinating bees. Rolling across the valley floor from the Breede River to the feet of the rocky Langeberg range, Merwenstein is perfectly placed to make the most of the Robertson winelands. And once the car is suitably packed with clinking bottles there's everything from guided river trips and golf to horse riding and hot springs to enjoy. Heidi is an expert on the area and will happily take guests to a local crèche she helped set up or on a tour of nearby Bonnievale. She's also a great cook and rustled up a feast of traditional SA fare on my visit. "Here we don't decorate your plate, we fill it!" an aproned Hugo told me. Gloriously full, I slept like a log in my huge room. All four spots here have patios looking onto the garden. Come the morning I was out across the lawn for another birding walk (90 species to spot), savouring every moment at one our most relaxing finds. *Hier wird Deutsch gesprochen.*

Rooms: 4: all en-suite shower including one family suite with double bed and adjoining room with single bed and cot.
Price: R250 - R275 pp. sharing. Single supplement plus R50.
Meals: Full breakfast included. Dinner R120 pp.
Directions: Use the same turn-off as for the Merwespont Wine Cellar, 8km from Bonnievale on the road to Swellendam.

Les Hauts de Montagu Guest Lodge

Myriam and Eric Brillant

Route 62, Montagu 6720
Tel: 023-614-2514 Fax: 023-614-3517
Email: info@leshautsdemontagu.co.za Web: www.leshautsdemontagu.co.za
Cell: 083-529-3389 (Myriam); 083-528-9250 (Eric);

If you set your sights solely on staying in Montagu itself you would completely miss this little oasis of all things fine and French nestled three kilometres further along the road. As I slunk slowly up the long driveway past the helipad (sadly the Greenwood chopper was in for a service), Les Hauts De Montagu revealed itself in all its glory. It is not difficult to see why Eric and Myriam (both Congolese by birth but with years of Parisian industry experience) instantly fell *'tête over talons'* with this place; its setting is sensational. Perched high on the hillside it enjoys expansive views of the valley and its ripening vines. The main Cape Dutch farmhouse dates from 1865 and it has taken two years of painstaking restoration to bring the dilapidated building back to life. Inside, under 21 huge beams that hold up the roof, I dined on food that was fabulously French - garlic snail ravioli and creamy blue cheese with green fig preserve to name just two of the five scrumptious courses. With stomach bursting at the seams I crunched more heavily than usual along the loose stone path past beds of lavender to my cottage. A soaring chimney encourages the fire beneath on cold winter nights, while the huge glass doors allow refreshing breezes on hot summer ones. The glorious outside shower the following morning meant washing in the full view of Montagu… I was thankful it was those three kilometres away!

Rooms: 6: 1 twin, 3 kings and 2 queens, all with en-suite baths with outside showers.
Price: R400 - R550 pp sharing. Single R600.
Meals: Full breakfast included. Restaurant on premises, set 5-course menu R180.
Directions: Pass Montagu, stay on R62 for 3km. Hauts de Montagu on R. Helipad and airstrip also available.

Map Number: 4

Mimosa Lodge

Fida and Bernhard Hess
Church St, Montagu 6720
Tel: 023-614-2351 Fax: 023-614-2418
Email: mimosa@lando.co.za Web: www.mimosa.co.za
Cell: 083-787-3331

Continuing the Swiss influence at Mimosa, Bernhard and Fida took over this two-storey Edwardian townhouse in the middle of mountain-marooned Montagu two years ago now (and counting). It helps that I adore Art Deco as there's a lot of it about: chandeliers, wardrobes, cabinets, revolving bookcases, chairs re-upholstered in daring colours. The bedrooms bear little resemblance one to the other. Some are in the house, others in the dazzling flower garden, with its herbs and vegetables, orchard and black marble swimming pool. Colours are used with imagination throughout, some bold, some demure, but all give a true sense of luxury and space. Each suite has a CD player and all the rooms have a host of little extras: a decanter of Muscadel, books, magazines, fresh fruit, chilled water for example. An old shop counter has become the bar where guests congregate (and salivate) before dinner. Bernhard is a chef extraordinaire who used to run restaurants in Jo'burg and is well known in his native Switzerland. By the time you read this he will be blending his own Mimosa wine, the perfect accompaniment to cuisine prepared using only the freshest of ingredients, many originating from Mimosa's own lovingly-tended garden where more than 200 plant species thrive. I am very happy to be able to continue recommending Mimosa for a special treat. *Children by arrangement. Off-peak dinners by arrangement.*

Rooms: 16: 7 twins, 9 classic rooms, all with en/s bathrooms; 7 with bath & separate shower, 5 with shower, 4 with bath/shower.
Price: R405 - R725 pp sharing. Singles R554 - R1,022.
Meals: Full breakfast included. Dinner (table d'hôte) in the restaurant R145 - R155.
Directions: From Ashton side on R62, Church Street is 3rd on left after entering Montagu. From Barrydale, Church Street is 5th turning on right. Mimosa Lodge is clearly sign-posted.

Villa Victoria

Keith and Yvonne Foster
26 Berg Street, Montagu West 6720
Tel: 023-614-3219 Fax: 023-614-3219
Email: info@villavic.com Web: www.villavic.com
Cell: 083-227-5476

An offer of home-made lemonade (and that's home-made in the lemons-from-the-garden sense) won't guarantee entry into our book, but it's a pretty good start. Barely was I through the door at Villa Victoria than Keith, back from a hike and happily padding around in his socks, slipped a glass of the ice-cold, citrus nectar into my hand and ushered me onto a blissfully shaded verandah. When it comes to keeping cool, the Victorians knew what they were doing and this house, with its high, Oregon pine ceilings and large airy windows, is perfectly designed for escaping the scorching, summer sun. The Fosters themselves are effervescently energetic. Keith has built two wonderfully light attic guest bedrooms, a separate staircase up the outside of the house, a new verandah and a garden shed for good measure. Yvonne has been just as busy. When not working at the local farm school teaching crafts and running the library they set up (she'll happily take you there to visit), she's usually beavering away in her painstakingly-clipped garden. It's a stunning array of colour from which I proudly identified petunias, sweet-peas, lavender and the lemon tree before my thin knowledge of flowers petered out and I sheepishly returned to my lemonade. Please, if you are in this area, don't miss Villa Victoria. It's a true gem and its owners utterly delightful.

Rooms: 2: both doubles, one with en/s bath and separate shower, the other with en/s bath and hand shower.
Price: R220 – R300 pp sharing. Singles on request.
Meals: Full breakfast included.
Directions: From Worcester or Oudtshoorn take R62 to Montagu. Arriving in town on Long St, turn into Barry St. Continue to the end and bear L over a bridge. Berg St is second on the L.

Collins House

Tessa Collins
63 Kerk St (Church St), Prince Albert 6930
Tel: 023-541-1786 Fax: 023-541-1786
Email: collinsh@tiscali.co.za Web: www.collinshouse.co.za
Cell: 082-377-1340

Collins House stands out on Kerkstraat, unusual as a fine two-storey Victorian townhouse among so many Cape Dutch gable buildings. The open-plan kitchen/sitting room is the warm heart of the house - check out the beautiful tile and wood floor - and when I arrived Tessa was in her 'office', an old desk in the middle of the room, creating wire topiary and listening to the cricket on the radio. There are french doors out to the flower garden, and the very large swimming pool and air-con in all the bedrooms are a blessing during Karoo summers. The town is full of Cape Dutch national monuments and snoozes right at the foot of the spectacular Swartberg pass. You must not fail to experience this and Tessa takes guests up there with evening drinks - or you can hire your own scooter in town. Collins House is long on luxury. Bedrooms are upstairs (almost a rarity in itself in South Africa) and you are mollied and coddled with fine-quality linens and lotions. Tessa herself has been with us from the start, is refreshingly outspoken and likes grown-ups who she can have a drink with and get to know. Luxury is one thing, but character is inimitable... and Tessa and Collins House have that in spades. *No children. DSTV is available in the upstairs guest sitting room.*

Rooms: 4: 3 twins, 1 with en-suite bath, 1 with shower and 1 with bath and shower; 1 double with en-suite bath.
Price: R250 – R400 pp sharing. Single supplement R100.
Meals: Full breakfast included and served till 9.30 am.
Directions: On Kerkstraat in the middle of town.

Onse Rus

Lisa and Gary Smith
47 Church St, Prince Albert 6930
Tel: 023-541-1380 Fax: 023-541-1064
Email: info@onserus.co.za Web: www.onserus.co.za
Cell: 083-629-9196

The official pamphlet does a good job of conveying the delights of Onse Rus, but it modestly fails to bear testament to the biggest plus, the Smiths themselves. They fell in love with Prince Albert and the 150-year-old Cape Dutch Onse Rus in 1999 and their enthusiasm for both town and house has not abated since. Guests who have come down over the Swartberg Pass are given a whisky for their nerves and trips to The Hell, a famously isolated community 57km down a dirt track, are easily arranged. Back at the house, the large living room is hung with a permanent exhibition of local artists' work. The five thatched bedrooms all have private entrances, high ceilings, white walls and simple Karoo furnishings. One used to be part of the bakery, another was the printing room for a local newspaper. The house has some history! Outside there's a brand new swimming pool (a thing of particular beauty in such a hot climate) and also a gazebo, a focal point for relaxing in the garden. Here guests are brought food and drink while leisurely hours are whiled away with good books. If the weather permits – which it usually does – you can sit out on the verandah and enjoy fig ice cream in the shade of the Cape ash and Karoo pepper trees.

Rooms: 5: 3 doubles and 2 twins (one twin sleeps 4). 4 with en-suite shower, 1 with en-suite bath and hand-shower.
Price: R280 - R350 pp sharing. Singles prices enthusiastically given on request.
Meals: Breakfast included. Light lunches and coffee shop open. Traditional dinners on request
Directions: On the main street (Kerk or Church St) on corner of Church and Bank Sts.

Dennehof Karoo Guest House

Ria and Lindsay Steyn
20 Christina De Witt Street, Prince Albert 6930
Tel: 023-541-1227 Fax: 023-541-1124
Email: ria@dennehof.co.za Web: www.dennehof.co.za
Cell. 082-456-8848

New owners, but with the same ethos, a genuine Karoo experience. The set-up remains unchanged... an 1835 Cape Dutch farmhouse and outbuildings on the edge of town, infused with great personality. An entrance hall with hand-painted floorboards and bright yellow irises leads to a beautiful tiled room where a zebra-print sofa strewn with pillows sprawls beneath a gilt mirror. There's more Karoo country chic in the leopard-skin armchairs, upholstered chairs and dairy cabinet with cow-print crockery. Bedrooms are in the house or (erstwhile!) dairy and cow sheds with their whitewashed clay-and-straw walls, green doors and gable ends. Mine was just how I like it, creaking with character: 24-pane window, aged yellowwood shutters, worn wood floors, yawning timber ceiling and iron four-poster. The bathroom was just as big, with claw-foot bath, alcove shelving and shower spilling out a waterfall. On a somnolent stone stoep dozed a collection of chairs, a cushioned daybed and a reclaimed pew. Table settings sparkled in the sunlight, beyond which desert hills appeared through the feathery pepper trees. Then there's the Karoo hospitality. Negotiating the tractor in the road, we all joined the fun at the annual farm show before returning to an Afrikaans dinner of local lamb eaten *en famille*. Truly memorable. *Private customised tours throughout E. and W. Cape can be arranged.*

Rooms: 4: 3 doubles, 1 with en-suite shower and bath, 1 with spa bath and shower and 1 with shower, 1 twin with en-suite shower. Also 1 suite with its own sitting room and kitchen.
Price: R250 - R400 pp sharing. Single supplement plus 25%.
Meals: Full breakfast included. 3-course dinners by prior arrangement from R120 pp.
Directions: From Oudtshoorn, head north over Swartberg Pass. Turn left at T-junction into Prince Albert, Dennehof signed on right.

Aloe Cottage

Marlene and Laurie Knowles

Magrieta Prinsloo Road, Prince Albert 6930
Tel: 023-541-1128 Fax: 023-541-1128
Email: aloecottage@aloecottage.co.za Web: www.aloecottage.co.za
Cell: 082-553-2840

Tortoise feed, ostrich toes, buttons, elephant feet, quiver trees and sausages. Ring any bells? No, me neither. That is until my whistle-stop tour of Marlene and Laurie's rather special 8-acre Karoo botanical garden. Normally guests do the tour in more leisurely fashion in the late afternoon, before sundowners and a chance to chat to Marlene and Laurie. But it was a crisp, wintry morning when I arrived and the chill in the air seemed most out of keeping with the mass of desert succulent plants before me - over fifty varieties of aloes in all. What began as a retirement project is now a full-time preoccupation. As I discovered, Aloe Cottage delivers exactly what it says on the wrapper. The pale-green building even cunningly blends in with the surrounding plants that give it its name. Inside, honey-lemon rooms are light and airy with large antique mirrors; one bedroom has a brass bed and the twins have headboards made by a local craftsman. The kitchen is fully kitted-out with mod cons and in the homely living area there's a select library of botanical and birding reference books. The house is built on a hill overlooking Prince Albert and the views from the stoep out to the surrounding Gordonskop Nature Reserve and the Swartberg are in all directions and tend to take the breath away. After a morning spent foraging for new succulent finds, this is the perfect spot to exhaust the afternoon eyeing the finger-like shadows of the aloe-tree branches as they elongate with the setting sun.

Rooms: 1 cottage: 1 queen and 1 twin (extra-length beds), both with en-suite showers.
Price: R260 - R400 pp sharing. Minimum stay 2 nights.
Meals: Self-catering, though breakfast basics (and a few other goodies) are provided and replenished. Restaurants in Prince Albert are within walking distance.
Directions: From the Oudtshoorn/De Rust side, drive down Main Street, turn L at the phone booth on the left-hand pavement into MP Street, cottage is 500m along road on RHS.

Lemoenfontein Game Lodge

Ingrid Köster
Beaufort West 6970
Tel: 023-415-2847 Fax: 023-415-1044
Email: lemoen@mweb.co.za Web: www.lemoenfontein.co.za

Lemoenfontein, in the shadow of the Nuweveld Mountains, is one of those places where whatever your mood on arrival – and after a tiring drive down the N1 mine was ropey - a calmness envelops you like magic vapour. I was suddenly enjoying a cool drink on the vast wooden verandah, gazing over measureless miles of veld and chatting happily to Ingrid about the history of the place. It was built as a hunting lodge in 1850, then became a sanatorium for TB sufferers (the dry Karoo air was beneficial), a farm and finally (and still) a nature reserve. Everything has been done well here, no corners cut and the result is a most relaxing, hassle-free stay. Rooms are stylish and understated with top-quality fabrics and completely comfortable beds. Outside, lawns, a pool, bar and braai area and the veld are all segregated by high dry-stone walls. You *must* go on a game drive through the reserve before dinner - to look at all the buck and zebra of course, but also to be out in such scenery as the sun goes down. And one final thing: dinner when we got back was at first mouth-watering, then lip-smacking. A real South African experience. *All rooms are air-conditioned.*

Rooms: 12: 7 doubles, 5 with en-suite bath and shower 2 with just shower; 5 twins, 2 with en-suite bath and shower and 3 with just shower.
Price: R310 - R350 pp sharing. Single supplement R85.
Meals: Full breakfast included. A set dinner is available every night.
Directions: From the N1, 2km north of Beaufort West. Turn onto De Jagers Pass Road at the Lemoenfontein sign. Go 4km up dirt track, following signs.

Ko-Ka Tsara Bush Camp

Diana Köster
Loxton Road, Beaufort West 6970
Tel: 023-415-2753 or 023-414-3313 Fax: 023-416-1667
Email: info@kokatsara.co.za Web: www.kokatsara.co.za

Drive slowly. Wild animals', announced a sign as I turned into the craggy gorge below the Nuweveld Mountains. On cue, a herd of wildebeest emerged from the crunchy-dry undergrowth to inspect the stranger. Seemingly satisfied, they allowed me to continue into the heart of the 30,000 acres of Karoo veld, where stone-and-thatch A-frame chalets are dotted camp-style around a dung-strewn lawn – evidence of zebra and buck coming to graze the night before. Even my tracking skills were up to that diagnosis. Sliding glass doors open into the stone-floored chalets and a rustic wooden ladder leads up to the kids' galleried sleeping area. Although each has a fully-fitted kitchen and a private braai and camp-fire area, the guests basking by the pool when I arrived were busy digesting the breaded zebra fillet, marinated in garlic, ginger and soy sauce that they'd enjoyed in the star-lit boma the previous evening. As well as guided game drives up the hairy-looking mountain pass, or a gentler self-drive 'game amble' in a converted golf buggy, Ko-Ka Tsara is nirvana for bird-watchers. Alongside rare 'Big Four' birds such as the cinnamon-breasted warbler and the African rock pipit, there are 195 other species to keep eyes peeled for. A camp for lovers of the great outdoors.

Rooms: 7 chalets, all with 2 beds and two singles in the loft. All chalets have en-suite showers.
Price: R450 - R700 dependent on number of people and time of year. Game drives R90, self-drive game-buggy R100 per hour.
Meals: Full breakfast R50, 3-course dinner R95. Light lunch on request.
Directions: Take N1 from Cape Town. Go through Beaufort West. Turn left at Loxton and Ko-Ka Tsara sign (opposite Wagon Wheel Motel) and travel for 7km.

Eastern Cape

Oyster Bay Lodge

Hans and Liesbeth Verstrate-Griffioen

Oyster Bay, Humansdorp 6300
Tel: 042-297-0150 Fax: 042-297-0150
Email: info@oysterbaylodge.com Web: www.oysterbaylodge.com
Cell: 082-700-0553

Here's yet another film-set masquerading as a B&B… this one is for the beach scenes! Hans and Liesbeth have the very envy-inducing run of three and a half kilometres of pristine beach to themselves, the fine white sand of the dunes as pure as it is wind-driven (but for the odd monkey footprint). They have fifteen horses, eight of which are rideable, which roam free on the 235 hectare nature reserve, and the first time I visited there simply wasn't time for a beach ride. So I dreamt hard for two weeks and managed to dream it into reality, returning to experience for real the wind in my hair, salt air in my face and sun shining down… amazing. But there's more: Hans and Liesbeth have made hiking trails from the sand dunes through the fynbos where you'll have a chance to see some of the 140 species of bird on their land and maybe vervet monkeys. I could hear them, but didn't quite catch a glimpse. Your stay is very personable and relaxing with use of the swimming pool and self-catering facilities if you choose. Otherwise, supper could be some Oyster Bay rump steak from their cattle farm or the fresh catch of the day. Come here for the empty beach, the horses and walks along an unspoilt coastline. *Day-tours can be taken to nearby Tsitsikamma Nature Reserve and Baviaanskloof.*

Rooms: 4: all kings: 2 in the house, both with en-suite bath & shower; 2 in separate chalets with open-plan, free-standing bath & shower & private verandah with sea view. 3 also have kitchenette facilities.
Price: R300 - R550 pp sharing, depending on season. Booking advisable, but walk-ins welcome.
Meals: Full breakfast included. Lunches by arrangement. 3-course evening dinner R125.
Directions: From Cape Town on N2 turn off at exit number 632 Palmietvlei and follow signs to Oyster Bay Lodge. From Port Elizabeth take exit to Humansdorp and then follow signs to Oyster Bay Lodge.

34 Lovemore Crescent

Monica Johnson
PO Box 85, St. Francis Bay 6312
Tel: 042-294-0825 Fax: 042-294-0825
Email: dolfinvu@intekom.co.za Web: www.b-b.co.za
Cell: 082-695-3395

34 Lovemore is an unpretentious B&B and an absolute delight. This has everything to do with Monica's warm hospitality and the character of her home, built 20 years ago, though the beachside location is an added bonus. A cuppa appears on arrival and you are then shown up to your quarters, two large rooms under a high thatched roof, with a living area between them, all looking out to sea. The aloe-filled back garden is a bird-watcher's paradise where even the neighbours pop over for the viewing. The front garden has weaver-birds' nests in the trees and possibly Africa's most southerly baobab tree, a tenacious little thing brought down from Zimbabwe by the family in the '80s. And on the other side of the garden there is another separate flat, which can be rented on a B&B basis or as a self-catering unit (but you'd be missing out on an unforgettable breakfast of delicious home-made breads, scones, jams and all...). It lacks the sea views, so Monica feels duty-bound to offer it at give-away prices. With a sweeping vista across St. Francis Bay, where southern right whales can be seen in season and dolphins year round, you cannot fail to relax here. Keen surfers will be interested to note (they will in fact salivate over the news) that Bruce's Beauties are at the end of the garden.

Rooms: 2 rooms in the house: 1 double with en/s shower and 1 twin with private shower and bath; 1 flat sleeping up to 6 with 1 bathroom.
Price: Rooms in the house: R250 - R300 pp sharing. Flat: R180 pp self-catering, R210 with breakfast.
Meals: Full breakfast included for B&B in the house. Flat, as above.
Directions: From the Humansdorp road take 1st right into Lyme Rd South, then 3rd right onto St. Francis Drive, then 5th left onto Lovemore Crescent. 34 Lovemore is sign-posted at each of these turns. 34 is the last house on the left.

The Dunes Guest Farm

Chantelle and Brent Cook
PO Box 25, St. Francis Bay 6312
Tel: 042-294-1685 Fax: 042-294-1687
Email: reservations@dunesstfrancis.com Web: www.dunesstfrancis.com
Cell: 082-324-3484

After fourteen years in the madding metropolis of LA, St. Francis Bay represents a vivid and welcome contrast for Chantelle and Brent: 600 hectares of thrumming nature on the doorstep and tranquillity in abundance. At the end of a sandy road through coastal fynbos the guest house sits surrounded by indigenous garden with thick grass - the kind that crunches underfoot - aloe trees and strelitzias. Brent is a walking guide and takes guests through the farm on foot. He explains what they are doing for nature conservation while pointing out and expanding your knowledge of any critters spotted en route, including zebra and various species of antelope. A two-hour walk takes you to Thula Moya (the adjoining coastal reserve), via bird-watching hides and waterholes. Here, tea, scones, lunch or a well-earned sundowner will be waiting before you're whisked back to the comforts of the guest-house. Reminiscent of an old Cape farmhouse, the guest-house is part of the conservation effort with its Oregon wood floors, doors and window frames all reclaimed from an old school. The theme of comfortable splendour extends into the bedrooms, with their marble counter tops, percale linens on beds, underfloor heating, ball-and-claw baths and French doors, which open onto the verandah.

Rooms: 4: all doubles with en-suite bath and shower.
Price: R475 - R675 pp sharing. Winter specials available on request.
Meals: Full breakfast and afternoon tea and scones included. Light lunches R16 - R34. Dinners by arrangement.
Directions: From N2 take St. Francis Bay exit. Follow signs to St. Francis Bay onto R330. Past St. Francis village and follow signs to the right.

Thunzi Bush Lodge

Mark and Trenwyth Pledger
Maitland Road, Maitlands, Port Elizabeth 6018
Tel: 041-372-2082 Fax: 041-372-1181
Email: thunzi@telkomsa.net Web: www.thunzibushlodge.co.za
Cell: 072-597-4810

Ex-engineer Mark has been building tree-houses since he was 3 (well, as soon as he could co-ordinate his hands with any intricacy) and Thunzi's flawlessly planned and finished chalets are standing proof of his skill. Many personal touches are integrated within; baths wrapped in wooden decking, sinks stationed on sealed, sniffle-free sneeze-wood (strangely enough, a beautiful wood that makes you sneeze when you work with it); and a medley of wholesome games and entertainments that more than compensate for the lack of TV. The completely private cabins, linked only by gravel walkways, peep timidly through indigenous forest onto the De Stades River Wetlands where an abundance of birds have been listed. Over 352 wacky-named species flock to this eco-diverse area where coastal forest, thicket and wetlands meet (try narina trogon, African rail, Knysna lourie and the often-heard buff-spotted, red-chested and striped flufftails for size). Thunzi Bush Lodge is unique in its Maitland 'bush and beach' nature reserve location. Spurred by curiosity I popped the 2k's down the road to check out Maitland's impressive duned beach, the most isolated and untouched Port Elizabeth has to offer. Here you can hike, snorkel, whale-watch, sand-board (oh yes - the dunes really are *that* big), saddle up the Pledgers' level-ranged horses and/or go power-kiting (!). Personally a lamp-lit dinner beneath the star-lined silhouette of canopy would be enough, but I suppose one really should work up an appetite first.

Rooms: 3 chalets: 2 twin/kings, both with en-suite bath & shower; 1 family unit with 1 queen & 1 twin room with en-suite bath and shower.
Price: R375 - R750 pp sharing.
Meals: Full breakfast included. Light lunches and 3-course dinner on request. R90 - R110 for dinner, an extra R85 for private open-air dining experience.
Directions: Thunzi Bush Lodge is signed from the N2. More detailed directions can be emailed on request.

Aquasands

Richard and Deborah Johnson

No. 7, 11th Avenue, Summerstrand, Port Elizabeth 6001
Tel: 041-583-3159 Fax: 041-583-3187
Email: greenwood@aquasands.co.za Web: www.aquasands.co.za
Cell: 082-462-6774

Aquasands is glamorous. Deborah, in red lipstick and linen dress, is glamorous. By the time I left, even I felt a bit glamorous too. She is a food stylist and husband Richard is a philatelist (a stamp dealer - but glamorous too!); they excel in their acute sensitivity to each guest's needs. And their open-plan contemporary home is a repository for an ever-changing, rotating collection of fine art. The guest rooms, with their own separate entrances, are blessed with crushed velvet or silk bedspreads, percale cottons and mohair blankets, red gerberas in fish-bowls and cactus-style soap dishes, an echo of the real cactus garden out there next to the tranquil koi fishpond. Breakfast is served on the architecturally spectacular grey, slate-tiled patio under steel and wood, offset with vibrant splashes of pink, purple and cobalt paint blocks. This is surrounded by a lush garden where palm trees intermingle with indigenous plants and giant aloes... and beyond is the ocean, with safe bathing and sandy beaches a mere two minutes' walk away. If that's too far there's always the large heated saline pool, sauna and steam room within flopping distance of the breakfast table. I met Grandpa too - another asset of the house - a champion fly-fisherman with photos to prove it. Come here for a holiday and not just a stopover!

Rooms: 4: 3 king/twins and 1 queen. All with en-suite bath and shower.
Price: R400 - R600 pp sharing. Singles from R450.
Meals: Full breakfast included. Dinner available by arrangement.
Directions: From Cape Town take N2 to Port Elizabeth. Take exit 751B at sign for Settlers Way, follow signs to Summerstrand. Keep left onto Marine Drive along the sea front until 11th Avenue.

Halstead Farm

Maryke and Clyde Niven
Jan Smuts Ave, Addo 6105
Tel: 042-233-0114 Fax: 042-233-0251
Email: halsteadfarm@iafrica.com Web: www.halsteadfarm.com
Cell: 082-727-0484

When I arrived at Halstead my visit coincided with Maryke's two boys returning home with husband Clyde from a game of bicycle polo. Bicycle polo? That's just what I thought, but it seems it's becoming all the rage with the kids in Addo these days. The Nivens are etching into Addo culture much like Clyde's great-grandfather FitzPatrick did before him. (I'm not supposed to mention that, but Fitzpatrick is the chap that put Addo on the map by kicking off developments in citrus farming.) Four generations later and Maryke has now had her own vision, with the development of the B&B side of things. By keeping it small (only two suites) she provides a down-to-earth and very personal stay. You will receive first-class service where every little detail from car-washing to laundry has been considered. Little notes of history play throughout the apartments... an antique cot here, a piano there and the bathrooms have free-standing baths. The house was built in Provençal style before the turn of the last century and the décor reflects this with its rustic terracotta tones. Breathe in the trimmed tree-lined lawn and muse upon days gone by, nested in your outdoor sofa; or read a book at an umbrella-shaded table. A warm family-based feel presides here, which you can soak up as easily as the sun. *Horseback safaris are a popular way to experience the Addo Elephant Park, which is just 10 minutes away. Big Five experience can be arranged.*

Rooms: 2: 1 luxury family suite with en-suite bath and shower and 1 twin/king suite with en-suite bath and shower.
Price: R280 - R450 pp sharing.
Meals: Full breakfast included. Meals available at local restaurant.
Directions: From Port Elizabeth take R335 to Addo. Drive for 50km then turn left onto the R336. 4.5km down the road turn right into Jan Smuts Ave and follow the signs to Halstead Farm.

Lupus Den Country House

Priscilla and Noel Walton
Addo, near Sunland 6115
Tel: 042-234-0447 Fax: 042-234-0447
Email: info@lupusden.co.za Web: www.lupusden.co.za
Cell: 072-1814-750

Priscilla and Noel have not needed to learn any tricks about how to host. They are just naturally hospitable people who make you feel instantly at home and relaxed. When I arrived, lunch was waiting on the table and with a cool drink in hand I already felt part of the furniture. Priscilla and Noel have been living in their farmhouse for 40 years now – although the land it stands on has been in the family's hands since 1894 – and have recently made some adjustments to make the rooms all the more comfortable for their guests. Their citrus and cattle farm is found on the friendly dirt roads between Addo and Kirkwood. And when I say friendly, I mean locals waved hello to me all the way there! The garden, surrounded by citrus groves, blooms with bougainvillaea and an abundance of other flowers and trees. The tiled swimming pool – the type I am particularly fond of – and an enormous tipuanu tree are two of the gardens' greatest assets, while vine-shaded terraces are the perfect places of repose after a rendezvous with the elephants in Addo (only 20 minutes away). When staying at Lupus Den you can be a tourist by day out in the parks and feel a local when back in the fold. Breakfast includes freshly-baked bread (naturally). A true farm B&B with home cooking – hard to beat.

Rooms: 5: 1 twin & 2 doubles, 2 en-suite bath & shower, 1 en-s shower. Also 1 garden cottage with 2 bedrooms, both en-s full bathrooms & a bed-sitter in between for the use of 1 or both bedrooms. Each bedroom has own entrance & patio.
Price: R230 - R300 pp sharing. No single supplements. Children under 5 no charge. 6-9 yrs 25% adult rates. 10-12 yrs 50% adult rates. Teenagers (13 up) full price.
Meals: Full breakfast included. 3-course dinners (R90) and light lunches (R35 - R40), both by arrangement. Reduced rates for children.
Directions: From PE take R335 towards Addo. Cross railway in Addo, then turn L into R336 towards Kirkwood. At Sunland turn R at Lupus Den B&B sign & follow signs.

Broadlands

Rob Whyte
R336, Kirkwood 6120
Tel: 042-232-0306 Fax: 042-232-0306
Email: Info@broadlandsch.co.za Web: www.broadlandsch.co.za
Cell: 082-445-8837

Broadlands had me won over before I had even negotiated the drive: citrus orchards on either side, an avenue of palm trees, pink, purple and orange bougainvillaea, roses in profusion, an explosion of colour. The sweet aroma of nectar filled the country air. The lake opening out from the house overhung by weeping willows and orange grevillias beyond made my munching on home-made cookies all the more pleasurable. I can imagine the serenity at night, with the lanterns lit at the end of the deck and light dancing on the water. The farm here has been in the family since 1885 and apart from the thousands of citrus trees and the pack-house, it looked quite different back then. Today, luxury rooms with chaise-longues, Victorian baths and an anglicised sitting room and fireplaces provide well-appreciated comfort. Freshly-squeezed orange juice for breakfast is, of course, a certainty. The house is just 25 minutes drive from the Addo Elephant Park and for an African bush experience in the real Africa, Rob will take you up to his nearby mountain lodge for a night spent in the wilderness with sounds of the wild experienced from the traditional boma. Alternatively he'll take you on a sundowner game drive amongst kudu, nyala and zebra.

Rooms: 4: 2 kings, 2 twins, 3 with en-suite bath and shower, 1 with en-suite bath.
Price: R450 - R490 pp sharing. Singles + 50%.
Meals: Full breakfast included, picnic lunches and dinners on request (3 courses R110).
Directions: From PE take R75 and take second turn-off to Kirkwood onto R336. After 10km turn right onto a dirt road for 200 metres.

Camp Figtree

Maryke and Clyde Niven
Zuurberg Road, Addo 6105
Tel: 042-233-1291 Fax: 042-233-0251
Email: campfigtree@iafrica.com Web: www.campfigtree.com
Cell: 082-654-9555

Built following the same design as the colonial buildings at Pilgrims Rest, Camp Figtree is a slice of 1920's history perched remotely and solidly on top of the stunning Zuurberg mountain range. As I rumbled along the winding dirt track, rolls of landscape unfolded all around me like a paper flower in water. A reassuring "not far now…" sign made me smile as I thought of the seemingly endless kilometres of dust I had just kicked up. Sandwiched between the 12,000 hectares of the Riverbend Conservancy to the south, and Addo Elephant National Park to the north, Camp Figtree is a pirouette of dizzying views. The sheer intoxicating peace of the position will have you plopping into the pool to recover your senses. The khaki trousers of this outfit are held up by Kathy and Richard, a couple with a great deal of affection both for their guests and their surroundings… and no little cooking expertise too. Beneath the shade of a giant fig tree you will be treated to top-notch food and drink... or in a traditional fireside African boma. There is a long list of activities available from horse-riding, elephant-spotting and trekking to educated star-gazing. Pine Pienaar specialises in astronomical photography and will happily be your night-sky guide. With antique dressing-table, free-standing Victorian bath and sweeping curtained beds this place is a sophisticated mix of fine things and simplicity at the heart of nature. *Big 5 experience can be arranged.*

Rooms: 6: 2 twin/king rooms, 2 family suites and 2 luxury tents; all have en-suite bath and shower.
Price: From R695 - R1,250 pp sharing fully catered.
Meals: Full breakfast, lunch, dinner and even high tea all included.
Directions: From Port Elizabeth on the N2 take the R335 through Addo. Turn left onto Zuurberg Road. Follow the dirt track. As you climb the hill you pass through a steep sided rocky area. The turn off to Camp Figtree is soon after on your left.

Map Number: 5 & 6

The Elephant House

Clive and Anne Read

PO Box 82, Addo 6105
Tel: 042-233-2462 Fax: 042-233-0393
Email: elephanthouse@intekom.co.za Web: www.elephanthouse.co.za
Cell: 083-799-5671

The bush telegraph gave advance notice of the many charms at Elephant House. Many tourists and other guest house owners had urged us to visit, with a sincerity you could not ignore. It's a stunning house, the brainchild of one night's sleepless pondering by Anne who mapped the whole thing out in her head – a small, lawned courtyard surrounded on three sides by thatched and shady verandahs. The house is in a sense inside out. The drawing room leads to a dining room outside on the verandah (with antiques and Persian rugs). All the bedrooms open onto the verandah too and dinner (advertised with an African gong) is served there on silver and crystal. Evening meals are lit to stunning effect with lampshades made of Tuareg bowls. Lawns, indigenous trees and the racehorse stud (Clive used to run one in Natal) surround the house and when I was there the paddocks were full of mares with their foals. The bedrooms are luxurious with antique furniture, carpets, thick duvets and deep beds; and morning tea or coffee is brought to your bed, if so desired. There are also the Stable Cottage and the Family Suite, which, separate from the main house, retain the same charm, but are just a little cosier. The Elephant House also runs open-vehicle game drives in Addo, a few minutes away, morning and afternoon. *There is now a seasonal on-site masseuse who can conduct treatments inside or outside (Mon - Fri, Oct - May).*

Rooms: 11: 9 rooms in the house; 4 twins and 4 kings, all with en-suite bath and shower. Also 2 cottages that both sleep 4.
Price: Seasonal. R690 - R1,265 pp sharing. Cottages R400 - R550 pp sharing.
Meals: Full breakfast included in Elephant House. Self-served Continental for Stable Cottage. Lunch & dinner provided. 3-course dinners R150 – R170.
Directions: From P.E. R335 through Addo 5km on the road towards the park - you will see a sign off to your left for The Elephant House.

Hitgeheim Lodge

Marietjie and Archie Hitge

Sunland , Addo 6115

Tel: 042-234-0778 Fax: 042-234-0787

Email: hitgeheim@agnet.co.za Web: www.hitgeheim-addo.co.za

Hitgeheim means 'home of the Hitges'. Alternatively in Dutch it means 'big secret', one which I'm about to let slip... oops! This is a mystical place that whispers of peace and privacy, a place where a pair of wild grysbok or 'Bambis', as Archie calls them, feel safe to stroll nonchalantly among the aloes in the garden. The intimate cluster of thatched units show off the local area with dark slate tiles in the bathrooms and moody ostrich-leather chairs. Marietjie and Archie have made no secret of the wondrous views over citrus farms out towards Addo Elephant Park. Hitgeheim is rigged up to appreciate them with outdoor showers, viewing points and windows everywhere. It was far too nippy when I stayed for an outdoor anything, but a deep wallow in the free-standing bath at sunset more than made up for it. 'Langman' - meaning 'tall man', Archie's nickname for Monwabisi, the long-legged, wide-smiling lad that works there - will show you to your room and point out many special features of Hitgeheim including the wine cellar, "one of the best rooms in the house". Archie will happily give you a tour of his vast farm, the only place in South Africa where you can hand-feed pure-bred African buffalo (usually the most dangerous of the big 5) and stroke a zebra. The Hitges will welcome you into both their home and their big secret.

Rooms: 5: 2 kings, 2 twins and 1 queen, all with en-suite bath and shower. 4 also with additional outdoor shower.

Price: R450 - R850 pp sharing.

Meals: Full breakfast included. 5-course set dinner R200 per head. Braais by arrangement. Light lunches also available.

Directions: Heading away from Port Elizabeth on the N2 take the R335 exit towards Addo. Continue on the 335 through Addo then turn left onto the 336. After 6km turn left onto a gravel road and continue to follow the signs to Hitgeheim.

Nanaga Guest House

Malcolm and Leigh Mackenzie

Nanaga Farm, Alexandria 6185
Tel: 041-468-0309/0353 Fax: 041-468-0920
Email: nanaga.farmstall@mweb.co.za Web: www.nanaga.co.za
Cell: 082-730-1701

Trundling up the cow-lined driveway I felt - sad to relate - as if I had achieved some kind of celebrity status with all those many soft brown eyes fixated on my progress. Nanaga Guest House, a quaint, creaky-floored cottage, thrives within the borders of a working Friesland dairy farm, which you can explore at your leisure. Malcolm and Leigh, ex-finance and stockbroker people, found picking up the family farming business a challenge, but have passed both the hospitality and milking tests with flying colours. The high-ceilinged rooms in the original family farmhouse are refreshed with pale walls, offset by vibrant bedspreads and colourful cushions. A free-standing Victorian bath perches elegantly on clawed feet in one room while a corner 'super-soaker' shows off in another. All open onto a cheerful kitchen and lounge animated with throne-like stripy chairs that encourage guests to sit down and exchange stories. For the young and active there are a sizeable swimming pool and a tennis court; for the hungry there is the famous farm-stall. Nanaga Farm Stall is renowned and its produce selection has flourished over its 30 years of trade. Now you can munch not only your breakfast, but anything from the 13 different types of pie (lamb and mint is their speciality, but I joyously indulged in a good ole chicken filling) to a butter-drenched roosterkoek (the Eastern Cape's tasty answer to a croissant). Yum basically.

Rooms: 3: 1 king/twin, 1 twin and 1 double. All en-suite, 2 with bath and shower, 1 with shower only.
Price: R200 - R300 pp sharing.
Meals: Breakfast served at the family farm stall a short drive away. Other meals on request from R50.
Directions: From P.E. travel 50km along N2 to the R72 turn-off to Port Alfred. At the T-junction turn R. Farm signed 200m on R.

Lalibela Game Reserve

Rick Van Zijl
90 km on N2 from P.E.,
Tel: 041-581-8170 Fax: 041-581-2332
Email: res@lalibela.co.za Web: www.lalibela.co.za
Cell: 083-660-6052

A twig snapped, and my eyes were transfixed on the gently swaying branches beneath me. Whatever was down there had no idea I was up here in Treetops, the aptly-named tented camp of Lalibela. That's what I loved about this place, it blends so seamlessly with its surroundings. Camp hostess Cornelia (welcoming fruit cocktail in hand) had promised me on arrival I wouldn't need to go on a game drive to see animals. The watering-hole right below the focal fireplace on the main deck proves a thirst-quenching draw for all the big five and a whole lot more. I decided to ignore her advice and go on one anyway (well it would have been rude not to) and was rewarded with a ravenous rhino, the tiniest baby impala, and until you've seen zebras frolicking you haven't lived! The four camps of Lalibela are so spaced out you never know anyone else is ever there. Treetops promises (and it delivers!) intimacy and luxury with four thatched-roofed, canvas-walled safari tents connected by raised wooden walkways. The larger Lentaba boasts secluded chalets and striking indigenous gardens, while Mark's Camp, with its mass of thatch and wood, is one for the kids. While a big five safari may not appeal to them, the sweet safari they are taken on certainly appeals to me. Who needs leopards when you've got lemon sherbets!

Rooms: 23 rooms in 4 separate camps. All doubles or twins, plus 3 family suites, all with showers and/or baths.
Price: R2,250 pp sharing. Single supplement R1,125. Price includes all meals, all drinks and game activities.
Meals: All meals included.
Directions: 90km from Port Elizabeth on the N2 highway towards Grahamstown until you see the Lalibela sign (tar road all the way).

Reed Valley Inn on Amakhala

Rod and Tracy Weeks

Amakhala Game Reserve
Tel: 042-235-1287 Fax: 042-235-1041
Email: reedvalley@bulkop.co.za Web: www.amakhala.co.za
Cell: 082-783-2506 (Tracy)

Reed Valley Inn just oozes history. The 1806 homestead, complete with wattle and daub walls and wonky floors, sits on the old mail wagon route from PE to Grahamstown, where weary messengers would change horses and quench thirsts. Following in their hoofsteps (but in a car), I found Rod and Tracy had made some slight changes since the farm came into Weeks' family hands in 1898. There was no 'Big 5' game viewing in those days, and what was once the inn are now charming guest quarters, with the original roof and a gaping fireplace retained. I hear your cries of anguish: "But where do we get our booze then?" Don't despair… Rod has merely moved the pub next to the dining room, far more convenient. Before joining Rod and Tracy for supper in the colossal, chandeliered and wooden-floored dining room (unless it's being served under the stars out in the bush) you can soak up the history on display in the pub. Old farming tools dangle from the walls alongside black-and-white photos of the farm from the 1920s, and a selection of pipes and a chessboard await those of a more ruminative disposition. Days of course are spent out on the range looking at animals. The perfect stopover before I was back in the saddle and galloping on towards Grahamstown.

Rooms: 4: all doubles or twins on request, all with en-suite bath and shower.
Price: R1,500 per person all-inclusive with light lunch, dinner, B&B plus 2 game activities. Dinner B&B R650 pp. Single supplement 30%.
Meals: Full breakfast included. Lunch and dinner available.
Directions: From PE take N2 for 60km towards Grahamstown and see sign to Reed Valley on right.

Leeuwenbosch

Bill and Rosemary Fowlds
Amakhala Game Reserve, Off N2 between Port Elizabeth & Grahamstown,
Tel: 042-235-1252 Fax: 042-235-1252
Email: leeuwenbosch@amakhala.co.za Web: www.amakhala.co.za
Cell: 083-383-2921

Leeuwenbosch has gone from strength to strength since the first edition and remains a real South African find offering an unbeatable colonial safari experience. Firmly established as the senior partner in the Amakhala Game Reserve, it is a place full of zest and character, which has steadily been building its portfolio. There's a whole lot more in the game reserve now and with lion, rhino, cheetah and elephants as new additions the 'big five' is complete. Game drives and river cruises for birding and fishing are a must and if you are staying for a few nights a bush dinner is also recommended. Meals are generally served in the Dutch settler's house and remain intimate, convivial and delicious. For their accommodation, guests can either choose the Victorian mansion with its antique furniture, antique full-sized billiard table and antique photographs of Fowlds ancestors, or the newly converted contemporary game lodge. This now houses four luxury rooms, with a wide veranda for lounging. Bill's tiny cellar pub remains an intimate forum for story-telling and a mini-chapel rounds off the Leeuwenbosch 'village', constructed in time for William Fowlds junior's wedding. The world's first stegosaur discovery site (1845) has recently been added to the reserve. All the family chip in to make your stay personable and memorable.

Rooms: 8: 4 rooms in the manor house, 2 twins, 2 doubles all with en-suite bathrooms. 3 twins, 1 double in lodge all with en/s shower and bath.
Price: R1,195 - R1,980 inclusive package of 2 reserve activities (game drive, river cruise, night drive, canoeing, guided walk) breakfast, lunch & dinner. Dinner B&B from R650. Off-season & last-minute specials.
Meals: Full breakfast included and served until 10.30 am. All meals included in the package.
Directions: From P.E. take the N2 to Grahamstown (do not take Paterson) for 67km where you'll see signs for Leeuwenbosch on your right only 1.5km beyond Shamwari turn on the left.

The Safari Lodge on Amakhala

Justine and Mike Weeks

PO Box 9, Paterson, 6130, Amakhala Game Reserve
Tel: 042-235-1608 central reservations Fax: 042-235-1041
Email: safari@amakhala.co.za Web: www.amakhala.co.za
Cell: 082-448-2971

As I soaked in my double bath, candles lit, the late sky glowing pink with pleasure, birds twittering, bush buck barking in the surrounding hills and lions roaring from afar (or so I chose to think...), it crossed my mind that this was perhaps not the toughest assignment of my life thus far. Amakhala Safari Lodge is surely the luxurious way to experience the game parks of the Eastern Cape. Beds, equipped with mosquito nets, are super-comfortable and there's a sofa area inside each thatched hut whose canvas fronts and terraces look onto the valley brush and the waterhole below. The bedrooms and the communal hut are decorated with Cape antiques and furniture carved from the wood on Mike's farm. Mike and Justine aren't always at the camp, but Mnoneleli and Riaan, their rangers, are sure to take good care of you. After a delicious meal – usually served round the fire outside – and a good night's sleep, an early wake-up call takes you to the Addo Elephant National Park to admire its ponderous pachyderms at close quarters. Game drives to Amakhala Game Reserve (now a big five reserve) follow in the afternoon, with its beautiful and varied scenery of bushveld, savannah, cliffs and animals... lots of animals, including the big five. *Day trips to the neighbouring Shamwari Game Reserve are included in a 3-day package. Closed June. Children 9+.*

Rooms: 6: 4 doubles with en-suite double baths with shower attachment and outside showers, 2 luxury with private plunge-pools.
Price: R1,480 - R1,580 pp sharing (winter). R2,380 - R2,580 pp sharing (summer). Singles plus 30%. All-inclusive (meals, local beer & house wine, safari activities).
Meals: All included.
Directions: From PE take N2 for 60km towards Grahamstown. Turn left on gravel road to Paterson and follow signs.

The Cock House

Richard Anker-Simmons and Jean-Louis Fourie
10 Market St, Grahamstown 6140
Tel: 046-636-1287 Fax: 046-636-1287
Email: cockhouse@imaginet.co.za Web: www.cockhouse.co.za
Cell: 082-820-5592

The Cock House offers a friendly welcome and fine dining in the setting of a historic old house in downtown Grahamstown. Nelson Mandela has stayed three times and current President Thabo Mbeki has also been a guest (their visits are recorded in photos on the walls of the bar in case you don't believe me). Former owner Belinda Tudge worked hard with her late husband Peter to build up a business to be proud of, and it is really nice to see a staff who are so obviously genuinely proud to work there. With new owner Richard, manager Jean-Louis and his team carrying on the Cock House tradition of friendly hospitality there is always an opportunity to strike up a conversation in the delightful yellowood bar. The house dates back to 1826 and was one of the first built in Grahamstown. A stone-floored verandah stretches along the front of the house (mirrored by a wooden balcony upstairs) and the interior is full of yellowwood beams and broad-planked floors. I can recommend Norden's restaurant, which offers an international cuisine with a South African flavour and has its own herb garden, using local and seasonal ingredients wherever possible. The home-made bread is a particular treat. The two large rooms in the main house have glass doors opening onto the balcony and the seven converted stables open onto the garden. Personal and fun.

Rooms: 9: 6 doubles, 3 twins; 7 with en-suite bath and shower, 2 with en-suite shower.
Price: R330 - R420 pp sharing. R390 - R480 singles.
Meals: Full breakfast included and served any time. Lunch and dinner available in Norden's restaurant (except Monday lunch). Dinners from R120.
Directions: From P.E. take 2nd exit from N2 signposted "Business District/George Street". Take off-ramp L, turn L at bridge into George St. Continue down long hill into Grahamstown. At 4-way stop with Market St turn R and you will see the Cock House on the right corner.

Map Number: 6

Rivermead

Karen and Paul Davies
Bond Street, Grahamstown 6140
Tel: 046-636-2727 Fax: 046-636-2728
Email: helbom54@global.co.za Web: www.rivermead.co.za
Cell: 082-343-5665

As the heavy gates groaned open, I had no idea what to expect from Rivermead, so efficiently was the property concealed behind them. I parked by the (all-weather) tennis court and climbed the brick path that wends its way through beautiful terraced gardens and lush lawns, past stone steps that descend to the swimming-pool terrace (salt-water), and up to the titanic trees that shade the entrance. From this summit, the views over the trees of the Rhodes University campus and the Grahamstown valley are nothing short of imperious. On the opposite hillside is the 1820 Settler Memorial (I'm told it resembles a ship, but you have to squint quite a bit…). Naturally the most is made of these views throughout the house, with solid, sliding glass doors and private verandahs attached to all the bedrooms. Cool, tiled floors sweep you through the extensive open-plan kitchen, dining and lounge area with their black granite work surfaces and whitewashed walls. Space is in abundance. Karen and Paul have provided the finest linens on beds, marble tiles and glass doors in the bathrooms and there are mod cons aplenty. The suites both have sitting rooms too. But for all the luxury Rivermead is still at its heart a very friendly bed and breakfast. So there you are, that's what's behind those gates.

Rooms: 3: 2 suites with double beds and lounge area with sofa-beds, 1 with en-suite shower, 1 with en-suite bath and shower; 1 double with en-suite shower.
Price: R280 - R375 pp sharing. Singles R350 - R450.
Meals: Full breakfast included. Self-catering option available for other meals.
Directions: From High St, turn R into Somerset Street. Turn L into Leicester St (immediately before St. Andrew's Prep School). Continue until Bowles St. Turn R. Rivermead is signed from here. Map can be faxed or emailed.

Dovecote

Angela Thomas
17 Worcester St, Grahamstown 6139
Tel: 046-622-8809 Fax: 046-622-8809
Email: anthomas@imaginet.co.za Web: www.grahamstown.co.za/dovecote/
Cell: 082-695-4262

From the charming garden cottage off her quiet Grahamstown street, Angela runs a good old-fashioned B&B: very comfortable and very friendly. Even as I drove up Worcester Street, I knew I was going to like Dovecote – joggers, dog-walkers and garden potterers all offered a nod and a wave. Angela, an avid bridge player, was the most friendly of the lot, opening up her cottage to guests simply because she loves doing it. And guests quickly become devoted. Her most famous returnee, Emeritus Archbishop Desmond Tutu, often stays when he's in town – there's a photo of him and his wife standing in the Dovecote garden. Perhaps it's this small garden with pebbled paths and a stone table in the shade of the bougainvillaea; perhaps it's the quiet privacy of the studio-style cottage, with its stable door and small kitchenette; or perhaps it's Angela's delicious home-made baking that lures him back time after time. Big, warm, freshly-baked scones were just one small scratch on the surface of Angela's impressive breakfast repertoire. I surreptitiously held one back to savour later in the day, they were so good. All of this has certainly whetted my appetite for a return visit.

Rooms: 1 cottage with twin beds and sleeper-couch and en-suite shower.
Price: R175 - R190 pp sharing. +R20 single supplement.
Meals: Continental breakfast included. Selection of restaurants in Grahamstown.
Directions: On N2 from PE take first Grahamstown exit signed Beaufort Street. At lights turn left into Summerset Street. Go over three stop-streets and as road curves left, turn left into Worcester Street.

Settlers Hill Cottages

Marthie and Don Hendry

71 Hill Street, Grahamstown 6140
Tel: 046-622-4243 Fax: 046-622-4243
Email: settlershill@imaginet.co.za Web: www.settlershillcottages.co.za
Cell: 082-809-3395

Marthie Hendry's passion for Grahamstown and its history is infectious and will envelop you too if you stay in one of her delightful cottages which were originally inhabited by British settlers in the 1820s. Built in the city's original artisan quarter close to the evocatively named Artificers Square, Jasmine, with its separate garden cottage, and Belhambra cottages creak with charm and character. Marthie's pride and joy is the most recent addition to her collection, Settlers Hill Manor. This Victorian house has been recently renovated and has shining yellowwood floors and big rooms with en-suite bathrooms, plus a rose garden that has upped its roots and moved from the front to the back because of the continuing trials and tribulations of rose-planting in South Africa. The decoration throughout is a blend of original features and modern where these matter (i.e. in the bathrooms and kitchens...), but the notable lack of ostentation only adds to the authenticity. You will be hard pushed to take any of it in, however, if you attempt everything on Marthie's Things-to-Do-in-Grahamstown list, which is as long as a man's arm. She loves taking people around the imposing Victorian buildings in town or to the witch-doctor shop nearby, where a Xhosa herbalist can mix you up some good luck potions.

Rooms: 4 cottages: 2 are self-catering; Jasmine Cottage and Settlers Hill Manor are B&B, and have 7 en-suite bedrooms.
Price: R275 - R330 pp B&B. R200 pp self-catering.
Meals: Full breakfast included for B&B. There are a number of restaurants within walking distance.
Directions: Marthie meets guests at 71 Hill St (which is on the same street as the Cathedral).

Château Blanc

Ann White

32 Westbourne Road, Kenton-on-Sea 6191
Tel: 046-648-1271 Fax: 046-648-1271
Email: annwhite@telkomsa.net Web: www.kenton.co.za
Cell: 083-354-8189

I imagine Ann standing on her balcony, drinking in the Bushman's River that opens out onto the Indian Ocean before the house, the fine, white sand, the turquoise-blue water, the dunes, an intoxicating vision that fills the senses, and thinking, "I really should share this with as many people as I can!" Ergo Château Blanc. She moved here from a farm near the Winterberg Mountains and, as she says; once a farm lass, always a farm lass. She has brought her heartfelt hospitality and baking with her (I had some yummy carrot cake) and she has even secreted a bonsai herb and vegetable garden where you wouldn't have thought one could exist. She has no lawn or vines but just three paces from her house is the beach where blue river meets blue ocean meets blue sky and gives you the best kind of garden you could wish for. In the area you can try out a variety of water-sports (water-skiing, boating, canoeing, surfing, diving), fishing, golfing, horse-riding, or simply enjoy a sunbathe and picnic on the beach. Any notions you may have that an old chateau is cold and draughty will soon be dispelled as you are assured of the warmest of welcomes in Ann's modern, comfortable and contemporary home. Here you are simply a guest within unpretentious surroundings with a light-filled room and an ocean view. 100% personable B&B at its best.

Rooms: 2: 1 double with en-suite bath and shower, 1 twin with private bathroom. Single party bookings only.
Price: R250 - R300 pp sharing. Whole cottage available from R1,500 - R2,000 per day.
Meals: Full breakfast included. Dinners by arrangement. Restaurants nearby.
Directions: From PE take R72 and turn right into Kenton-on-Sea. Go down Kariega Road until 3-way stop, turn right down River Road and continue until the river. Turn left into Westbourne Road.

Oyster Box

John and Jane Damant

19 Elliot Rd, Kenton-on-Sea 6191
Tel: 046-648-2658 Fax: 046-648-2685
Email: jcd@intekom.co.za
Cell: 083-539-5797 or 082-807-8842

It took less than a minute from the moment I walked through the door of the Oysterbox for my bags to disappear along with John in one direction, and for me to disappear along with Jane out onto the verandah. There was no time to waste. With the sun plunging ever deeper behind the horizon, the quotidian solar spectacular was well under way. And then in a flash of fiery reds, and oranges it was all over. "Not all that impressive a blaze tonight," John pipes up having joined us on the decking. He is clearly a man who has spent a lot of time out here. This enchanting couple are understandably proud of their home high on the Kenton hillside. Its towering position provides an unrivalled view of the Bushman's River mouth, and all the comings and goings from the Indian Ocean. Both of the elegant rooms enjoy to the full all that the views have to offer with huge glass doors, and private seating areas. The gargantuan suite upstairs even opens out onto its own balcony. Inside white-tiled floors cool sand-baked feet after a hard day on the beaches, while fluffy, hand-embroidered towels are provided for refreshingly powerful showers. With tummy rumbling I sat down to a dinner of the finest Karoo lamb… but for a digestif I was back outside, unable to resist an extra helping of those superlative moonlit views.

Rooms: 2: both doubles with full en-suite bathrooms.
Price: R250 pp sharing. Singles R300.
Meals: Full breakfast included, other meals on request. 3 course dinner R55. Light lunch R20.
Directions: Turn into Kenton, drive to Ocean Rd and turn R. Continue along to yellow circle, turn R into River Rd. 1st turn on L into Elliot Road, property on right.

Whitnall's

Gail and Mike Whitnall
36 Elliot Road, Kenton-on-Sea 6191
Tel: 046-648-2138 Fax: 046-648-2138
Email: whitsend@wol.co.za
Cell: 072-231-0451

Gail, Kenton physiotherapist by day, farmhouse wife every other week and hostess to her guests whenever she has any, seems to magic out of nowhere a cafetière of piping hot coffee and a selection of the finest cakes this side of the Bushman's River. And she's insistent I try each and every one... and I am sadly weak with cakes. This is a lady who seems instinctively to know exactly what her guests require, especially when it comes to kids (there are board games for the bored, boogie-boards for the beach). This is self-catering where everything can be catered for. Don't feel like cooking after a hectic day of sunbathing and paddling? Gail and her team will come in and do it for you. Can't be bothered rustling up the breakfast? Gail will be there again, serving up either inside on the dining room, or outside on the stoep. I personally would be outside all the time. The garden is a riot of life with an abundance of colour, birds, sundials, lush grass, and swaying palms. Gail and Mike perform no mean feat keeping it this way with Kenton's unkindly winds. The Latin-tagged trees have adopted many weird and wonderful wind-blown poses that work to shelter this little haven, perfect for peaceful days around the plunge pool. Whitnall's may be a matter of metres from the beach, but it would still take more than that to tear me away from this sun-soaked idyll.

Rooms: 1 cottage with 2 doubles and 1 twin; 1 with en-suite bathroom, 1 en-suite shower room.
Price: R200 pp sharing self-catering. R250 pp B&B.
Meals: Dinner on request.
Directions: Turn into Kenton, drive to Ocean Rd and turn R. Continue along to yellow circle, turn R into River Rd. 1st turn on L into Elliot Road. Follow road along, property last house on left.

Sibuya Game Reserve

Nick Fox
39 Eastbourne Road, Kenton-on-Sea 6191
Tel: 0861-SIBUYA (742892) Fax: 046-648-2114
Email: reservations@sibuya.co.za Web: www.sibuya.co.za
Cell: 083-648-2020

Nick and the team greeted me quayside in Kenton, then transported me upstream on a wholly exciting journey into the wild. I felt like one of those early adventurer-pioneer chappies. You may be only half an hour from Kenton, but you'll think you're in another, pretty idyllic world of singing birds, splashing fish and rustling leaves. The flat-bottomed boat will take you to your new home, an intimate tented camp where just four tents, on stilts and protected above with a wooden roof, are scattered among the trees, sharing the space with hammocks and hanging chairs. Beds inside are enticing with crisp, white cotton sheets and oh-so-snug green-fleece blankets for chillier nights. But Sibuya is all about being outside, even when it comes to your en-suite bathroom. A flight of stairs takes you up into a wood-decked affair where you can shower and wash your teeth while looking into the bush and wondering if anything is watching you watching them. By night the camp relaxes in the mellow glow of paraffin lamps and roaring log fires, while a fine feast of game is prepared for you. Nights will pass star-gazing and strange-sound-identifying, while days can be spent on game drives or messing about on the river. A unique reserve experience!

Rooms: 4 tents: all double or twin, and 3 with en-suite shower, 1 with en-suite bath and separate shower.
Price: R1,150 pp sharing. Singles R1,650. Price includes boat transfers, game drives, all meals and drinks.
Meals: Breakfast, picnic lunch and dinner included.
Directions: 120km from Port Elizabeth & 150km from East London on R72. Turn into Kenton and follow the signs.

Coral Guest Cottages

Cynthia and Alf Kleinschmidt

Jack's Close, Port Alfred 6170
Tel: 046-624-2849 Fax: 046-624-2849
Email: cynthia@coralcottages.co.za Web: www.coralcottages.co.za
Cell: 082-692-3911

Staying in Cynthia and Alf's settler's cottage was like being transported back in time, a charming old structure with an unlikely and rather romantic history. Once upon a time, in the mid-1800s it housed the consulting rooms for a Doctor Jones-Phillipson, having previously been transported to Port Elizabeth from England, then to Grahamstown and then by ox-wagon express to Port Alfred. Our own Alfred, of the Cynthia-Alf variety, discovered the cottage in disrepair and decided to dismantle it, treat the wood and resurrect it body and soul in their front yard. Quite a mission but well worth the effort! So thank you Alf for your entrepreneurial spirit. Now guests can sleep in a well-travelled Oregon pine cottage, which is quite an exclusive experience. Cynthia's daily and delicious contribution is breakfast, her speciality in both variety and eclectic style. She can cook different breakfasts every day for two weeks, so what you have depends on her creative inspiration on the morning in question. I sampled her eggs benedict africano with cheese sauce and grated biltong, but you may get her crêpe speciality with potatoes, mushroom, bacon and sausage. The beaches nearby are not to be missed so make sure you allow enough time to enjoy them in a relaxed way.

Rooms: 2: 1 twin and 1 double, both with shower.
Price: R225 (winter) - R265 (summer) pp sharing. Singles +R40.
Meals: Full breakfast included.
Directions: Off the R72 in Port Alfred.

The Lookout

Louise and Alan Corrans

24 Park Rd, PO Box 2809, Port Alfred 6170
Tel: 046-624-4564 Fax: 046-624-4564
Email: info@thelookout.co.za Web: www.thelookout.co.za
Cell: 073 273 2912

It was only after I returned to the office that I found Louise's answer-phone message inviting me to join her and Alan for lunch. Shame.... I know I would have eaten well. And also as it turned out, I'd only limited time to explore everything the Corrans have done with their perfectly positioned pad. After sifting through the old photos, I can see that they've done a lot. Not for nothing is The Lookout so named, with a sight line down to the Indian Ocean over the head of a toy town Port Alfred fragmented over its harbour islands below. Each of the alluring suites downstairs opens directly onto the garden, where a royal palm and an aloe bainesii sway above the pool. While the Corrans may be up in the world (they live on the 1st floor), that doesn't mean they have forgotten about you down below. In fact they'll come knocking on your door every morning with your breakfast basket, a system Louise and Alan have now perfected. Although each guest has their own tiled verandah from which to soak up the views, I can recommend a natter around the sun-baked braai area, where patio doors lead through to the pub where I would be on 'The Lookout' for a cooling drink to match a magnificent sunset.

Rooms: 3 units: 1 king with en-suite shower; 1 twin with private bath and shower and open plan dining/kitchen/lounge area; 1 twin with en-suite shower and open plan dining/kitchen/lounge area. All have sofa-beds.
Price: R220 - R280 pp low season. R330 - R400 pp high season. Extra guests on request.
Meals: Full breakfast included. Other meals self-catering.
Directions: R72 from PE into Port Alfred. Turn first left after bridge into Pascoe Crescent, then immediate right into Park Road. House is signposted on the right.

Sheilan House

Joan Buckley & John Beaumont
27 Prince's Ave, Port Alfred 6170
Tel: 046-624-4076 Fax: 046-624-4722
Email: mikeb@sheilanhouse.co.za Web: www.sheilanhouse.co.za
Cell: Joan 082-894-1851; Mike 082-895-9671

I've never really thought of myself as a trend-setter," a beaming Joan divulges as she welcomes me through the door of ultra-modern Sheilan House. Instantly my eyes are drawn upwards to an intricate web of white-painted beams fanning out around the roof. The architect has done a stunning job of converting what was just a humble bungalow into this super-cool enclave and now similar designs are beginning to pop up all over Port Alfred. High vaulted ceilings dominate throughout, while an abundance of glass and light heightens the sense of serenity. The bedrooms too have a Zen-like quality with their white walls, white tiled floors, and in some, white wardrobes and white furniture - minimalist and peace-inducing without ever being Spartan. Pastel-shaded duvets add the only colour they need. Bathrooms are big, the showers enormous, while each of the four rooms benefit from their own private gardens for those times when you just want to get away from it all. Breakfast the following morning provided an ample opportunity to sample Joan's speciality, springbok carpaccio. As I munched mouth-watering morsels in the terracotta-tiled, glass-walled dining room, I looked out across the neat garden to an alluringly blue swimming pool. A kingfisher sat on the decking calling a mate for a quick dip or so I understood it. If the weather had been nicer, I would have happily obliged.

Rooms: 4: 3 doubles & 1 twin. All en-suite, 2 with bath and separate shower, 2 with shower only.
Price: R350 - R450 pp sharing. Singles on request.
Meals: Full breakfast included. 2-course evening meal on request from R60.
Directions: On the R72 cross Port Alfred Bridge heading in Port Elizabeth direction and turn L into Wesley Hill. Then take 3rd turning to R into Prince's Ave. Pass two streets on left and property on left.

Fort D'Acre Reserve

Mel and Rory Gailey

Fish River Mouth, Port Alfred 6170
Tel: 046-675-1091 Fax: 046-675-1095
Email: mel@fairgame.co.za Web: www.fortdacre.com
Cell: 082-559-8944

When the sun's gone down, you're running late and, whether you admit it or not, are ever so slightly lost, some sort of a signal is much appreciated. On cue, the Fish River Lighthouse that stands in the middle of the reserve lit up the night sky like a beacon to guide me in (or so I like to think). The lodge, where guests stay, is a mammoth thatched affair, entered via heavy, sliding glass doors from a pretty redbrick garden path. It's immediately obvious that this was a lodge designed for hunters: the rustically tiled floor is strewn with animal skins and the local taxidermist has not been idle. Even the great central hearth is framed by elephant tusks. A galleried landing overlooks the communal lounge, where a cavernous leather sofa almost prevented me from making it to bed that night. The next morning I was able to see the Fort D'Acre Reserve in all its glory. Opening the curtains in the bay windows that dominated my bedroom, I looked beyond the milling herd of zebra to the Great Fish River stretching out below me towards the Indian Ocean and the reserve's private stretch of beach. I enjoyed my breakfast on the sun-drenched terrace, but the open-walled, thatched, outside bar could be equally appealing. Oh, and just in case you were wondering, the fort was built by the British during the wars against the Xhosa. *Guided horse rides through the reserve and onto the beach now available at additional cost.*

Rooms: 4: 3 doubles and 1 twin, all with en-suite showers.
Price: R450 pp sharing. Game drives an optional extra.
Meals: Full breakfast included. Dinner by arrangement or selection of restaurants nearby.
Directions: On R72 20km from Port Alfred towards East London. First turning to right after Great Fish Point Lighthouse.

Umngazi River Bungalows & Spa

Terry and Tessa Bouwer
PO Box 75, Port St Johns 5120
Tel: 047-564-1115/6/7 Fax: 047-564-1210
Email: stay@umngazi.co.za Web: www.umngazi.co.za
Cell: 082-321-5841

The wild coast may be South Africa's most spectacular and yet least touristy region with its rocky coastline, indigenous forests, secluded coves and many river mouths. And all this is on your doorstep at Umngazi, a lively family holiday resort where the only time you will spend indoors will be to sleep and eat. The relaxed and informal lodge is on the banks of the Umngazi Estuary so you can choose between swimming in the pool, the river or the sea, fishing off rocks or boats, and walking in the forests. Bird-watching cruises are also organised for sunset. Ferries transport guests over to the beach from a river jetty. Meanwhile, back at home you will be missing out on tennis, snooker and table tennis. I guarantee that a week here, however lazy you are, will see the colour back in your cheeks and a bit of muscle on the arms and legs. And your sense of time will go haywire. Children are well catered for with trampoline, fort, sandpit and designated dining room. You have a choice of sea-, river- or garden-facing cottages and there are three honeymoon suites with working fireplaces, sliding doors onto private patios, sea views, a big spa bath and double outside shower. Weekly fly-in packages are available Friday to Friday from Durban where you fly at 500 feet above sea level along the beautiful coastline - a wonderful experience to start a holiday. *The new spa offers (among other things), Swedish massage and a peppermint sea twist wrap while you look out on 180-degree views of the Indian Ocean.*

Rooms: 65 bungalows: twin or double on request, all have en/s bathrooms, most with baths & showers.
Price: R430 – R660 pp sharing all-inclusive. Fly-in package R5,600 – R6,570 pp includes flight, 7 nights, all meals & transfers from Virginia Airport. Pick-up/transfer from Durban Int R200 pp.
Meals: All included.
Directions: From the south, Umngazi lies 90km due east of Umtata. From the north, via Flagstaff and Lusikisiki to Port St Johns on a tarred road. There is also a transfer service from Umtata and a private flight service between Durban and Port St Johns.

Lelieklooof Valley of Art

Dries and Minnie De Klerk
Burgersdorp 9744
Tel: 051-653-1240 Fax: 051-653-1240
Email: sanart@intekom.co.za

What a place! Magnificent Bushman art and high-altitude wilderness to nourish the soul; log fires and home-cooked meals to look after earthier parts. Dries and Minnie have landed on their feet at Leliekloof, a farm adjoining their own property which they acquired a few years ago. The river here has chiselled a tortuous gorge through the sandstone and ironstone hills and the many caves host thirteen remarkable sites of Bushman art. Dries took me for an exhilarating morning drive and we visited two of them, Eland and Dog Caves. The quality of the paintings is superb, Dries a full reservoir of information about both the images and artists. There is also a 2-day scenic 19km hike around the valley, and a large dam for canoeing and trout fishing. Art apart, the countryside will extract from you superlatives you never knew you had. Single guests usually stay, for reasons of sociability, at the De Klerks' farm, while others have the run of Leliekloof House nearer the valley. The magnificent main room is 22 metres long, with sitting area, yellowwood bar, fireplace and huge antique Oregon pine dining table. You can self-cater, but given the stellar quality of Minnie's food (and the variety of things to do), I strongly suggest that you ask her to prepare your meals. Two nights minimum stay recommended. There is also a two-day scenic 19-km hike around the valley, and two large dams for canoeing and trout fishing.

Rooms: 1 farmhouse with 3 bedrooms (2 dbl & 1 twin, 2 en-suite bath, 1 en-s shower) plus a loft sleeping 4; 1 extra bedroom with bath & shower. 1 booking only at a time.
Price: Full board rates: R380 - R440 (for 3 or more). R400 - R460 for 2 people. Self-catering & B&B options available. Singles on request. 1 couple/group accepted at a time.
Meals: Breakfast, lunch and dinner included. Dinner is 3 courses including bottle of wine.
Directions: 6km south of Jamestown on N6 turn towards Burgersdorp. Turn R after 10km. After another 5.5km fork R & Leliekloof is another 1km. Map can be faxed.

Map Number: 6

The Stagger Inn

Robin and Berta Halse & Sean and Ann Bryan
Carnarvon Estate, Sterkstroom 5425
Tel: 045-966-0408 Fax: 045-966-0408
Email: carnarvon@worldonline.co.za
Cell: 082-445-1032

So nice to arrive somewhere and instantly know that the people there will make your stay all the more enjoyable. I wasn't even asked if I'd like lunch… it was assumed and presented. Tea? That came too. Smiling, warm faces are a given at the Stagger Inn and all three generations of the family that help on the estate exude a contagious enthusiasm for it. So here you are in the great outdoors with 25,000 acres of pristine wilderness at your beck and call. You can bird-watch, fish for rainbow trout and large-mouth bass, swim in the weirs of clear spring water, go boating on the dams, do some clay pigeon shooting and spot some of the fifteen species of antelope on game-drives (also lynx, jackal, genets, black eagles, fish eagles and vultures). Or you can just walk among the indigenous shrubs and wild flowers. Ruddy-faced and hungry from the fresh air and activities, guests cosy up by the blazing log fire before a hearty, healthy dinner of home-cooked produce fresh from the farm (cows, sheep, pigs, sawmill and a dairy). And then to bed, hunting-lodge-style in farmhouses with comfortable (rather than luxurious) rooms for a well-needed night's sleep. As I discovered in the morning, the quality of light up here is a phenomenon, and the views breathtaking. The rolling ridge-country and grassy plains reach as far as the eye can see Make sure you stay for long enough.

Rooms: 6: 2 doubles, 2 twins with en-suite bathrooms; 2 doubles for self-catering with en-suite shower.
Price: R300 – R400 pp dinner B&B.
Meals: Full breakfast and dinner included.
Directions: From Queenstown, take N6 for 50km and turn right on the R344 towards Dordrecht and follow signs to Stagger Inn (gravel road for 13km).

Redcliffe Guest Farm

Johnnie and Carol Morgan
PO Box 137, Tarkastad 5370
Tel: 045-848-0152 Fax: 045-848-0152
Email: info@dtours.co.za Web: www.dtours.co.za

Johnnie and Carol kindly adopted me for the night when I couldn't - or rather didn't want to - leave their unspoilt country idyll in the depths of the Winterberg Mountains. Not many tourists have yet found the Winterberg, but surely it is only a matter of time. This is an escape from everything apart from cows, sheep, birds and the natural environment that supports them. The simplest way to enjoy the area is to go for a hike across the rolling grassland hills. The gorge on a neighbouring farm is, I think, the most spectacular spot I have been privy to in South Africa and it goes virtually unvisited. The plateau folds in on itself and plummets hundreds of metres down, waterfalls dropping from terrace to terrace. Or you can go swimming, trout-fishing, mountain-biking, horse-riding, bird-watching, or play tennis back at the house. Carol may cook you her speciality stuffed leg of lamb for dinner and Johnnie will happily show you around his shearing shed. He is especially proud of his merinos whose pure, white wool is used to make smart Italian suits. Guests here have all the space they could need both outside and inside the five-bedroom farmhouse, including a light-filled sun room. A real home and the area of highland farms is still to be discovered even by the more adventurous overseas traveller.

Rooms: 1 farmhouse: 1 double and 4 twins, 3 en-suite and 2 with private bathrooms.
Price: R525 pp lunch, dinner, bed and breakfast minimum 2 people, R150 pp self-catering minimum 3 people. Phone to discuss group prices.
Meals: Breakfast, lunch and dinner on request. Self-catering also an option.
Directions: On R344 between Tarkastad and Adelaide. Directions faxed or emailed.

Cavers Country Guest House

Kenneth and Rozanne Ross
R63, Bedford 5780
Tel: 046-685-0619 Fax: 046-685-0619
Email: ckross@intekom.co.za Web: www.cavers.co.za
Cell: 082-579-1807

I can't be the first to call Cavers an oasis, but it is irresistible. There in the distance a stand of tal oaks shimmers unconvincingly in the haze. And then suddenly you are among well-watered anc mature gardens, an Eden of lawns and vivid flowers. The fine stone, ivy-encased farmhouse was built in 1840 and has been in Ken's family for four generations. The bedrooms, with wooder floorboards, high ceilings and voluptuously draped windows, are refined and elegant. From one of the upstairs rooms I got an impression of living in the trees with an hadeda nesting at eye leve and yellow orioles twittering and fluttering about. Two grand upstairs rooms with pressed-meta ceilings have balconies overlooking the profusion of flowers below. The thatched cottage also has long views over the lawns and up to the Winterberg Mountains. Rozanne is a maestro in the kitchen, cooking with fresh produce from the farm and the surrounding area and all her meals are mouth-watering feasts. The memory of that salmon cheesecake is even now a Pavlovian trigge that gets the mouth watering. There is a clay tennis court, hiking and riding or even cricket on the magnificent ground nearby. Swimming is in the pool or a big round reservoir.

Rooms: 5: 4 rooms in the manor house: 2 twins & 2 king/twins, 2 en-suite shower, 1 bath, 1 shr & bath; 1 cottage has 1 twin & 1 double sharing bath & shower
Price: R300 – R450 pp sharing.
Meals: Full breakfast included. Dinner and light lunches on request.
Directions: 8km from Bedford on the R63 towards Adelaide, turn left at the sign and follow the dirt road for 8km.

Die Tuishuise

Sandra Antrobus
36 Market St, Cradock 5880
Tel: 048-881-1322 Fax: 048-881-5388
Email: tuishuise@eastcape.net Web: www.tuishuise.co.za

Unique accommodation indeed! Sandra has a raptor's eye for historic detail, laced with an antique dealer's nose and the heart of an interior designer - unparalleled in my experience of South Africa. There are 25 houses along Market Street, all antiquely furnished to reflect different styles, eras and professions. The houses were once lived in by bank managers, teachers, wagon makers etc, and you step into their 19th-century shoes when you stay - although the bathrooms, perhaps, retain a little more modernity. Each house is an antique shop in its own right, but modern comforts include fans, heaters and fireplaces. I was lucky enough to visit them all and it is no exaggeration to say I was struck dumb - reason enough for Sandra to have gone to the effort (some might feel). The hotel, a Victorian manor at the end of the street, has a further 19 rooms similarly done out in the style of the time and sherry is served in the drawing room before buffet dinners (my Karoo lamb was delicious). Sandra and her daughter Lisa are dedicated to presenting South African history in a way you can touch and feel. They do cultural performances epitomising the Xhosa and Afrikaner culture - ask in advance. *Closed 24th & 25th December.*

Rooms: 25 restored 19th-century houses, each rented out as one 'unit'. There is also a hotel.
Price: From R270 - R300 pp sharing. No single supplement.
Meals: Breakfast served 7 - 9 am in summer, 7 - 10 am in winter. Traditional dinners available.
Directions: From PE take N10. When you arrive in Cradock at 4-way stop turn left into Market St. Die Tuishuise is 3rd block on left.

Wheatlands

Diana and Arthur & Kirsten and David Short
Route R75, PO Box 325, Graaff-Reinet 6280
Tel: 049-891-0422/4 Fax: 049-891-0422
Email: wheatlands@wam.co.za Web: www.wheatlands.co.za
Cell: 082-414-6503 or 072-251-9022

Guests at Wheatlands are thoroughly spoilt. I had read that the main house had been built on the profits of ostrich feathers in 1912 (a so-called 'feather palace'). I'm not sure why, but this led me to expect a humble farmhouse… and to get my shoes muddy finding it! But no. I found instead a gigantic manor house with a façade dominated by three extravagant gables. The house, designed by Charles Bridgeman, mingles Cape Dutch and Edwardian styles with a lovely white-pillared verandah at the back and then a green lake of lush lawn where heritage roses grow like weeds. Park your wagon (or whatever you are driving these days) in the huge sandy courtyard and enter a long, cool, wood-panelled hall, an instant pleasure as you leave the desert heat of the Karoo. It's an appropriate home for the piano, all the antique furniture and the Persian rugs. The corridors are lined with books, there is a snug for reading and guest bedrooms are not converted outhouses, but an integral, lived-in part of the house. There are wonderful wanders to be had in the revelation of a back garden. The Shorts are astoundingly nice people, brimful of the hostly arts. Diana and Kirsten cook delicious dinners, which are eaten at one large oak table. Arthur, meanwhile, is a serious wool and mohair farmer and cricketer… they even have their own ground.

Rooms: 3: all twins, 2 with en-suite bath and shower, 1 with private bath and shower.
Price: R300 - R350 pp sharing.
Meals: Full breakfast and dinner included (Karoo lamb a speciality).
Directions: 42km on the R75 south of Graaff-Reinet, Wheatlands turn-off to the left, 8km up a gravel road.

Abbotsbury

Sue and Gordon Scott
PO Box 551, Graaff-Reinet 6280
Tel: 049-840-0201 Fax: 049-840-0201
Email: abbotsbury@cybertrade.co.za Web: www.abbotsbury.co.za
Cell: 072-486-8904

A three-kilometre drive on a dirt track takes you up into the land that time forgot, a small, perfectly-formed valley that the Scotts call home. Sue and Gordon are there to greet you in their improbably lush and well-tended garden, which seems immune to the Karoo sun's forbidding glare. An ingenious old water furrow running down from the dam must take some of the credit for this, although a fence has also been added to protect the garden's aloes and roses from midnight-feasting kudus... of which there are plenty despite the privations. Gordon, in fact, has a game-viewing vehicle (a battered old Landcruiser) and will take you in search of the ten species of antelope and other Karoo wildlife on the farm - or you can hike up the mountains yourself. Back at base, guests either stay in a lovely old cottage, circa 1880; or a twin-bedded suite attached to the Scotts' own, even older house; or the new luxury garden suite with its sweeping views of the garden and wild valley in the distance. None lack for character, with polished yellowwood floors, restored old furniture and photographic prints and artwork on the walls. Sue takes your supper orders when you book so as to have a fresh farm supply at the ready (springbok and Karoo lamb specialities) and you are served in your own private dining room with solid silver cutlery and bone china. Breakfasts are also a royal affair. *Nearby: the sculpture garden of the Owl House, historic Graaff-Reinet, and the awe-inspiring views of the Valley of Desolation.*

Rooms: 3 units: 1 cottage with double & en-suite twin and separate bath with shower attachment; 1 cottage with king and en-suite shower; 1 twin suite with en-suite bath and shower.
Price: R255 - R320 pp sharing B&B.
Meals: Full breakfast included. 3-course dinner on request: R75 - R90.
Directions: 27km north of Graaff-Reinet on N9, turn left onto 3km farm track to Abbotsbury.

Cypress Cottages

Hillary Palmé
76 Donkin St, Graaff-Reinet 6280
Tel: 049-892-3965 Fax: 049-892-3965
Email: info@cypresscottage.co.za Web: www.cypresscottage.co.za
Cell: 083-456-1795

After a hot - and particularly bothersome - drive to this historic Karoo town, it came as a huge relief to wearily step through Cypress Cottage's heavy wooden doors and immerse myself in the quiet coolness lurking within. Minutes later, cold beer in hand and propped up on a stoep with a magnificent mountain view, my recent hardships evaporated into the heat-hazed sky. Both cottages are of the beautiful early 1800s Cape Dutch variety and are understatedly decorated with a (highly developed) taste for the natural and comfortable. Thus, the bedrooms display high reed ceilings, solid pine and slate floors, antique chests, fresh flowers and free-standing baths. Fresh and perfectly wholesome breakfasts are laid up on the terraces - free-range eggs from the house chickens, succulent figs, peaches, prunes and apricots straight from the orchard. You can escape the heat by splashing in the bore-hole-fed reservoir that has been converted into a swimming pool. Across the sleepy street, a familiar smell wafted over from the other cottage, where guests were merrily braaiing under the shade of its vine-covered pergola. The main garden is an extraordinary feat of will and clever engineering - desert has been transformed into an oasis of lush vegetation despite the difficulties of brackish water. Historical Graaff-Reinet is worth at least two day's stopover in my opinion - Cypress Cottages many more.

Rooms: 6: 4 doubles and 2 twins. All with en-suite bathrooms. All with air-con and heating.
Price: R250 - R400 pp sharing. Singles on request.
Meals: Full breakfast included.
Directions: From south enter town and pass police academy on L and go over bridge. Two filling stations on L - take road between them (West St). Follow to very end, turn R into Donkin St, guest house first on L. From north: R at T-jct (Caledon St). 4th Left is Donkin St. House last on R.

KwaZulu Natal

Plumbago

Mick and Libby Goodall
546 St Ives Ave, Leisure Bay
Tel: 039-319-2665
Fax: 039-319-2665
Email: begood@mweb.co.za
Web: www.plumbagokzn.co.za
Cell: 082-561-6993

I think the coast of KwaZulu Natal gets better and better the further south you head, and Leisure Bay is testament to that. It's just stunning, and, buried in the banana plantations between bush and beach, is easily missed by those hammering along the N2 to more on-the-beaten-track destinations. Plumbago itself is on the crest of a hill on sandy St Ives Avenue (just off Torquay Avenue, naturally), a gentle stroll from the sea. It's an airy double-storey home, hidden from its neighbours by the thick foliage of Libby's indigenous garden, indigenous that is "except the rosemary and the lemon tree for G&Ts," she admits. The birds are amazing and hop around right under your nose, and while they chattered in the trees, we chattered (over lunch) at a long, central dining table made from an old jetty post. Downstairs the house is open-plan with large windows, high ceilings and soft, blue walls – the perfect antidote to sizzling summer days. Upstairs a wrap-around verandah keeps the main bedroom equally cool and if you do get over-heated you can just jump in the outside shower. There are endless sea or land-based activities to keep you busy in the area, but with a beautiful beach on hand, well, I'd be just as happy focusing on some serious R&R.

Rooms: 2: both doubles, one with bath and shower, one with bath, outside shower available to both.
Price: R250 – R300 pp sharing.
Meals: Full breakfast included. Other meals on request.
Directions: Follow N2 and R61 south from Durban towards Port Edward. About 5km north of town take the Torquay Ave/Leisure Bay turn off. Follow Torquay Ave to the crest of hill and turn L into St Ives Ave. Plumbago is 100 yards down on the R.

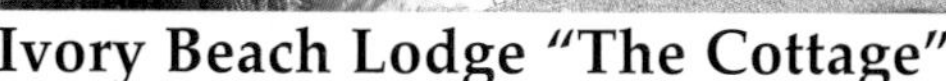

Ivory Beach Lodge "The Cottage"

Massimo and Nicci Negra

379/1 Outlook Road, Southbroom 4277
Tel: 039-316-8411 Fax: 039-316-8411
Email: masniki@venturenet.co.za Web: www.ivorybeachlodge.co.za
Cell: 082-440-9489 or 082-331-3202

Sybarites and nature lovers will find equal delight at Ivory Beach Lodge, the Indo-African style home of Massimo and Nicci Negra. Built on a secluded beach, with vistas of pounding surf and densely-vegetated dunes, guests are accommodated in 'the cottage', a self-contained bungalow which floats in a leafy canopy of trees in the steeply sloping garden. A footpath from the property leads onto seemingly endless golden miles of mostly people-less beach. Organic thatch, wood, rough walls and pigmented floors blend seamlessly with luxurious furnishings. A well-equipped kitchen and decking along the seaboard side make alfresco dining a delight, with whales and dolphins making regular appearances. The property has a salt-water rock-pool and sun deck. This stretch of coast is dubbed "the golf coast" and Ivory Beach backs onto the fifth tee of one of many excellent golf courses along the coastline. The Negras' award-winning trattoria, La Terrazza, is the obvious place to eat, a 20-minute stroll from the homestead. In July (or so!) billions of breeding sardines come to the coast, trailed by giant flocks of seabirds that dive-bomb the frothing feast. Thousands of dolphins join in too and there are tours out to watch the phenomenon. As for 'the cottage', it remains one of the best beach houses I have ever visited.

Rooms: 1 cottage: 1 king and 1 twin sharing a double shower. Fully-equipped kitchen for self-catering and a sitting room.
Price: R400 - R500 pp sharing. Children under 12 half price.
Meals: Fruit, coffee and milk provided. Continental breakfasts by arrangement. For lunch and evening meals their restaurant is 800m down the road.
Directions: Take the N3 south. Exit at Southbroom South, travel 400 metres, turn first right into Outlook Rd and follow for 2km (approx). Look for number 379/1 down a driveway on your left.

Map Number: 7

Wailana Beach Lodge

Rene and Reney Tobler
436 Ashmead Drive, Ramsgate 4285
Tel: 039-314-4606 Fax: 039-314-4606
Email: wailana@iafrica.com Web: www.wailana.co.za
Cell: 082-379-0922

The pace of life at Wailana is about as relaxed as you'll find anywhere on KZN's sub-tropical south coast and when I turned up Rene Tobler (pronounced as in Toblerone) was moseying around in shorts and flip-flops trailed by his chirpy young daughter/assistant Joya. He's a well-travelled chap and after countless trips to Thailand and Laos – his eyes light up at the slightest mention of them - he's swapped his Swiss homeland snow for SA sun and a modern, chill-out zone, hidden among the palms just a stone's throw from the Indian Ocean. This is a place to kick back and mooch whether you're slabbed out on the pool-side deck, ploughing through a good book in the hammock or inventing cocktails in the half-inside, half-outside bar. I loved the bright colours and arched doorways, and the individuality of each room. How to choose between them? On the upper deck I liked the sea-view, sea-blue Captain's Cabin, but wanted the open shower that tumbles from the Master room's bathroom ceiling. And then there's the Oriental room down below with its koi carp prints and driftwood swing on the balcony. Oh… I don't know. How about a night in each? There's so much more I could tell you, but I'd be cheating if I uncovered everything, so you'll just have to visit and discover the rest for yourself.

Rooms: 5: 2 kings, 3 queens. 3 rooms have bath and shower, 2 have shower only.
Price: R300 – R490 pp sharing.
Meals: Full breakfast included.
Directions: From N2 and Durban take the R61 south until Margate/Ramsgate off-ramp (exit 29). Head towards the sea. Turn L at T-junction. Pass Spar and Total garage then turn R onto Ashmead. Wailana is 200m on, on R.

Map Number: 7

Lindsay Loft

Caroline and Pepi Jankovich

26 Lindsay Avenue, Morningside, Durban 4001
Tel: 031-207-1634 Fax: 031-208-3227
Email: caroline@lindsayloft.co.za Web: www.lindsayloft.co.za
Cell: 083-190 0963

If your loft is anything like mine it's a dark and dusty dumping ground for old junk. Caroline's loft, I can enviously assure you, is NOTHING like mine. It's enormous. Walls are whitewashed and go up forever, floors are tiled to keep it cool in summer and there's a lengthy, decked verandah, of which more later. Actually no, I can't wait. The verandah is great, accessed from both the living- and bedrooms it peaks through the trees and across the city from its hill-top look-out. Bottle-brush, mango and avocado all tickle its handrail and you're encouraged to pick the fruit to avoid it crashing down onto the neighbour's tin roof. Sadly, my visit was a little early for those fresh treats so I was duly filled up with tea and toast instead. Back inside, the bedroom is cavernous and calming with (besides a bed of course) caramel armchairs and a beautiful old writing desk. The living area too is dotted with mahogany antiques and separated from the kitchen by a breakfast bar. For the chef, there's all the cooking kit you need and Caroline will supply the essentials to get you started. This is a great base from which to explore KZN. The Drakensberg mountains are a few hours inland, the game reserves a short drive up the coast and there are excellent beaches and golf courses.

Rooms: 1 double/king with en-suite combined bath and shower with optional spare single bed for extra family member in adjoining room.
Price: R300 - R500 pp sharing.
Meals: Starter supplies provided.
Directions: From M4 to Durban take exit 2, Moore Rd. Follow to traffic lights and turn R into Manning Rd which becomes Essenwood Rd. 100m after feeding into Montpelier Rd take Lindsay Ave up a steep hill. Lindsay Loft is just over the brow.

Ntengu Lodge

Andrew and Kathryn Buchanan
24 David McLean Drive, Westville, Durban 3630
Tel: 031-266-8578 Fax: 031-266-8026
Email: ntengu@intekom.co.za Web: www.ntengulodge.com
Cell: 083-777-2644

That Andrew was sloping around barefoot was an immediate sign of the pace of life at Ntengu: gloriously slow. A couple of recently-arrived guests were sipping a chilled glass of wine, installed in poolside wicker armchairs; another, here on business, was tapping at the computer in Andrew's office. Everyone seemed happily ensconced as if in their own homes. Like so many of the owners in this book here is a man "too creative for the corporate world" who has opted for a change of track and these days spends his time hammering and sawing in his workshop, building striking kiaat wood furniture to fit his house. And he's got his work cut out after expanding from one to six rooms in as many years. Ntengu Lodge is a two-storey house squarely planted on one of the jungly ridges that fold back from Durban's beachfront. Up here the trees rustle with a constant breeze that makes for a welcome escape from sweltering city-centre summers. In fact, the city couldn't feel further away. The breakfast room opens onto the decked pool and a wall of greenery, and from wrought-iron bedroom balconies there is a stunning view down into the Palmiet Nature Reserve that protects the surrounding hillside. Staff are easy smilers, service is impeccable, rooms have silk curtains, walk-in showers or other twists of luxury. Andrew is also the chef, adding the ability to excite your tastebuds to his many talents.

Rooms: 6: 2 king/twins with en-suite shower; 2 queens, 1 with en-suite bath and shower and 1 with en-suite bath/shower; 2 doubles, 1 with en-suite bath and shower and 1 with shower only.
Price: R335 pp sharing. Singles R480.
Meals: Full breakfast included. Dinner on request.
Directions: From Durban follow N2 north towards Stanger. After 20km take N3 towards Pietermaritzburg. Take next exit, M32 to Pavilion Shopping Centre and turn R at the top of ramp to Westville. Continue 2.1km to T-junction, turn R for 1.2km to BP station. Turn L into David McLean Drive and house is number 24 on L.

Map Number: 13

Fairlight Beach House

Bruce and Michele Deeb

1 Margaret Bacon Avenue, (Corner South Beach Rd), Umdloti Beach 4350
Tel: 031-568-1835
Fax: 031-568-1835
Email: bdeeb@mweb.co.za
Web: www.fairlight.co.za
Cell: 082-775-9971 or 082-443-8529

I got my first taste of Bruce and Michele's laid-back hospitality as soon as I arrived. It was another hot KZN day and I was bustled off for a joyous dip in the sea just across the road – "We can talk later". And we did. This newly-refreshed 'inspector' was soon sipping a cold beer by the pool and tucking into some delicious Lebanese pastries and thoroughly South African boerewors as Bruce tended the braai. The garden behind the house is dominated by two large milkwoods, a great place to shelter from the sun, although there are also sun-loungers around the swimming pool. The front of the house has a wooden deck running all along it, from where you can watch the surfers - all the rooms open onto it. Dolphins love the surf, too, and if you're lucky you can swim with them. Bruce can lend you a boogie board and flippers. Inside, it is effectively a family home and luxury guest house rolled into one – plenty of light and air as befits a beach house, family snaps on the wall and a warm, welcoming vibe to it. Rays of positive energy emanate from Michele, Bruce and their long-standing housekeeper Maria. Soak it up, then go forth and fish, surf or swim with a big smile on your face. Ten miles of heaven, a.k.a. Umdloti Beach, are but 40 paces from the house. *Durban and the airport are both within half an hour's drive.*

Rooms: 6: 4 with en-suite bath and shower, 2 with just shower (all are fully air-conditioned and sea-facing).
Price: R350 – R500. Singles from R450.
Meals: Full breakfast included. Limited self-catering facilities available.
Directions: N2 exit to Umdloti. Follow down to roundabout. Keep right past Total garage and Fairlight is 500 metres along South Beach Rd.

Uthula

Candy Jessel and Avril Tucker

26 Milkwood, Zimbali Forest Estate, Umdloti Beach 4422
Tel: 031-568-2104 Fax: 031-568-2104
Email: cjessel@t-online.de Web: www.zimbali.de
Cell: 082-349-7380

Uthula" means peace in Zulu and if you don't leave this house feeling peaceful I'll personally pay you a refund. Well, I might.... Down to the hanging chains that replace plastic drainpipes, every architectural detail has been meticulously thought out to create a two-storey haven of Zen-like tranquillity. It's part of the private Zimbali estate, just north of Durban, where homes have been built to melt into rather than stand out from their surroundings. Candy's house overlooks sand and surf and has a private stairway leading down to the beach. Either side of the covered entrance, water trickles into a Japanese pond, home to some 30 koi carp. Inside, the roof-high hallway is lined with family prints of Candy as a nipper. Dark, mahogany woodwork and cream-coloured walls run throughout. Two of four bedrooms face seaward and wall-to-wall windows upstairs and down mean the whole house can be opened to the huge deck and fabulous weather through the summer months. I absolutely loved it and reckon it is just as suited to a gang of pals as to a family (the kids will love the pool and bunk-beds). Candy's mum, Avril, looks after the place and meets you on arrival. She's hugely friendly and helpful and will organise a cook or buy enough starter goodies to keep the wolf from the door (or pool). Golfers, by the way, have their own golf cart (included in the price) to go out and play from the doorstep. *And new since the last edition, a spa room.*

Rooms: 5: 2 kings with en-suite bath and shower, 1 twin with en-suite shower, 1 double and a room with bunk-beds with shared bath and shower.
Price: R3,500 - R4,500 per night dependent on season.
Meals: Self-catering, but a cook is available.
Directions: From N2 take turn-off at Tollgate "Tongaat" then turn R towards Westbrook beach. At end of road take first L at circle towards Ballito (M4). At 2nd circle take 2nd L. After 2km take 3rd L at 3rd circle into Zimbali Forest Estate. Enter gate keeping on road until entering 2nd gate. Take 1st R into Milkwood and house is number 26.

Map Number: 14

The Dune Guest House

Michelle, Richard and Glenda de la Hey

45 Bellamont Road., Umdloti Beach 4350
Tel: 031-568-2089 Fax: 031-568-1067
Email: enquiries@thedune.net Web: www.thedune.net
Cell: 083-407-3397

Whether it belongs to Richard, Glenda or daughter Michelle, the family-run nature of this guest house guarantees a friendly face to greet you on arrival and ease you into the view-bedazzled lounge. If you're lucky you may even catch a glimpse of son Mark, who is a yachtsman and might have the best job in the world; if not you'll just have to settle for glimpses of whales and dolphins. Both father and son are established photographers, amongst other things, and you can tell they certainly have an eye for the perfect picture, as The Dune is a panoramic paradise. Monkeys, mongooses, blue duikers and birdlife love the indigenous garden and rightly so. All the pale stone-floored rooms are softly finished in creams and browns while wicker and bamboo headboards and furniture give it that sugar cane country feel (perhaps an ode to Richard's sugar farming days). Enjoy your own private deck and ocean views or cook up some fun in the sociable braai area, kitted out with all the self-catering gizmos you could need. From the glass-captured butterflies in the lounge to the still-life marlin in the newly-licensed bar, everything seems to hold a story or fragment of de la Hey family life. I was privileged to meet the whole gang when I stayed and felt almost as if I'd been granted a family membership by the time I reluctantly left.

Rooms: 4: 2 twin/kings, 1 queen and 1 honeymoon suite; 2 with en-suite bath and shower and 2 with en-suite shower only.
Price: R300 - R400 pp sharing.
Meals: Full breakfast included. A shared braai facility and kitchenette is available for those that may wish to self-cater.
Directions: From Durban take the N2 North Coast/Stanger. Take the Umdloti/Verulam off-ramp. At the stop street turn right towards Umdloti, driving under the highway and over the M4. Turn left into Bellamont Road (you will see a dophin sign) and left again at the T-junction. The Dune is no.45 on right.

Map Number: 14

Nalson's View

Wendy and Kelvin Nalson
10 Fairway Drive, Salt Rock
Tel: 032-525-5726 Fax: 032-525-5726
Email: nalsonsview@3i.co.za
Cell: 083-303-1533

After a long, long (long, long) day on the road I finally emerged from my car at Nalson's, wild-eyed and mud-besmattered. I couldn't have pitched up anywhere more perfect. Kelvin and Wendy welcomed me as if I had been living there for years. This was my room, these my beers and friends… I owned the place didn't I? A fantastic shower washed off the mud (don't ask) and I was invited to dinner. I couldn't tell who were guests, who were family friends, such is the open-house air of friendship here, and the meal was out of this world. Kelvin and Wendy have an oyster and mussel licence (guests can go with them and pick their own) and these were by FAR the best I've had in SA. Nalson's is one of those places where guests stop over for one night and have to be prised out of the place days later. Breakfast was sensational (both local baker and butcher are true servants of the community!) and, joy oh joy, freshly squeezed fruit juice. Guests who make the correct decision to stay more than one night will get involved in the sea activities – dolphin- and whale-watching on boats, fishing, bird-watching and the ten kilometres of beautiful Christmas Bay Beach. There's plenty to do on dry land too including golf galore, walking-distance restaurants and the Sibaya casino just 10 minutes away. *Ask about children.*

Rooms: 4: 2 doubles, 1 family and 1 double/twin; 3 with en-suite shower, 1 with en-suite bath and shower.
Price: From R300 pp sharing. Singles on request.
Meals: Full breakfast included and served when you want it. Dinners by prior arrangement. Price depends on what you have.
Directions: From Durban take N2 north. Take exit 214 (Salt Rock/Umhlali). Right at T-junction signed to Salt Rock, follow road round to the right past Salt Rock Hotel (on your left). Fairway Drive is next right.

Seaforth Farm

Trevor and Sharneen Thompson

Exit 214 off N2, Salt Rock, Umhlali 4390
Tel: 032-525-5217 Fax: 032-525-4495
Email: ttastym@iafrica.com Web: www.seaforth.co.za
Cell: 082-770-8376

Seaforth Farm is a full-blown treat of a guest house. Trevor and Sharneen have many interests, talents and motivations and Seaforth is a constant source of stimulation. Trevor is an official tour guide and will advise you on the 'must-do's' in the area. Dolphin trips are very popular with guests. One is whisked out through the surf on a "Rubber Duck" and if lucky, one can get close up to these wonderful creatures that abound along this stretch of the coastline. Sharneen is a water-colourist and has also won medals for flower-arranging, so the house blooms with extravagant displays and paintings. Trevor is a skilled craftsman and much of the furniture has been made in his workshop (his latest piece, a huge lychee-wood bed) – and it is highly accomplished work. The garden is lush and wild and envelops everything at Seaforth in tropical colour. There are brahman cattle, chickens, pawpaw and pecan trees, and the dam and its abundant bird life. Trevor is coaxing it in with a cunning plantation of pond weed, lilies and islets, and you can bird-watch from a hide overlooking the dam. The guest house provides large, well-equipped bedrooms, a pool and thatched summerhouse with dam- and sea-view for heavenly breakfasts and candle-lit curry evenings. Finally, the staff have a stake in the success of their venture. A pioneering guest house indeed.... *Zulu spoken.*

Rooms: 4: 1 family cottage with 2 bedrooms, each with en/s shower; 2 doubles and 1 twin with en/s shower and bath.
Price: From R290 pp sharing B&B. Family suite (sleeps 5) from R720.
Meals: Full breakfast included.
Directions: From Durban take the N2 north. Exit on the 214 signed Salt Rock. Go 200m and take the 1st right into Old Fort Road, then 1st left into Seaforth Ave - the house is at the end.

Map Number: 14

The Chase

Jane and Jonathan Chennells
PO Box 45, Eshowe 3815
Tel: 035-474-5491 Fax: 035-474-1311
Email: thechase@netactive.co.za Web: www.thechase.co.za
Cell: 083-265-9629

Jane and Jonathan have so much to offer their guests that you hardly have to leave the premises. The weather-boarded house is gargantuan (Mrs Chennells senior had a penchant for large, open spaces) with long views of the farm's sugar cane plantations on overlapping mounds of distant hills. On clear days you can even see 90 degrees of sea. (They also have ducks, chickens, cows, sheep and goats like a proper farm should, of course.) The garden is an orgy of barely controllable tropical growth, lush and colourful (check out the tulip tree and the Indian mahogany), its trees often weighed down by parasitic ferns and creepers. Birds are equally irrepressible and there are 70 species in the garden and 280 (!) in the Eshowe area. Kids will love the walled-in swimming pool (13 metres long) where you can swim by floodlight at night too. A hammock swings from a tree, a trampoline is stretched at ground level and there is a hard tennis court. Chennells Chase is an involving, very comfortable, incredibly good-value family home, with huge amounts of space inside and out. Pack a sense of humour and a pair of binoculars.

Rooms: 2: 1 double with en-suite bath; 1 twin with en-suite shower. Also a self-contained farm cottage with 3 bedrooms and 2 bathrooms.
Price: R200 – R300 pp sharing. Singles R300 – R400. Self catering in the cottage (sleeps 5) R450 – R550.
Meals: Full breakfast included (except in the cottage - by arrangement only) and served any time.
Directions: From Durban take N2 north for 1 hour. Turn off at Dokodweni off-ramp. Half an hour to Eshowe. Take first left signed to Eshowe, house 1.8km signed on left.

Zimbete Country House

Anne and Nick Nicolson

PO Box 1141, Empangemi 3880
Tel: 035-791-1991 Fax: 035-791-1991
Email: nickanne@iafrica.com Web: www.zimbete.co.za
Cell: 083-632-0195

Zigzagging through the sugar cane, you probably won't spot Nick and Anne's house until you're actually there. It's surrounded by a tropical garden, bursting with indigenous and exotic plants (and consequently birds - 278 species in fact, including the palm-nut vulture). The palm trees are vast and billowing bougainvillaea engulfs the farmhouse. Finally reaching the front door and Zimbete's inner sanctum, I was amazed to hear the plants were all put in just twenty years ago. But then this place is brimming with surprises, not least the family history. Anne and Nick are both descended from Natal settler families (and are both history buffs). Anne's great-grandfather fought in the Zulu wars before becoming chief architect, city engineer and mayor of Durban all at the same time (clever chap!). Nick – farmer of nuts and veg and bird and tree fundi – is a local lad too. His family are everywhere and visitors to famed food-house Cleopatra Mountain Lodge will meet his sister Mouse Poynton. Food is a major theme at Zimbete too. Anne has a range of devilish desserts and after one of her dinners you'll be glad of a room just a few yards down the corridor. They're great by the way, each with a garden view. But my favourite was a diminutive garden cottage hidden in the vegetable patch between the leeks and the lettuce – eyes peeled for Peter Rabbit. Whether it's for the glorious farm setting, fascinating company or awesome food, Zimbete Country House is well worth stopping for.

Rooms: 5: 4 queens, one with shower, others bath and shower; 1 twin with bath and shower.
Price: R375 – R450 pp sharing.
Meals: Full breakfast included. 4-course dinner on request: R150.
Directions: From N2 take R102 at Zululand University exit north towards Empangemi. After 4km turn R towards Felixton. Zimbete is signed 100m further on to the L.

Wendy's Country Lodge

Tony, Wendy, Gavin and Jenny Udal

3 Riverview Drive, Mtubatuba 3935
Tel: 035-550-0407 Fax: 035-550-1527
Email: wendybnb@iafrica.com Web: www.wendybnb.co.za
Cell: 083-628-1601

As I wove my way through a labyrinth of fine flowers and tropical plants searching for Wendy's reception I was tickled with feelings of expectation. Tony's family were the first Scottish settlers to arrive in the area (in 1850) setting early cogs in motion for the sugar cane industry, while Wendy's family were the first British occupancy in 1810. The original 1920s sugar estate house seems to have bottled the experience of their ancestors in true colonial and romantic style. "It's a love project, a total love project," Wendy tells me as she talks me through the regeneration of all that has gone before. Being soaked in such history makes for some interesting antiques and items; in fact the place was like a veritable museum, beautiful, wooden rocking-chairs, old military trunks, original stained-glass panels in the doors and traditional white cotton, lace-trimmed curtains. Antiquity, however, doesn't mean you miss out on any mod cons. All rooms have mozzie nets, bathrobes and air-con. You can swim in the heated pool, bird-watch in the amazing garden or mingle with other guests around Tony's bar, feasting on peanuts from the giant snack jar. Game drives, fishing and aquatic adventures are run from the lodge by Wendy's son, ensuring a true family feel and easy access to St. Lucia Wetlands and Umfolozi-Hluhluwe Game Park. Wendy also promises she'll take you to 'Friends' for dinner... trust me, you'll love it.

Rooms: 8: 2 queens and 3 twins, all with en-suite bath and shower; 1 double and 1 twin with shower only; and 1 family unit let as a whole with 1 double, 1 twin and shared shower.
Price: R235 - R400 pp sharing. R600 - R800 for family unit (sleeps 4). Singles on request.
Meals: 3-course dinner available every night apart from Sunday in 'Friends' restaurant R100 - R125. Light lunches also available of request.
Directions: From Durban take the N2 north to Mtubatuba turn - follow to the T-junction. Go right where you'll see a sign to Wendy's and follow the signs to the house.

Maputaland Guest House

Jorg, Penny and Gisela Orban
Kabeljou Ave, No. 1, Greater St Lucia Wetlands Park, Zululand 3936
Tel: 035 590-1041 Fax: 035-590-1041
Email: bookings@maputaland.com Web: www.maputaland.com
Cell: 082-940-7380

Maputaland Guest House is great value and the perfect launch pad for exploring the World Heritage Site, beaches, reefs and big game of the area. Jorg, who is very modest about his talents, is the bird fundi (430 local species live locally!) and a registered professional game guide too, while his wife Penny runs the house with a helping hand from mum Gisela. The lodge is recently built, homely, relaxed and perfectly comfortable. But you're hardly here to stay indoors! Join a trip into the nearby Umfolozi-Hluhluwe Reserve, or up to Sodwana Bay where sister Nikki (a dive master) will rig you up for a scuba experience. St. Lucia Wetlands Park offers a multitude of eco-systems, existing back-to-back and guaranteeing the most varied of wildlife viewing. Amazingly, Jorg also likes to explore the streets of St Lucia itself, taking his guests on night safaris. Hippos, impala and on rare occasion even leopards can be seen wandering about the pavements. Bush babies and chameleons come out during the cicada hours too. Jorg does a cracking 'bonnet breakfast' (he assures me it's NOT road-kill) for those that go with him on day tours (starting at 4 am and getting back at 6pm - yep - good value alright). Ask about turtle-watching tours (two rare breeds come here), deep-sea fishing and fly-casting for huge game fish (which Jorg sometimes also cooks on the braai). Exciting and incredibly friendly with it.

Rooms: 6: 2 doubles and 3 twins with en-suite bath and shower; 1 family unit with extra bed and en-suite bath and shower.
Price: R250 - R300. Singles from R350. Full-day safaris from 4am - 6pm from R475. Half days from R375.
Meals: Full breakfast included. Dinners by arrangement. Full-day tours include breakfast and lunch. Half-day tours include breakfast only.
Directions: From Jo'burg (7 hrs): take N2 through Bethal, Pongola etc and past Hluhluwe. Turn off to Mtubatuba then left on R618 to St Lucia. From Swaziland (3 hrs): join N2 from Pongola/Mukuzi and head for Mtubatuba. From Durban (3 hrs): N2 towards Mtubatuba, right on R618 to St L. Signs in St. L for guest house.

Sunset Lodge

Shelley and Rodney Klomfass

154 McKenzie Street, St Lucia 3936
Tel: 035-590-1197 Fax: 035-590-1135
Email: info@sunsetstlucia.co.za Web: www.sunsetstlucia.co.za
Cell: 082-974-7318

You hold up a bit of biltong or sausage and they just swoop down and take it" Rodney beams as daughter Skyelar, a flurry of blonde curls, peeps shyly from behind his legs. He was talking about the resident yellow-billed kites. Particularly partial to hand-feeding they feature in the tamer segment of St. Lucia's impressive wildlife spectrum. The 'wise-to-watch-from-a-distance' segment includes crocs, hippos and even on occasion leopard, which you can appreciate from the Klomfasses' back garden as the views stretch right out over the estuary. The six self-catering chalets have been built in classic American log-cabin style, a spin-off from Shelly and Rodney's travelling days, and seem to suit their situation perfectly. Lightly African themed inside, fully serviced daily and kitted-out with full kitchen, air-con and TV (which you won't need to watch) they have everything you could ask for in a place to stay. You can braai on your own private verandah or play 'count the hippo' from the deck-lined swimming pool. If you're after adventures further afield than your own daring back yard (buck and hippos have been known to come and sit on the lawn) your hosts will gladly 'make a plan' to suit. "We have the best of everything here," I'm told, and as a pivotal point for big game, beaches, bush walks and bird life they are certainly not wrong.

Rooms: 6 chalets: 1 double with shower only, 4 that sleep four (a double and a twin in each with full en-suite bathroom) and 1 that sleeps up to 5.
Price: R495 - R750 per two-bedroom chalet. R350 - R550 for 1 bedroom chalet.
Meals: Chalets are fully equipped for self-catering.
Directions: From the N2 take the turn-off to Mtubatuba then the R618 to St. Lucia. As you enter St. Lucia village over the bridge turn right at the round-about onto McKenzie street and Sunset Lodge is at the end on your right.

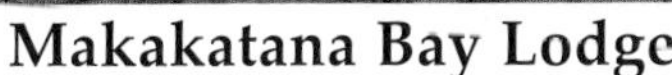

Makakatana Bay Lodge

Hugh and Leigh-Ann Morrison

Mtubatuba 3935
Tel: 035-550-4189 Fax: 035-550-4198
Email: maklodge@iafrica.com Web: www.makakatana.co.za
Cell: 082-573-5641

Makakatana Bay Lodge is sensational and I can do little to improve on these photos, which do not lie. If only we had space for ten shots, to show you every aspect of the lodge: the gleaming wooden interiors; the bedrooms (including the wonderful honeymoon suite), connected by walkways through the forest, with their gargantuan slabs of glass and warm, earthy African colours; the pool encased in decking and raised above the grasses of the wetlands; the lake itself and the extraordinary St Lucia waterways. Guests are taken on drives into the wetlands to search for birds (360 species!), crocodiles and hippos. You can also be taken to the beach for snorkelling and swimming or out on a game drive to a nearby reserve before returning to a sumptuous dinner with your hosts in the outdoor boma. Safari drives to Hluhluwe Game Reserve are also available if you have a hankering to see the Big 5. The family's old 'Crab House' is the only part of the lodge not raised above the tall grasses. This was once a storeroom for crabs caught in the lake, now a wine cellar with a giant tree growing out of its roof. Huge sliding doors throughout the lodge open onto wooden decks with views over the lake, and the absence of railings just adds to the feeling of openness to nature. The lodge is beautifully welded to its environment. An absolute treat.

Rooms: 6: 1 honeymoon suite with extra single bed, 2 king suites, 3 twin suites; all with en-suite bath and outside shower.
Price: Standard R1,895 - R2,395 pp sharing, Honeymoon Suite R2,100 - R2,850 pp sharing. Singles R2,450 - R2,995. All-inclusive, dependent on season.
Meals: Fully inclusive of all meals and safaris. Dinner, bed and breakfast option also available - enquire for rates.
Directions: Take N2 north from Durban for 250km to Charter's Creek. Follow road for 15km (14km on tar) to fork. Take right fork and follow signs to Makakatana Bay Lodge (4 more km or so).

Map Number: 14

Hluhluwe River Lodge

Gavin and Bridget Dickson

Greater St Lucia Wetlands Park, Hluhluwe 3960
Tel: 035-562-0246/7 Fax: 035-562-0248
Email: info@hluhluwe.co.za
Web: www.hluhluwe.co.za

A short drive through dense bushveld takes you to this friendly, informal lodge overlooking the shores of Lake St Lucia. On arrival, I dumped my kit in a wood-and-thatch chalet and headed straight for the big deck, the centrepiece of the lodge, for a drink and some orientation. The view is straight across the Hluhluwe River flood plain. There's a pool lost in the trees near the Zulu boma (for evening braais), but most will want to make full use of the all-seeing, all-knowing guides (including sometimes Gavin himself) who will take you exploring in this remarkable region. The river is just there for canoe safaris (hippos and crocs are commonly sighted and always a great variety of birds) and you can take boat trips around the lake, eyes peeled for all sorts of land game coming in to drink. There are drives through the Wetland Park sand forests, but I visited nearby Umfolozi-Hluhluwe Park. And what a trip, my first real game drive and we spotted a leopard! You can also go on botanical trips or guided walks to old fossil banks and (astounding) bird-watching excursions in the park. Whatever you choose this is an intimate, sociable place, where small numbers and very knowledgeable guides make the experience personal and rewarding. The focus is on the topography, the birdlife and the wetland environment as a whole, rather than just the 'Big Five.'

Rooms: 12: 8 twins & 2 family rooms, all with en/s shower; 2 honeymoon suites (pictured) with shower & bath. For honeymoon suites, ask when you book.
Price: R1,300 – R1,600 pp DBB and one game drive. From R1085 – R1,385 pp sharing for DBB. Winter Special 1 April to 31 July R1,040 - R1,280 pp sharing DBB + 1 game drive. Prices from R856 to R1108 pp sharing DBB. Extra activities from R295.
Meals: Full breakfast, dinner and high tea included. Lunch on request from R65.
Directions: From N2 take Hluhluwe off-ramp & pass thro' Hluhluwe town. Take R22 signed Sodwana Bay. 3.4km after crossing railway turn R onto D540. Follow 5km signs to lodge. Gate guard will also direct you.

Bushwillow

Julian and Liz Simon
PO Box 525, Hluhluwe 3960
Tel: 035-562-0173
Fax: 035-562-0473 Email: info@bushwillow.com
Web: www.bushwillow.comCell: 083-651-6777

Game reserves can be an expensive stopover, so for visitors on a tighter budget we've uncovered some more affordable gems that still offer great access to local highlights. Bushwillow is one such, set in the Weavers Nature Park. With 150 hectares to explore (on foot) you'll spot plenty of wildebeest, zebra and giraffe, setting the mood for the 'Big 5' at Umfolozi-Hluhluwe or the St Lucia Wetlands just half an hour away. It's hidden in the sand forest and can be reserved for your exclusive use, so you need only battle friends and family for deckchair space (often the toughest battle of all). I arrived to whoops and squeals from the pool on a blisteringly hot day, and was only too glad when Julian shepherded me inside to the cooling waft of the ceiling fans. The three forest-green chalets blend into the bush perfectly, cunningly positioned a stone's throw from a waterhole so you needn't go further than the deck to spot the local wildlife. Bedrooms are peacefully private and just a few steps along the boardwalk from the living area, with its granite worktops for Mary-Ann, the chef, and a eucalyptus dining table that supports her excellent meals. It seems they've thought of everything.

Rooms: 3: 2 twins and 1 king chalet all with bath and shower.
Price: R450 - R750 pp sharing. Bookings can be reserved to one group at a time.
Meals: Self-catering or meals on request. Breakfast R50, dinner R125.
Directions: From the N2 take the Hluhluwe off-ramp and pass through Hluhluwe town. Take the R22 towards Sodwana Bay. Continue 16km after crossing the railway line and Weavers Nature Park is on the L. Bushwillow is signed within the reserve.

Thonga Beach Lodge

Paige and Brett Gehren
Isibindi Africa Lodges, Mabibi 3815
Tel: 035-474-1473 Fax: 035-474-1490
Email: res@isibindiafrica.co.za Web: www.isibindiafrica.co.za
Cell: 082-466-8538

   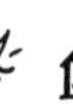 

I had been eagerly looking forward to my visit to Thonga Beach Lodge since before I had even left Cape Town. I knew it would be great because all the Gehrens' places are (see Isibindi Lodge, Kosi Forest Lodge and Rhino Walking Safaris). So, typically, when I did finally arrive thousands of KZN kilometres caught up with me and, lying down for an afternoon snooze, I didn't wake until six the next morning! Sundowners at Lake Sibaya and a gourmet dinner all passed me by, but I was raring to go for a sunrise stroll. The sky was a soft pink, the surf breaking onto footprint-free sand and looking back to the lodge I could just make out the thatched tops of each rounded room, twelve in all, poking out through milkwood brush. Thonga Beach is sandwiched between forested dunes and ocean, an hour's sandy drive and 4x4 trail from the nearest tar road. Huts are connected by snaking, wooden walkways and in mine a huge mosquito net hung from high rafters, separating the bed from the bathroom, a design marvel in itself. One single piece of sculpted concrete flows past glass-bowl sinks and chrome taps into an oval bath. This is as luxurious and romantic a destination as you'll find anywhere, but it's super-relaxed too. Mike, Nikki and all their staff are hugely friendly, the birding, diving, walking and wildlife are superb and – a rare bonus – it's majority community-owned so your pennies help support the local economy.

Rooms: 12: 9 twins, 3 doubles, all with bath and shower and sea or forest view.
Price: R1,800 - R2,150 pp sharing. Includes all meals, guided snorkelling, guided walks and kayaking. Spa treatments and scuba diving prices available on request.
Meals: Full board.
Directions: From Durban take the N2 north to Hluhluwe and then follow signs to Kosi Bay. 30km beyond Mbazwana follow signs right to Coastal Forest Reserve. Thonga car park (and lodge pick-up point) is 32km on along sandy road.

Kosi Forest Lodge

Patrick Paige and Gina Bugbee

Isibindi Africa Lodges, Kosi Bay Nature Reserve, PO Box 1593, Eshowe 3815 Tel: 035-474-1473 Fax: 035-474-1490
Email: res@isibindiafrica.co.za
Web: www.isibindiafrica.co.za
Cell: 082-466-8538

Kosi Bay is the sort of place that novelists map out and then construct adventures in. You are picked up by a four-wheel drive, which can negotiate the sand tracks criss-crossing the region. You park up not just your car, but also the modern world you are now leaving. There is no tar and no electricity here. Instead you enter a landscape of raffia palm groves, primary sand forests, mangroves, water meadows, interconnecting lakes (yes, hippo and crocodile like it too and are regularly sighted). And then there is the sea and the mouth of the river for diving, swimming and fishing in 'perfect, white sand coves with huge overhanging trees' (says the lodge brochure). The reed-thatched camp itself perfectly balances the wild (your chalet is in the middle of a boisterous forest) with the romantic (candlelit meals and outdoor baths and showers). I loved the deep stillness of the early-morning guided canoe trip and other activities include reef-snorkelling, turtle-tracking, forest walks and bird safaris. I consider Kosi Forest Lodge one of the most rewarding (and therefore best-value) places I have stayed in SA. I recommend a minimum of two or three nights. New hosts (and joint owners) Patrick and Gina are lovely people and bring with them a new level of personal hospitality.

Rooms: 8: 1 family 'bush suite'; 6 twins and 1 honeymoon double; all with outdoor bath and shower and additional covered shower.
Price: R1,120 - R1,390 pp sharing. Singles plus 30%. Transfer from police station R15 pp. Children under 12 half-price. DB&B rates on request.
Meals: All meals included. Guided canoeing on the lakes and walks in the raffia forest also included. 1 full day excursion included in stays of 2 nights or longer.
Directions: From Hluhluwe take N2 north past Mkuze. Turn R signed Jozini. In Jozini thru' town, L over dam & follow for 37km. Turn R at T-jct & follow for 67km to Kwangwanase. R at Kosi Forest sign & follow tar road to R & up slope to police station compound. Turn L & park under trees.

Map Number: 14

Tamboti Ridge

Denise and Brian Blevin
Between Pongola and Mkuze, Golela T-junction, Pongola 3170
Tel: 034-435-1110 Fax: 034-435-1008
Email: shayalodge@saol.com Web: www.shayamoya.co.za/tamboti
Cell: 083-269-9596

What a relief! After days of inland dryness I'd made it to the Pongola valley, a lush expanse of well-watered sugar cane farms, dripping with bougainvillaea. And at its heart, Tamboti Ridge, smiling Blevins and a restorative glass of iced juice. Phew. These two are super-relaxed and this shows in a wholesome B&B. Here, there are plenty of farm-based activities for the children and also access to next-door Shayamoya (also owned by the Blevins) for top nosh, fishing and game drives on the Pongola Reserve. Brian runs his farm as holistically and organically as possible, producing everything from sugar and vegetables to yoghurt and cheese for the guests. You can watch the cows being milked, ramble across the farm or fish for bass at the dam. Otherwise, the jacaranda-shaded lawn and pool are ideal for lazing. In the heat of the day I fancied nothing more than a good book on the room-side deck, gazing through a sub-tropical garden to the river far below. But time was not on my side. I had a date at Blevin project number two! A welcome place to water the horses and break long journeys between Jo-burg and the KZN reserves and resorts.

Rooms: 4: 3 twins and 1 double, all en-suite with bath and shower, plus air-conditioning and fans.
Price: R280 - R320 pp sharing B&B. Singles on request. R225 pp for game drives and river safaris. Tiger fishing R600 per boat per half-day.
Meals: Full breakfast included. You can also eat lunch and dinners at the main lodge: 3-course meals from R125 (excluding wine). Self-catering option also available.
Directions: When travelling north on N2, 40km past Mkuze, turn L at signs directly at Golela junction. When travelling south on the N2, 30km past Pongola, turn right onto the farm, almost directly opposite the turn to Golela and Swaziland border post.

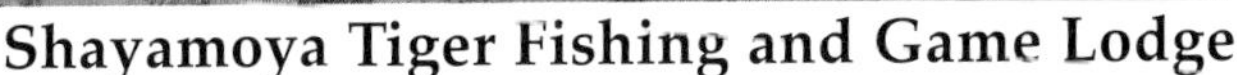

Shayamoya Tiger Fishing and Game Lodge

Denise and Brian Blevin
PO Box 784, Pongola 3170
Tel: 034-435-1110 Fax: 034-435-1008
Email: shayalodge@saol.com Web: www.shayamoya.co.za
Cell: 083-456-8423

Sometimes, 230 words are just not enough. Shayamoya is the Blevins' fantastic game lodge, offering all the luxuries you could want, but with the family-run atmosphere of a homespun B&B. After a blissful slosh in the pool (research, you understand) I was soon sharing a beer with Brian in the bar and planning a morning fishing trip (more research). From its hilltop look-out the lodge surveys the vast Pongolapoort Lake and 10,000 hectare reserve. Alongside boat cruises, elephant monitoring, rhino walks and game drives - as if that wasn't enough – the tiger fishing is superb. But hook and line could wait. First came supper, dining under the stars on fillet steak and a shiraz from the new cellar (wine tastings and food are yet more strings to the Shayamoya bow). You can see across to Swaziland from the dining-room deck, as I could from my chalet, a hexagonal affair with cobbled outdoor shower and funky, ceramic hippo plugs. Come dawn, Nandi, the resident spotted eagle owl, woke me up and I was soon driving past giraffe and wildebeest to the lake with ranger Douglas. For some reason, despite a display of great skill, I caught absolutely nothing, while fellow fishermen were hauling them in truly agricultural fashion! They were staying on the Blevins' twelve-sleeper houseboat "Shayamanzi". That's for rent too, by the way, and with any luck, I'll be chucking my line from that next year.

Rooms: 10 chalets: 2 premium kings, 8 standards including 2 doubles and 6 twins. All rooms have bath and outside shower.
Price: Dinner bed and breakfast rate R880 - R1,045. Singles + R250. Self-catering option available for groups of 6, R380 pp. Cost of additional activities available on request.
Meals: Dinner and full breakfast included. Lunch available on request at additional cost.
Directions: When travelling South on the N2, 27km past Pongola, take the Golela/Swaziland turning to the left. Travel for 2km until you reach the entracnce on the left. From Durban, take N2 North, 40km beyond Mkuze turn right towards Golela.

Map Number: 14

Isandlwana Lodge

Pat Stubbs
Isandlwana 3005
Tel: lodge: 034-271-8301/4/5, res: 011-537-4620 Fax: 034-271-8306
Email: lodge@isandlwana.co.za Web: www.isandlwana.co.za
Cell: 082-789-9544

Isandlwana Lodge is *the* place to relive Anglo-Zulu War history and approaching through the dust I could see its namesake hill from miles away. The rocky outcrop was throwing a long shadow across the valley, just as it did on January 22nd 1879 when 25,000 Zulus attacked the British soldiers encamped on the hill's eastern slope. The story of the ensuing battle is fascinating and the lodge eats and sleeps it. Rob Gerrard, an ex-Gordon Highlander, leads tours that include nearby Rorke's Drift. Even the lodge itself is designed around a Zulu shield, a thatched, tapered structure that wraps around the hillside and looks across the Isandlwana battlefield. Though steeped in history, it has a refreshingly modern feel. Upstairs, the lounge and bar have leather sofas, ceiling fans and high-backed, iNguni dining chairs. All twelve rooms are downstairs off a winding, rocky corridor, with very private balconies for enjoying the incredible view. Pat has furnished the lodge in a pleasingly subtle blend of hand-printed bedspreads, copper lampshades and slate-tiled, chrome-tapped bathrooms. Having arrived here from Florida and a life of "peanuts and insurance," she has taken to hosting as a duck takes to water. Once you've waltzed through her to-do list of battlefield tours, walking trails, 300 bird species, cultural tours, horse riding, swimming and gourmet dining, you'll have happily spent at least three nights here.

Rooms: 13: 5 doubles and 7 twins all with showers. Also self-catering guest house with 3 bedrooms, 6 people max.
Price: From R1,190 (low season) pp sharing, singles R1,490 for dinner B&B. Battlefield tours R300 per tour. Other activities quoted on request.
Meals: Price includes dinner, bed and breakfast.
Directions: From Durban take the N2 north to Eshowe then the R68 through Melmoth and Babanango. Turn L at 4-way stop in Babanango. Travel for approx 45km to turn-off to Isandlwana Lodge, then another 9km on dirt road.

Isibindi Zulu Lodge

Brad and Anél Mack
Isibindi Africa Lodges, Rorke's Drift, Dundee 3000
Tel: 035-474-1173 Fax: 035-474-1490
Email: res@isibindiafrica.co.za Web: www.Isibindiafrica.co.za
Cell: 082-466-8538

Driving up to Isibindi in the early evening, the way ahead was intermittently illuminated by a spectacular thunderstorm. It seemed to be following me. Ignoring the portents, I pressed on Homerically to claim my prize, a night at the wonderful (the first line of my notes just reads 'Wow!') Isibindi Zulu Lodge. It's on a hill in the middle of a 2000-hectare nature reserve on the Buffalo River, with six secluded chalets looking out over the bush, a modern spin on the traditional Zulu beehive hut. The best view is reserved for the pool, a great place for daytime dozing before an afternoon game drive with lodge managers Brad and Anél. Both have been passionate about the wild since they were knee-high to a bushbuck and Brad is a talking encyclopaedia on anything that moves (and most things that don't too). The game wasn't playing ball on our evening outing but we heard plenty of snuffling about in the twilight as we walked back under the stars to the lodge (the game vehicle wasn't playing ball either!). For those not balmy about the bush there are Zulu dancing evenings laid on, daytime tours of the Anglo-Zulu battlefields or even a rafting and abseiling camp on the reserve for the adventurous. From nature, history and culture to adrenaline-pumped excitement... Isibindi has it all.

Rooms: 6: 4 twins, 1 double, 1 honeymoon beehive suite; all with en-suite bath and shower.
Price: R1,075 - R1,150 pp sharing. Singles plus 30%. Price includes 3 meals & 1 game activity per day. Battlefield tours, Zulu homestead visits, Zulu cultural evenings & rafting extra.
Meals: Full board includes breakfast, lunch and dinner and all teas and coffees.
Directions: Take R33 from Dundee for 42km, then turn left onto dirt road at Isibindi Eco Reserve/Elandskraal sign. Follow signs to Isibindi which is 21km from main road.

Map Number: 13

Mawelawela Game and Fishing Lodge

George and Herta Mitchell-Innes

Fodo Farm, PO Box 21, Elandslaagte 2900
Tel: 036-421-1860 Fax: 036-421-1860
Email: mitchellinnes@mweb.co.za Web: www.mawelawela.co.za
Cell: 083-259-6394 or 082-734-3118

George and Herta are a natural, down-to-earth couple whose veins of hospitality run deep… and staying with them is to enjoy a few days awash with incidental pleasures. Herta, a bubbly Austrian, moved out to South Africa 28 years ago and married George, who is a beef farmer – his boerewors is delicious. He is also a keen historian and leads tours out to the site of the battle of Elandslaagte. His study is full of Anglo-Boer war prints and weighty tomes including a collection of the London Illustrated News. (Ask him to show you his father's beautiful collection of bird-eggs too.) If you stay in the main house the rooms are very comfortable and the bungalow across the jacaranda-filled garden is perfect for families or groups. A short drive away from the farm itself you'll find the thatched hunters' cottage on 1500 wild hectares set aside for game. There is a trout dam at the front into which George has built a waterfall, and there are a shower and a plunge pool to one side. The cane-sided shady braai area faces dam-wards and you can watch the eland and kudu come to drink in the evenings. Finally a toast to Herta's cooking which is wonderful! Many of the ingredients are home-grown and all is served on her collection of fine china and family silver. *Bookings essential.*

Rooms: 4: 2 twins (1 with en/s bath, 1 en/s bath & shower); 1 apartment with double, twins & single (self-catering or B&B); 1 self-catering game lodge sleeps 7.
Price: B&B R250 pp sharing. Singles on request.
Meals: All meals are in the main house. Full breakfast included. 3-course dinners (excluding wine) R80. Main and coffee R50.
Directions: On N11, 35km from Ladysmith, 70km from Newcastle. Also entrance on R602, 35km from Dundee towards Ladysmith.

Oaklands Country Manor

Jamie and Anna Bruce
PO Box 19, Van Reenen 3372
Tel: 058-671-0067 Fax: 058-671-0077
Email: info@oaklands.co.za Web: www.oaklands.co.za
Cell: 083-304-2683

Jamie was in the British army for many years but bar the military memorabilia that pops up in flags and prints there's no regimentation at Oaklands. Instead the colonial manor is an intimate country hotel set in 260 acres of heavenly highveld countryside that teems with rock art and birds. Kids are well catered for (Jamie and Anna adore them) and when I visited four large ones - namely the Combined British Services - had descended for the weekend. Jamie is super keen on his polo and had organised a tournament of horse-backed fun, kicking off with a delicious (and very well-lubricated) dinner in the friendly Oaklands pub. The following morning a jaded but jolly British team impressed all with a hopeless performance at the home-grown "polo-pit squash" field. For the non-horsey among you, there are Boer War battlefield tours, a balustraded pool, mountain bikes and a tennis court (with umpires chair to provoke argument). The stone-walled rooms are fun, converted from old stables and outbuildings. All are different in style, but consistent themes are colourful duvet covers, bright African art and stunning views from the patios. Tucked away behind the trees is the new 'Ukhubona' lodge. Light and airy, with high-ceilings and warm terracotta walls it has a delightful yet understated 'african' feel. Here you're in the wilds among mountains, craggy cliffs and paddocks full of galloping horses, and I guarantee you'll love it.

Rooms: 13: 7 twins, 6 doubles, all en-suite baths and shower over bath. Self-catering house sleeps 6: 1 queen en-suite large bath, 2 twins sharing shower, fully-equipped kitchen & outdoor braai.
Price: May - Oct: R540 pp sharing, R570 singles. Nov - April: R660 pp sharing, R690 singles. 'Ukhubona' self-catering lodge is R1,500 per night.
Meals: Full breakfast and dinner included. Lunch is also available. All meals can be provided for those staying in the self-catering lodge.
Directions: Take the N3 to Van Reenen, turn right at the Caltex garage. Go 7km down a dirt track - Oaklands is signed to the right.

Montusi Mountain Lodge

Anthony and Jean Carte
Off D119, Alpine Heath,
Bergville 3350
Tel: 036-438-6243
Fax: 036-438-6566
Email: montusi@iafrica.com
Web: www.montusi.za.net

Montusi feels a bit like a hotel, which just happens to be run by your aunt and uncle. You know... you haven't seen them for years, but no sooner have you stepped from the car than they've got your bed sorted (well, your thatched, Conran-style, country cottage complete with fireplace, selected DSTV and view!) and are fixing you a sundowner on the patio. Yes, the views are every bit as good as the photo suggests. Ant bought wattle-strangled Montusi Farm in the early 1990s. Being a man of X-ray vision, he saw through the undergrowth to a lodge perfectly positioned to catch the surrounding view, he saw fields of galloping horses and he saw lakes to fish in. So he did away with the wattles (via a community project) and a new Montusi emerged. Meals are superb... some examples: lamb with chargrilled lemon and mint, ostrich fillet with garlic and marinated peppers, malva pudding, custard cups. There are many ways to burn off the calories with limitless hiking, horse-riding for all levels of experience, mountain-biking and fishing. But best of all is ex-skiing pro Chris's circus school! It is as professional as they come, with trapezes, bungies, nets, ropes and they sometimes put on shows too. Montusi impressed me because it's a happy family run place with plenty of style. *Golf and massages available locally. Picnics at waterfalls can be arranged.*

Rooms: 14 cottages: 4 are kings with en-suite bath and another twin with en-suite shower next door. 10 are kings with shower and bath.
Price: R715 - R780 pp sharing. Singles plus R100. Price includes dinner and breakfast.
Meals: Full breakfast and 4-course dinner included (wine extra).
Directions: If coming from the south head north through Pietermaritzburg, Estcourt and turn left signed Northern Drakensberg. Continue for 80km through Winterton and Bergville on R74. Follow signs (some small) to Montusi.

Ardmore Guest Farm

Paul and Sue Ross

Champagne Valley, Winterton 3340
Tel: 036-468-1314 Fax: 036-468-1241
Email: info@ardmore.co.za Web: www.ardmore.co.za
Cell: 083-789-1314

Just in time for scones and tea on the lawn, the rain clouds parted, the sun put its hat on and I was able to savour the stunning views of Champagne Castle (second highest mountain in SA at 3377m) and the Cathkin Peaks before me. The Drakensberg National Park begins just down the road so bring your hiking boots. Ardmore is a super-relaxed, freewheeling sort of place. Sociable and delicious dinners, eaten by lantern light at long tables in the yellowwood dining room, draw on the farm's organic produce - eggs from happy, roaming chickens and fruit, vegetables and herbs from a pesticide-free garden. Paul will tell you all about the art here, all created by the local Zulu community, much of it from the new Zulu cotton-weaving factory and the world-renowned Ardmore Pottery at the end of the garden. There is masses to do: hike to waterfalls and mountain peaks; watch the rare bald ibis that makes its home here; fish, canoe, mountain-bike; the game farm nearby (1/2-hr drive) offers cheap horse-riding to see the rhino, zebra and giraffe; the Drakensberg Boys' Choir performs on Wednesdays at 15h30; and there are 230 rock-art sites in the area too. The small thatched rondavels are sweet and cosy and the bigger ones have fireplaces. Garden furniture is set out under the giant liquid amber tree, an important focal point for the property, where you can take tea and contemplate the mountains.

Rooms: 5 rondavels: 3 large doubles with en/s bath and shower; 2 small with en/s shower; 2 x 2 bedroom cottages: 1 double & 1 twin with en-suite bath & shower.
Price: Dinner, bed and breakfast: R285 - R360 pp sharing. Holiday rates (Christmas and Easter) R320 - R395. Singles R360.
Meals: Full breakfast and dinner with wine included.
Directions: From the N3 take the R74 to Winterton and go south along the R600 towards the Central Drakensberg for 18km. You'll see a sign on your left, 5km up partly dirt road for Ardmore.

Spionkop Lodge

Lynette and Raymond Heron
R600, Drakensberg and Battlefields Area, Ladysmith 3370
Tel: 036-488-1404 Fax: 036-488-1404
Email: spionkop@futurenet.co.za Web: www.spionkop.co.za
Cell: 082-573-0224/5

A magnificent storm was exploding over the Drakensberg Mountains when I visited and it was a relief soon to be tucked up in an armchair by the fire with a dog at my feet. Raymond is a convivial Scot who grew up on the far side of the Zambezi. He's a registered guide, raconteur par excellence and an expert on the tragic movements of the Battle of Spionkop, a keystone in the Anglo-Boer war. You only have to go to the characterful bar and you'll be sitting right where General Buller camped with 27,000 men (Winston Churchill and Mahatma Gandhi among them). The lodge is built on the old Spearman farm and is now a 700-hectare eco-reserve with 278 bird species and a mass of flowering aloes in June and July. You can stay either in bothy-ish stone cottages, which are comfy and snug with fireplaces for winter and verandahs for summer; or in the colonial farmhouse with its polished floorboards and library full of history books (plus a sunroom to read them in). But the main heart of the lodge is the 108-year-old stone, converted barn, now a massive glass-walled dining room with sinuous blonde branches creeping from floor to ceiling. You'll get to know it pretty well. As well as the history, there are game drives, fishing, birding and bushman art enough to keep you entertained for a week.

Rooms: 8 doubles, all en-suite with bath and shower. Plus 2 self-catering cottages: Aloe has 2 double beds and a bath; Acacia has 3 bedrooms and 2 bathrooms.
Price: R830 – R930 full board pp sharing. Aloe R790 per night. Acacia R990 per night.
Meals: All meals included in B&B price. Meals optional for self-caterers: R65 for breakfast, R50 for lunch and R110 for dinner.
Directions: 20 mins off N3 from either Durban or Jo'burg. See web site for map.

Sewula Gorge Lodge

Graham and Santie McIntosh & Jacquie Geldart

Off R103, 18km from Estcourt, Estcourt 3310
Tel: 036-352-2485 Fax: 036-352-2868
Email: info@sewula.co.za Web: www.sewula.co.za
Cell: 082-824-0329

The pictures do not exaggerate. This glorious thatched lodge lives beside a rocky-river gorge filled with cascading waterfalls (the main one is 20 metres high) and swimming pools. As soon as I arrived I realized I had made a significant mistake. I had not organized to stay the night at Sewula and had missed my opportunity to swim under the waterfall looking at the stars. The emphasis is on relaxation and seclusion and only one party stays at a time. Staff live away from the lodge and there is absolutely no-one about except you, a very rare treat (even by GG standards). For this far-too-low-really price, you can pretend you own this truly heavenly place. It is self-catering, but with any domestic hardship extracted. For here, not only does nature spoil you, but the staff do too, by washing up, servicing the rooms and lighting the log fires. Under the thatched pitch of the main lodge roof are the kitchen, bush-chic sunken sitting room, a giant fireplace, an oversized chess set and much wildly original carpentry and functional sculpture. Similarly lovely are the cottages, which have sleeping lofts for children and face the falls. You can walk to an iron-age settlement, battle memorials and great fishing spots. Jacqui is a stellar host and constantly thoughtful. 100% (as the locals say)! *The rock art sites and white-water rafting are within an hour's drive.*

Rooms: 4 cottages (max 8 adults & 10 children): 3 have en/s shower, 2 of which have outdoor shower too; 1 cottage has en/s shr & bath. One booking at a time.
Price: Min. R680 for the whole place per night self-catering. R340 pp for extra guests, but children half-price if sleeping in loft.
Meals: Restaurants are nearby.
Directions: Exit 143 on N3 from Durban to Mooi River. Take R103 to Estcourt, 20.3km from off-ramp, take right turn onto dirt road to Malanspruit and follow signs to Sewula Gorge Camp.

Zingela

Mark and Linda Calverley
PO Box 141, Tugela River
Tel: 036-354-7005/7250 Fax: 036-354-7021
Email: zingela@futurenet.co.za Web: www.zingelasafaris.co.za
Cell: 084-746-9694

Hiking, fishing, abseiling, rafting, swimming, game-viewing, hunting, quad-biking, horse-riding… perhaps I'd be better off listing the things you *can't* do at Zingela. Mark and Linda are delightful and, over twenty years or so, have built up their home/riverside bush camp to offer everything and anything, all the more astonishing given their location. This really is wild country. From a rendezvous in the wee village of Weenen it was an hour's 4x4 drive (not for the faint-hearted) past isolated Zulu villages and down to the Tugela River - worth every bump. There are five palatial double tents overlooking the river, all open to the elements. Showers are more outside than in, branches provide the towel rails and each tent has hefty, iron-framed beds and beautiful wooden furniture from Zanzibar. Those on the romance beat will love the "hitching post" with doubtless the world's largest headboard, a vast, mattress-to-canvas slab of sandstone. There's electricity and gallons of hot water but Zingela is essentially bush living ("don't-forget-the-loo-roll-or-matches kind of country," says Linda). When I visited the place was alive with families (there are zillions of kids' beds in extra dormitory tents). Some youngsters were preparing for a rafting adventure and everyone was thoroughly enjoying the endless fresh air, filling grub and lashings of good, wholesome fun.

Rooms: 5 tents: 3 doubles and 2 twins, all with shower.
Price: R650 – R750 includes all food plus game drive, abseiling and rafting. Quad-bikes, horse-riding and stalking are extra.
Meals: Full board.
Directions: Faxed or emailed on booking, or just phone en route.

Sycamore Avenue Treehouse Lodge

Bruce and Gloria Attwood
11 Hidcote Road, Hidcote,
Mooi River 3300
Tel: 033-263-2875
Fax: 033-263-2134
Email:
sycamore@futurenet.co.za
Web: www.sycamore-ave.com

Tree-houses! Need you read any further? There are not many who can weave a whole house into the branches of a giant pin oak, but Bruce has done it not once, not twice, but three times and when I visited he was busy stretching his imagination around yet another house in the trees, the Planequarium, an exciting 'under the water and up in the air' themed wooden extravaganza. All three of the original arboreal retreats are standing strong and are hidden from the house by foliage each set above a magical garden below (where couples love to get married) and overlooking miles of rolling fields beyond. Bruce is a functional sculptor and his weapon of choice is wood. You'll spot his work all over the Midlands, but it's here that he's really gone to town, or rather, tree. From beds to bread bins to window hooks and hinges, everything is crafted from beautifully grained cedar or wattle, or whatever he can lay his hands on. The third addition, Bottle-tree House, is magnificent. Its spiral staircase winds up from a bottle-walled sitting room to the queen-sized bed, and set into the bedroom is an outdoor jacuzzi. Just picture it... enjoying a good soak to the sound of orioles, although you might have to turn the bubbles off first. A 100% unique, must-try experience. *Well placed for arts/crafts region and Giant Castle.*

Rooms: 4 treehouses: 1 queen & 2 doubles, all with jacuzzis and all have showers. The new Planequarium treehouse has 2 double rooms, both with en-suite toilet and basin, shared shower and jacuzzi.
Price: R400 - R550 pp sharing. Single supplement +50%.
Meals: Full breakfast included. Dinner by arrangement: 3 courses from R95 (excluding wine).
Directions: Take exit 152 off N3. From south turn right, from north turn left onto the R103 Hidcote Rd. Travel for 2km and Sycamore is signed right.

The Antbear

Andrew and Conny Attwood
Fernhust Farm, Moor Park – Giants Castle Road, Estcourt 3310
Tel: 036-352-3143 Fax: 036-352-3143
Email: aattwood@antbear.de Web: www.antbear.de

Thank goodness Andrew and Conny gave up the corporate rat race in Germany for B&B'ing. They renovated the old farmhouse and, like all the buildings at The Antbear, it is thatched and sits on a hilltop surveying the Drakensberg peaks. Andrew is a canny chap. The lodge and rooms are home to his chairs, tables, doors, staircases, towel holders, candle-sticks - the list of working wooden sculptures runs and runs. Just across from the lodge's leafy, colonnaded front patio an old tractor shed has been converted into four other bedrooms. Billowing white curtains frame the view and the rooms have intriguing fireplaces and plenty of humorous sculpture. The first room is superb with a staircase that climbs the right-hand wall, a loft bed-platform in the thatchy peak on the left and a six-foot causeway between the two. There's masses to keep you occupied in the area with birding, rock-art sites, river-rafting, battlefield tours and local arts and crafts. Each night weary guests congregate at the huge yellowwood table (Andrew-carved, naturally) to swap tales of their day's adventures. Homely and 100% organic (unless the horses, tortoises, chickens or geese haven't raided Connie's garden!); the food here is amazing with authentic flavours borrowed from Zulu neighbours or from around the world. All in all, you'd be a fool to stay for only one night.

Rooms: 5: 4 en/s doubles in renovated tractor shed, 3 with showers, one with bath; 1 separate double with en/s jacuzzi bath and shower.
Price: Dinner, bed and breakfast from R440 - R640 pp sharing. No singles supplement.
Meals: Lunch and picnics on request from R40 pp. Dinner usually 3 courses (excluding wine).
Directions: Take exit 152 on the N3 signed Hidcote for 7km. At T-junction turn right towards Giant's Castle. After 14km turn right towards Moor Park onto dirt road. After 5.5km you will see The Antbear sign to the right. The thatched cottages are 2km up the farm road.

Map Number: 13

Engeleni Lodge

Graham and Sue Armstrong
Rosetta 3301
Tel: 033-267-7218 Fax: 033-267-7103
Email: engeleni@futurenet.co.za Web: www.engeleni-lodge.co.za
Cell: 082-854-2338

To fully experience all that the KZN Midlands has to offer, this place should be high on your 'must-do' list. For not only is Sue a delightful host, but she is also an experienced, home-grown tour-guide who is dying to share her local knowledge with you. So whatever sparks your fancy, from private gardens, horse-studs, San rock paintings, air-ballooning (take-off point, the lawn) or Zulu spiritual healing... Sue will sort it out. There are also superb birding and fishing opportunities right here on the farm. And the accommodation is tip-top too. After years spent outcast and overgrown, the lodge has been welcomed back, and wonderfully restored and now radiates country warmth from each room. Full of beautiful original artworks and with fishing rods and binos dotted around, Engeleni is one of those places where I immediately felt right at home. From the huge wood-panelled kitchen with wagon-wheel light-fittings hanging from the rafters, to the flower-filled dining room, cosy pub, cheery bedrooms, book-filled corridors and snug living room (with traditional Gallic fishing-boat above the log-fire!), this deceptively large house, dwarfed by its magnificent setting, is a knock-out. I absolutely loved the smaller, slightly more 'African' Mayfly too; so cosy that Sue sometimes uses it as her own secret R&R retreat. Romantic couples, keen beans and lazy idlers all... I'd recommend you stay at least two nights.

Rooms: Engeleni Lodge: 5 king/twins, 1 with en-suite shower, 2 with en-suite shower & bath, 2 rooms share bath; Mayfly Cottage: 1 king/twin with en-suite double shower.

Price: R250 - R275 pp sharing. If less than 5 people R1,500 per night for Engeleni Lodge.

Meals: Full breakfast R65 or continental R45. Lunch is R65. Dinners are flexible though generally R120 for 3 courses.

Directions: From Durban/Jo'burg, take Mooi River Toll Plaza off N3. L onto R103 to Rosetta, then turn R into Kamburg Rd for 18km. R into D314, then continue for 3.7km on registered dirt road following signs to the lodge.

Map Number: 13

Stocklands Farm

Eve Mazery
4 Shafton Rd, Howick 3290
Tel: 033-330-5225 Fax: 033-330-5225
Email: edulink@iafrica.com Web: www.stocklandsfarm.co.za
Cell: 082-975-2298

The warm welcome that I received as I tumbled out of my car, late and weary, is undoubtedly typical of Stocklands. As my cognitive faculties jolted back to life over a restorative beverage, it became obvious that Eve and Roland are natural hosts; thoughtful, funny and relaxed. They have put a lot of love and plenty of style into the wonderful old house. The argument goes that half-measures are not really in keeping with Stocklands, and you can see their point. The walls of the original 1850s house, for example, are over 50 centimetres thick and the belhambra tree at the front of the house is no-less-than enormous. Birds come in droves – they love Roland's indigenous trees and bank upon bank of stunning flowers. I loved the fuchsia tree myself (it flowers in January). Down near the tennis court there is a koi pond and many guests like to savour a slow, hot afternoon in the thick shade on a blanket here after a picnic. The four rooms, like the cottages, are meticulously decorated to individual themes. Eve has found hand-embroidered linen and original works by local artists to decorate and nothing is left out. Choose from a range of breakfasts including the Vegetarian, the Sunrise, the Decadent and… the Sensible! *Game can be viewed right next door, by the way. French spoken.*

Rooms: 4: 2 suites & 2 bedrooms, 1 en-suite bath, 3 en-s shower. Also 2 cottages: 1 with 3 bedrooms & 2 bathrooms, 1 with 2 bedrooms, 1 shower.
Price: R230 - R260 pp sharing. Singles on request. Self-catering R140 - R180 pp.
Meals: Full breakfast included or you can self-cater in the cottages. Excellent café next door & more in area.
Directions: From Jo'burg take N3 to Durban. Take first exit to Howick signed Howick/Tweedie. At Stop sign turn left to Howick. Through lights to bottom of hill, turn L to Karkloof. 100m turn R into Shafton Rd. Stocklands is 1km. From Durban take N3 to Jo'burg. Take 3rd Howick turn-off as above.

Inversanda

Tom and Lucinda Bate

Howick 3290
Tel: 033-234-4321 Fax: 033-234-4751
Email: bate@nitrosoft.co.za Web: www.inversanda.co.za
Cell: 082-781-3875

I have to admit, I cut a pretty ungainly figure on an early morning ride through forest and field with Tom and Lucinda - my fourth-ever horse-back experience. Holding on for dear life, I was undoubtedly passenger rather than driver as I bounced up and down on Dablamanzi (unnervingly translated as the "wave parter") but, as with my entire stay here, I loved it. Hemmed in by mountains and a meander of the Mgeni River, Inversanda is in a world of its own but in easy reach of the major routes. All four Bateses (plus assorted hounds) are utterly charming and you're encouraged to participate in their farm and life as much or as little as you like. Being their lone visitor, I joined the family and neighbours for dinner and was soon involved in a hard-fought game of after-supper "Articulate". When not farming cattle, buried in chartered surveying or battling to conserve their stunning surroundings, Tom and Lucinda are serious horse-lovers and breed and school polo ponies. Polophiles are more than welcome for a weekend knock-about on the makeshift, riverside pitch. Otherwise you can fish, walk or swim pretty much anywhere you want. The farmhouse itself (1800s) goes on forever and guests have their own wing, a pot-planted patio with stunning views across the valley, two enormous twin rooms and a basic kitchen. I loved the drawing room, where there's a hearthside, bottomless red sofa for the saddle-sore and enough firewood to spit-roast an elephant.

Rooms: 1 self-catering wing of the house with two twin rooms and shared bath and shower.
Price: R200 - R250 pp self-catering.
Meals: Meals available on request.
Directions: Faxed or emailed on booking.

Valemount Country Lodge

Dalene and Lance Bailey
PO Box 45, Underberg 3257
Tel: 033-701-1686 Fax: 033-701-1687
Email: info@valemountafrica.com Web: www.valemountafrica.com
Cell: 082-828-8921

The Sani Pass is as thrilling/hair-raising a drive as you'll enjoy/undergo in SA, so thank goodness Lance and Dalene are on hand to put a stiff drink in your hand at the bottom. The Baileys came here from Johannesburg just a year or two ago and they couldn't look more at home in their new surroundings. Their home is a thatched, sunny-yellow slice of tranquillity that spreads out across a regimented English country garden, between pine and English oaks and stunning copper beeches. The rooms all have bags of space, working fireplaces and patios facing the garden or surrounding woodland. You can wander wherever you like, ambling along winding, wooded footpaths, fishing for trout in the lake or bobbing about in the heated pool. That's the latest addition and Lance proudly showed me the three separate 'Martini seats' and jacuzzi jets. He and Dalene have a real eye for detail (they even cut the grass in the forest for you!) and have all sorts of plans for paths here and gazebos there, while quietly harbouring romantic visions of a mini-cheese-factory, although "we've got to learn to make cheese first," he acknowledges. If you've spent the day clattering around the dirt roads, I can't think of anywhere better to rub the dust from your eyes and relax.

Rooms: 6: 2 luxury kings, 2 standard twins, all with en-suite bath and shower; 2 double self-catering units with en-suite bath and hand-shower.
Price: From R245 pp sharing. Singles on request.
Meals: Full breakfast included. Dinner (R110) on request.
Directions: From N3 off-ramp 99 take R617 110km to Underberg. Continue for 8km towards Swartberg and Valemount is signed on the left.

Penwarn Country Lodge

Peta Parker

PO Box 253, Southern Drakensberg, Underberg 3257
Tel: 033-701-1777 or 1341 or 1342 Fax: 033-701-1341
Email: info@penwarn.com Web: www.penwarn.com
Cell: 083-305-3009

Penwarn is simply fantastic. There are two places to stay here (I'm afraid that the cave is no longer an option). The main lodge was converted from an old dairy and fertilizer shed into colourful sitting rooms, a bar and wonderfully comfortable bedrooms. And then there is magnificent Mthini Lodge complete with wooden deck overlooking the main dam, grazing game, horses, cattle and the mountains beyond. I stayed here and was up fishing at the crack of dawn (well, before breakfast at least). You can try your luck pretty much anywhere and kit and lessons are provided. In fact, the list of activities at Penwarn is exhaustive (and exhausting!): tubing on fast-flowing rivers or swimming in pools fed by waterfalls; bird-watching (lammerguyers may join you at the Vulture Restaurant); mountaineering or abseiling (tricky cliffs everywhere); and game drives where tame eland will approach you. I headed out on horseback after a pile of scrambled eggs and rode through herds of zebra and wildebeest before trotting off to inspect 1,500 year-old bushman art. Peta and her staff (or family, I couldn't tell) are great fun but all too-often overshadowed by TV celebrity Nimrod, a (very) tame otter partial to sausages, dog wrestling and baths (close the door or he'll be in yours!). Penwarn is a magical and brilliant place, run by the best.

Rooms: 11: 7 suites at Indabushe Lodge, 4 suites at Mthini lodge. All have en-suite bath and/or shower. (No cave dwelling anymore – sorry!).
Price: Full board is R800 - R950 pp sharing.
Meals: Full breakfast, lunch, 4-course dinner and all snacks are included. Wine is not. Canoeing is free.
Directions: Take Exit 99 off N3 marked Underberg, Howick South and travel 110km west to Underberg, going through Boston and Bulwer en route. Take the Swartberg Road out of Underberg and after 5km turn right onto Bushmansnek Road (dirt track). After 16km turn L to Penwarn (drive is 4km long.)

Map Number: 13

Free State & Lesotho

Die Ou Stal

Piet and Zenobia Labuchagné
38 George Street, Zastron 9950
Tel: 051-673-1268 Fax: 051-673-1268
Email: dieoustal@tiscali.co.za
Cell: 082-416-7832

In a place like Zastron, it's vital to find yourself a guide to show you the unknown gems that lurk around every corner and to recount the astonishing tales of yesteryear. Look no further than Piet. His enthusiasm for the geology and pre-history of Africa is infectious. After the whistle-stop tour of intriguing local rock formations, spiced up with ancient bushman legends, I'll never look at a cliff face in the same way again. Had I stayed longer, I'd have been begging him to take me on a day trip to nearby Lesotho, but alas I had to leave even before one of Zen's sumptuous suppers of bobotie or chicken pie. At least I had time to sit on the stoep outside the converted stables that are now the guest rooms and watch a lightning storm hammer away at the Lesotho mountains – a majestic sight indeed. The bedrooms are simple, cosy affairs with whitewashed walls and doors that open into a small kitchen. Breakfast, however, is served at the large dining table in the main house, atop wooden floorboards and next to a fridge surely dating from before fridges were invented (also wood): this intriguing feature is now a drinks cabinet. In a town that's won awards for its friendliness (driving around with Piet, the whole town and his uncle Joe came out to give us a wave), Zen is champion of champions.

Rooms: 2: 1 double with en-suite bath and shower; 1 twin with en-suite shower.
Price: R250 - R350 pp sharing.
Meals: Full breakfast included. Dinner on request: R50.
Directions: From N6 turn onto R26 and follow signs to Zastron. In town, turn right opposite the corner of the church into Mathee Street, then take third left into Berg Strat and see signs.

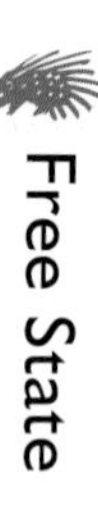

Springfontein House

Graeme Wedgwood
32 van Riebeeck Street, Springfontein 9917
Tel: 051-783-0076 Fax: 051-783-0425
Email: wedgie@icon.co.za Web: www.springfontein-guest-house.com
Cell: 082-450-6779

Graeme used to run Smithfield House, which he brought to life with cultivated, Epicurean zeal. Well, the same applies here at his new home. Those with a taste for fine living will find a kindred spirit in Graeme, a man whose love of house and garden, countryside, good company, food and wine now sets the tone at Springfontein House. He was once a gallery owner in Johannesburg – a far cry from his first, 26-year career as a London stockbroker – and his personal art collection includes a rather racy Battiss, an inky Sekoto and other originals by South African artists, both established and emerging. African rugs, powdery sofas, bowls of dried rose petals and side tables proffering porcelain complete the sandy-coloured sitting room. Through glass doors is a slate-floored, frond-filled sunroom and an incarnadine dining room, with Georgian tables and silver candelabras. In the bedrooms the curtains are silk, the towels soft and the comfy beds have crisp linen, plump pillows and mohair throws. Outside, white walls dazzle and creepers climb above the stoep; there's a bricked patio and colourful flower-beds, a pool and a series of fishponds. But the reason you come here is to be looked after, and arriving from the biscuity veld, you'll feel lucky indeed. *Graeme will explain about biking, hiking, rare bird-watching, fishing, sailing on Gariep Dam.*

Rooms: 5: 3 queens, 1 with en-suite bath/shower, 1 with en-suite shower and 1 with full bathroom en-suite; 2 twins, 1 with en-suite bath/shower and 1 with full bathroom en-suite.
Price: From R200 pp sharing. Singles on request. Booking advised.
Meals: Full breakfast included. 3-course dinner available on request R75, excluding wine.
Directions: Heading north on the N1 turn off at Springfontein South sign. Follow road, becoming Settler St. Van Riebeeck St is on your left, and Springfontein House is at the end on right. For those travelling south on the N1 come off at Springfontein North exit and follow the signs.

De Oude Kraal Country Estate

Gerhard and Marie Lombard
Nr. Bloemfontein 9300
Tel: 051-564-0636
Fax: 051-564-0635
Email: info@oudekraal.co.za
Web: www.oudekraal.co.za
Cell: 082-413-1798

Sprawled over 2,400 hectares of flat veld, the farm at De Oude Kraal was a hive of Boer War activity. British officers lived here in the final stages of the conflict as the countryside was swept clean between the infamous blockhouses, one of which can be found in a secluded corner. As I arrived, guests were saddling up for a riding tour to study the history, see the ostriches and check the sheep - there are also springbok and blesbok to be seen on the farm. At night this is the perfect site for star-gazing beneath clear, unpolluted night skies. But not before enjoying one of Marie's fabulous traditional six-course dinners in the pine-floored dining room, complemented by a fine wine from Gerhard's award-winning cellar (and it's well worth asking him for a guided tour). With wider waists and tickled taste buds, guests waddle back to their rooms to make some space for the traditional 'boere' (farm) breakfast awaiting them the following morning. Rooms range from simple but cosy stone-floored affairs in the converted shearing shed to luxurious four-poster suites with private patios overlooking the smooth, tree-lined lawn. Some of the bathrooms are features in themselves, my favourite boasting an open shower in the centre of a bare-rock room, the spa-bath sunken into a rock bed and filled via a mini-waterfall. A word of warning: don't wear your best tie in the old railway sleeper-wood bar. Gerhard's collection numbers 803 and counting.

Rooms: 10: 4 "standard", 2 with en-suite bath, 2 with en-suite bath and shower; 2 "luxury", both with en-suite bath and shower; 4 "executive", all with en-suite bath and shower.
Price: R385 - R495 pp sharing. Singles R450 - R560.
Meals: Full breakfast included. 6-course gourmet dinner R165 excluding drinks. Light lunches on request.
Directions: From Bloemfontein, travel 35km south on the N1. Take off-ramp 153, and then follow the signs (7km from N1).

Bishop's Glen

Ted and Bits Quin

PO Box 9, Glen 9360
Tel: 051-861-2210 Fax: 051-861-2210
Email: bishopsglen.ea@connix.co.za
Cell: 082-374-4986

It's a particular pleasure to stay in a place where the owners give of themselves as unstintingly as Ted and Bits do. I love the fact that they join you (you join them?) for both dinner and breakfast – this is what staying in somebody's home is all about. Nine of us sat down to a sumptuous dinner in the evening and added new resonance to the word 'convivial'. The house dates back to 1813, and the dining room still has some of the original yellowwood timbers. All is lived-in yet elegant, with beautiful wooden furniture and family portraits in abundance. Earlier we had gathered on the plant-encrusted verandah, looking out over the lush garden and its 200-plus bird species, before moving to the sitting room where Ted's 27 (I counted) cattle trophies fill up one wall. My bedroom was impressively large and timbered, with pretty linen and a substantial array of novels. No old travel magazines here! Bits (a childhood friend called Pieces is out there somewhere) does not take last-minute bookings – she likes to be prepared - so make sure you ring well in advance to reserve a night in one of the Free State's finest, homeliest bolt-holes. *There is also a game farm, with many different antelopes.*

Rooms: 3: 1 double and 2 twins; all with en-suite shower, 1 with shower and bath.
Price: Dinner, bed and breakfast: R400 pp sharing. Singles on request.
Meals: Full breakfast included. Also dinner: 3 courses with pre-dinner drinks and wine at table.
Directions: Faxed or emailed on booking. Bishop's Glen is 20km north of Bloemfontein off-ramp 213 from N1.

St Fort Country House

Ernestine Goldblatt
Clarens 9707
Tel: 058-256-1345 or 058-256-1101 Fax: 058-256-1250
Email: info@stfort.co.za Web: www.stfort.co.za

Scrape the mud off the old walking boots and start limbering up. St Fort is a hiker's dream with trails leading through fields of bleating sheep that surround the house, up craggy koppies and jutting overhangs to Mushroom Rock (a rock, you will be surprised to learn, that is shaped like a mushroom). Or, for those with excess energy to burn, there's a day hike to caves decorated with bushman paintings. Rolling up the drive past the trout-fishing dam and towards the kaleidoscopic garden, dominated by purple larkspurs, I noticed guests sheltering from the afternoon sun on the brick-pillared verandah, locked in a game of bridge, too weary to walk or fish. Inside, Oregon pine floors creak underfoot, and framed photos chart the history of the farm from when a stern-faced Mr. Walker moved here from his St Fort estate in Scotland during the Boer War. Light floods into the lounge through a sprawling bay window, as in the cavernous master bedroom, and both rooms are kept snug in those harsh Free State winters with thick Persian rugs. Self-caterers have a small kitchen, or use the original farm kitchen, with a table big enough for all-comers. Otherwise, Ernestine will zip over in the morning to prepare a breakfast feast, but with the option of haddock or even 'uitsmyter' – ham on toast, topped with tomato, scrambled egg and cheese, for those who didn't know.

Rooms: 5: all doubles or twins on request, 1 with en-suite bath and shower, 4 with en-suite showers.
Price: R240 - R270 pp sharing. Singles R280 - R330.
Meals: Full breakfast included. Self-catering option available or restaurants in Clarens.
Directions: From the N5 take the R712 signed to Clarens. Pass Clarens and turn R on the R711 Fouriesburg Road, continue for approx 5km, and St Fort is on the left.

Map Number: 13

The View

Ryk and Bea and Sasha Becker
20 Bell Street, Harrismith 9880
Tel: 058-623-0961
Fax: 058-623-0961
Email: rmbecker@internext.co.za
Web: www.harrismithaccommodation.co.za
Cell: 082-775-7381 (Bea); 082-921-3624 (Ryk)

How better to while away a sticky afternoon than by nesting in a rocking chair behind teak pillars on a shady verandah, overlooking a lush garden, slowly draining a pot of tea? Bea and Ryk have found a magic formula simply by being themselves at home! The actual view of the title is now interrupted by an abundance of verdure, but I for one was glad of the green shade and the peaceful sounds of twittering birds hidden among the branches. Inside, a portrait of Bea's big-bearded great-grandfather, President of the Free State (deceased, of course), overlooks the social epicentre of this family home. The lounge, complete with creaking wooden floorboards, vibrant rugs and daringly bright sofas, sweeps through folded-back doors into the dining room where the heavy table awaits those staying in for dinner. And I thoroughly recommend you are among them. You would travel a long way to find a better meal and you'll miss out on Ryk spilling the beans on what to do in this area where he grew up. Before heading up to my goose-feathered bed for my best night's sleep in years, no visit to The View would be complete without being introduced to the rest of the family: four springer and two cocker spaniels. *Son-in-law Simon can arrange stargazing visits to his farm and other local activities.*

Rooms: 3: all doubles with en-suite bath and/or shower. 1 room has private bathroom.
Price: R200 - R275 pp sharing. Singles R280 - R350.
Meals: Full breakfast included. Dinners on request from R95 pp.
Directions: From Jo'burg side into Warden Street (main street) go around church. 7 blocks from church turn R into Bell Street. From Durban & Bloem, on entering Harrismith turn away from Spur/Engen garage into King Street. Turn L into Warden Street at 1st stop-street. Bell Street is about 10 blocks from here on L.

Malealea Lodge and Pony Trek Centre

Mick and Di Jones

Malealea, Brandhof 9324
Tel: 051-436-6766 Fax: 051-436-6766
Email: malealea@mweb.co.za Web: www.malealea.com or www.malealea.co.ls Cell: 082-552-4215

You shouldn't need an excuse to go to the kingdom of Lesotho, but if you do, look no further than Malealea Lodge. Here in the country's heartland – no phones, no mains electricity - Mick and Di have created a fascinating environment through a combination of their own personal warmth, native knowledge and a wealth of natural and cultural attractions. Malealea thrives on its interaction with the neighbouring village, but this is no plasticky 'Cultural Village' experience. The lodge is entered via the area's trading station, horses for treks of up to six days are hired locally (you stay in the villages you visit), and children will guide you on hikes. In the evenings, you listen to a local choir, before a band plays with home-made instruments. It's worth travelling off the high roads to experience moments such as these! Communal suppers are served canteen style - backpackers and ambassadors rub comradely shoulders – before the pub and firelit stoep drag you away. Later your torch guides you back to thatched rondavel or farmhouse-style accommodation – try to stay as near to the front as possible. I arrived in the afternoon rain but woke up to the most stunning of mornings, with the mist lying low down in the valley, and the peacocks crowing arrogantly at everyone. I loved this place. Two nights are an absolute minimum. *Best visited between December and May.*

Rooms: 40: 8 doubles and 32 twins all with en-suite shower.
Price: Rondavels R240 pp sharing, farmhouses R190 pp sharing. Single supplement 50%.
Meals: Full breakfast included. Lunch R50. Dinner R70 for as much as you want. Horse treks R200 pp per day. Village accommodation R45 pp. Day rides from R100 pp. Communal kitchen.
Directions: Faxed or emailed on booking.

Map Number: 12

Northern Cape

Papkuilsfontein Farmhouse

Willem and Mariëtte van Wyk, Jaco and Alrie
Nieuwoudtville 8180
Tel: 027-218-1246 Fax: 027-218-1246
Email: info@papkuilsfontein.com Web: www.papkuilsfontein.com

I'm going to stick my neck out and say that this is my favourite place to stay in South Africa! And here are my reasons.... You stay in an old stone cottage, surrounded by rock, gum tree and wildlife, not another human in sight. The quality of peace and stillness defeats description. Gas-fired plumbing for baths, hurricane lamps for light - many guests have refused to come back if Willem installs electricity. Then there's the small matter of the gorge and waterfall, which I would have kept secret if I wasn't insistent on your visiting the farm. Your jaw will drop 180 metres into the canyon. Take a picnic to the deep rock pools for swimming above the waterfall (or there's a pool next to the cottages) and you can climb down into the gorge in an hour and a half. The wild flowers in season are sensational even by Namaqualand standards; the plantlife, divided between Cape fynbos and Karoo succulent, a botanist's dream; steenbok, klipspringer, porcupine and dassie love the terrain and have NOT been specially introduced. Alrie is an excellent cook (breakfast a string of surprises). It's a magical place that not many know about and the van Wyks are all lovely, friendly people who seem unable to put a proper price on what they have to offer! You should stay at least two nights. There's also a restored corrugated-iron cottage for those who need their electricity!

Rooms: 2 stone cottages sleeping 4 and 6: one with bath and outdoor shower and the other with shower. 1 cottage with one twin and one double, one with en/s bath and one with en/s shower.
Price: R225 - R270 pp sharing. Single rates + 50%. Minimum cost per cottage per night in flower season: Gert Boom R625, De Hoop R470.
Meals: Full breakfast included. 3-course dinners R110.
Directions: From CT take N1 then N7 to Vanrhynsdorp. Turn off onto R27 to Nieuwoudtville. Turn right into town, and straight through onto dirt road for 22km. The farm signed to the right.

Guest House La Boheme

Evelyne Meier
Post Net Suite 101, Private Bag X5879, 172 Groenpunt Rd, Upington 8800
Tel: 054-338-0660 Fax: 054-338-0661
Email: laboheme@mweb.co.za Web: www.labohem.com
Cell: 083-383-8288

La Boheme claims its rightful place in this book on many counts: its fantastic view from a green, green lawn over the Orange River flood plain; its cool-blue pool; its palm trees that rustle in the hot breeze; and the fantastic dinners served on the verandah at a candle-lit, communal table (undoubtedly one of the best meals I have had in South Africa!). But all of these things play second fiddle to Evelyne herself, who is hugely friendly and energetic and a wholly exceptional host. A cultural blend herself, half-Hungarian and half-Swiss, her guest house also melds various ethnic styles. There are only three rooms here, guaranteeing the personal touch and each offering something different. I had a trendy-Africa, honeymooners' room with a huge bed of sculpted 'decocrete' and its own patch of outside with iron chairs. Next door has a private patio too, but more of a Caribbean feel and for those wanting a little more space and a touch of Asia there's a separate garden cottage with its own kitchenette and gravel garden surrounded by lush plants. I highly recommend you find your way to Upington, which is an Orange River oasis in the middle of the Kalahari Desert. Not many do. The Kgalagadi Transfrontier Park (Kalahari-Gemsbok Park) is just a couple of hours away, Augrabies Falls less than that, and local vineyards and river cruises closer still. *Languages spoken: French, German, Italian, English and Hungarian.*

Rooms: 3: 1 king with en/s bath and shower, 1 queen with separate bath and shower, 1 cottage with queen and twin sharing a shower.
Price: R336 - R546 pp sharing. Singles R526 - R956.
Meals: Full breakfast included. 3-course dinners available for a minimum of 3 people by prior arrangement (24 hrs notice): R160. All drinks are extra.
Directions: In Upington take Schröder Street towards Olifantshoek, N14, under railway bridge and past Gordonia hospital. 1.7 km after hospital, turn R to Engen garage. Turn immediately L (Groenpunt Road). Continue 2.5km to red & white Telkom tower and guest-house is on the right.

Riviera Garden B&B

Anneke Malan
16 Budler Street, Upington 8801
Tel: 054-332-6554 Fax: 054-332-6554
Email: ariviera@upington.co.za Web: www.upington.co.za/ariviera
Cell: 072-447-6750

Riviera is a true patch of paradise on the banks of the impressive Orange River, a patch it's taken Anneke a lifetime to find. It was the garden that I loved above all, a lush parade of palm trees, roses and agapanthus and racing-green grass that cools even the most overheated of travellers (as I certainly was when I visited). The lawn flows like a tributary past the pool, right to the water's edge and a secluded, white bench at the end of the garden, the perfect spot to sit and contemplate the river's flowing depths. It's from here that guests hop onto a cruise boat at six o'clock for evening river trips, bobbing downstream, washing down the sunset with a G&T before ambling into town for some dinner. The evenings can be as hot as the days in this part of the world and you'll be glad to find the two cool garden rooms hidden among the greenery with their hefty beds and bags of cupboard space for longer stays. From national parks (Upington is a gateway to the Kalahari Desert and Namibia) to vineyards there's plenty to keep you busy here and it's a must-do stop on any tour of the unspoiled Northern Cape.

Rooms: 2: 1 twin with bath and shower, 1 double with extra single and bath.
Price: R215 pp sharing. Singles on request.
Meals: Breakfast R35. Dinner on request.
Directions: Follow main roads right into the centre of Upington. From Schroeder St turn onto River St towards the river, that leads into Budler St and Riviera is number 16 on the right about half way down.

A La Fugue

Jacqueline Castella
40 Janggroentjieweg, Upington 8800
Tel: 054-338-0424 Fax: 054-338-0084
Email: pujcastl@mweb.co.za Web: www.lafugue-guesthouse.com
Cell: 082-789-9324

Chaud, hot, heiss! Upington was knocking on almost 40°C when I visited, so Jacqueline definitely had the right idea, meeting me at the car in pink swimming costume and sarong. Positively melting after hours on the road I was invited to flump myself down on a plant-shaded pillow by the pool and was fed a glass of iced tea. What initially struck me about A La Fugue, as I was led along a rose-lined and plant-dotted path, was the tropical garden, absolutely dazzling in the intense sunshine. Named after great composers, each of La Fugue's bungalows has their own unique identity. Rossini and Rusticana, two quaint wooden chalets, seem to originate from the Swiss element of your host, while studio bungalow Mozart and family unit Vivaldi perhaps embody the classic French side. The two B&B rooms in the house (Chopin and Bach), soothing in golds and creams, are found along a short landing where Jacqueline's stunning model daughter beams warmly from the wall. Dinner and breakfast, touched with a little foreign pizazz, are served outside on one of the bright mosaic tables (your hostess has a distinct flair for mosaics and you will find examples in many unexpected places). It's a good thing each room has its own outdoor seating area as with such a garden you won't want to sit inside. Personally I would rarely be found far from the thatched African-themed poolside lapa and loungers. Jacqueline is fluent in French, English and German by the way.

Rooms: 5: 2 self-catering studios, 1 self-catering family unit and 2 B&B double rooms. All with en-suite shower and own separate entrances.
Price: R225 pp sharing B&B. Enquire about singles and self-catering prices.
Meals: Full breakfast included in B&B price, R55 if self-catering. Dinners on request (preferable 24 hrs notice) R170 inclusive of all wine and drinks.
Directions: Emailed or faxed on request.

Map Number: 10

Witsand Nature Reserve

Northern Cape

Bertus Bester
R64 Kimberley to Witsand,
Postmasburg 8420
Tel: 053-313-1061/2
Fax: 053-313-1061/2
Email:
witsandkalahari@telkomsa.net
Web:
www.witsandkalahari.co.za
Cell: 083-234-7573

There are few places beautiful enough to get me out of bed before seven. At Witsand, in the southern Kalahari, I sprang into action at five. At the foot of the Langberg Mountains, this provincial nature reserve is a 3,500ha gem, dominated by a 65-million-year-old dune system that 'roars' as you walk on it. The sky-scraping, grass-dotted ridges of sand vary in colour from blinding white to golden tones and tanned reds, dwarfing the six-man chalets that are hidden in the bush below. Ten spots offer plenty of air-conditioned comfort, fully-equipped kitchens and a huge, tree-shaded braai area with ancient railway-sleeper dining tables for jolly star-lit nights. I spent an afternoon soaking up the scenery, guided by resident expert Jeanene, who has a fascination for creepy-crawlies and pointed out springbok, oryx, and desert birds galore (there's a great bird hide). Bertus and Yvette run the show and very kindly welcomed a lone GGer into their home for supper. Self-catering is usually the order of the day, but I'd recommend opting for the Kalahari Experience, which includes hearty meals, wine and guided walks. If you're feeling particularly adventurous there's even room for a bit of cycling or sand-boarding (!). This is a truly spectacular place and my solo, crack-of-dawn walk through dunes ruffled only by wind and animal tracks is a memory that will last as long as I do.

Rooms: 10: all family chalets with a double room, 2 twin rooms and shared bath, shower and toilet. Camping options also available.
Price: Dinner B&B plus guided walk for R925 pp. R220 pp self-catering. Min R630 night for chalets at weekends. Dune board hire R100.
Meals: Dinner, B&B available. On-site shop sells basic foods.
Directions: From Upington take the R64 to Groblershoop. Before entering the town turn left towards Griquatown. Travel 59km on this road. Turn left at Witsand turn-off onto a gravel road for 45km and follow the signs.

Kuilfontein Stable Cottages

Penny and Leigh Southey

Kuilfontein Farm, Route N1, Colesberg 9795
Tel: 051-753-1364 Fax: 051-753-0200
Email: kuil@mweb.co.za Web: www.kuilfontein.co.za
Cell: 082-552-2488

A drink is always welcome in the middle of the blazing Karoo and I was gasping when Penny poured mine in the chilled-out guest lounge. Kuilfontein has been in Leigh's family for five generations and is still a busy dairy and sheep farm. Surrounded by a vast hinterland of arid fields it's hard to believe it's only 1.2 kilometres from the N1. The white-washed Stable bedrooms are all named after race-horses, the theme continuing inside with newspaper clippings and framed shots of 'Danny Boy' or 'Equilateral' (among others) in action. French doors lead from your own verandah onto gleaming screed floors sporting locally-made furniture, as well as the odd family heirloom, while brightly-coloured walls and fine-quality linen create a homely feeling. The 'Feed Room' has been appropriately converted into a dining/breakfast room. The Southeys' own dairy means fresh yoghurt and milk appear for breakfast amongst other goodies. I would have loved to stay and experience the 'home-grown' Karoo lamb or venison for dinner before trundling onto the 'upside-down trough bar' also housed here. A tall wicker stool is the perfect spot to park yourself for some cheerful banter, beverages and hilarity (as experienced by a previous 'inspector'); unfortunately for me it was not meant to be, but there is nothing stopping you from booking in and sampling all Kuilfontein has to offer. A popular stop-over point, but this farmstead is worth staying a lot longer for.

Rooms: 8: 5 standard double bedrooms, 2 luxury double rooms and 1 family suite, all with en-suite showers.
Price: R270 - R350 pp sharing. Singles on request. Children 6+ on request.
Meals: Full health breakfast included. 3-course dinner R100 - R120.
Directions: 12km south or Colesberg, 60 km north of Hanover on N1.

Gauteng

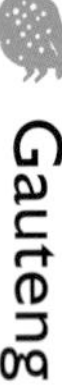

Melrose Place Guest Lodge

Sue Truter
12a North St, Melrose 2196
Tel: 011-442-5231 Fax: 011-880-2371
Email: melroseplace@global.co.za Web: www.melroseplace.co.za
Cell: 083-457-4021

Once ensconced behind the electric gates at Melrose you have entered an Eden-in-the-city. The verandah overlooks a large flower garden and enormous swimming pool, all shaded by trees. Eight new rooms don't crowd it at all. It is such a pleasant environment that you may find yoursel shelving projected tasks for a day's lounging about. My room was a suite attached to the mair house, with mounted TV, huge bed (built up with cushions and pillows), a big bathroom anc double doors onto the garden. The high levels of luxury in all the rooms are not reflected in the rates. Sue is the sweetest of hostesses, quick to smiles and reacting sensitively to the mood anc wishes of each guest. On the night I stayed we had a braai with an amazing array of meat dishes and salads which appeared from nowhere, and Sue's team will cook dinner for anyone whc wants it every evening. Her aim is to maximise the number of happy campers staying. This is her home after all, complete with kids, dachshund and a parrot in its 40s. While guest contentmen is running at 100 per cent, it's difficult to see what else she can do. *Laundry provided on request. Nearby: Wanderers cricket ground, Rosebank and Sandton shopping precincts and many restaurants. Airport transfers arranged by Sue.*

Rooms: 14: all en-suite (1 bath only, 4 bath and shower, 9 shower only); includes two cottages.
Price: R390 - R440 pp sharing. Singles R595 - R650
Meals: Full breakfast included. Lunches (R45) or dinners (R90) by arrangement.
Directions: Ask for a map when booking. Or a map is on the web site.

Liz at Lancaster

Liz Delmont
79 Lancaster Ave, Craighall Park, Johannesburg 2196
Tel: 011-442-8083 Fax: 011-880-5969
Email: lizdel@megaweb.co.za Web: www.lizatlancaster.co.za
Cell: 083-229-4223

Liz's place on its own is our idea of a B&B (more on that later), but throw in Liz as well and you get something special. In my limited experience she is an anomaly among South Africans, having no great interest in rugby, football or cricket, and this despite being surrounded by a sports-mad family. Liz taught art history and post-graduate tourism development at Witwatersrand University for over 20 years, and is a fascinating person to speak to about South Africa both past and future... and about Jo'burg. She will point you in all the right directions for a genuine, heartfelt and hard-to-come-by insight into her home city. But guests at Liz's also have plenty of space in which to do their own thing. The big, comfy rooms are either side of the main house, with their own entrances and parking spaces and now come kitted-out with internet access and satellite TV. Two more have been added since our last book; that is to say, Liz has given over even more of her home to her guests. A separate cottage has its own kitchen and sitting room. They all open up onto their own private patios, where breakfast is generally served, with potted plants climbing up the walls and plenty of shade. Between them is a rose-filled garden, while at the front of the house is yet more green space around the pool. Finally, a mention for the friendly staff, who have a stake in the venture.

Rooms: 4: 3 doubles (1 with kitchen) with en/s bath and shower, plus 1 cottage with kitchen and sitting room.
Price: R265 - R340 pp sharing. Singles R430 - R540.
Meals: Full breakfast included. Dinners on request but very close to Parkhurst and many restaurants.
Directions: Jan Smuts Ave runs down the middle of the city and Lancaster Ave is off it. Directions on web site.

The Peech Hotel

James Peech
61 North Street, Melrose, Johannesburg 2196
Tel: 011-537-9797 Fax: 011-537-9798
Email: reception@thepeech.co.za Web: www.thepeech.co.za

It was supposed to have been swaying palms on Bali beaches, but instead we've got jacaranda trees in a Johannesburg suburb," says James. Even the worst of navigators could tell his plans had wandered somewhat off-course. But, whatever was intended, the glamorous Peech Hotel is a magnificent addition to this vibrant city. In proportion, always leaning towards the generous (large pool, big rooms, huge beds, mammoth baths that fit two people and monster porcelain and 'raindance' showers), it is also small enough not to lose any of its intimacy (the staff even address you by your name). This once-humble, thatched home has been transformed into an open-plan, contemporary oasis, its modernity announced by suede square stools with brilliant cushions. The bedrooms are blessed with feather duvets, Oregon pine floors, flat-screen TVs, Ipod SoundDock, WiFi and electronic safes. These are sophisticated spaces you will enjoy spending time in. Barely a day goes by, it seems, without something being written about The Peech. When I was there the talk (most of it coming from me) was all about Maxwell's, the newly-opened restaurant. Grilled Mozambiquan crab drizzled in a lime dressing and washed down with a zingy SA chardonnay was frankly sensational and I will not forget it in a hurry. Next-door you can reduce any guilt at the 24/7 mega-gym with its 50m lap pool and cardio-machines of torture to which guests get exclusive access. The Peech, though I hesitate to say it, is a peach.

Rooms: 6: 5 doubles or twins and 1 suite with separate lounge. All have full en-suite bathrooms.
Price: R1,100 per room per night.
Meals: Breakfast included and restaurant on site.
Directions: On website or can be emailed/faxed when booking.

Random Harvest Country Cottages

Linda De Luca & Liezel Dreyer
Plot 57 Nooitgedacht, Mogale City 1740
Tel: 011-957-2758 Fax: 011-957-2399
Email: deluca@icon.co.za Web: www.rhn.co.za
Cell: 082-553-0598

I would make an ideal dictator...," Linda worryingly confessed shortly after I had crept through the gates and into this Narnia of saplings and shoots, "...of the environment that is," she thankfully added. There's clearly no room for democracy in Linda's world when it comes to saving the nation's plants. This self-confessed nature addict set up the Random Harvest indigenous nursery, the first of its kind, 16 years ago. Back then everyone said she was mad but now people flock from miles around to pick up their fashionable fynbos. "I think I preferred it when I was mad," chuckles Linda. This 50-odd-acre site is a world away from the city it sits in. Paths battle with plants over rights of way, and key in hand I navigated my way through a sea of green, winding past rondavels of chickens before tasting 'Yellowwood', my cottage for the night. A cosy little thatched affair with everything you could possibly want (huge bed, snug living room, secluded patio) and more besides, including a bottle of the freshest farm milk - the cows that produced it munch in a field around the corner. Sitting on my lawn surrounded by plants (indigenous only, of course), staring at the stars and listening to the frogs, it was hard to believe that I was in Africa's largest city.

Rooms: 8: all 1-bed cottages with showers, some have baths. 6 have self-catering option.
Price: R275 - R325 pp sharing B&B.
Meals: Full breakfast included. Dinners and braai packs on request from R50. Many restaurants nearby.
Directions: Directions can be faxed or emailed on booking.

North West Province

Hideaway at the Farm

Mike and Sabine Manegold
Pelindaba Road 10, Broederstroom, Hartbeespoort 0240
Tel: 083-476-0507 Fax: 012-205-1309
Email: info@hideawayatthefarm.com Web: www.hideawayatthefarm.com
Cell: 083-476-0507

I couldn't imagine a less contrived and more relaxing place. Mike is a laid-back nurturing soul (and reformed advertising executive) with a real commitment to and passion for South Africa and this spirit reigns at the farm. With views to the Hartbeespoort Dam and magical Magaliesberg - Johannesburg's playground and natural magnets for water-sport and hiking enthusiasts - the farm consists of a four-bedroom farmhouse, the best of which boasts large, sliding glass doors leading on to the pool. Across the drive are the rondavels: slate floors, fleshy walls and towering, thatched ceilings. Though the farm no longer yields any produce, it "farms people" instead. Charming Benjamin runs the place whilst Chef Michael and assistant Deliwe, renowned for culinary wizardry, cook up homely Swiss/African fare in the open-walled restaurant below. This is a truly memorable spot to dine with its live jazz events, cavernous fireplace and billowing cloth-panelled walls. When it's not open - trust me, go once and you'll go every night - all rooms have cooking facilities and there's also the braai area marked out by Sabine's dream symbols. But for me, the real reason to come to the farm is because it is filled with the optimism of the new South Africa. Swiss-born Mike has a wealth of knowledge about his adopted country but to listen to Benjamin's balanced tales of the Apartheid years is to witness the new hope for South Africa first-hand. An enriching experience.

Rooms: 6: in farmhouse: 3 doubles & 1 twin, all separate with en-s showers & private terraces; also 2 rondavels, each with double & en-s bath/shower.
Price: R225 - R365 pp sharing self-catering. Singles on request. Weekly and monthly rates available.
Meals: Self-catering. Fridge stocked with breakfast supplies. African-Swiss restaurant on site (traditional Swiss food) for other meals and a good number of restaurants within a ten-minute drive.
Directions: From Johannesburg follow signs to Randburg and N1 heading north-west. Take R512 past Lanseria Airport toward Hartbeespoort Dam. At T-junction turn left and the farm is signed on the left.

Map Number: 20

La Bastide

Marianne and Hans Donker
Main Road, Skeerpoort, Hartebeespoort 0232
Tel: 012-207-1938 Fax: 012-207-1940
Email: donker@netactive.co.za Web: www.hartebeespoortdam/labastide
Cell: 083-297-1122

As the sun baked down on the surrounding armies of sweet-smelling lavender, Marianne busied herself with the king of coffee-makers in the kitchen and I sat, dogs at feet, on the stoep, staring at the mass of swirling black objects circling in the sky. "One of the world's largest colonies of vultures lives right up there," explains Marianne worryingly, as she pops down a cup of perfectly percolated Colombian and points to the peak of the majestic Magaliesberg Mountains. Did they know something I didn't? The view of the Skeerpoort Valley from here would put sight in a blind eye, while staying at La Bastide is a restorative for the entire body. Marianne's husband Hans is a master-builder by trade (accomplished painter and exotic Turkish pot importer when at a loose end) and only the finest of fine materials have gone into making this, his latest masterpiece. Exposed dry-stone walls and weather-weary wood lend the property an aged charm and each of the delectable guest cottages have been filled with period pieces... But Hans still manages to bring them bang up to date, unable to resist slipping onto the walls the odd contemporary painting from his impressive portfolio. Country-style kitchens have everything you could ever want, including use of a newly-planted herb garden. The area has so much on offer (hot-air ballooning, golf, hiking, horse-riding) and La Bastide is the very comfortable base from which to try it all out.

Rooms: 4: 2 cottages, both with 1 bedroom, 1 with queen, 1 with twin; both have full en-suite bathrooms; also 2 queen rooms in main house with shared bathroom.
Price: R600 per cottage per night sleeping 2 (R800 sleeping 4). R350 for room in main house.
Meals: Breakfast and other meals on request. Plenty of good restaurants nearby.
Directions: Halfway to Sun City from Jo'burg on R512. Follow R512 until T-junction at Broederstroom. Turn L & continue 17km to next T-jjct at Skeerpoort. Turn R onto R560 & La Bastide is 800m on L (look for yellow signpost 19-21).

Map Number: 20

Jaci's Tree Lodge

Jan and Jaci van Heteren

Madikwe Game Reserve, PO Box 413, Molatedi 2838
Tel: 014-778-9900 Fax: 014-778-9901
Email: jaci@madikwe.com Web: www.madikwe.com
Cell: 083-447-7929, reservations 083-700-2071

Lion spoor's been spotted - a pride on the hunt. With hearts racing in anticipation, we bounce along a sandy track hoping to find them first. When we do, we watch in breathless awe as they saunter by less than a metre from us, senses fixed on their prey: then there's an elephant, who charges and they scatter. We're still abuzz when we return to our already-run baths and chat animatedly around the boma fire at dinner. Jaci's has this effect on you. Wonderfully indulgent, this is one of Tatler's favourites. Beyond the foyer's tree-pierced, blonde-thatch roof lies an expansive restaurant overlooking riverine forest and separated from the chic bar by a four-sided open fire, which together keep you in long cocktails and gourmet food. Relax the excess off in a hammock; alternatively there's a pool and gym. Save your gasps of delight for the tree-houses. Sitting six metres above ground and linked by a rosewood walkway, their glass doors concertina open onto private decks. Vibrant colours form a backdrop for a bed festooned with silk cushions, burnt-orange suede beanbag and swollen stone bath with handmade copper pipes. But Jaci's trump card is the rangers, whose enthusiasm creates a wonderful, wild adventure. What a job they have - daily taking breath away. Further along the river bank you'll find Jaci's Safari Lodge, opulent canvas and stone suites. Ideal for romantic safaris and children of all ages welcome and specially catered for.

Rooms: 8 tree-houses, each with king-size bed and bath and outdoor "jungle" shower.
Price: R1,995 – R3,295 pp sharing.
Meals: All meals and game drives included.
Directions: Only 1.5 hours' drive from Sun City or a 3-hour drive from Johannesburg. Daily road and air transfers from JHB and Sun City. Ask for details when booking.

Mosetlha Bush Camp

Chris, June and Caroline Lucas

Madikwe Game Reserve
Tel: 011-444-9345 Fax: 011-444-9345
Email: info@thebushcamp.com Web: www.thebushcamp.com
Cell: 083-653-9869

Mosetlha puts the wild into wilderness; no doors or glass here as they would hinder the feel and dust of Africa permeating your very core; no worries either as you leave them at the gate. Facilities are basic but real; guests draw their own hot water from a donkey-boiler before proceeding to the shower. Recently the kitchen was extended and a new thatch and stone lapa has been added for guests to read, relax and compare sightings, but the authenticity remains untainted. The wooden cabins are comfortable, but used only for sleeping - you are here for the wilderness experience of the outdoors. Chris's passion for conservation and his environment shines through and is contagious (which reminds me to say that the area is malaria-free). His guests depart much the wiser, not only because of the game drives, but also because of the superb guided wilderness walks. Yes, the Madikwe Game Reserve (70,000 hectares) has the so-called 'Big Five,' but a game lodge worth its salt (such as this) will fire your imagination about the whole food chain. Even the camp itself is an education - all sorts of birds, small mammals and antelopes venture in. Come for a genuine and memorable bush experience. *Children welcome from 8 years old up.*

Rooms: 8 twins sharing 3 shower/toilet complexes.
Price: All-inclusive from R995 per person. Alcoholic and fizzy drinks extra.
Meals: All meals and refreshments (tea, coffee, fruit juice) included.
Directions: Detailed written directions supplied on request or see website.

Mpumalanga

Wetlands Country House & Sheds

Ann Felton

83 Van Riebeek St, Wakkerstroom 2480
Tel: 017-730-0101 Fax: 017-730-0124
Email: wetlandscountryhouse@telkomsa.net Web:
www.wetlandscountryhouse.co.za Cell: 082-371-5121

Being hailed as an English rain god wherever I went it came as no surprise that I timed my visit to Wakkerstroom with one of the biggest downpours the town had seen in years - Wetlands Country House indeed. It was a relief therefore to see Philip patiently peering out of the window, awaiting my arrival, umbrella at the ready. A couple of mad dashes back and forth from the car later I found myself safely secluded inside, hot tea in hand. Wetlands is a wonderfully luxurious country retreat. Local Ine stone walls are everywhere, both inside and out, while reed roofs help keep the rain off. The cattle were evicted long ago from their shed around the corner and in their place have come huge wicker-framed beds, free-standing Victorian baths, wrought-iron fires, and large cushion-embroidered sofas. But it took the day after the night before to really enjoy what this place has to offer. With the storm having lumbered off into the distance I was free to roam the magnificent grounds accompanied by Charlie the labrador. Trails disappear off in all directions, through thickly-canopied woods, past a dam struggling with the previous night's excess, and along a river raging with excitement. Wakkerstroom is one of the world's bird-watching Meccas and a couple of highlights are red-chested flufftails and grey crowned cranes. *Gliding and micro-lighting also available.*

Rooms: 7: all doubles with full en-suite bathrooms.
Price: R250 - R300 pp sharing B&B. Group prices negotiable. Singles R300.
Meals: 4-course meals for groups R100. Light meal served for couples R65.
Directions: Drive straight through Wakkerstroom on the main road and Wetlands Country House is on the left.

Bushwise Safaris

Tim van Coller and Peter Winhall

Crocodile River, overlooking Kruger, Marloth Park, PO Box 909, Komatipoort 1340

Tel: 083-651-7464 (Lodge) Email: info@bushwisesafaris.com

Web: www.bushwisesafaris.com Cell: 083-555-0181 (Peter)

I defy you to find a more knowledgeable and enthusiastic raconteur on life in the African bush than Peter. I defy you to find anyone more insane than Tim, currently canoeing solo down the Zambezi, fending off hungry crocs. Bushwise seems an apt name. I'm certainly more bush-savvy after two action-packed days here and, cliché though it may have become, truly felt like I was leaving old friends when the time came to pack my bags. But charging rhino won't keep me from coming back. The lodge couldn't be better placed, on the portals to Swaziland and Mozambique, with the open-walled, thatch-roofed bar overlooking the Crocodile River and Kruger Park that stretches out beyond. It's here that hippos wallow and elephants drink (in the river, of course, not the bar). The distant roars of lion add sound effects to Peter's childhood tales from the Rhodesian bush as guests huddle around the boma fire to enjoy one of Donna's feasts under the stars. With so much to do, I was up at three the next morning, grabbing my binos ready for a nerve-tingling walk in the Kruger. Turns out the binos were superfluous – another story for Peter to recount to future guests, or save for the latest chapter of his memoirs. I recommend at least three nights if you want to become as bush-wise as me.

Rooms: 5: all twins or doubles, 4 with en-suite showers, 1 with en-suite bath.
Price: R1,650 pp including all meals, full-day drives in open vehicles in Kruger, guided tours of Panorama Rte & day trips to Maputo/Swaziland, airport transfers (KMIA). R650 pp DB&B only.
Meals: All meals included, drinks extra.
Directions: Directions emailed on booking.

Serenity Luxury Forest Lodge

Leila Campbell
Sherlock Farm, Malelane 1320
Tel: 011-726-8579 (res) or 013-790-2000 (lodge) Fax: 011-482-8448
Email: jantay@netactive.co.za Web: www.serenitylodge.co.za
Cell: 082-856-5595

Leila had told me cryptically over the phone that to get to Serenity I would have to leave Mpumalanga without actually going out of it. I finally understood what this riddle meant as I drove along the rough stone driveway. Dry and arid browns slowly gave way to lush and youthful greens. The blue of the sky diminished under an ever-thickening canopy of trees. Red duikers darted about, while vervet monkeys sat and watched me pass in quiet contemplation. I hesitate to use the word, but Serenity really is an oasis in an Mpumalangan desert. High in the Drakensberg Mountains, deep, dark, wooden walkways snake through the trees, past tumbling indigenous bush and burbling waters. It is the only indigenous forest lodge anywhere in Mpumalanga, and its geographical position means it actually enjoys a KwaZulu Natal eco-system with its accompanying birds and butterflies. 1000-year-old matumi trees dwarf everything around, and provide bountiful shade from the scorching sun. The water has been tested and Leila assures me that "it's cleaner than anything you can buy in a bottle!" Thatched-roofed, wooden chalets hide among the trees, and provide a luxurious place to rest weary legs after a hard day hiking on the multitude of trails. Open-sided and yet completely private, from the bed there's a near-360 degree view. From romantic candlelit dinners on the decking to picnics in the woods, I challenge you to come here and not be captivated.

Rooms: 9: 6 doubles, 2 twins, 1 family unit (sleeps 4). All with full en-suite bathroom.
Price: R950 - R1,250 pp sharing, Dinner B&B. Singles + 25%.
Meals: Full breakfast, dinner, high tea and welcome drinks on arrival included in price.
Directions: From Nelspruit continue along N4 to Malelane. Turn R at sign to Malelane Estates. 12km on paved road, follow signs to Serenity.

Chez Vincent Restaurant and Guesthouse

Vincent and Sara Martinez

56 Ferreira Street, Nelspruit 1200
Tel: 013-744-1146 Fax: 013-744-1147
Email: bookings@chezvincent.com Web: www.chezvincent.co.za
Cell: 082 331 1054

After weeks in the bush I was truly... well, bushed, but couldn't have been better looked after by Vincent and Sara. They are great people and theirs the perfect staging post during any journey through this part of the world (a must by the way). Nelspruit is a hub town, gateway to Mozambique and Swaziland, and also the Kruger National Park. Some guests come over from Maputo for shopping or even just for dinner chez Vincent, while others are international visitors stopping over before entering the park. All, including myself, go mad for Vincent's South African-influenced French cuisine in the intimate restaurant, hung with paintings by local artists. He's originally from Toulouse and over an after-dinner bottle of wine he and Sara sympathetically listened to me prattle away in bad French gone rusty. Physically and grammatically exhausted I made a beeline for bed and one of the best nights' sleep I've had in South Africa. Rooms here are pretty much brand-new, all light-filled, air-conditioned and some opening out onto the swimming pool. Each has Sara's choice of funky colour splashes (lime green, turquoise, yellow, pink and orange) and I had one of the five family suites, complete with a full kitchen, sofa-bed and shower so huge you could lie down in it... so I did. Delicious food, relaxed atmosphere, very nice hosts and an opportunity to do some shopping before disappearing into the bush.

Rooms: 11: 6 doubles with en/s showers and bath, 5 family rooms each with 1 double, bathroom with shower, sofa-bed, lounge and fully-equipped kitchen.
Price: R259 - R280 pp sharing. Singles R350.
Meals: Full breakfast included. A la carte restaurant on premises.
Directions: Take N4 to Nelspruit and turn right into Ferreira St at Absa Square. At end turn right (still Ferreira St) and immediately left into service road, Chez Vincent is 4th house on the left.

Tomjachu Bush Lodge

Ann & Chris Bach

Valbonne Farm, Uitkyk Rd, Nelspruit 1200, Reservations: Intnl + 27 11 803-9908, SA 0861-111-4792 Lodge: 013-744-0203 Fax: 011-807-9133
Email: reservations@tomjachu.com or tomjachu@mweb.co.za
Web: www.tomjachu.com Cell: lodge 082-704-4804

Sitting on the huge stoep sheltered from the midday sun, I drank in the unsurpassable views of the Bekker Mountains (even locals think it's the best vista for miles) in the company of my amiable hosts Ann and Chris. Originally built for the family (Thomas, Jack and Hugo provide the Tomjachu name), the house has been lovingly converted without losing any of its homely charms. This means you'll find guests meandering in and out of the huge kitchen, perhaps helping Ann and Chris with the nightly feast of succulent game. Opulent, chequered sofas crowd around the fireplace of the main lounge, while in the rooms of the lodge you'll find big beds with hand-embroidered linen... but my favourite was the separate Rock House just around the corner. With massive glass doors it offers unbroken views of the countryside, so much so that, "people just never want to get out of bed," Ann informs me. Creamy walls throughout are punctuated with dashes of Africana, from safari hats left behind by guests to prints of the local wildlife. Tomjachu is a satisfyingly relaxing place where even the animals are chilled. Kudu nibble the pots plants, while Fluffy and Buffy, the tame ostriches (if there's such a thing), regularly drink from the pool.

Rooms: 9: 5 in lodge (2 with sitting rooms) & 3 cottages (2 with own pool), 5 twins & 4 doubles. All en-suite, 4 with baths, the rest with showers.
Price: R320 - R495 pp sharing B&B. Self-catering option R295 - R495.
Meals: 3-course home-cooked meals by arrangement R135. Also breakfast picnics & hampers. Game drives in open safari LandRover available.
Directions: From Nelspruit turn R from N4 into Kruger St (ABSA bank on R). Continue into Ferreira St to Uitkyk area. Follow road 5km to end of tar, 1.7km of dirt then turn L & follow signs to Tomjachu.

Kavinga Guest House

Stuart and Ros Hulley-Miller
R37 Nelspruit/Sabie Rd, Nelspruit 1200
Tel: 013-755-3193 Fax: 013-755-3161
Email: kavinga@mpu.co.za Web: www.kavinga.co.za
Cell: 083-625-7162

Thick orchards of avocados buffer Kavinga farmhouse and its green lake of lawn from the outside world. Ros assembles a country breakfast on the stone-tiled verandah, which is latticed with rare jade vine and camouflaged by plants and flowers. If you are like the majority of the Hulley-Millers' guests you will spend a good deal of time there, lying on wicker furniture and deck chairs or flopping indolently in the pool while Ros dispenses indispensable drinks. Generous bedrooms dotted around the grounds are classily decorated and pander to the 21st century with satellite TV, bar fridges and sumptuous bathrooms (with both shower and free-standing bath). The family unit has its own sitting room with a sofa bed to unravel for extra bodies. French windows open onto small, covered patios with broad views over the Lowveld. I think it was Walt Disney's Baloo the Bear who said: 'Float downstream, fall apart in my backyard'.... *Just 45km to the Kruger National Park.*

Rooms: 5: 3 doubles and 2 twins, all with en-suite baths and showers.
Price: R255 - R280. Singles R325 - R375.
Meals: Full breakfast included. Dinner by arrangement: R95 for 3 courses.
Directions: 11.5km north from Nelspruit on R37 towards Sabie. Sign to right.

Ambience Inn

Hannes Scholtz and Issy de Lira
28 Wally Scott St, White River 1240
Tel: 013-751-1951 Fax: 013-751-1951
Email: ambience@lantic.net Web: www.ambienceinn.co.za
Cell: 082-928-0461

I made my way through a canopy of flamboyant trees - in full red-blossom livery - and found Ambience Inn at the end of a quiet cul-de-sac where guinea fowl roam between properties. The house was built from scratch into an Aztec-style palladium. Terracotta-coloured columns and walls provide the entrance into a sub-tropical/indigenous garden of clivias, gingers, macadamias and a colossal kapok tree with cotton-wool flowers which Victorians apparently used to stuff their pillows. There is a refreshing and get-fit-worthy, fifteen-metre long lap swimming pool bordered by blue, mosaic tiles. On the guests' stoep is a manicured garden of mosses, tropical staghorn ferns and orchids clinging to old tree stumps. Hannes, a qualified horticulturalist and keen landscape gardener, has created a delightful forest meander at the end of the indigenous garden - an ideal nook for nature-lovers and bird-watchers alike. The bedrooms are comfortable with cool-for-the-summer screed floors and high ceilings. All of the rooms have private outdoor courtyards with al fresco showers and imaginative breakfasts are served on the stoep with canvas striped curtains hanging from the high mantle and wind chimes singing in the breeze. Take-out picnic baskets can also be provided for early starts into the nearby Kruger Park. Come evening, sunset viewings with Issy and Hannes overlooking Legogote are also a possibility.

Rooms: 6: 4 doubles and 2 twins, all with en-suite showers and outside shower.
Price: R275 pp sharing. Singles R350.
Meals: Full breakfast or picnic basket. Dinners on request and restaurants nearby.
Directions: From Jo'burg take N4 to Nelspruit and turn left onto R40. When in White River turn first left after first traffic light into Henry Morey Rd, then right into Frank Townsend Rd, then left into Wally Scott St.

Jatinga Country Lodge

John and Lyn Davis
Jatinga Road, Plaston, White River 1240
Tel: 013-751-5059 or 013-751-5108 Fax: 013-751-5119
Email: info@jatinga.co.za Web: www.jatinga.co.za
Cell: 082-456-1676

You know from the smile at the boom-gate and the cheerful greeting at the end of the gravel drive that all will be well at Jatinga. From the tiled foyer, you're led through an atrium hallway to a terracotta-tiled lounge. This is bathed in sunlight flooding through open French doors that lead onto a somnolent verandah. Here couples on cushioned wicker chairs take tea overlooking a glassy croquet lawn and a fabulous sub-tropical garden strewn with jacaranda petals. The large bedrooms, some modelled as modern rondavels, radiate from the 1920s homestead. Victorian rooms have outdoor showers, the Provençal house concrete baths so big they should come with a lifeguard. I stayed in the Colonial Suite and, clothes despatched for laundering, found I could enjoy my mini-bar ministrations from any number of positions: the oversized bed, the sofa, the claw-foot bath, the patio.... But the choices don't end there. You can browse safari journals in sofas like quicksand; perfect your heliotropic posturing by a pool shielded by ramrod palms; or sip sundowners on the deck above the White River. In the light-filled dining room with its cellar of top-notch wines I gleefully tackled the crab curry, my clean clothes preserved by a bib, the battle-scarred tablecloth not so lucky. You are so well looked after here you may forget that your safari adventure awaits.

Rooms: 20: 4 luxury suites and 16 superior rooms, all with en-suite bath and shower.
Price: R895 – R1,175 pp sharing. Singles R1,175 – R1,495.
Meals: Full breakfast included. A la carte restaurant serves breakfast, lunch and dinner daily. Gourmet picnic hampers on request.
Directions: From Nelspruit head to White River (approx. 20km) and proceed through town. Continue straight along the R538 to Karino/Plaston for 4.3km, from last traffic light, crossing over two railway lines. Turn right onto the Jatinga Road (dirt road). Travel for 1.9km to the Jatinga Gate.

Numbela Exclusive Riverside Accommodation

Michael Johnson and Tamasine Smith
White River 1240
Tel: 013-751-3356 Fax: 013-751-1380
Email: relax@numbela.co.za Web: www.numbela.co.za

 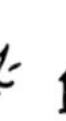 

I happened upon Numbela by chance on a day off and got lucky. Upon arrival I was met by a happy group of guests bringing the remnants of a picnic up from the river beach, and was soon joining them on the sandy bank for a drink. Just outside White River, the lodge is on a 200-acre wet-and-woodland wonderland that teems with birdlife and which you are free to explore. Two cottages are separated by a converted mill-house. One has a raised stoep with a swing-seat piled with pillows and the interior is all about flair. The main room is enlivened by earthy red and orange paint-work, the bedroom is dressed with blushing fabrics and the washed-blue bathroom comes with an outdoor shower. The smaller, thatched cottage near the river has chalky walls and claret-coloured floor with high ceilings, an Oregon pine kitchen, stable doors and an open fire. The bedroom is decorated with African artefacts, their origins explained in a thoughtful pamphlet. There's a welcome attention to detail, from the faultless design to the touches like refreshingly complimentary spirits and mixers and the delicious breakfast delivered to my patio. And you couldn't ask for more affable hosts than Michael and Tamasine. They are on hand to help with tasks great or small: organising Mozambique visas, balloon trips or spa treatments. These are people doing their own thing well. *Close to Casterbridge Farm shops and restaurants, golf courses and the Kruger gates.*

Rooms: 3: 2 self-catering/B&B cottages, 1 double with en-suite shower plus mezzanine single, 1 double & twin with en-suite bath and outdoor shower; 1 self-catering cottage with 4 twin bedrooms with en-suite showers, 1 private bath.
Price: B&B: from R380 pp sharing. Self-catering: from R660 for 2 people, R1,000 for 4. Singles on request.
Meals: Full breakfast included in B&B rate. Kitchen stocked with essentials including spirits and mixers (B&B only).
Directions: 20km north of White River on the R40 Hazyview road. The oval sign is clearly visible on the left. Turn left and follow the signs down a dirt road for approximately 1km to the gate.

Plumbago Guest House

Ilara & Robbie Robertson
R40 between White River and Hazyview, Hazyview 1241
Tel: 013-737-8806 Fax: 013-737-8852
Email: plumbagoguesthouse@mweb.co.za Web: www.plumbagoguesthouse.co.za Cell. 082-951 0467

Through wrought-iron gates at the end of a bougainvillaea-lined drive I found Plumbago - as pretty as the flower that shares its name. Set on an avocado and banana farm, it sits above the plantation watching over it and out to Kruger Park in the distance. When I arrived, 1940s jazz was swinging out from the radio, just the right aural accompaniment to the nostalgic, colonial-inspired setting. In the drawing room and bar, an eclectic collection of antiques, paintings and rugs are interspersed with vases filled with exotic flowers and extravagant palm-leaf fans that stretch up to the ceiling. The rooms have the same casual gracefulness about them with their subtle, natural tones, Jacobean print curtains, mahogany beds and abundance of vased and water-coloured flowers. With a large lived-in verandah, elegant pool and sauna in the beautifully tended garden there's plenty of opportunity to relax and mull over days gone by, particularly in Robbie's history-reading section in the tennis court's viewing lapa. But what really makes this place stand apart are the Robertsons themselves. On my visit, Ilara (who honed her culinary skills cooking for diplomats) was deciding on that evening's dinner menu whilst Robbie, who has his own construction company by day, was itching to go micro-lighting (you can go too) before being back for waitering duty later on. A young and active bunch, they are often busying about doing their own thing but are more than happy to share their passions with you.

Rooms: 3 garden chalets: 1 king/twin with en-s shower; 1 king with en-s shower; 1 king extra-length sleigh-bed with en-s shower and bath.
Price: R480 - R580 pp sharing. Singles +R150.
Meals: Full breakfast included. Dinner on request.
Directions: From Jo'burg, take N4 to Nelspruit and then on to White River. Go on R40 to Hazyview, Plumbago is signposted on right 34 km out of White River and 10km before Hazyview. 4hrs from Jo'burg.

Rissington Inn

Chris Harvie
PO Box 650, Hazyview 1242
Tel: 013-737-7700 Fax: 013-737-7112
Email: info@rissington.co.za Web: www.rissington.co.za
Cell: 082-327-6842

Informality and relaxation dictate at the Rissington Inn; you feel this even as you mount the broad steps to the verandah for the first time. Sun-lounging guests dazily contemplate the flower gardens full of frangipani; the swimming pool is a rectangle of cool aquamarine; the hazy valley shimmers beyond. In the evenings gourmet, incredibly good-value candlelit dinners are served by friendly staff. We have eaten with Chris on four separate occasions and never been disappointed, despite much creativity and daring in the dishes. High ceilings put the lid on well-designed rooms. The one I had was enormous with a Victorian bathroom and its own sitting area. But Rissington isn't the sort of place where you feel like hiding away or watching TV. Owner/mover/shaker Chris actually seems to LIKE seeing his guests doing what they want, dressed how they feel and making friends. When you arrive there is usually a gaggle of guests lined up at his wooden bar and you could easily mistake them for Chris's personal friends. They probably only arrived a few minutes before you. *Hazyview sits at the portals of the Kruger National Park.*

Rooms: 14: 2 queens, 3 with 2 queen beds, 3 queens with an extra single, 6 king/twins, all en-suite bathrooms. Garden rooms have outside showers.
Price: R325 - R580 pp sharing.
Meals: Full breakfast included and served till noon. Restaurant on-site for à la carte lunch and dinner.
Directions: 2km south of Hazyview on R40 White River Numbi Gate (KNP) Rd. On right coming from main Hazyview 4-way stop - see signs for Rissington and Kiaat Park.

Rock-a-Bye B&B

Lynda and Warren Bartholomew
R536 between Hazyview and Sabie, Hazyview 1242
Tel: 013-737-8186 Fax: 013-737-8039
Email: rockabye@telkomsa.net
Cell: 083-360-2991

Macadamia-shell gravel crunching under wheel, I ambled my way up the drive following the river's meander, a lush kaleidoscope of greens before me, simply beautiful. Previously sea-turtle conservationists, Lynda and Warren flung off their flippers five years ago and came here to craft their own inland idyll; in fact they have planted each plant and built every building themselves. And the gravel is no coincidence either, for this is now a macadamia nut farm. Amongst the flowers in Lynda's colour-speckled garden sit three thatched rondavels, each with a private, raised verandah gazing out at the forested valley ahead. With tree-canopy-high ceilings, wooden furniture and sandy walls, the rooms are understatedly 'African', except for the huge animals spirited to life on the walls. The murals are painted by Lynda's clever mother Pat, and my favourites are the dusty herd of zebra and the little bush-baby in the loo. En route to the cottage Lynda and I interrupted several bobbing hens (suppliers of your breakfast eggs) and passed a posse of papaya trees standing to attention (and bearing your breakfast fruit) and a rather jolly-looking tractor (providing nothing whatever for breakfast). Secluded in the trees the cottage inside seems skyscraper-high, with masses of room, plenty of books and dining areas inside and out on the bird- (and hippo- if you're lucky) viewing deck. With an adventure company right next door and Kruger just down the road, I'd recommend at least a three-night stay.

Rooms: 4: 3 rondavels, all twins, 2 en-suite shower, 1 en-s bath; 1 cottage (self-catering) with 1 queen en-s shower, 1 twin (3/4 size beds) en-s bath & outdoor shower, 2 singles in living room, well-equipped kitchen & dining room.
Price: R300 - R350 pp sharing. Singles R360. For the cottage R250 pp, children half-price.
Meals: Full breakfast included for B&B. Treetops restaurant & Pat's farm stall across the road.
Directions: Take N4 from Jo'burg to Nelspruit then R40 to White River. Carry on thro' Hazyview town & turn L onto R536 to Sabie. Rock-a-Bye signposted after 10km on R-hand side.

Map Number: 21

Graskop Hotel

Lella Smyth
3 Main St, Graskop 1270
Tel: 013-767-1244 Fax: 013-767-1244
Email: graskophotel@mweb.co.za Web: www.graskophotel.co.za

The irrepressibly-sunny Lella promised me this would be a hotel room tour like no other as she glided up the staircase. One tired '70s-style hotel has been transformed into an art gallery you can actually sleep in. Harrie the owner, of world-famous Harrie's Pancakes fame, and yes you can indulge in your every pancakey fantasy right next door, bravely invited the nation's contemporary artists to do whatever they wanted within the confines of each of the compact but comfortable rooms. As the key clanked the first door swung open to reveal its secrets: a TV replete with test-card sculpture on one wall, a pillow-safe complete with hanging keys sculpture on the other. "It's art, you're not supposed to understand it", Lella added helpfully. (The artist for this room is Cecile Heysteck.) A quilt of stuffed arrows points the way to sublime slumber in one room, while blown-glass plates rise like toadstools from the wall of another. My favourite is by the world-renowned photographic artist Abrie Fourie, who's colourful creation stripes the room in a barcode of segmented scenery, which even escapes out all over the door - seeing is believing! You will find more conservative rooms, but you won't escape the art, which is everywhere (there's even a gallery downstairs). The Graskop Hotel enchants around every corner. It started as a blank canvas, but it's quickly filling up, and I can't wait to see what wonders have been added by next year.

Rooms: 34: 19 in the main hotel building and 15 garden rooms. All have showers, some have bath with shower over. Secure parking.
Price: R250 pp sharing B&B. R280 singles.
Meals: Full breakfast included. 4-course meal available on request for larger groups R90.
Directions: From Nelspruit take the R538 to Hazyview then the R535 to Graskop. Hotel is the only 2-storey building in the town.

Map Number: 21

Idube Private Game Reserve

Sally Kernick
Sabi Sand Game Reserve 1242
Tel: 011-888-3713 Fax: 011-888-2181
Email: info@idube.com Web: www.idube.com

There are few establishments where the staff seem to have as much fun working together as at Idube. Be they guides, trackers, managers or chefs, the Idube crew exude a delightful sense of goodwill to each other and to all mankind. And it's not difficult to see why. Warthog roam through the camp, elephants pass nearby; there is space and greenery, beauty and beast. The land was bought in 1983 by Louis and Marilyn Marais and Louis sensibly built the swimming pool before designing and constructing the rest of the camp himself. Guests sleep in chalets dotted around the sloping grounds, while the thatched seating and dining areas look out over the Sabi Sand Game Reserve. A rope bridge over the river bed takes you to a hide where you can admire the Shadulu dam and its regulars without being admired yourself. Two game drives per day plus guided walks give you the chance to see what's happening elsewhere in the reserve and tracker Titus amazed us with his ability to read bent grasses and droppings. We took time out for sundowners by a dam, accompanied by a bull elephant and a bull hippo. There was much posturing and manliness, not least from me, before a return to camp for dinner (which was excellent!) and conviviality under the stars.

Rooms: 10: 2 kings and 8 doubles all with en/s bathrooms and outdoor shower.
Price: Winter (May to end Sept) R2,050 pp sharing. Summer (October to end April) R2,950. Single supplement +35%.
Meals: All 3 meals plus morning and evening drives and a guided walk included. Drinks and transfers extra.
Directions: 34.4km from Hazyview along R536 towards Kruger Gate. Follow signs off to the left. 19.5km along a dirt road.

Map Number: 21

Plains Camp

Nikki and Gerrit Meyer

Rhino Walking Safaris, Kruger National Park, Skukuza 1350
Tel: 011-467-1886 Fax: 011-467-4758
Email: info@rws.co.za Web: www.rws.co.za
Cell: 083-631-4956

This is where I fell for Africa: sitting outside my tent in the Kruger, sipping G&T (for the quinine, you understand) and watching game serenely traverse Timbitene Plain. This is the only private lodge where you can walk in pristine wilderness - nothing short of a privilege. From Rhino Post, the fabulous sister lodge on the Mutlumuvi river bank (where you can stay) you walk to Plains Camp. Here the refined, pioneer tents have dark wood furniture with brass hinges and leather straps, bathrooms with copper taps protruding from tree stumps and the largest, softest towels. During the day, you can doze on the chocolate-leather sofa or sip highball cocktails in the plunge pool. Pith helmets, surveying tools, maps and a gramophone add to the bygone feel and, to cap it all, the head ranger Gerrit is the sort over whom Karen Blixen might have swooned. Walking on rhino footpaths, the trails let you soak up both the scale and detail of the bush. No mad rush to tick off half-glimpsed Big Five, this – it's all about the quality of the sightings. That said, we encountered glowering buffalo, rampant rhino, lionesses on a hunt and had a pulse-quickening showdown with a bull elephant that I'll dine out on for ages. Afterwards we sent the sun down the sky and, wrapped in rugs, headed toward gas-lamp beacons for a never-ending feast. A safari fantasy come true.

Rooms: 4 twin-bed African-explorer style tents, each with en-suite loo, shower and overhead fan.
Price: R1,950 - R2,350 pp sharing. Ask about 3-, 4- or 5-night packages and single supplement.
Meals: All meals, house wines and beer, safari activities (primarily walking) and optional sleep-outs included.
Directions: From the Paul Kruger Gate follow signs to Skukuza Rest Camp & Rhino Walking Safaris. Drive past Skukuza on H1-2 towards Tshokwane and Satara. Cross Sabie and Sand rivers and after second turning to Maroela Loop, turn left signed Rhino Walking Safaris. Meet at Rhino Post Safari Lodge.

Mpumalanga

Iketla Lodge

Albert and Hennielene Botha

off R555, Ohrigstad 1122
Tel: 013-238-0190 Fax: 013-238-0190
Email: relax@iketla.com Web: www.iketla.com

Be relaxed… be peaceful' is Iketla's poetic English translation from the local Sotho dialect. Appropriately named, as it turns out. Surrounded on all sides by hills and rocky outcrops, Albert and Hennielene greeted me in the shebeen, where the late afternoon sun was gushing through the open sides, flooding the thatched, tiled dining area. For those that don't know, a shebeen is a drinking den and it's to this magnet that guests began to flock as they returned, brimming with exhilaration, from the day's adventures. Some had been exploring the Panorama Route, others had been walking guided trails through Iketla's 540 hectares of wilderness, inspecting all creatures great and small, and learning about the impressive range of birdlife and traditional uses of indigenous plants. They regaled us with their new-found knowledge and enthusiasm, with Albert, a bushman at heart, chipping in with many jewels of profounder expertise. A faint drumbeat interrupted the banter to signal supper, though my acute senses had already picked up the aroma of something sensational in the air… ostrich strips in a sherry sauce as it turned out. At daybreak I inspected my chalet, similar in style to the main lodge with rugged stone walls, a thatched roof and a verandah outside sliding glass doors. There I read my book and rested my bones, listening to the morning wildlife bring this African wilderness alive.

Rooms: 6 chalets: 3 doubles and 3 twins, all with en-suite showers and outside showers.
Price: R720 pp sharing. Singles +R160. Under 12 half-price.
Meals: Full breakfast and dinner included.
Directions: From N4 turn off at Belfast and follow R540 through Dullstroom to Lydenburg. Follow R36 through Lydenburg to Ohrigstad. 4km past Ohrigstad turn left onto R555. Sign to Iketla 6km further on right.

Swaziland

Phophonyane Falls Lodge

Lungile de Vletter
PO Box 199, Pigg's Peak
Tel: +268-437-1429 Fax: +268-437-1319
Email: lungile@phophonyane.co.sz Web: www.phophonyane.co.sz
Cell: +268-604-2802

A South African visa is enough to see you popping over the border into the Kingdom of Swaziland and immersing yourself in 500 hectares of pristine nature. Phophonyane Lodge is perched high on a valleyside in thick indigenous forest with the constant background music of a thousand birds (230 species) and the rushing white water of the Phophonyane River cascading down the kloof below (waterfall-viewing walks are a must). You move between the main lodge and the various tents, cottages and beehives on cobbles and wooden walkways, past murals and rough wood sculptures, natural materials blending easily into the landscape. Some of the cottages have sitting rooms, private gardens, narrow wooden staircases up to bedrooms and balconies, big showers, kitchens et al. The safari tents with their private decks are simpler but more romantic. You are lost in the trees and I stayed in one of the two right down by the rushing water's edge, the best sleeping draught imaginable. The reserve is criss-crossed with hiking paths leading to natural rock pools for swimming, although there is the alternative of the recently-built saltwater pool. Phophonyane prides itself on its links with the local community, some of whom now entertain in the evenings with traditional Swazi-dancing. An invigorating experience and a two-night stay is a must. *4x4 drives to mountains and Bushman paintings available along with a new chalet on the Crocodile River overlooking the Kruger Park for Phophonyane guests.*

Rooms: 6: 3 cottages (2 sleep 4, 1 sleeps 2), 2 with shower, 1 with bath; 3 beehives (1 sleeps 3, 2 sleep 2), all en-suite with shower and king-size beds.
Price: Safari tents R330 - R350 pp sharing. Beehives R450 - R500 pp sharing. Singles R675 - R750.
Meals: Each unit is self-catering, except some tents. A la carte restaurant available and picnic lunches can be prepared.
Directions: 7km north of Pigg's Peak Town or 35km from Jeppe's Reef border post to sign posts then approx 4km of dirt road following the signs to the entrance.

Limpopo

Pezulu Tree House Lodge

Limpopo Province

Gilly and West Mathewson
Guernsey, Hoedspruit 1380
Tel: 015-793-2724
Fax: 015-793-2253
Email: pezlodge@mweb.co.za
Web: www.pezulu.co.za
Cell: 083-376-3048

The sorry victim of a tree-house-free childhood, I was intrigued by the concept of Pezulu - six different reed-and-thatch constructions spread among the trees surrounding the central building, which is itself entwined around a large amarula. They are all hidden from view behind branch and leaf, and many have bits of tree growing up through the floor to provide the most natural of towel rails, stools and loo paper holders. The 'houses' are named after the trees in which they sit: 'False Thorn' has a magnificent shower with views over the Thornybush Reserve – be prepared for inquisitive giraffe; while 'Huilboerboom' is a honeymoon suite set eight metres above ground (privacy even from the giraffe). Gilly's husband West conjured Pezulu out of the Guernsey Conservancy on the edge of the Kruger Park. There are no predators in this area, only plains game, so you and the buck can wander around the property in perfect safety. Activities on offer include the usual two game drives a day and/or guided hikes. They can also arrange microlight flights and visits to rehabilitation centres and the white lion breeding project... assuming they can persuade you down from the trees.

Rooms: 6: 1 family unit (1 double and 1 twin) and 5 doubles; 1 with en/s shower, 2 with separate bath, 3 with separate shower.
Price: From R595 dinner, B&B to R995 all-inclusive. Microlight flights (R375), white-water rafting, Kruger visits and other activities also available.
Meals: Fully inclusive of all meals and game activities. Drinks extra.
Directions: Ask when booking.

Gwalagwala

Dorian and Ann Harcourt-Baldwin

Guernsey Rd off the R40, PO Box 1499, Hoedspruit 1380
Tel: 015-793-3491 Fax: 015-793-0535
Email: gwala@netactive.co.za Web: www.gwala.co.za
Cell: 083-701-2490

Kitted out in khakis and walking boots I can't imagine Dorian as a Jo'burg banker, but that's what he was until a yearning for the bush got the better of him. This is a man who clearly loves every blade of grass on his 500ha reserve and his passion is easily understandable. Stocked with plains game, Gwalagwala is a stunning spot hidden away in the greenery of the Klaserie River and the most instantaneously peaceful retreat I found in this region. Deep (deep) in the bush, just yards from the gurgling waterway, Dorian and Ann have erected five huge tents, built onto raised decks, each with a tiled bathroom and reed walls. They're close enough to be friendly, but spaced enough for privacy, connected by shaded paths to the pool, boma and bar. And not just any old bar. Here drinks (and breakfast) are served 30 feet up in a circular tree house wrapped around a huge jackalberry tree. Why go to the birds when they can come to you? Purple-crested louries, the rare African finfoot... the bird list takes hours to unscroll. Canoeing and croc-spotting, antelope and acacia, this is the sort of spot that ignites in me an urge to one day own my own piece of Africa (and preferably a big, noisy Landrover to go with it).

Rooms: 5: 2 doubles and 3 twins; 3 with shower, 1 with bath, 1 with bath and shower.
Price: R1,150 pp full board, including 2 game activities, one of which is a "Big 5" game drive.
Meals: All meals included.
Directions: Faxed or emailed on booking or available on website.

Umlani Bushcamp

Marco Schiess

Timbavati Nature Reserve
Tel: 012-346-4028 Fax: 012-346-4023
Email: info@umlani.com Web: www.umlani.com
Cell: 083-468-2041

Rhino-tracking on foot; a rather exciting experience with a couple of bull elephants; sun-downers as the bush settles for the night... this is what safaris are supposed to be about. Umlani is set on a gentle slope above a dry river course (wet in spring) and no fence separates you from the Timbavati's more feral inhabitants. You do not, for example, leave your rondavel at night to investigate snuffling noises, and elephants regularly swing through the middle of the camp for a drink at the pool. You sleep in delightful reed-walled rondavels with thatched roofs (no bricks here), hurricane lamps (no electricity either), and you shower *au naturel*, but in complete privacy. Marco and his wife Marie ran the camp by themselves for a decade until the demands of a young family compelled them to find like-minded managers. After the evening game drive everyone sits out on the deck by the bar, or in the boma round the fire, mulling over what's just been seen, before sitting down to an excellent and often buzzy dinner at tables of 8. Thoughtful hosts and knowledgeable rangers provide the charming, human face of a full-on bush experience. I had many laughs during my stay, while another guest was in tears when she had to leave! Umlani is exceptionally personal and genuine and you live as close to nature as they dare let you.

Rooms: 8 doubles (2 sleeping 4); all with en-suite outside showers.
Price: R2,050 pp sharing. Singles R2,700. Children under 12, R1,540. 3-night special: R5,230 pp sharing, R6,880 singles, R3,950 kids under 12. 7-night special & winter special also on offer.
Meals: All meals, drinks and 2-3 game activities included.
Directions: You will get a map when you book.

Gomo Gomo Game Lodge

Van Zijl Manktelow
Timbavati Game Reserve, PO Box 1696, Nelspruit 1200
Tel: 013-752-3954 (reservations) Fax: 013-752-3002 (reservations)
Email: gomo@netactive.co.za Web: www.gomogomo.co.za
Cell: 082-568-6632

How do they do that? Every time we visit Gomo Gomo they manage to produce spectacular game action. This year, out on drive with ace ranger Morné, we scored a stunning hatrick: two lions lying in the long grass, lazily eyeing the leopard they'd chased up a tree, with a bull elephant sloshing in the waterhole behind (and no doubt the rhino and buffalo keeping score). This bush is not for taming! And the camp's pretty wild too. Yes there's electricity, but fans and bedside lamps complement, rather than compromise, the bush atmosphere. You sleep in rondavels or safari tents (I prefer the latter), some of which are river-facing and have private decks. A day in camp usually contains morning and evening game drives and a bush walk before guests gather for dinner in the boma and sit round a fire in as much of a circle as numbers allow. Want to or not, you will find yourself telling big-game stories (or at least big stories about game). The camp sits right by the Nhlaralumi River (swimming is a mite hazardous – fewer crocs and hippos in the pool) and the sounds of the night will stay with you (in a good way) for a long time. To top it all, the staff are an impressively enthusiastic team, a vital element, which makes the camp stand taller than others.

Rooms: 9: 5 brick-and-thatch rondavels (3 with 2 bedrooms), 4 with shower, 1 with bath; 4 luxury safari tents, all with en/s shower.
Price: R890 - R1,400 pp sharing. Singles +R400. Children under 12 half-price. One-off vehicle entry fee of R75. There is also a R90 per person conservation levy (subject to change).
Meals: Full breakfast, lunch, dinner and game drives included. Extras are your bar bill and any curio purchases.
Directions: From Hoedspruit take the R40 south for 7km. Go left at Eastgate Airport sign. Follow to the gates – signed Gomo Gomo in the park.

Motswari Private Game Reserve

Kathy and Steve Bergs
Timbavati, Hoedspruit 1380
Tel: 015-793-1718 Fax: 015-793-2365
Email: marketing@motswari.co.za or motswari@webmail.co.za
Web: www.motswari.co.za

Watching a leopard devour an impala at a distance of just a few yards is a special game viewing experience by anybody's book (except perhaps another impala's) - particularly when you're lucky to be there at all. It was late and I had been stood up for the night (the cheek of it), but like the stars that they are, Kathy and Steve came to my rescue. These two have been in the game game for years and are among the friendliest characters you'll meet in this book. They're bush-lovers through and through and they actually met at Motswari in the 1980s. After a brief stint away when Kathy ran an English school and Steve played with explosives (don't ask), they're back. And you can see why. The lodge is great, with a rocky pool, open bar and dining room all spread out across the green banks of the Sohebele River, deep in the Timbavati reserve. Along with a herd of bush-happy guests I ate supper under the stars at a long poolside table, talking cats with the rangers. Appropriately, each room's named after an animal and I was given "Cheetah", perhaps because of my lithe physique and feline cunning – or was it my searing pace? Anyway, they're all painted different shades of bush colours outside and whitewashed within with hefty mosquito-netted four-posters, satisfyingly chunky furniture and a plentiful supply of wildlife books and magazines to make yourself sound intelligent... just purrfect.

Rooms: 15: 1 king and 14 twins all with bath and shower.
Price: R1,950 - R2,900 pp. Singles +R900. Price includes 2 game drives, game walks and meals.
Meals: All included.
Directions: From Hoedspruit take the R40 south towards Klaserie. Turn L at Timbavati and Hoedspruit Eastgate Airport signs. Continue straight to main gate (20km on tar/dirt road). Motswari is signed 32km in from the gate.

Mfubu Lodge & Gallery

Olga Kühnel and Jack Colenso
Balule Nature Reserve, Phalaborwa 1390
Tel: 015-769-6252 Fax: 015-769-6252
Email: olina@telkomsa.net Web: www.mfubu.com
Cell: 073-416-0451 (bad signal at lodge)

I've been deeper into the bush, but rarely has it seemed so penetrating. There are no fences here, just the guarantee of hot water, cold beer and animals that come to you. At dinner we ate the best Jansson's Temptation this side of the North Sea and awaited curtain-up. Silently hippos trotted onto centre stage, a brilliant moon silhouetting them against the white canvas of an alluvial beach. Nowadays the Olifants River eases like oil, so in the morning we ran the gauntlet, wading through its crocodile-infested waters. (Well, someone knew someone who thought they heard one here once). Safely on the other side, we clambered aboard a Land Rover, mingled with rhino, buffalo and giraffe and watched birds from a hide. On longer drives, Jack has been known to cook eggs on a shovel. Easy for a WW2 flying ace who's building himself a plane. "I've got all the parts," he says, "all I need is a miracle." The lodge itself sits on the riverbank, a trio of thatched cabins with fans, electric lights and tented fronts, connected by a walkway which weaves amongst trees. Further off, there are two cottages with kitchens, game-viewing platform and art gallery – Olga collects local art and encourages guests to paint, pen or ponder. It's not so much "shamrackle" (one of Olga's spoonerisms) as delightfully unrushed. Our friends in the bush.

Rooms: 5: 3 twin cabins sharing two bathrooms; 1 twin timber cottage and 1 double stone cottage, both with own showers.
Price: R590 pp. Single supplement R100.
Meals: Full breakfast and 3-course dinner included. Drinks not included.
Directions: From Jo'burg N12, from Pretoria N4, through Witbank to Belfast. Left on R540 to Lydenburg, then R36 through Strijdom Tunnel following signs to Phalaborwa. Turn right onto R530 to Mica. 22km from Mica on R530 turn R on dirt road following Mfubu signs (about 9km).

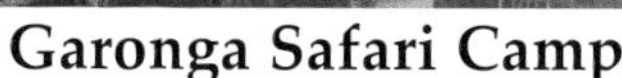

Garonga Safari Camp

Bernardo Smith

Greater Makalali Game Reserve, Hoedspruit 1380
Tel: Res: 011-537-4620 Fax: Res: 011-447-0993 Camp: 015-318-7902
Email: reservations@garonga.com Web: www.garonga.com
Cell: Camp: 082-440-3522

Garonga is as close to Heaven as most of us ever get. Bernardo has succeeded in creating a luxurious, yet completely relaxed, North African oasis in the middle of the South African bush: terracotta colours, thick earthen walls, cushions on low beds and billowing white fabrics. The pace is slow and unpressurised, the perfect relaxed environment for honeymooners, couples celebrating anniversaries or for just about anyone who needs to make it up to someone else. Game drives are always available, but you may prefer to lie in under the high, white-tented canopy of your amazing room, dreaming of the candlelit bath taken under the stars on the previous evening with a bottle of wine; or of the sensational food you have enjoyed and hope still to enjoy. Alternately you can choose a more solitary, more exotic night's sleep twenty minutes from camp on a platform high above the water. Still stressed? Then return to Garonga and fall asleep in one of the hammocks or be pampered by the resident aromatherapist while gazing languidly over the nearby waterhole. Probably the most romantic place to stay in this book. *Children welcome from 8 years old and up.*

Rooms: 7: 4 king/twins and 2 doubles with indoor and outdoor shower; 1 bush suite with bath, shower, outdoor shower and air-conditioning.
Price: R1,595 - R7,200 pp.
Meals: Breakfast, lunch and dinner included, as well as picnics, sleep-outs and bush bath, house wines and beers, soft drinks and laundry.
Directions: Directions will be given to you when you book.

Blue Cottages Country House

Pieter & Maria Van Der Merwe

Olifants River Estate, Hoedspruit 1380
Tel: 015-795-5114/5750 Fax: 015-795-5931
Email: info@countryhouse.co.za Web: www.countryhouse.co.za
Cell: 082-851-3802

Pieter and Maria recently became the new owners of Blue Cottages, individually-wrapped rondavels and cosy-looking cottages set amidst a lush jungle of indigenous and tropical trees. Luckily they were just as enthusiastic about our book as I was about their magical little spot. Crane and Quail are small, round and thatched, whitewashed on the outside with blue doors and smothered in Virginia creeper. Inside, delphinium-blue walls, quaint cottage furniture and just enough space for a bed - sweet as pie. The private bathroom is in a separate hut just a few steps away. Crane and Garden Cottage come replete with delightful sitting rooms and kitchen(ette)s and all rooms keep their cool with air-con and overhead fans. Bedrooms, sitting rooms and the terrace are decorated with a showcase of superb African artefacts, the best pieces from the well-established Monsoon Gallery. Food is another bonus; choose from the fresh fusion-cuisine menu in their ever-popular afro-chic restaurant or perhaps enjoy a tasty home-cooked dinner served on the verandah by lamplight. Whichever you decide, a traditional or 'health' breakfast will great you in the morning. A delightful (re-) discovery and a good base for the Blyde River Canyon (truly magnificent!) and the Kruger Park.*All rooms have air-con or overhead fans.*

Rooms: 4: 2 rondavels: Crane (with double & 2 sleeper-couches in living room) & Quail (with twin room); both have private outside bath/showers; Garden Cottage (1 double, en-s shower); Farm Suite (sleeps 5, en-s bath & shower).
Price: Crane: R239 pp sharing, R270 single; Quail: R177 pp sharing, R234 single; Garden R359 pp sharing, R416 single; Weavers Nest Suite; R302 pp sharing, R359 single. Self-catering option in Crane and Garden Cottages.
Meals: Breakfast included. Dinner R95 for 3-course meal.
Directions: On the Hoedspruit to Lydenberg road (R527) 28km from Hoedspruit.

Coach House Hotel and Spa

Guy Matthews

Old Coach Rd, Agatha, near Tzaneen 0850
Tel: 015-306-8000; reservations: 015-306-8027 Fax: 015-306-8008
Email: info@coachhouse.co.za; reservations@coachhouse.co.za
Web: www.coachhouse.co.za Cell: 083-627-9999

The Coach House *is* a hotel, but it is a rare achievement in the genre to retain such a friendly and personal atmosphere; this is down to a dynamic Guy Matthews and his attentive team. You are encouraged to slow down, switch off, breathe in the air and maybe take a snooze on your own patio. The setting is spectacular, although the Drakensberg hid coyly behind the mist when I stayed. The food is also delicious and comes mostly from the surrounding farms. There is a floodlit croquet lawn (if you can muster the energy), a keyhole-shaped pool, a new spa with heated pool number two, a substantial gym and a variety of treatment rooms. You can also go hiking in the grounds (560 hectares, mostly dedicated to macadamia and pecan nut plantations) or sample the joys of the little nougat factory, the snooker room with views of the lowveld, the sitting room with roaring fires, and the oldest (109 years!) money jukebox in the world. Since the first edition people have continued to speak highly of the Coach House and it deserves its excellent reputation. *No children under 14. Kruger National Park is 100km away. Close to the Coach House: Rooikat Forest Trail, Debegeni waterfalls, and township and cultural tours.*

Rooms: 41 rooms, all with en-suite bathrooms.
Price: R675 - R975 pp sharing (B&B). Single room R950 - R1,259 (B&B). Includes use of sensorium and a complimentry drink.
Meals: All meals available in the restaurant. Casual breakfasts R120. 5-course set-menu dinners R250 (wine extra) or à la carte. Dress smart-casual.
Directions: Ask when booking.

Kurisa Moya Nature Lodge

Ben De Boer and Lisa Martus

Houtbosdorp, near Magoebaskloof, PO Box 280, Haenertsburg 0730
Tel: 015-276-1131 Fax: 015-276-1131
Email: info@krm.co.za Web: www.krm.co.za
Cell: 082-200-4596

Log cabins in an indigenous forest, a beautiful Ben-crafted cottage overlooking mile upon mile of mountains and veld, or a rustic, thick-walled farmhouse.... Ben and Lisa offer the lot and the hardest part of your stay will be choosing where to lay your head. For me it was just a stop-off sadly, with a lazy couple of hours on the verandah being filled in on available attractions (tea plantations, waterfall walks, massages, fly-fishing, Kruger expeditions...) and filled up with lunch and lime juice. All three destinations are self-cater-friendly, but homespun "meals on 4x4 wheels" are on hand. It is a family-owned affair run by Ben and assorted siblings and spouses. They've worked tirelessly to tread as lightly as possible on their mountainside environment and that's what makes this such a tranquil place to stay. The stilted cabins (my favourite) are hidden by a dense canopy of afro-montane forest and their decks are the ideal spot for a lamp-lit braai or bino-less birding. Fortunately one of SA's top two guides, the affable David, is on hand to properly introduce you to Knysna turacos, black-fronted bush shrikes and some 300 other species that are on show when they choose to be. Pulling out of the drive, I really wished I'd stayed the night. Ten minutes down the road one of my tyres exploded. I really, really wished I'd stayed the night. *Massages, fly-fishing, sunset 4x4 drives and bird walks available on site.*

Rooms: 4 venues: 2 forest cabins sleeping 2 adults and 2 kids each, sharing a shower; 1 cottage sleeping 2-6, sharing shower; 1 farmhouse with 2 doubles and 3 twins, all with en-suite bath and/or shower.
Price: R300 - R350 self-catering, R500 - R600 full board. Children under 12 half-price.
Meals: Breakfast R70, lunch R80, supper R120.
Directions: From Jo'burg take N1 north to Polokwane and then R71 to Tzaneen. After 20km turn L at first traffic lights, continue for 27km and turn R onto the farm.

Lesheba Wilderness

Limpopo Province

Peter and Kathryn Straughan & John and Gill Rosmarin
Louis Trichardt/Makhado 0920
Tel: 015-593-0076
Fax: 015-593-0076
Email: magic@lesheba.co.za
Web: www.lesheba.co.za
Cell: 083-444-0456 or 083-266-9502

Kudu!" a shrill cry from pint-sized ranger Erinn as we bounce along to a family supper. Kathryn and Peter's daughter may be a mere nipper but she's an A-Z on the incredible array of life to be found in their mountaintop kingdom. And a kingdom it is. Creeping up to 4,400ft, I was amazed to reach not a rocky ridge but a huge plateau with its own mini-mountains, grassy plains and thick-bushed gorge. Kathy's parents own this 2,600ha game farm and over eleven years the family have rebuilt a dilapidated Venda village, created a secluded bush camp, started a traditional arts and crafts school, discovered seven rock art sites... and raised three kids. The village is stunning, a gaggle of clay-red rondavels regenerated with the help of Venda artist Noria Mabasa. She sculpted dozens of figures around the clustered bedrooms and huge kitchen/dining room that gazes across the bushy heights. In my room - one of two fabulous suites with inter-linked bedroom, bathroom and kitchen - a curvaceous mermaid stretched seductively around the bath. In the other, the outdoor shower springs from a standing man's ear. This is a magical, see-it-to-believe-it kind of place and a hiker's paradise. Come the morning we were back in the pick-up when Kai's voice crackled across the radio (daughter number 2). What was it? A rhino? A rarely-sighted leopard? "Mummy, Mummy, Erinn threw me off the bed." A false alarm.

Rooms: Venda village (sleeps 13): all rooms with en-suite showers: 2 luxury king suites with huge rock baths, indoor and outdoor showers & kitchen. Hamasha Bush Camp (also exclusive) sleeps 8; all rooms with en-suite showers.
Price: R850 - R1,250 full board. Self-catering or semi-catering on request.
Meals: All game drives, guided rock art walks are included. Horse-riding trails are available. Courses in the 'Centre of Indigenous Knowledge' school extra.
Directions: Take N1 north from Jo'burg to Louis Trichardt. At first crossroads in town turn L onto R522 towards Vivo. Continue for 36km and Lesheba is signed R down a gravel road.

Map Number: 20

Jembisa Bush Home

Neil and Natasha Whyte

Waterberg 0530
Tel: 014-755-4415 Fax: 014-755-4444
Email: info@jembisa.com Web: www.jembisa.com
Cell: 082-570-8474

Jembisa is simply the perfect family safari destination; a home from home kitted out for toddlers to teenagers and planted in some of the most spectacular bush you'll see. Despite palatial proportions the stone and thatch house could not feel more welcoming, its titanic living and dining room providing a central attraction, strewn with well-loved sofas and completed with a honky-tonk piano and vast fireplace. Rhodesian teak staircases sweep up each side to immense bedrooms and no less than five bathrooms, and whether you're flying solo (like me) or a team of ten, you'll enjoy cart-wheeling through them. It all feels distinctly English, sipping tea on the verandah, swinging racquets on the floodlit tennis court and thumbing through the volumes of a snug library. But venture a little further and this is most certainly Africa. At the foot of the garden, beyond salt-water pool and shaven lawns, a huge deck juts from the hillside gazing proprietarily across the Palala River, a deep, snaking watercourse sliding through the forest far below (favoured spot for wallowing hippo and catchable yellowfish). You won't see the boundaries of the reserve from the deck – particularly when face-down, enjoying a massage treatment. It covers some 3,000ha (an awful lot of acres) and is packed with trackable game from rhino to leopard and hyena. *Also perfect for small groups looking for exclusive use of a safari camp.*

Rooms: 6: 1 king, 2 queens & 2 king/twins all en/s bath and shower; 1 twin bunk-bed sharing bath and shower.
Price: Bookings on an exclusive basis. R1,950 pp includes all activities on the game reserve. Kids under 12 half-price.
Meals: All meals and drinks included.
Directions: From Jo'burg take N1 north. After Warmbaths take R33 via Nylstroom to Vaalwater. In town turn R to Melk River. After exactly 40km turn L to Lapalala and Melk River school. 8km on turn R to rhino museum. Continue 4km and gates are on R.

Windsong Cottages

Phil and Juliet Calcott & Charles and Nina Baber
Boschdraai Farm, Vaalwater 0530
Tel: 014-755-4425/4000 Fax: 014-755-4946
Email: windsongcottages@telkomsa.net
Cell: 084-405-8865 or 083-276-0518

The Babers and the Calcotts are an utterly charming clan and the most open-hearted, generous people you'd hope to meet, let alone be entertained by. Lucky then was I during my stay to have the whole family from top (Charles - legend in own lifetime) to littlest toe (young Peter, grandson and future doppelganger) all to myself. Equally brimming with character are their cottages, three of which are shaded by jacarandas in green-fingered Nina's stunning garden. Higgledy-piggledy, with packing-box doors, wonky doorframes and home-made bricks, they too have been growing organically over the years, much like the extended Baber family. Each has heaps of space and shares the fantastic braai area sunken into the lawn under the trees. Ticking all the right boxes for a multi-family getaway is Kudu Lodge, which sits across the farm pondering three beautiful dams. One of Charles's adages, 'a short pencil is better that a long memory' never felt so true than when I came to scribbling down the things there are to do here. Top of the list is Charles's world-famous farm tour which he leads in partnership with Richard The Lionheart - Windsong's trusty black lab; and then there's hippo-watching, horse-riding, jungle-gyming, fishing... and so on ad infinitum. Come meal times Juliet dishes up delicious, homely fare that always comes with extra servings of good cheer and a big dollop of laughter. This place is *truly* a destination in itself - absolutely 100%.

Rooms: Windsong Cottage: 1 twin & 2 triples en-s shower, 1 triple en-s bath & dressing room; Rose Cottage: 1 double & 1 twin with shared shower; Butterfly Cottage: 1 double en-s bath; Kudu Lodge sleeps up to 16 with a mix of doubles, twins and bunks.
Price: R180 - R280 pp for the cottages. Kudu Lodge is R100 - R230. Children under 12 half-price, under 2's free. Fun and active baby-sitting and child-minding on offer.
Meals: Self-catering and B&B. Breakfasts are an extra R40. Dinners R60 and lunches R50 on request.
Directions: 30 minutes from Vaalwater. Directions emailed on booking.

Ant's Nest

Ant and Tessa Baber
Vaalwater, Waterberg 0530
Tel: 014-755-4296 or 014-755-3584 Fax: 014-755-4941
Email: antsnest@telkomsa.net Web: www.waterberg.net
Cell: 083-287-2885

Ant's (and Tessa's) Nest is a true bush home run by a truly great team. It's a one-party-a-go destination in the malaria-free Waterberg where the only rule is "do what you want". Built centre stage in a natural amphitheatre, bedrooms are arrayed in and around the home on Baber family land. There's a colonial feel to the Indian furniture and shaded verandah, but it's not in the least bit stuffy. In fact, it's one of the most relaxed and child-friendly places I've found, and there are activities galore. Top of the list are the horses, some 40 of them, from the novice's plodder – for those who still think them uncomfortable in the middle and dangerous at both ends – to the challengingly frisky. And horse-back is the best way to see the game (particularly the rare antelope like oryx and sable), while wallowing in the new 15-metre pool can also be pretty effective when Irwin the rhino and other animals come to munch the lawn or drink at the waterhole. Otherwise there are traditional game drives or walks, visits to meet Ant's dad Charles (a legend in these parts) and his cattle stud, tours of rock art sites or Iron Age villages... and always piles of gourmet food to come back to. Really, with so much on offer, why bother coming for less than a week?

Rooms: 4: 3 kings with en/s bath and shower, 1 family unit with 3 single beds and shared bath and shower.
Price: R2,090 - R3,000 pp. Kids R780 - R1,500. Prices vary according to number of people and are fully inclusive of all activities whilst on the game reserve.
Meals: All meals and drinks included.
Directions: From Jo'burg take N1 north. After Warmbaths take R33 via Nylstroom to Vaalwater. Head through town and turn R opposite Total garage to Elisras/Lephalale. After 10km turn R to Dorset. Ant's Nest is signed on L 11km on.

Map Number: 20

Ant's Hill

Ant and Tessa Baber
Vaalwater 0530
Tel: 014-755-4296 or 014-755-3584 Fax: 014-755-4941
Email: antsnest@telkomsa.net Web: www.waterberg.net

...And for those in search of a more classic lodge experience with all the same activities, there's Ant's Hill just up the road (and hill, obviously). This too is a family-friendly, exclusive-bookings venue and you're encouraged to use whichever of the five rooms you fancy. The troop staying when I visited were doing just that; Mum and Dad plus young twins in the huge family suite, a teenager above the lodge, overlooking the bush, and a ten-year-old in the hillside honeymoon suite! The main lodge, rooms and salt-water pool all teeter on the edge of a gorge that's a lush, green home to baboons and the ideal spot to watch the sun set over the Waterberg (G&T in hand, of course). All the stone and wood here comes from the reserve, with twisted wild olive boughs hauled in to make door frames and fireplaces. The whole place has a truly homely feel, stuffed with Kenyan furniture, Ant's paintings, brightly-coloured cushions and royal-sized beds. Paul, your incredibly friendly host, runs the show with wife Daleen and baby Ruben. *Activities in the game reserve are included in the rates. Other activities in the area are available at extra cost.*

Rooms: One-group booking only. 5 rooms in total: 2 kings, 1 twin, 1 family cottage with 1 king & 1 twin room; all with bath and shower.
Price: R1,800 - R3,000 pp. Kids R780 - R1,450. Prices vary according to number of people and are fully inclusive of all activities whilst on the game reserve.
Meals: All meals and drinks included.
Directions: From Jo'burg take N1 north. After Warmbaths take R33 via Nylstroom to Vaalwater. Head through town and turn R opposite Total garage to Elisras/Lephalale. After 19km turn R at Ant's Hill sign onto dirt track heading uphill and follow Ant's Hill signs.

Map Number: 20

Makweti Safari Lodge

Dawn and Alan Kisner
Welgevonden Game Reserve, Waterberg, Vaalwater 0530
Tel: Res: 011-837-6776 Lodge: 014-755-4948 Fax: Res: 011-837-4771
Lodge: 014-755-4950 Email: makweti@global.co.za
Web: www.makweti.com Cell: 083-280-9801

Hosts Wayne and Vicky are the life and soul of this fantastic lodge and I just can't believe we didn't find them sooner. Not only has Wayne a sixth sense for game-finding, he also knows a lot about dung. At any given moment he'll leap off the game vehicle to explain the inner workings of an elephant or the mind-set of a dung beetle, and that's what stands out on his drives. Not only were our sundowners abruptly curtailed for an exciting lion hunt, but he also opened our minds to the full mosaic of bush life. From enormous browsers to tiny insects, it's a fascinating jigsaw that leaves you wondering only where we fit in. Makweti is buried in the Welgevonden private reserve on the undulating, malaria-free Waterberg range, and with fences dropping all the time there's an ever-expanding array of greenery and game on your doorstep. That doorstep overlooks a stunning gorge and summer waters tumble past the lodge, beneath a springy rope-bridge that leads to thatched chalets. Mine was sumptuously private, hidden in the bush with a well-decked-out deck peering through the undergrowth. Indoor and outdoor showers and a free-standing tub ensured I was clean as a whistle before moseying down to the main lodge, where a reed-filled fish pond divides the bar and bookshelves from the dining room. Here we spent much of our time, scoffing sweet potato, tomato tartlets and kudu loin with onion marmalade. Makweti is an unfenced camp - so expect the unexpected.

Rooms: 5: 4 doubles and 1 twin all with bath and shower.
Price: R1,980 – R3,300 pp sharing. Includes all meals, accommodation, safaris and local taxes.
Meals: All meals provided. Drinks extra.
Directions: 260km from Jo'burg. Directions faxed or emailed on booking, or on website. Car transfers available. Flight transfers can link to Mpumalanga airport for Kruger and Mozambique stays.

Mozambique

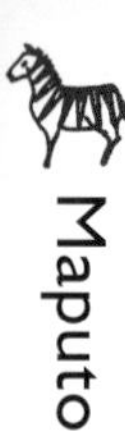

Casa Lisa Lodge

Bruce and Michelle Buckland
CP472, Maputo
Tel: +258-82-304-1990
Email: buckland@teledata.mz

It was here, with a refreshing dry breeze wafting across the pineapple fields, that my Mozambican adventure began. I couldn't have chosen a more rustic destination, or such a charming, laid-back couple as Bruce and Michelle to launch me full stomached into an epic journey. At Casa Lisa you won't find luxuries like electricity points or glass in windows (a blessing as it turns out), but you will find comfort, friendliness and good cheer – far superior substitutes in the heat of Southern Africa. Built around a central tree trunk (where Bruce's hat with 'The Boss' emblazoned across the front dangles from a branch), it is the reed-walled, reed-roofed bar where the heart of Casa Lisa beats. Michelle can often be found ploughing her way through a paperback, waiting anxiously for the chicken delivery from Maputo to trundle up the long drive, while The Boss potters behind the reed and wood bar with the sheepdogs lolling at his feet. As fortune had it, the chicken-man arrived in the nick of time and I enjoyed the famous chicken supper I'd heard so much about. Washed down with the local brew, I retired to my reed and concrete chalet to snuggle up behind the mosquito net and read by candlelight. A perfect stopover to rest those weary driving legs.

Rooms: 15 chalets sleeping 1-11 people. 10 with en-suite showers, 5 with private bathrooms.
Price: $17 - $22 pp. Children under 12 half-price.
Meals: Full breakfast $5. Dinner $8.50 for 3 courses, $5 main course only. Lunch by arrangement.
Directions: On EN1, 48.5km from junction of EN4 onto EN1 (Xai Xai road, north of Maputo).

Casa Barry

Malcolm and Peggy Warrack
Tofo Beach, 4320
Tel: 082-808-5523 Fax: 031-767-0111
Email: peggy@dbnmail.co.za Web: www.casabarry.com
Cell: +258-232-9007 (Lodge)

Just what the doctor ordered after a seven-hour slog along the recently upgraded roads of Mozambique. I couldn't wait to dump my bags and stretch my aching legs on the clear sands of Tofo Beach that arched away into the distance. In the protected lukewarm bay, a fleet of small (and rather rickety-looking) fishing boats were being hauled from the water's edge, overflowing with wriggling goodies from which the lodge's chefs make their selection for the restaurant. Following my nose, I headed to the stilted wooden deck protruding from the reed-roofed bar, offering a bird's-eye view of the comings and goings on the beach. This is clearly the place to be, with diners and drinkers soaking up the atmosphere as the sun goes down to the sound of some good ol' classics warbling in the background. Successful fishermen fired up the braais for a family feast on their verandah before sinking, satisfied, into a deep sleep under the reed roof of their wooden chalet. Seems these folk had an action-packed day behind them. Nevertheless, I rose early to find them strapping on scuba gear or untangling fishing lines as a couple of riders cantered along the deserted beach. John runs the scuba centre and is an oracle on everything from reefs, giant manta rays and whale sharks. Linked to the scuba centre are two internationally accredited marine scientists who are also a world of knowledge and available at all times to discuss the treasures of the deep.

Rooms: 20: 12 chalets sleeping 4-6 with private shower rooms and kitchens; 8 casitas with en-suite showers.
Price: R900 per day for 4-sleeper chalet. R1,150 per day for 6-sleeper chalet. R180 pp for casitas.
Meals: Full breakfast R30. Self-catering or restaurant on premises specialising in local seafood.
Directions: Map on website, directions can be faxed.

Deacra

Barry Deacon
Vilankulos
Tel: +258-293-84076 or +258-293-82048 Fax: +258-293-82048
Email: casarex@teledata.mz or info@bhs.co.zw Web: www.deacra.com
Cell: +258-82-530-7792

I arrived at Deacra to find its beachfront, self-catering houses relaxing in the company of their individual private gardens and swimming pools. Following their cue, I later chose a shady spot to doze beneath one of the huge palm trees that nod eagerly towards spectacular views of the archipelago, all of which felt exclusively mine. I imagined hours of fun sipping cocktails on the verandah and debating what it would be like to really own just one of those islands, Bazaruto perhaps, or maybe Magaruque? Hmmm... perhaps ask the very hospitable Buddy and Cally. They are based on-site to give a warm welcome and can be called upon at a moment's notice if you need to know anything at all about Vilanculos or the Bazaruto archipelago. Although just a 3km (by 4x4) away from Vilanculos and all the conveniences it supplies (shops, banks etc), do amass all your food and kit before arriving - trust me, once here, it won't feel easy to leave. And why should you? The houses come fully-prepped with top-quality linen, mosquito-nets, and kitchen mod cons aplenty adorn the vast wooden worktops of the equally vast kitchens. This really is a self-caterer's haven, so make the very most of being able to do your own thing at your own speed, or lack thereof. With fishing (ever caught a squid?), diving (or swum with one?), windsurfing and water-skiing, Deacra provides both tranquillity and adventure.

Rooms: 3 twin bedroom self-catering houses all with en-suite shower, fully-fitted kitchens and outdoor shower.
Price: $350 per house per night. A $200 refundable breakage deposit will also be expected on arrival.
Meals: Fully self-catering.
Directions: On entering Vilankulos, turn left at main T-junction, follow for around 2km to next T-junction on Beach and turn left again, from here carry straight on for another 4.5km on sand road – you will come across beige Deacra masonry houses on right-hand side. Turn right and proceed to caretakers house at the end on the right-hand side.

Casa Rex

Melonie Glyn-Woods and Ray Monson
Beir 19 Outubro, Vilankulos
Tel: +258-293-82048 Fax: +258-293-82048
Email: casarex@teledata.mz Web: www.casarex.co.zw

I've never met Rex, but you only have to stroll round his house to feel that you know him. He built it ten years ago, single-handed, hand-crafting the furniture from heavy, mahogany-like local wood. He's dotted the house with flotsam and jetsam washed up on the beach below (not any old rubbish – a ship's wheel, lovingly restored, and a port-hole fitted into the front door were my favourites). A remarkable chap. And a remarkable place, run by the super-relaxed Ray and Mel... the most charming couple this side of Maputo? A few minutes sprawled on the deep black-slate verandah and, if you're anything like me, you'll quickly fall as deeply in love with the place as they have. And who can blame us? This shady haven plays host to the best restaurant in town (the thought of squid and stuffed crab as fresh as the ocean itself set my hunger pangs twanging), overlooking an oasis of a garden, drenched in colour, with views (and a path) down to the ocean. Pink bougainvillaeas hide the garden rooms and palms, overflowing with coconuts, stretch skywards above the crystal pool. The rooms, scattered among the greenery, provide welcome relief from the African sun with their cool, tiled floors and whitewashed or exposed walls. Rex may have built perfection.

Rooms: 7: 4 doubles, 1 with en-suite bath and shower, 3 with en-suite shower only; 1 triple (3 single beds) and 2 twins (family rooms) all with en-suite showers. 6 new air-conditioned doubles will be opening in August 2006.
Price: $75 - $95 pp. Single supplement $20 in high season.
Meals: Full breakfast included. A la carte restaurant on the premises, approx $25 - $30.
Directions: 850km north of Maputo on EN1, turn right at Vilanculos sign in Pambara. In Vilanculos turn left at the main T-junction and left again onto the sand road when you get to the sea (Casa Rex is signposted here). Casa Rex is 800m on right.

Map Number: 28

Nkwichi Lodge

Patrick Simkin
Manda Wilderness, Lake Niassa
Email: info@mandawilderness.org Web: www.mandawilderness.org
Cell: 082-709-792

Ed's petrol crisis in Vilanculos made visiting Nkwichi (several tanks further north) impossible, so trusted friend of the firm Dorothy McLaren took up the baton and told us all we needed to know. Bewitching stuff. When we talk about venues being destinations in themselves, this is what we mean: Lake Malawi (or Niassa as it's known in Mozambique), hundreds of miles of gin-clear water, bound in by thick, indigenous forest. This really is true wilderness and the adventure starts with the transfer, buzzing in on a charter flight, chugging in on the M.V. Ilala steamer or sailing to a squeaky, white sand beach on the Nkwichi dhow. This is the only lodge on the Manda Wilderness Reserve and with beds for just 14 guests you'll cross paths with nothing but the wildlife - otters, zebra, monkeys and eagles included. There are endless snorkelling spots, waterfall walks or sailing and canoeing expeditions available while hammocks are on hand for the readers, snoozers and lunch-time boozers. All 6 chalets are built of natural materials, artfully dotted within Nkwichi's invisible boundaries. Massive beds, great big armchairs and deckchairs at every turn invite you to relax and absorb the surrounding beauty, before digging into wholesome meals, heaped with locally-grown veg. The only tricky bit is deciding where to eat: the waterside deck, the lofty dining room or will it be in the shade of a 2,000 year old baobab tree…?

Rooms: 6: 5 chalets doubles and 1 chalet split into 2 (1 double, 1 twin). All en-suite/outside bathrooms & 'eco-loos' (soon to be flush toilets).
Price: African residents: US$180 per night per couple. Internationals: US$360 per couple. Singles $90 - £150.
Meals: Transfers each way: from Likoma Island = $25 pp. From Cobue $20 pp. From Mbueca $10 pp. All meals and activities included in the rates.
Directions: From Malawi, charter plane from Lilongwe to Likoma Island (45 mins) & then transfer by boat (40 mins). Or take Ilala ferry from Chipoka on Fri, arriving Sat. From Lichinga in Mozambique, 4-hr, scenic road transfer to Mbueca & 15-min boat transfer to lodge. 4X4 is needed. Lodge can organise vehicles & drivers.

Map Number: 28

Namibia

Namibia is a big country and knowing where to stay has always proved a problem for independent travellers there in the past. Until now, despite the wealth of information on accommodation available, there has never been any help in making the choice, i.e. while many brochures are distributed for free at the airport etc, there was no selective and evocative guide-book hand-picking places with charm and leaving out the rest. Which is were we come in.

I knew the accommodation gems were there somewhere... but where? What I really needed was a resident expert to show us the way…

Just when I was pondering this very issue, Lily emerged out of my email inbox like the genie from the bottle, and our wishes were granted. She has lived in Windhoek for a few years now and has spent a great deal of that time travelling to every out-of-the-way corner of the country staying at lodges and B&Bs. In fact she tells me that, with her husband at the wheel, they have driven 60,000km in just two years. Her interest was not merely that of the holiday-maker, although her enthusiasm for the wonders of nature to be found across Namibia is certainly catching. She had already written two books on accommodation in Thailand and The Phillipines. By the time we were in contact she already knew which places we wanted for the most part.

The photos (most of which were taken by Lily) and descriptions tell their own tale. It looks entirely enticing… edible almost!

This is the first countrywide guide to great places to stay in Namibia with all the information you need for independent travel freely available within the pages of this book. As always the places to stay that Lily has chosen are all run by friendly enthusiastic people. This is the sine qua non of GG selections. But beyond this you will see a huge variety in styles of accommodation, in rates, in geographical position etc. Our view is always that great places to stay are found right across the price spectrum. And that a great guide-book will offer you all sorts of different excitements while never compromising on the essence of hospitality.

If you are about to make use of this part of our guide-book, well, frankly I am jealous!

The next part of this introduction is by Lily herself.

DRIVING IN NAMIBIA

You can drive a saloon car on many roads in Namibia: the main tarmac roads from Windhoek to Swakopmund, to Etosha or to Rundu/Katima Mulilo/Kasane; and also on the many excellent dirt roads of the country. But you will definitely feel more comfortable with a 4x4 on the dirt roads. If it rains a 4x4 is definitely the best plan. However, in some parts of Damaraland (for example), if the river is flooding (a rare occurrence), even with a 4x4 you might wait from a few hours to a few days for the water level to drop. That is Namibia for you! So it is always a good idea to check with the place you are going to visit to see if you're going to need a 4x4 and if, during the rainy season, the rivers can be crossed. (In Kaokoland you would need GPS, but the only accommodation that we have in

Kaokoland, Serra Cafema, is accessible only by plane.)

All the dirt roads are very well signposted, quite amazing in the middle of nowhere! In my experience, the best map – even if it is not always perfect - is "Map Studio Tourist Atlas - Namibia" published by Struik, and this can be bought in CNA. This map is also very useful as it indicates the fuel stations.

Take care to refill your tank every time you find a fuel station, as there are not that many in some parts of the country.

CAR HIRE

If you get enough time to visit and have a tight budget, it is much cheaper to rent a car in South Africa than in Namibia…but you will have to drive a long way. For example Cape Town to Windhoek is about 1400km. You can make interesting stops on the way, of course, but the distances generally in Namibia are huge.

PRICES IN NAMIBIA

Accommodation is Namibia is more expensive than in South Africa, despite the fact that it is generally not as sophisticated. This is a pity, but you have to consider the fact that the guest farms or small lodges are often very remote, and that makes everything more logistically difficult and therefore expensive to run. For example in some places the owners have to drive 2 hours - or sometimes even 4 hours! - to do their shopping. So be prepared to spend a little more, but I never met anyone who felt that Namibia was bad value for money.

In Namibia there is a wonderful sense of wilderness. You can drive for hours without passing another car. The average size of a farm, for example, is 8,000 hectares! As you drive through most of the country you will see amazing landscapes of red sand dunes, fascinating rock formations and many animals and plants that don't exist anywhere else. The Caprivi Strip is very different – lush and green - and it is cheaper than Botswana and Zimbabwe although you will see the same kind of wetland terrain and wildlife.

MOBILE/CELL PHONES

In Namibia, many places have no coverage for cell phone. They work in the main towns (Windhoek, Swakopmund, Rundu, Katima Mulilo) but more whimsically in other parts. A word of advice: try calling from the highest point of the road or guest farm.

TELEPHONE NUMBERS

To call Namibia from the UK dial 00264, then drop the 0 from the local code. The numbers given in the Namibian chapter are all from within Namibia.

WILDLIFE

On the main roads you will see signboards with symbols of a kudu crossing, or a warthog crossing etc…This might seem quaint, but one day in a 100km stretch we counted 50 warthogs on the bend of the roads! Many accidents occur because of kudu or oryx crossing the road – this occurs mostly at dawn, but not only. Or on dirt roads. As they are often excellent, people forget that they are driving on a dirt road and go too fast. It is advisable to keep your maximum speed down to between 80km and100km an hour on dirt roads.

TIPPING

* In restaurant you give 10%, and if you pay by credit card, you write down the tip you want to give and add it to the bill.

TIME OF YEAR

All seasons are nice in Namibia, so there is no obvious best time to visit. It depends what you are looking for.

Winter in Namibia is approximately from June to end of August. During the day it is 20 to 25 degrees, very agreeable for hiking. At night, the temperature can drop to 4 degrees, or even to around zero.

Summer is approximately from November to March. It can be pretty hot during the day, 30 degrees or more in some desert areas.

In good years, there is a small rainy season in November. The main rainy season usually starts in January and ends in April, but in some regions, such as the south the rains come only every 2 years or even less frequently, and never last long. Except in the Caprivi, you will never have whole days of rain. The rain lasts for one or two hours a day. Namibia is beautiful after the rains, all green and blooming. It is hard to imagine that it's the same country that was so dry and yellow before!

But during the rains it is more difficult to see animals.

In the Caprivi, when the rain starts, the elephants go deep into the forest, but the hippo are still there and it is a good season for birding. It is very hot and humid during the rainy season in the Caprivi.

In Swakopmund, it is cool most of the time all year round (14 to 18 degrees during the day) and misty, except during summer where the temperature is very pleasant. Namibians love to go to Swakopmund to escape the heat. The sea is generally freezing (around 12 degrees) – that's what I think, anyway, but some people don't seem to mind! - because of the Benguela current. That explains the huge seal colony in Cape Cross. In summer the water can reach the dizzy heights of 20 degrees.

Lily.

The Hilltop Guesthouse

Angela Curtis and Allen Uys
12 Lessing Street, Windhoek
Tel: 061-249-116 Fax: 061-247-818
Email: hilltop@iafrica.com.na Web: www.thehilltophouse.com
Cell: 081-127-4936

Hilltop is a Bavarian-style building (1958) constructed, unsurprisingly, on a hill in a quiet *cul-de-sac*. The house is surrounded by a wooden balcony and guarded by a majestic araucaria that stands aloof in the garden. Formerly a photographic studio, it was transformed by Angela and Allen into a guesthouse full of character. They have retained the old-world look of the interior with its Oregon-pine floors, wood-lined semi-circular doors and dark, colonial furniture - these contrast strikingly with the ecru walls decorated with watercolours of animals. The Honeymoon suite is charming, with an antique fireplace remodelled in earthenware tiles. Antique charm, certainly, but you have every modern convenience as well. Meals are served in your room or on the garden terrace near the swimming pool looking out at the view over Klein Windhoek. Allen adores cooking and he also takes care of the service himself. His cuisine is light and creative: I feasted on an excellent spiced leek consommé followed by a tasty chicken curry with couscous and vegetables. Angela's specialities are the raising of white shepherd dogs - to whom she'll take great pleasure in introducing you - and making gourmet desserts (in that order). Both are absolutely charming hosts and very happy and able to advise you on your travel arrangements. And guess what? At Hilltop, you have both freshly-squeezed orange juice and great coffee for breakfast… details perhaps, but indicative of the approach here.

Rooms: 7: 1 single, 3 doubles and 2 family rooms; 1 single in a separate cottage.
Price: N$550 pp sharing, singles N$660 and family rooms N$1,800. Rates valid until December 2006.
Meals: Full breakfast included. Prices vary from N$25 to N$90 for other meals.
Directions: Take Nujoma Drive from international airport. Turn R at Nelson Mandela Ave, L at Robert Mugabe Ave, L again at Lilien Crohn St and L again at Langenhoven. Then take a R into Promenaden Rd and a final R into Lessing St.

Casa dell' Ama

Marutsca Breitenmoser and Christine Bays
66 Amasoniet Street, Windhoek
Tel: 061-234-131 Fax: 061-234-683
Email: marutsca@euronovelties.net Web: www.euronovelties.net
Cell: 081-278-5975 or 081-294-2821

Marutsca and Christine are two extraordinary, energetic young women, who succeed in combining their work with the perfect running of their guesthouse. They dreamed of a place unlike any other and this dream has certainly been realised. More than a guesthouse, this is a private house put entirely at your disposal, a place where you are welcomed as a friend with great sincerity and kindness. The house belonged to Marutsca's godfather and it has been renovated from top to toe to create a sophisticated home in minimalist style. The whole house is open to you: the ultra-modern kitchen, the living room, and the television/music room where there is even Internet access. The two enormous bedrooms are refined and cheerful at the same time with their sponge-painted walls the colour of desert sands and wooden furniture designed especially for Casa dell' Ama. A huge terrace in mineral tones of ochre and red with a lapa and superb free-form swimming pool provide perfect vantage points for the extraordinary view over the Otjihavera Mountains. It is amazing to consider that you are in Windhoek! As if this wasn't enough, Marutsca and Christine cook to perfection with a palette of menus - Swiss, Moroccan, Indian - and imaginative decoration that varies according to the menu. If available, they will happily organise a "sunset braai" in the hills for you or accompany you on shopping trips. What more could you wish for?

Rooms: 2 bedrooms with en-suite bath and shower.
Price: N$500 pp sharing + VAT. No single supplement.
Meals: Full breakfast included. Lunches and dinners on request from N$85 to N$145 per menu.
Directions: From international airport, take Sam Nujoma then turn right into Nelson Mandela, right to Kuiseb and left into Omuramba. From here turn right to Eros St and finally turn left to Amasoniet.

Map Number: 16

Londiningi Guesthouse

Nathalie Nosjean
11 Winterberg Street, Eros, Windhoek
Tel: 061- 242-378 Fax: 061-226-201
Email: londiningi@mweb.com.na Web: www.londiningi.com
Cell: 081-128-1017

Nathalie recently left France to move to Windhoek and has opened a very friendly guesthouse, which in just a few months has become extremely popular. You will have little trouble understanding why when you stay. Although this is undeniably excellent value for money, Nathalie's personality has much more to do with her success. She is full of energy, good humour and generosity, doing everything she can to put you at ease and to help you in arranging your trip, or in solving any small problems which may arise. You quickly feel at home and some guests feel so comfortable here they don't want to leave. Apart from this, Nathalie is a *cordon bleu* chef specialising in French cuisine. Comfortably settled on the verandah in the company of other guests, I savoured the asparagus in Hollandaise sauce, a roast served with little bundles of green beans with bacon and, to finish, a vanilla sorbet with a raspberry coulis. There are many details which make this place special: the painted murals by a local artist on the patios of some of the rooms, the large map of Namibia painted in naïve style on the wall of the terrace by a guest, the small baobabs made of wire which hold the tea and coffee sachets in the bedrooms. The garden is green, the pool irresistible and this is just a great place to start and end your Namibian adventure.

Rooms: 8: 1 x 2-bed family suite with en-suite bath and shower; 2 bedrooms with en-suite bath and shower; 5 bedrooms with en-suite shower.
Price: Suite N$850. Double room N$400. Single N$300.
Meals: Full breakfast included. Dinner N$100, Lunch N$60 and packed lunch N$50.
Directions: From international airport, take Sam Nujoma, turn right into Nelson Mandela, right to Kuiseb St, left into Omuramba Rd, right to Eros Rd, left to Swarberg, then first left to Winterberg St.

Vondelhof Guesthouse

Yvonne and Craig Gibson

2 Puccini street, Ausspannplatz, Windhoek
Tel: 061-248-320 Fax: 061-240-373
Email: vondelhof@mweb.com.na or reservations@vondelhof.com
Web: www.vondelhof.com

As you approach Vondelhof your eye is first captured by the green turret of the old house in the middle of the garden. The atmosphere here, informal and convivial, is down to Yvonne who so effortlessly puts her guests at their ease with attention that is at once personal and relaxed. She looks after everything, from the booking to the cooking, with the help of Craig, who is not averse to a bit of cooking himself when the spirit comes upon him; and she is always ready to listen to you, to help with reservations or trips into town… she will even share her recipes with you! There are several menus but it is the first guest's order that determines the day's menu. So there's a tip for you! The hake in sweet and sour sauce is very good. There's another. The outdoor patio, at the centre of which is the swimming pool, is the focal point from which radiate the reception area, low buildings harbouring the bedrooms and the restaurant. Guests come to the verandah to have a drink, dine, to write or simply to relax. The rooms are comfortable, each slightly different from the others with original crete-stone walls the colour of sand. They are simply, but tastefully furnished with tall wooden giraffes, basketwork and African fabrics. One of the rooms in the main building has a large wooden deck overlooking the gardens. Children will be delighted to find a jungle gym in the garden.

Rooms: 8: 7 double rooms and 1 triple room all with en-suite bathroom.
Price: N$362.50 pp sharing. Single N$515. Triple N$290 pp sharing.
Meals: Full breakfast included. Light lunch from N$17.50. N$110 for a 3-course dinner.
Directions: Follow Sam Nujoma Drive from international airport. Go underneath the railway line, turn right onto Hosea Kutako Drive then turn left into Puccini street.

Okambara Elephant Lodge

Christian and Uschi Schmitt
Off D1800, Windhoek
Tel: 062-560-217 Fax: 062-560-217
Email: okambara@iway.na or info@okambara.de Web: www.okambara.de
Cell: 081-128-0669

What a pleasure to enter this bucolic garden, where birdsong thrills among the jacarandas, eucalyptus and bougainvillaea and the orange trees and palms of its orchard. A long-haired donkey and her foal, followed by two calves and some sheep, cross the road just in front of our car. Children will love this place, even more because they can swim in the huge, natural swimming pool hidden high up among the foliage. Christian and Uschi also took a plunge when they came to Namibia on holiday 15 years ago, fell in love with the country and decided to move here with their two little girls. Christian's pleasure was evident as he took me on a long game drive through his property to find the white rhinoceros and elephants that he himself introduced. You have a very good chance of seeing a wide variety of animals. The accommodation is very comfortable, whether you are in the round, thatched chalets that are set to one side for a little seclusion, or in the main house. The latter, designed by Christian's father, has echoes of a stone castle with its red rough-cast turrets. However, the interior, with its high wooden beams, has a distinctly African flavour. The perfect place to enjoy a drink is enconsed in one of the comfortable leather sofas arranged near the fire where there's a library of interesting nature books to choose from. The terrace at the back of the house faces a waterhole where kudu often come to drink. Uschy herself excels in the warmth of her welcome and in her *bellissimmo*(predominantly Italian) cooking.

Rooms: 6: 2 cottages and 4 rooms in the main house: 2 double rooms with en-suite shower and 2 family rooms with 2 bedrooms sharing an en-suite shower (1 with living room).
Price: N$640 pp sharing. No single supplement. Game drives: N$150 pp.
Meals: Full breakfast, light lunch and 3-courses dinner included.
Directions: Take B6 (Windhoek/Gobabis), turn onto D1808, then onto D1800 direction Witvlei for 20km before turning right to Okambara (7km).

Guest Farm Kiripotib

Hans Georg and Claudia von Hase

On D1448, Windhoek
Tel: 062-581-419 Fax: 062-581-419
Email: hans@kiripotib.com Web: www.kiripotib.com
Cell: 081-243-2628

This is one of the rare places in Namibia where you can learn how a livestock farm operates and Hans, a third-generation Namibian farmer, is an erudite teacher with a passion for his work. He also has experience as a safari operator, and can advise you in the organisation of your trip and has plenty of anecdotes about his own travels to tell. Claudia manages the jewellery design studio and the Karakul carpet weaving (the Karakul is a sheep if you didn't know). Her creations are displayed in an adjacent shop… and they are decidedly difficult to resist! In addition to their diverse talents, Hans and Claudia are sensitive hosts with a desire to take care of their guests. The guest farm has an artistic atmosphere with a liberal sprinkling of good humour. The thatched lounge in front of the house is where everyone congregates for good home-cooked meals, which make use of home produce from the farm. The buildings and the swimming pool are surrounded by indigenous trees, such as baobabs, African olives and acacias with Madagascan periwinkles at their bases. Claudia's artistic talent - art pieces in African woods, basketwork from the north and colourful Karakul carpets from the studio - is evident in the décor of the rooms and the two new chalets. These recent additions are more independent, roomy and light-filled spaces, but all face out onto the flat, golden Kalahari landscape.

Rooms: 7: 3 rooms, 2 chalets (can sleep 3), all with en-suite shower; 2 budget safari tents with en-suite open-air shower.
Price: Chalets: N$498 pp sharing, singles N$599, triples N$450; rooms: N$425 pp sharing & singles N$499; safari tents: N$315 pp sh & singles N$380. Tour of farm at sunset included.
Meals: Full-breakfast included. N$70 light lunch. N$105 dinner.
Directions: From Dorbabis take dirt road C15/MR33 direction Uhlenhorst. At Klein Nauas pass an old white tower. From there drive straight for about 12km on D1448.

Bagatelle Kalahari Game Ranch

Fred and Onie Jacobs
On D1268, Mariental
Tel: 063-240-982 or 061-224-712 Fax: 063-241-252 or 061-224-217
Email: bagatelle@reservation.destination.com
Web: www.bagatelle-kalahari-gameranch.com

On my arrival, the raucous cries of peacocks in the midst of the red parallel-running sand dunes of the Kalahari made me wonder if I had a touch of sunstroke! But it is just that Onie has a passion for animals: 38 peacocks, 7 cats who lounge at the entry in a wicker basket (taking turns in pairs!), 9 dogs, 4 cheetahs entrusted by the Cheetah Conservation Fund and several orphaned animals that Onie feeds by bottle … a delight for children. The lodge is the former home of Fred and Onie and with all their furniture and décor still in place, the atmosphere is warm, personal and relaxed. The library, near the fireplace, is filled with books about Namibia. You serve yourself from the fridge in the kitchen or from the bar, writing down what you take. Each of the different spaces of the lodge opens onto the next until you reach a shaded verandah overlooking the pool and the open-air lapa. In the evenings, everyone gathers here to enjoy a good dinner in a convivial atmosphere, seated at candlelit tables that are arranged in a semi-circle facing the campfire. The air-conditioned chalets are all very comfortable, but it is the Dune chalets that command superb views over the Kalahari landscape of red dunes dotted with acacias. Each Dune chalet bathroom is equipped with a wonderful bathtub set in an alcove so that you can contemplate glorious sunsets whilst lying in your bath, sipping a chilled glass of wine!

Rooms: 10: 4 Dune chalets with en-suite bath and shower and 6 Strohbale chalets with en-suite shower.
Price: N$800 pp sharing for Dune chalet and N$700 pp sharing for Strohbale chalet (additional adult possible in Strohbale N$400). Single supplement N$300.
Meals: Full breakfast and tea time included. N$60 light lunch. N$120 dinner (buffet style).
Directions: Accessible from Kalkrand and Mariental. On D1268, 25km from the intersection with the C20, and 40km from the intersection with the C21.

Klein Aus Vista

Willem, Piet and Johan Swiegers

2 km West of Aus on the B4, Aus
Tel: 063-258-021 or 063-258-116 Fax: 063-258-021
Email: ausvista@namibhorses.com Web: www.namibhorses.com or www.gondwana-desert-collection.com

The dynamic Swieger brothers had just completed construction of an elegant restaurant facing west towards the sunset when I visited. The Aus Mountains that border the dunes of the Namib Desert are spectacular and a paradise for hikers with numerous trails covering the 52,000 hectares of the private Sperrgebiet Rand Park. The flora is exceptionally rich after the winter rains. For those who seek solitude, the Eagle Nest chalets at the foot of an impressive chaos of granite rocks, yet a mere 7km from reception, are nothing short of fantastic! The rocks have been integrated into the buildings, hugging the chalets or emerging in the interiors in the most unexpected places. Each chalet is different: 'The Rock', my favourite, is perched on the side of the hill between two enormous boulders. The stone interiors are cavernous, rustic and imaginative, each with a fireplace for cold, winter nights. In the kitchen, the table is already set and the fridge is full of cold drinks. Come the evening, the fiery rays of the setting sun touch both the rocks and the chalets in dramatic fashion. The rooms and the new chalets adjoining the reception are in brief walking distance to the on-site restaurant/bar where a cosy, relaxed atmosphere resides. Many will take the opportunity to drive out and see the wild horses of the Namib; a herd is always assembled at a waterhole 20km away on the road to Luderitz. *Various excursions can be booked at reception to explore Klein Aus Vista's own park or the neighbouring Namib Naukluft Park.*

Rooms: 12: 8 self-catering chalets in 'Eagles Nest Rock'; 4 rooms in 'Desert Horse Inn.' Another 20 chalets at 'Desert Horse Inn' from 1st July 2006.
Price: Eagles Nest Rock Chalets: N$450 - N$595 pp sharing B&B, N$795 single B&B; Desert Horse Inn: N$395 pp sharing B&B, N$460 single B&B.
Meals: N$45 breakfast, N$75 lunch, N$130 dinner.
Directions: Accessible from Aus (2km) and from Lüderitz (115km) on B4.

Sandrose B&B Guest House

Christine and Erich Looser

15 Bismark street, Lüderitz
Tel: 063-202-630 Fax: 063-202-365 Email: haussandrose@iway.na
Web: www.suedafrika.net/unterkunft/sandrose_gh.htm
Cell: 081-293-8512 or 081-241-5544

The eerie film-set atmosphere of the town of Lüderitz, nestled into the wind-sculpted dunes and rocks and looking out to a turbulent sea, produced a strong desire in me to find somewhere cosy to stay the night... and nearby diamond 'ghost' town Kolmanskop, where the sand has reclaimed the houses, even more so! Thankfully you couldn't find a more fitting place than Sandrose, a cocoon of well-being in the centre of Lüderitz. The striking yellow façade of Christine and Erich's turn-of-the-last-century house sets the tone. Christine has decorated the house and guest rooms with style, retaining the spirit of the colonial German homes of Lüderitz. The rooms are built around a sheltered plant-filled patio, a real oasis in the desert. Each is comfortable and bright with its own private terrace and equipped for making breakfast. Still, it would be a pity to miss the excellent ones that are prepared in the dining room, with its antique pine furniture and walls adorned with friezes and photographs. The table too is a delight for the eye with its colourful hand-painted ceramics. On the ground floor she has her very own pretty craft boutique and it's here that you'll see her wonderful agate collection, all harvested from the beach - now there's a hint for collectors! Christine is a thoughtful hostess and has prepared lists of places you may like to visit. She is always happy to help you with your arrangements. *There is an Internet corner in the reception.*

Rooms: 3 units: 'Grosse Bucht': self-catering house with 2 bedrooms, lounge, en-suite shower & extra 5th bed; 'Bogenfels': self catering suite with 1 double room & private outside shower & toilet (very close); 'Halifax': 1 double room & en-suite shower with breakfast facilities.
Price: Grosse Bucht N$150 pp sharing (or N$400 if only 2 people). Bogenfels and Halifax N$180 pp sharing and singles N$340.
Meals: Full breakfast on request (N$50). Restaurants near by.
Directions: Bismark Street is the main road of Luderitz.

Namibrand Family Hideout

Andreas and Mandy Brückner

Farm Stellerine, Namibrand Nature Reserve, District Maltahöhe
Tel: 061-226-803 (office hrs) 081-127-2957 (after hrs) Fax: 061-220-634
Email: ambruck@mweb.com.na Web: www.hideout.iway.na
Cell: 081-127-2957

It is difficult to find a more authentic, serene place than this house in the middle of the Namibrand Nature Reserve. Difficult too to find a more magical landscape with its extraordinary red dunes punctuated with acacias and boscia and inhabited by oryx, kudu, zebra, hartebeest, ostrich, springbok... Thanks to Mandy and Andreas, the Stellerine Farm, established in 1945 but later abandoned to the desert sands, has been renovated simply and equipped with the essentials while keeping the atmosphere of the past. It is now open for guests to live within the beauty of Namibrand. The house has the relaxed atmosphere of a holiday home with its rough-cast white walls, cotton fabrics and rattan furniture. This is certainly a place for nature lovers, but it is also especially suited for families with children - there are board games, books and dune boards aplenty. The guest book brims with children's drawings and comments of approval. Here you'll find a deafening silence, views over the desert and dunes, oryx and springbok coming to drink at the waterhole just 20m from the terrace and superb starlit nights. You can explore the dunes behind the house either on foot or in a 4x4 vehicle. A circular track enables you to cross this incredible landscape in about 3 hours (deflate your tyres to 120 KPA). In case of any problems, the management of Tok Tokkie Trails, on the neighbouring farm, will be able to help you.

Rooms: Self-catering farmhouse sleeping 8-10: includes 2 doubles & 1 room sleeping 4 (possible to sleep 2 extra people in lounge); 2 showers & fully-equipped kitchen (gas fridge/stove, solar lamps). Guests must provide own bedding altho' pillows/towels can be arranged at extra cost.
Price: N$560 - N$1,365 per night for the entire house, dependent on size of group, country of residence & length of stay.
Meals: Fully self-catering. Bring all your own food, beverages and firewood for braai and hot shower. First shop is in Maltahöhe, about 100km away.
Directions: 110km south of Sesriem, accessible from Solitaire, Maltahöhe or Helmeringhausen, on C27. After leaving the main road, it is 16km from the gate, passing Tok Tokkie Trails. Information sheet & map provided on confirmation of booking.

The Desert Homestead and Horse Trails

Andrew and Melissa Gillies
Maerua Park, Windhoek
Tel: 063-683-103 or 061-246-788 Fax: 063-683-104 or 061-243-079
Email: homestead@africaonline.com.na or sosses@iafrica.com.na
Web: www.deserthomestead-namibia.com Cell: 081-127-7161

The owners took their 22 horses, saddles and harnesses, their dogs and their cats, and moved even closer to the Sossusvlei dunes to recreate something of the atmosphere of the former Desert Homestead. The structures all face the superb views over the golden plains and the Tzaris Mountains. The restaurant is perched on a promontory and dinner is usually served elegantly on the terrace at individual tables by candlelight under the starry night sky. The menu is written up on a board: the evening I stayed there was green pea soup with delicious rolls straight from the oven, ostrich kebabs with spinach and then cheesecake. The vast semi-circular room with its high ceiling, combining both living area and interior dining room, is full of atmosphere with old farm tools hanging above the stone bar counter and comfortable sofas arranged around a cast-iron fireplace - the grey cat certainly seems to appreciate it. From the dining room, you can see the meal preparation through a large opening to the modern kitchen. I always like that sort of confidence from a kitchen. In the morning, lively conversations among the staff are heard and everyone, from managers to waiters, is smiling and friendly. The bungalows built down below are light-filled and cheerful, with pretty, wooden furniture and designer bathrooms. Excursions to the Sossusvlei dunes 32km away can be arranged as well as nature drives, guided walks and sunrise or sunset horse rides.

Rooms: 20: all bungalows with en-suite shower.
Price: N$1,150 per double room. N$700 singles. N$1,500 triples.
Meals: Full breakfast included. Early morning packed breakfast possible. From N$20 to N$55 light lunch. N$120 dinner.
Directions: Along C19, 32km south east of Sesriem and 3km north of the junction of the C19 and D854.

Zebra River Lodge

Rob and Marianne Field
Tel: 063-693-265 Fax: 063-693-266
Email: marianne.rob@zebrariver.com Web: www.zebrariver.com

Some places, and Zebra River Lodge is one, seem to be blessed by the gods! From the road there is no hint of the dramatic beauty of this 13,000-hectare property in the heart of the Zaris Mountains. Having visited several times, I have still not explored all of the hiking trails there; the most spectacular of these crosses a canyon almost as deep as that of Fish River (just 60m less), at the end of which is a spring surrounded by centenary ficus. The limestone mountains are beautifully striated and form terraces where comiphora and moringa trees grow. Not only is this some of the most beautiful landscape in Namibia, but you will also be delighted by the warm and friendly welcome from Marianne and Rob. In the evening, everyone gathers in the living room, filled with a variety of objects, that give it great eclectic charm - antique pine furniture, dishes, old coffee-grinders, bouquets of dried flowers and Rob's own superb photographs of the dunes. You find the same atmosphere in the décor of the rooms. Marianne's cooking is very good and it is a pleasure to stay on and chat beside the fire, enjoying the excellent wines chosen by Rob. He has a passion for the fascinating geology and palaeontology of the region. If you request in advance, Rob will take you to the Sossusvlei dunes or into the Namib Naukluft National Park.

Rooms: 7 double rooms and 1 self-catering cottage with 2 bedrooms (sleeps 5).
Price: N$600 pp sharing. Singles N$700. N$350 per night for the self-catering cottage (minimum of 2 nights).
Meals: Full breakfast, light lunch and 3-course dinner included.
Directions: Accessible from Maltahöhe, Duwisib, Sesriem, Bullsport. Zebra River Lodge is on the D850, 19km from the intersection with the D854 and 10km from the intersection with the D855.

Barchan Dunes Retreat

Hannetjie and Willem Van Rooyen
On D1275,
Tel: 062-682-031 Fax: 062-682-031
Email: barchan@iway.na Web: www.natron.net/tour/barchan-dunes

Barchan Dunes is one of my favourite places in Namibia. Hannetjie, with her natural charm and Willem, with his sense of humour, are truly great hosts and their friendly welcome is reinforced by the enthusiasm of their dogs who rush to meet your car; and they in turn shortly followed by the two pet meerkats, Koerie and Vlooi! The generously-sized cottages, each decorated in a different theme, are built into the crescent-shaped hollow of the dunes that overlook a serene landscape of mountains and rocky outcrops in the distance. In the evening, dinner is served communally in the elegant dining room. This is a highlight, as much for the quality and quantity of Hannetjie's culinary skills (make sure you prepare for this by dieting beforehand!) as for the good conversation. Willem generously serves some excellent wines - you find your glass refilled as if by magic - and it is all included in the price. The retreat merits a stay of at least two nights to appreciate the beauty of the surrounding area and simply to pamper yourself. Don't miss walking in the canyon among the ghostly silver trunks of the moringa trees. Willem can organise excursions into the dunes of Sossusvlei, 1-hours away (book in advance). Late in the afternoon, Willem takes you on a game drive to see the 40 oryx on his farm or to contemplate the sunset, drink in hand, from a viewpoint on the rose-coloured dunes. "Another boring day ends in Africa!" he concludes with a laugh.

Rooms: 6: 2 rooms inside the main house, 3 cottages and 1 self-catering cottage. All have en-suite shower.
Price: N$759 pp sharing. Self-catering N$650 for the cottage per night. No single supplement. Farm drive also included in rate.
Meals: Full breakfast, coffee and cake in the afternoon, 3-course dinner, malt and soft drinks, included in the rate.
Directions: On D1275. Accessible from Walwis Bay take C14, turn L on D1275 "Nauchas" for 15km; or from Rehoboth take C24, in Nauchas turn R to D1275 to Spreetshoogte Pass. After pass it is 20km.

Map Number: 15

Lagoon Lodge

Hélène and Wilfried Meiller
88 Kovambo Nujoma Drive, Walvis Bay
Tel: 064-200-850 Fax: 064-200-851
Email: french@lagoonlodge.com.na Web: www.lagoonlodge.com.na

Lagoon Lodge is bright yellow, doffing the cap to Provence where its proprietors come from. Only the street separates the lodge from the lagoon, which is bordered by a promenade where residents come to walk at the end of the afternoon to admire the sunsets, often superb here. Hélène and Wilfried are both passionate about Africa and have travelled the continent widely with their daughter. In 1999 they left France without much regret and moved to Walvis Bay, taking with them their beautiful antique furniture and a good stock of blue and yellow cotton fabric. It is obvious from the attention to detail - perfectly coordinated colour schemes, household linens hand-embroidered by Hélène - that the owners have put their hearts into furnishing their lodge. The eight comfortable rooms are each different in terms of colour, theme and décor. Wilfried, who is also a talented woodturner, has created much of the furniture and decorative objects himself. A lovely conservatory has recently been added to the dining room and protects the sea-facing living room. Hélène and Wilfried will welcome you warmly and are particularly helpful in spontaneously offering their assistance to reserve a tour by boat or canoe on the lagoon, or in a 4x4 to the dunes. They will readily offer to take you to town in their car if they are available. Only breakfasts are served, but they are delicious, with croissants home-made by Hélène!

Rooms: 8 rooms (including 3 family rooms good for 2 adults & 2 kids) with en-suite shower.
Price: N$470 pp sharing and N$590 single. N$1,020 family room.
Meals: Full breakfast included. Restaurants nearby (for good seafood in a great seafront setting try 'The Raft').
Directions: At the entrance of Walvis Bay follow directions to Sandwich Harbour. Kovambo Nujoma Drive borders the lagoon on your right, and Lagoon Lodge is the yellow house just on your left. Secure off street parking.

Sam's Giardino

Samuel Egger

89 Anton Lubowski Ave, Swakopmund
Tel: 064-403-210 Fax: 064-403-500
Email: samsart@iafrica.com.na Web: www.giardino.com.na

Samuel Egger, who holds a Swiss diploma in hotel management from Lausanne, is no newcomer to the world of hospitality and this is immediately apparent. He has trained his team to be completely interchangeable: each member of the staff takes it in turn to cook the 5-course menu no less! A tasting of South African wines is offered at the beginning of the evening in the impressive cellar, while the new kitchen is very modern with a bay window opening partly onto the living room. Food and drink are an important part of the experience here. Sam takes care of his guests' comfort with friendly good nature, giving them a map on arrival, showing them all the points of interest and making reservations for activities and restaurants. Sam's Giardino, a comfortable house built in German style with a glass-wall in front, is found in the midst of its own bijou garden with rose trees and a fishpond. The rooms are spread out over two floors and decorated in tones of red and green. The atmosphere throughout is convivial, the guests gathering in the living room to watch National Geographic CDs or browsing in Sam's excellent library - another of his passions. However, dinners are served with flair at individual tables. The last of Sam's passions, and this you will understand, is Einstein, a brainy pedigree Bernese hound who Sam refers to as the Public Relations Manager. He is a real star and muscles in on every photo!

Rooms: 10: 9 with en-suite shower and 1 family room with 3-4 beds and en-suite shower.
Price: N$440 pp sharing. N$640 Single. Dogs and cats also welcome if well-behaved! (by prior arrangement).
Meals: Swiss breakfast included. N$135 for 5-course dinner. N$70 wine tasting at 6:30pm.
Directions: In Swakopmund, from Sam Nujoma turn left into Moses/Garoeb street, then left again into Anton Lubowski Ave. 20 minutes on foot from town centre.

The Stiltz B&B

Danie Holloway
Strand Street South, Swakop River, Swakopmund
Tel: 064-400-771 Fax: 064-400-711
Email: info@thestiltz.in.na Web: www.thestiltz.na
Cell: 081-127-2111

You enter the Stiltz as if through a secret door to a well-guarded kingdom of sea, wind and surrounding dunes, and yet it is just a few minutes' walk to the centre of town. Built high up on stilts on the edge of the dry Swakop River's bed, the wooden, thatch-roofed chalets are linked together by walkways. If possible, ask for a chalet facing the sea. The architect, Dannie Holloway - who is clearly partial to elevated structures having built The Raft at Walvis Bay, The Tug at Swakopmund and Etongo Wilderness Lodge - has created something magical here. At night, you are lulled to sleep by the sound of the waves and in the morning you wake to contemplate the wild tamarisk bushes as pink flamingos fly overhead. All the chalets are big and bright and are colourfully and stylishly decorated. Wood, sometimes collected from the riverbed, has been used throughout, from the light, twisted wood of the sofas to the large double bed. The bathrooms are made from rosewood, glass, stainless steel and coloured ceramic tiles and you have a wonderful shower with a large showerhead. Breakfasts, served in the honeycomb, polygonal structure of wood and glass, are superb. At the moment, Dannie is managing The Stiltz himself, but he expects to hand over to a manager to allow himself time and space to create another masterpiece.

Rooms: 9 chalets: 3 twins, 4 doubles, 1 honeymoon and 1 family (sleeps 4), all with en-suite shower.
Price: From N$523 pp sharing to N$620 pp sharing. Singles from N$765 to N$867.
Meals: Full breakfast included. Selection of restaurants including The Tug (good seafood) 5 mins away.
Directions: In Swakopmund, from Sam Nujoma, turn left into Strand Street (along ocean), pass "The Tug" restaurant and the aquarium, turn left at Gull's Cry, then The Stiltz is on your right.

Brigadoon Guest Cottages

Peet and Yvonne Venter
16 Ludwig Koch St, Swakopmund
Tel: 064-406-064 Fax: 064-464-1954
Email: brigadoon@iway.na Web: www.wheretostay.co.za/brigadoon.htm

Brigadoon is a charming Victorian-style house found in a quiet street just five minutes' walk from the beach, the lighthouse, the museum and boutiques of the town centre. Bruce and Bubble, the owners, are Scottish by birth but the architecture is distinctly German. Brigadoon is named after their family farm in Namibia, though it comes originally from the Broadway musical set in Scotland… which perhaps you've seen? I am welcomed in like a long lost friend by the manager, Peet, who showers me with kind advice on where to dine and what to do in this quaint town (he even made a restaurant reservation for me). The rooms are arranged within the confines of a delightful little garden. Some on the ground floor of the house face a pretty garden path whilst the others sit at the far end of the garden. Each room is different and has its own charm. All are cosy, impeccably neat, and prettily decorated with wooden wardrobes, pedestals and oregon cupboards dating from the 1930's, and botanical or bird drawings on the walls. Some rooms consist of a bedroom and a small kitchenette/living room, while some are slightly larger with a basic kitchen facilites. In the morning, all the ingredients for a good, healthy breakfast are served on your own terrace overlooking the garden. It's your turn to do a little of the work by heating the water for your coffee or tea and toasting the bread. An excellent way to start the day.

Rooms: 9 garden cottages & rooms: include 1 family suite with 2 singles in main room & 2 bunks in alcove; 6 doubles and 1 self-catering cottage. All have fridge, toaster, kettle & stoves/microwave.
Price: On request. From N$600 per double per night.
Meals: Breakfast included.
Directions: Ludwig Koch St is the last road before the main beach parking area. Proceed past the police station towards sea front and turn R. Second house on the R.

Etusis Lodge

Gerald & Inge Hälbich
On P1954, Karibib
Tel: 064-550-826 Fax: 064-550-961
Email: etusis@iway.na Web: www.etusis.com

We arrived at Etusis Lodge on Easter Sunday and the large rectangular table, where communal meals are served, was decorated with coloured chocolate Easter eggs, which made a rather surreal picture in the April heat. After our departure, there were distinctly fewer eggs - I am completely, and unfairly, unable to resist chocolate! Etusis is a traditional German lodge, run by Gerald and Inge since it opened in 1994. The owner, M. Ledermann, who lives in Germany, fell in love with the Otjipatera Mountains where the lodge was built. He decided to buy the farm and build the lodge to preserve the environment, especially the Hartmann's mountain zebra, and to share it all with his guests. In terms of geology, the history of Etusis is very interesting and amateurs will find all the information they need on the website. The tourmaline mine, abandoned today, is open to novice collectors - we searched without success, but even the ordinary rocks you find here are very beautiful. Numerous hiking and escalade trails crisscross the 20,000-hectare game reserve. You can also explore it on horseback and on a game drive with Gerald. Tents and charming bungalows with mezzanine floors are independently arranged and well spaced out along the dried riverbed that sparkles with white marble and is linked by pathways bordered with lawns and punctuated by cactus and yuccas. The main house with its thatched roof is roomy and bright with pink bougainvillaea clinging to the stone walls. Ideal night skies for star-gazing, telescope

Rooms: 12: 5 double tents with shared facilities; 7 bungalows with en-suite shower (sleeps up to 4 people with additional child's bed available when necessary).
Price: Tent: N$550 pp sharing, N$650 single. Bungalow: N$850 pp sharing, N$975 single. Sundowner game drive in a 4x4 vehicle extra N$100.
Meals: Full breakfast and dinner included.
Directions: Turn onto the C32 from Karibib for 19km, then right onto P1954 for 16km.

Erongo Wilderness Lodge

Roger Fussell and Lindy van den Bosch

10km off D2315, Omaruru
Tel: 061-239-199 Fax: 061-234-971
Email: info@erongowilderness.com Web: www.erongowilderness.com
Cell: 081-128-0951

At Erongo Wilderness, the main dilemma is deciding where you will find the most beautiful view: from the verandah of the stilted tents, from the restaurant, from the plunge pool or from one of the surrounding hills. On reflection, I think it must be from the top of the hill where you will be taken for a sundowner, just fifteen minutes' walk from the lodge. Here the view is magical, when the rock glows with the colour of warm amber. The lodge is situated in the Erongo Conservancy and is in complete harmony with the landscape in a valley surrounded by spectacular granite outcrops. Sometimes the rocks are round and smooth while at others they assume Dantesque forms with trees emerging from them, as if made of stone themselves. The tents rise in tiers on the hillside, each quite independent and connected to the others by wooden walkways. The bathrooms are partly open to the nature outside. The restaurant is perched on a promontory, accessible by an easy walk and with rest benches provided! Welcoming and informal, the interior is decorated with beautiful, rustic railway-sleeper furniture, basketwork, seeds and African masks. Candlelit dinners with delicious Italian flavours are served stylishly at individual tables. Roger, Lindy and Mike are discreet hosts yet attentive at the same time. They work between Erongo Wilderness and an extremely pretty guesthouse, Olive Grove, they own in Windhoek. Two of the nicest addresses in Namibia.

Rooms: 10: all tents with en-suite showers.
Price: Low season N$850 pp sharing, no single supplement. High season $970 pp sharing and N$1,180 single. All guided walks included in this rate.
Meals: Early morning tea, coffee and muffins, full breakfast/brunch, coffee and cake in the afternoon and 4-course dinner included.
Directions: Follow the C33 from Karibib or Otjiwarongo towards Omaruru. 3km on the Karabib side of Omaruru, take the D2315 West. After 10km of gravel road, turn left into the Erongo Wilderness Lodge gate.

Map Number: 15

Farm Rüppell

Jan and Petro van Rensburg
On D2337, Otjiwarongo
Tel: 064-672-90178 Fax: 064-672-90178
Email: ruppell@iway.na Web: www.farmruppell.com

If you would like to participate in the life of a Namibian farm, Farm Rüppell is probably the most authentic you'll find. Jan and Petro are utterly delightful hosts... of course, a prerequisite for inclusion in this guide. The house, constructed in 1914, has plenty of character with its pretty ochre-yellow façade, beautiful antique clear pine furniture and frieze-decorated walls. Petro has furnished it all with great taste: trunks artistically arranged in the entrance, bouquets of dried flowers in earthenware vases, small dishes filled with petals, abstract compositions of wood roots, and antique photographs. The bedrooms, each different, are cosy and romantic. The kitchen is open to the dining room and is the atmospheric focal point of the house, with its collection of boxes on the shelves, its antique oven and tempting mealtime aromas. The goats' cheesecake – Petro raises the goats – and the souflée omelette were both a delight! The verandah where you dine faces the imposing granite massif of Omaue, 1.5km long, which we went up in the 4x4 for a sundowner, an occasion crowned on that evening with a gorgeous rainbow. From the summit, you can see as far as Brandberg and Spitzkoppe. You can walk along the river - dry during most of the year and bordered by majestic ficus and combretums - or climb the surrounding granite outcrops.

Rooms: 5: 3 with en-suite shower and 2 rooms sharing 1 bathroom.
Price: N$450 pp sharing. N$550 singles.
Meals: Full breakfast and dinner included. Light lunch on request N$25.
Directions: Accessible from Omaruru or Otjiwarongo. From C33 turn onto D2337 for 12km. Stay on main track and pass through gate "Schoenfeld 8km."

Waterberg Guest Farm

Harry and Hannah Schneider
On C22, at the foot of the Little Waterberg, Otjiwarongo
Tel: 067-302-223 or 061-253-992/7 Fax: 067-302-223 or 061-221-919
Email: waterberg@iafrica.com.na or res@discover-africa.com.na
Web: www.discover-africa.com.na Cell: 081-124-6688

Returning from distant Caprivi, rarely has a room seemed to me so conducive to rest as the one I found here! From the dazzling walls to the immaculate quilts covering the soft beds draped with huge, square mosquito nets, white dominates everything and highlights the pieces carefully chosen by Hannah: basketwork, ostrich egg lamps, photographs of birds and pretty African wooden statues. There are fuchsia blossoms on the embroidered towels in the bathrooms - these also a study in white. The dinners are served in the large, welcoming main room with comfortable sofas around the fireplace, coloured kilim carpets, a library filled with books about Namibian wildlife and natural history, not to mention the impressive bar which occupies one entire wall! For those of independent inclination, two new creatively designed chalets have been built about 200m from the house, hidden in the bush. At four o'clock, tea and home-made cakes are served in the lapa, amidst bougainvillaea, hibiscus and pink and red impatience. Near the swimming pool there is a small waterhole where the animals come to drink in the evenings. From a distance, the majestic silhouette of the Waterberg Plateau dominates the scene. You can discover on foot or on game drive the 42,000 hectares of this farm located at the foot of the Small Waterberg. You can drive to the Waterberg National Park, just 18km away, or to the Cheetah Conservation Fund at Otjiwarongo. Hannah and Harry will organize these activities for you.

Rooms: 6: 4 double rooms, 1 with bath and shower, 3 with shower only and 2 bush chalets with inside and outside shower.
Price: N$500 pp sharing. Singles N$580.
Meals: Full breakfast included. Other meals available on request. N$110 dinner.
Directions: Travelling north from Okahanja on the B1, 29km before Otjiwarongo, turn right (east) onto C22, in direction of Okakarara/Waterberg. Travel 30km and find Waterberg Guest Farm signboard on your right.

Aloegrove Safari Lodge

Johan and Ivy Döman
On C2438, Otjiwarongo
Tel: 067-306-231/2 Fax: 067-306-231 or 067-302-577
Email: aloegrove@iway.na or aloegrove@mweb.com.na
Web: www.aloegrove.com Cell: 081-127-4103

From Aloegrove, perched on a hill like a watchtower, you can enjoy magnificent 360-degree views over a vast shrubby savannah plain and in the distance to the Waterberg Plateau. You can be assured here of the attentive presence of Ivy and Johan who live in the farmhouse opposite, while still feeling very much chez vous. The pretty stone house with its glass conservatory, dining room, bar, drawing room and billiard table, is fronted by a shaded verandah, and the whole place is put at the disposal of its only guests. The cottages meanwhile are also built on the crest of the hill, very independent, and the brand-new ones set up for self-catering are particularly nice and roomy. Aloegrove is a great place to revitalise in the middle of some absurdly peaceful countryside and in a warm and informal atmosphere. You dine in the evening near an enticing wood fire, where braais (or barbecues if you still are not up with the lingo) often form the basis for good family-style meals prepared by Ivy. Johan meanwhile can take you off on game drives or to visit the farm. Several hiking trails crisscross the property, allowing sightings of birds and wild animals, particularly from the hide above a waterhole, 2km away - we saw a herd of eland when we were there. The Cheetah Conservation Fund of Otjiwarongo, 25km away, is accessible from the property without having to rejoin the main road system. But anyway Johan and Ivy have their own rescued animals: two lions, two leopards and two cheetahs.

Rooms: 6 chalets: 3 doubles with en-suite shower and 3 self-catering with en-suite bath/shower and braai area.
Price: N$590 pp sharing and N$610 single. Self-catering N$330 pp sharing and N$350 single.
Meals: Full breakfast and dinner included in the non self-catering rate. N$45 Light lunch (must pre-book). Meals are available and meat on sale at the lodge for those in self-catering.
Directions: Accessible from B1 Otjiwarongo to Otavi. On B1, 18km after Otjiwarongo, turn right onto C2438, then follow the signs to "Aloegrove" for 18km.

Wabi Game Lodge

Mark and Christina Egger

Along D2512, Waterberg, Otjiwarongo
Tel: 067-306-500 Fax: 067-306-501
Email: wabi@iafrica.com.na Web: www.wabi.ch

At Wabi, you are right on top of the Waterberg Plateau. After a 20-minute ascent by car, the road follows the edge of the escarpment with its superb views of high, rocky peaks of red sandstone eroded into fantastical shapes and laced with the clinging vines of climbing figs. Don't forget the cooler so you can toast the spectacular sight of the towering rock at dusk. Filled with enthusiasm for their property, Mark and Christina have reintroduced many animal species: two white rhino, five buffalo, a number of roan antelope, waterbuck, nyala, lechwe, giraffe and even three hippos. Wabi also hosts visiting hunting parties and it is an interesting place to discuss conservation issues. Christina is full of energy and is responsible for looking after the needs of her guests and for the preparation of the meals, which are served individually. You still have the pleasure of chatting with Mark and Christina over a drink at the bar before dinner. The park surrounding the house is a verdant delight: above the carefully tended lawns the acacias are filled with the sounds of hornbills, touracos, babblers and glossy starlings while, at their bases, blue plumbago, fuchsia, hibiscus, laurel roses and other roses form colourful flowerbeds. A bougainvillaea-laden arbour leads to the four well-equipped, air-conditioned suites. It is difficult to tear yourself away from the swimming pool, which overlooks the waterhole, but then, why should you? After all, you are on holiday.

Rooms: 6 cottages; each with bedroom, living room and en-suite-bath and shower.
Price: N$850 pp (no single supplement). For more than one night: N$650 pp. Price also includes 1 game drive.
Meals: Full breakfast, light lunch, 3-course evening dinner and soft drinks included.
Directions: From B1, 23km before Otjiwarongo, turn right to C22, in direction of Okakarara/Waterberg for 41km, then turn left onto gravel road D2512 direction Waterberg Plateau Park, for 54km. Wabi is well sign-posted on your left.

Gabus Game Ranch

Heidi and Heinz Keuhl
On D3031, 10km from Otavi,
Tel: 067-234-291 or 067-242-201 Fax: 067-234-290
Email: kuehl@mweb.com.na Web: www.natron.net/tour/gabus/
Cell: 081-127-9278

Heinz is for the outdoors and me for the cooking!" Heidi tells us laughing. What she doesn't say, but we quickly discover, is that they both have wonderfully warm hearts. The farm has been in Heinz's family for four generations and he has lovingly constructed a small family museum in a barn. The couple have two young children, all with names beginning with H like their parents, and so children are most welcome here! On the ranch, wildebeest, giraffe, waterbuck, mountain zebra have been introduced and you can see them during the game drive with Heinz. Behind the now-ruined original farm house, which is found at the base of a petrified cascade, the limestone rocks of the Uiseb Mountains are marvels of colour and form. Three varieties of comiphora trees, green, orange and red, grow at the foot of these mountains. Heinz shows us the deep cave of an old leopard that he sees two or three times a year and whose claw-marks are clearly visible on the trunk of a gnarled tree nearby. Heidi is an excellent cook, full of surprises. In a traditional, typically German farm, who would expect to taste a delicious Thai Haw Moek (fish steamed in banana leaves)? A bougainvillaea-covered portico gives access to a little garden where the dining-room and the air-conditioned rooms, each different in style, are situated. And facing the swimming pool there is a waterhole where the animals come to drink.

Rooms: 6: 3 small chalets with 3 rooms and en-suite shower; 1 family room good for 1 couple and 3 children with en-suite shower; 1 double room with en-suite bath; 1 honeymoon with en-suite shower and outdoor Jacuzzi.
Price: N$780,00 per pp sharing (price applicable from Oct 06). 1 game drive included. Additional game drives on request N$100 pp.
Meals: Full breakfast, afternoon coffee and cake and 3-course dinner included. Light lunch served on request at N$45.
Directions: In Otavi take C39 direction Outjo, then turn on D3031 (Gabus is well signposted). Gabus is 10km from Otavi.

Ohange Lodge

Karla and Justus Brits
On B1, Otavi
Tel: 067-234-031 Fax: 067-234-356
Email: ohangejk@iway.na Web: www.ohange.com
Cell: 081 261 6738

My heart beats faster as we enter the ancient and tortuous tambuti and comyphora woodlands, the ground covered with sharp stones, with ferns and lilies growing between them. Let's hope the lodge is at the top of this enchanted place... and there it is, cocooned in the middle of hundred-year-old marulas, a couple of paradise flycatchers fluttering past and overlooking a waterhole where kudu, oryx, eland, ostrich, impala, blesbok and giraffe come to drink without fear. Behind, the pointed thatched roofs of the little red ochre cottages can be glimpsed through the trees. Karla and Justus, who were not expecting us, came forward smiling and immediately offered us coffee. They have made their dream come true recently by buying this property and reintroducing numerous animals to create a little paradise. At the end of the afternoon, during our game drive when the 4x4 begins to climb a steep track to the top of the mountain, Justus laughingly tells us that 'the honeymoon is over!" But, at Ohange, the honeymoon is never over: we are offered a surprise sundowner in the bush while admiring a spectacular sunset. In the evening, an excellent *braai* is served outside, overlooking the illuminated waterhole, followed by a night game drive when we see lesser bush babies, civets and spring hares. No leopards or cheetah that night, but in the morning we could see leopard tracks just behind the lodge.

Rooms: 10 cottages all with en-suite showers.
Price: N$1,120 double room. N$680 single room. Kids under 6 sharing with parents under 6 free, 7-12 years N$225. Game drive and night drive N$120 pp.
Meals: Full breakfast and dinner included. Light lunch N$65.
Directions: 30km north of Otavi on B1. 1 hour 15 mins from Etosha (Namutoni gate).

Roy's Camp

Marietjie and Wimpie Otto
Farm Elandslaagte, Grootfontein
Tel: 067-240-302 Fax: 067-240-302
Email: royscamp@iway.na Web: www.swiftcentre.com

And now for something completely different: a journey into the realm of fantasy. At Roy's Camp a leaning towards rusticity in the architecture and the amazing decoration chosen by Wimpie, a passionate craft artist, fuse here into pure poetry. You are welcomed into the lapa through mobiles of seeds, ostrich eggs and bones. You sit on imposing wooden armchairs, with arms fashioned from kudu horns, or at the bar on tree trunks covered in animal hide. The same degree of imagination is found in the thatched chalets, each different of course, in both shape and colour, and each with its own braai terrace. The dining room, its roof supported by tree trunks, is highly atmospheric in the evenings when oil lamps and pottered candleholders emit a strange light. Bouquets of dried herbs, antique tools and kitchen implements, jute curtains bordered with seeds, porcupine quills and feathers add further to the tone. The owners live next door but, having young children, have delegated the running of the lodge to very attentive managers. You can hike on two specially laid trails or go on a farm/game drive. Roy's Camp will help you if you want to get involved in other activities (traditional hunting and tracking trips, collecting veld food or making jewellery) at a Bushman village 86km away in the direction of Tsumke, and it is projected that by mid-2006 guided tours by 4x4 will be available.

Rooms: 5 chalets (2 family chalets) all with en-suite shower. Family chalets have 2 bedrooms that share 1 bathroom.
Price: N$355 pp sharing. N$415 single. N$300 pp in the family chalet.
Meals: Full breakfast included. Lunch and dinner N$95. Light lunch N$55. Braai packs from N$45 to N$60.
Directions: 56km north of Grootfontein on the B8 to Rundu. Turn left just after Tsumkwe turn-off. Roy's Camp is 1km off B8 and well signposted.

n'Kwazi Lodge

Valerie and Wynand Peypers

20km east of Rundu, Rundu
Tel: 066-686-006 Fax: 066-255-452
Email: nkwazi@iafrica.com.na
Cell: 081-242-4897

You will know when you meet her that Valerie Peypers has a heart of gold, whether you are one of her guests or one of the eight children from the nearby village whose education she decided some years ago to take responsibility for. At n'Kwazi you will not find superfluous luxury, but instead solid and original wooden thatched chalets, designed and built by Wynand in 1991. The constructions are spread out in the middle of a quasi-tropical garden - it rains a lot in the Kavango during the rainy season, as I can vouch for! The interiors have wooden panels lending the rooms the feel of a mountain refuge. The chalets looking onto the Okavango are my favourites, breezy on account of their high ceilings. The bar of the lodge - which also caters for a camping site - is very animated in the evenings when full. All the world seems to assemble there for sundowners and to share enthusiastically their stories of high adventure. Rundu is an almost obligatory stop when on the road for the distant Caprivi. Valerie serves up hearty family-style cooking, and keeps an impressive selection of pots and pans arrayed around an enticing wood fire, as well as anything between 4 and 30 people! You can bird-watch on the nearby flood plain, set off on a sunset cruise, or ride one of the horses you will see walking peacefully among the chalets, sometimes followed by the two orphaned duikers that Valerie has adopted.

Rooms: 13 chalets all with en-suite showers.
Price: N$325 pp sharing. N$410 singles.
Meals: Full breakfast included. N$115 dinner.
Directions: 10km north-east of Rundu on B8 turn left then follow the sign-posts for about 10km.

Ichingo Chobe River Lodge

Dawn and Ralph Oxenham

Impalila island, Ngweze, Katima Mulilo
Tel: 00-267-625-0143 or 00-267-713-02439 Fax: 00-267-625-0223
Email: ichingo@iafrica.com Web: www.ichingo.com or www.ichobezi.co.za
Cell: 00-27-82-903-2490

Ichingo's charm has as much to do with the nature of its wonderful setting as with the sense of humour and kindness of its proprietor Ralph. There is no unnecessary luxury at Ichingo, just the exuberance of nature and the enveloping roar of the rapids beside which the camp is situated. Getting there is an adventure in itself: leaving your car at Kasane, a motorboat takes you on a 15-minute ride to the camp, so well concealed by dense vegetation that I only noticed it at the last minute. The tents, each with a raised verandah, are surrounded by trees and twisting creepers. In the evening, guests gather for drinks around a large table under the wooden pavilion and chat away as if at home. If you encourage him, Ralph has an inexhaustible supply of stories about the region while Nicci's cooking is creative and absolutely delicious. After hearing us discussing croissants the day before, she baked some especially for us in the morning! But you will be pampered by all the staff. You can explore Chobe River with its wildlife and birds (more than 400 species) in individual motorboats with a guide. The sight of elephants coming down to one of their favourite bays is unforgettable. Ralph also operates a luxurious cruise boat allowing you to observe the elephants even from your bed. A tour of the Victoria Falls, 100km away, or a game drive into the Chobe National Park can also be arranged through Ralph.

Rooms: 10: 6 double tents with en-suite shower and a luxurious cruise boat with four air-conditioned cabins.
Price: N$2,250 pp sharing. Single supplement 10%. Includes transfers, all meals & all activities such as fishing and game-viewing by boat. Off-season discounts may be available Dec to March.
Meals: Full breakfast, lunch and 3-course dinner included.
Directions: If you arrive by car, the staff of Ichigo will meet you at Kasane immigration office (near the river) and will help you with all the formalities. Make sure that you have all the documents of the car to cross the border!

Map Number: 27

Ndhovu Safari Lodge

Horst und Ursel Kock

Divundu
Tel: 066-259-901 or 061-224-712 Fax: 066-259-153 or 061-224-217
Email: ndhovu@iway.na or reservations@resdes.com.na
Web: www.ndhovu.com Cell: 081-236-2542

On the banks of the River Okavango, opposite Bwawata National Park and only 4km for Mahango Park, you will find a tented camp secreted amidst tall trees, with a backing track of running water, the sporadic grunts of hippos and birdsong. The camp was bought and renovated in December 2004 by Horst and Ursel who upped sticks from their farm near Windhoek and headed for the green Caprivi. This was a place where, personally, I felt deliciously well! The lapa opens onto the river and is decorated with originality, the central living area made from rattan, littered with embroidered cushions from South Africa and framed by sculptured mirrors reflecting the water, which is omnipresent here. You dine in style at rustic rosewood tables, and off Zimbabwean ceramic dishes, hand-painted in naïve colours. Amateurs - and I am one - will be delighted to be able to buy these here. The tents all face the river, each one graced with a verandah and gaily decorated in pretty cottons. My night was punctuated by an atmospheric cacophony of animal calls, the croaking of frogs, the howls of hyenas and in the really wee hours the roar of a lion.... Horst, with unextinguishable enthusiasm, will take you out in his motor-boat to go fishing, or to bird-watch or just to be there, glass in hand, at the spectacular sunsets. Marango Park is particularly interesting as much for its fauna - rare roan antelope, lechwe, nyala, elephant, buffalo - as for its very varied landscapes which alternate between marsh, prairie, baobab groves and forest.

Rooms: 8 tents with en-suite shower. Tents n° 6, 7 and 8 are very private but farther from the lapa.
Price: N$795 pp sharing. N$300 single supplement.
Meals: Full breakfast and dinner included. N$85 lunch.
Directions: Coming from Victoria Falls (Katima Molilo) or from the Etosha National Park (Rundu) on the B8 turn south at Divundu onto D3403, towards the Mohembo border post between Namibia and Botswana for 20km. At signpost turn left towards the river through Kamotjonga Village, then follow black and white elephant signboards for 2km to lodge.

Mushara Lodge

Mariza and Marc Pampe
8km from Namutoni gate of Etosha National Park, Tsumeb
Tel: 067-229-106 Fax: 067-229-107
Email: mushara@iafrica.com.na Web: www.mushara-lodge.com

I arrived at Mushara with the first rains, an unforgettable moment in Namibia as a heavy perfume of dry grasses and scorched earth fills the air. Mariza and Marc built the lodge ten years ago, naming the lodge after the purple pod terminalia trees, 'mushara' in the local Ovambo language. The immense interior room with its high ceiling, incorporating the reception, bar and lounge, evokes a scene from *Alice in Wonderland* with the play of mirrors reflecting the garden and the ostrich egg chandeliers like stars. The wooden screens allow for cosy seating arrangements; leather sofas, kilim carpets, cashmere throws, paintings and drawings collected by Marc's parents and black-and-white photographs of elephants all combine to give the area a refined atmosphere. Under Mariza's supervision, dinner is an elegant affair of candles and white cloths - a pleasure for the eye as well as for the taste buds. The air-conditioned chalets are large and very comfortable, decorated with the same mix of modern and traditional Africa. I couldn't imagine how the two newer "Villa Musharas" could really surpass these already superb chalets, but an involuntary "Ah!" of admiration sprang to my lips as I walked in! A piece of advice: don't plan to do much else than bathe in all the luxury. My desire to hit the hiking trail was quickly subdued by the fact that a lion had been seen there some days before. The luxury of Mushara can make you forget you are at the entrance of the Etosha Park!

Rooms: 15: 10 doubles, 2 singles and 1 triple, all with en-suite showers. 2 luxury 'Villa Musharas' with living-room, bedroom, en-suite bath and shower.
Price: N$1,580 per double room. N$940 per single room. N$2,300 per triple room. 'Villa Mushara': N$2,320 pp sharing, singles N$3,328.70.
Meals: Full breakfast included. N$70 lunch or packed lunch N$55. N$150 3-course dinner. Full board included in 'Villa Mushara.'
Directions: Accessible from Tsumeb, after 73km on B1 turn left direction Namutoni gate. Mushara is 8km before the gate of the park.

Ongava Tented Camp

Cameron and Wendy Wilson

Etosha National Park, Sandton 2146
Tel: 064-404-459 or 064-402-434 Fax: 064-404-664
Email: travel@palmwag.com.na reservations@palmwag.com.na
Web: www.wilderness-safaris.com or www.palmwag.com.na
Cell: 081-269-7271 after hours

Rhino for breakfast, elephants for lunch and a sign of a leopard for dinner!" writes one of the guests. Animal sightings are never guaranteed, but you have the best chance of seeing them here where the guides make it a point of honour to find them. Nevertheless, after we had walked for three hours following the muddled tracks of two white rhino and their calves, the fact that our guide, Rio, found them was amazing. Meanwhile, back at the camp, other guests were watching (from the comfort of their armchairs) two other white rhino performing their ablutions in the waterhole about 20m away! There is almost always something to see at this waterhole where a veritable Noah's Ark passes by: kudu, oryx, cob, zebra. Sometimes lion come to drink and I can certify that they were roaring near the camp on the night I stayed. The Ongava Reserve of 30,000 hectares is populated with all the Namibian fauna except elephant, but these you will see in the Etosha Park, which borders Ongava. It is rare in Namibia to have such a strong feeling of being out in the middle of the African bush as you do in this tented camp, which is completely at one with nature. What contagious good humour from the cook (who excels in bread, brioches and cakes). And what attentive service from Wendy and Cameron! *Kids under 12 not allowed on walks & private vehicles for game drives required when kids accompanying parents.*

Rooms: 9 walk-in Meru tents with en-suite open-air shower.
Price: N$2,292 fully inclusive (meals, activities, daily laundry service). N$979 single supplement. Activities include guided game drive to Etosha pan or Ongava Game Reserve & guided walks.
Meals: Full breakfast, light lunch, 3-course dinner, drinks on game drives and house wine at dinner included.
Directions: Travel 99km from Outjo on C38, then turn left inside Ongama Game Reserve. The tented camp is 19km from the gate on a dirt road. Access by light aircraft possible.

Naua Naua Game Lodge and Safaris

Annette and Thomas Schaefer
Etosha National Park, Outjo
Tel: 067-687-100
Fax: 067-687-101
Email: info@nauanaua.com
Web: www.nauanaua.com

Naua Naua is a very comfortable lodge sitting among peaceful hills dotted with mopane and compyphora trees where the ground is carpeted with astonishing grey and red rocks. The white roughcast walls of the thatched buildings stretch out on a hill facing a waterhole down below where the animals come to drink. The cottages are spacious and light-filled, with high ceilings that ensure good ventilation. Some of them are well suited to families with a communal lounge. They are decorated in the African style with stone floors, Kiatt wood furniture, karakul wool carpets, basketwork, pottery and watercolours of animals. You will see telescopes almost everywhere, star-gazing being one of Thomas' passions. The second is cooking and he has trained his chef as well as often trying out new recipes himself. Annette and Thomas give personal attention to their guests and even dine with them, sharing themselves between two large tables when the lodge is full. They live in Germany, but, captivated by Namibia, they decided to open a game lodge a few years ago. At the end of the afternoon, you can watch the feeding of four cheetah from the Cheetah Conservation Fund and then drink a glass of champagne in the lapa at the top of a hill. . . one of the best ways I know to begin an evening! Day game drives are organised into Etosha and, by prior arrangement only, flights to Himba and Ovambos traditional villages.

Rooms: 6: 3 bungalows each with 2 en-suite bedrooms & shared lounge; 1 single room & 2 family rooms in main building; 1 self-catering farmhouse (4 bedr'ms/bathr'ms, 5km from lodge).
Price: N$765 pp sharing & N$950 singles. 3rd adult sharing room N$585. Rate includes cheetah feeding & sundowner (drink included). Self-catering farmhouse N$350 pp sharing twin room, N$600 single.
Meals: Full breakfast, tea/coffee/cake included. 3-course dinner N$160. Light lunch on request N$80. If self-catering, breakfast at the lodge N$60.
Directions: On C38 Outjo to Okaukuejo, about 25km before Andersson gate of Etosha, turn left on D2695 for 6km, then left on the farm road for 12km (well signposted).

Huab Lodge

Jan and Suzi van de Reep

On D2670, Outjo, Kamanjab
Tel: 061-224-712 or 067-687-058 Fax: 061-224-217 or 067-687-059
Email: reservations@resdes.com.na or info@huablodge.com
Web: www.huablodge.com Cell: 081-242-7375

Huab is steeped in serenity. In 1992, Suzi and Jan, both keen conservationists, decided to rehabilitate this hilly, overgrazed farmland of 8000 hectares in Damaraland. Waterholes were constructed and fences removed so that the desert-dwelling elephant and re-introduced giraffe, springbok and ostrich could roam free . . . and today the dream has become reality. Tall grasses sweep across the plains amidst mopanes and acacias and the animals have returned. The architecture blends perfectly with the surrounding countryside, and style and imagination are evident in the décor. The impressive oval structure of the lodge with its thatched roof has been built around the rocks, which even erupt into the middle of the room. It is open-sided so you feel part of nature. Everyone gathers here for excellent meals, served with style and enjoyed with your hosts around a large table made of Rhodesian teak sleepers, or to browse in the well-stocked library. The cottages are immense, bright and very comfortable, with huge bay windows and beautiful bathrooms, where you can contemplate nature while you shower. Everything is arranged to encourage relaxation: reflexology, aromatherapy, shiatsu treatments and massages and two thermal bathing pools. In Jan and his staff you will find knowledgeable guides who know how to captivate your interest for the small, but no less important, aspects of nature… what he calls 'the bushman newspaper'. There is a choice of day-trips or overnight trips to Grootberg, Himba Village, Twyfelfontein, Vingerklip or the Etendeka Mountains.

Rooms: 8 bungalows with en-suite showers amd separate en-suite loo.
Price: N$1,640 pp sh fully inclusive. N$550 for single supplement. Includes 3 activities (morning walk, nature drive & scenic drive) car wash & laundry service (if staying for at least 2 nights).
Meals: English breakfast, lunch, dinner and drinks included.
Directions: Halfway between Khorixas and Kamanjab on C35, turn west onto the D2670 at the Huab sign for 35km.

Grootberg Lodge

Simonetta and Dominic Du Raan
On C40, Maerua Park, Windhoek
Tel: 067-687-043 Fax: 067-687-044
Email: reservations@grootberg.com Web: www.grootberg-lodge.com

What a vista! The views over the Klip River valley from the lodge, roosting on the edge of the Grootberg Plateau, will delight you no matter where you stand: in the restaurant, the living room, your bedroom or on the terrace furnished with comfortable armchairs… even in your shower! The managers, Simonetta and Dominic, are a wonderful young couple, full of kindness and enthusiasm. Simonetta, who bubbles over with energy and good spirits, ensures that you want for nothing, while Dom is the one who takes you on game drives into the valley in search of the desert elephants or birdlife which he knows so well. You can also walk on the plateau at your own pace. The basalt stone walls of the buildings have the allure of a mountain refuge – by the way, the nights are deliciously fresh up here on the plateau – and the interior décor imparts a feeling of purity and well-being. A symphony of white tones contrasts well with the pretty, rustic Oregon pine furniture. In the vast long room which serves as living and dining rooms, tall mirrors at each end reflect the ecru sofas covered with bright plaid throws, individual pine tables, tree trunks and local stone décor as well as a huge bay window which opens out over the valley. Much more than a mere stopping place between Etosha and Palmwag, this is definitely a place where it is worth staying two days.

Rooms: 11 chalets with en-suite shower (2 of which are family chalets).
Price: N$1,470 double room. N$945 single room.
Meals: Full breakfast and 3-course dinner included.
Directions: On C40. Accessible from Kamanjab (97km) and from Palmwag Lodge (25km).

Palmwag Lodge

Jockel Gruettemeyer

Along C43, after junction with C40, Swakopmund
Tel: 064-404-459 or 064-402-434 Fax: 064-404-664
Email: travel@palmwag.com.na or reservations@palmwag.com.na
Web: www.palmwag.com.na Cell: 081-269-7271 after hours

Palmwag Lodge lies on the Uniab River, overlooking red ochre mountains silhouetted in the distance, and has the charm of an oasis with its reeds and tall palms rustling in the wind. This stop is more or less a must on any journey to Damaraland and Kaokoland and there is always a joyful liveliness here. The lodge has just been tastefully and harmoniously renovated, without losing its relaxed character. For your accommodation, you have the choice of the small bungalows overlooking the river, the stone cottages, the chalets with plunge pool, and, right at the end, the large attractive raised tents, which are my personal favourites. There is no lack of activities in this concession of 58,000 hectares: self-guided walks, 4x4 circuit with your own car (half-day), guided game drives in search of black rhino and desert elephant. The latter are often simply on the path leading to your tent or to the restaurant! Longer safaris or flights are also possible but must be reserved in advance. Another possibility is to spend two nights at the exclusive and remote Palmwag Rhino Camp, where you will track the black rhino on foot. It is all very romantic and exciting. Being 40m away from this animal sends your heart racing, but what an experience! The transfer from the lodge with a Palmwag Rhino Camp 4x4 vehicle to the camp takes two hours by road, passing through beautiful countryside.

Rooms: 44-bed lodge: 9 bungalows, 4 rooms; 2 family units (sleep 4) with splash pool on patio (1 x 1 bedroom, 1 x 2 bedrooms sharing 1 bathroom) & 5 luxury tents. All en-suite showers.
Price: N$745 - N$1,020 pp sharing. N$1,040 - N$1,425 singles.
Meals: Full breakfast and dinner included.
Directions: From Kamanjab on the C40 join the C43 to Palmwag Lodge. From Khorixas take C39, then C43. Access also possible from Swakopmund. Detailed directions can be email or fax.

Etendeka Mountain Camp

Dennis and Claire Liebenberg
Etendeka Mountain Camp, Sesfontein District, Kuneme Region; lodge and guest farm reservations PO Box 21783, Windhoek
Tel: 061-226-979 or 061-226-979 Fax: 061-226-999
Email: logufa@mweb.com.na Web: www.natron.net/tour/etendeka/

Fantastic. This word sums up the two days I spent in the 50,000-hectare Etendeka Concession. It is rare to find a place where environment and man-who-looks-after-it are so at one. For the past 15 years, Dennis has watched over Etendeka, modestly sharing his knowledge with guests, who leave with a hatful of fascinating experiences. You are in the heart of Damaraland's fabulous mountain landscape, a semi-desert region of plateaus and plains covered with boulders of red basalt and punctuated by groves of mopane and blue-tinted euphorbia. Either on foot or by 4x4, you will discover secret valleys and breathtaking views from the top of the plateau. Dennis will introduce you to the 'Etendeka Big Four trees' - cyphostemma, moringa, sesamothamnus and pachypodium - in all their weird and wonderful shapes. He is also passionate about birds, and there are many endemic to the area such as the herero chat, Monteiro's hornbill, Rüppell's korhaan and the rockrunner. Giraffe, kudu, oryx, zebra and springbok are commonly seen, and the desert elephant and rhino are also spotted from time to time. If you stay for three nights, perhaps Dennis will take you on the 'crystal walk'. You will sleep in harmony with nature in simple tents, furnished with what you need: a good bed with a cover for the pleasantly cool nights and an open-air shower. In the evening, before a communal dinner in the large tent, you can contemplate the stars. As I say, fantastic.

Rooms: 18 beds in 10 tents with en-suite open-air shower.
Price: N$1,450 pp sharing and N$1,800 singles. In triple tent N$1450 pp. Transfer to the camp, guided nature walk, scenic drive and full board included. No children under 8 years.
Meals: Continental breakfast, light lunch, afternoon tea and cake, a full bar, and 2-course dinner included.
Directions: Accessible from Kamanjab, Khorixas and Twyfelfontein. Pick-up point on the C40 to Sesfontein, at the Veterinary gate, just before Palmwag. Transfer time is 15h30 in winter and 16h00 in summer. Access by reservation only.

Kavita Lion Lodge

Tammy and Uwe Hoth

Off C35, Kamanjab
Tel: 067-330-224 Fax: 067-330-269
Email: info@kavitalion.com or kavita@iway.na Web: www.kavitalion.com

Tammy and Uwe's main project is the conservation of Namibian lions, and in pursuit of this they have founded the Afri-Leo Foundation. Initially the intention was to rescue five lions from the last of the Namibian zoos, but their objectives have widened to include environmental education and awareness programmes, research and 'farmer-predator conflict resolution'. They built the lodge ten years ago on a 10,000-hectare cattle ranch that they have converted into a wilderness area. These are people full of energy and conviction! The atmosphere at Kavita is informal, meals taken with your hosts in the thatched lapa, which is framed by bougainvillaea and opens onto the garden and its immaculate lawn. Tables are set out in the shade of wild olive trees. In the evenings, lanterns and bamboo torches illuminate the circle of stones of the boma and the pathways leading off to the cosy, thatched cottages built in stone. Stumps of wood in intriguing shapes are used everywhere as décor elements. Families can rent the original cottage near the lapa, which is brightly painted in yellow and is lovely with its grass patio. Apart from activities home on the range - game drives, introduction to the Foundation, guided or self-guided bird-watching walks - excursions can be organised, such as trips to Himba settlements, Damaraland/Kaokoland, Epupa Falls and Western Etosha National Park (to be booked at least 60 days in advance). *Due to the specific nature of the Afro-Leo project kids under 10 years are not able to view the lions.*

Rooms: 12: 8 thatched chalets with en-suite shower; 1 3-bedroom Family Cottage with en-suite showers, foyer, verandah and a separate family room.
Price: Chalets: N$895 pp sharing, N$1,200 singles; family cottage: N$700 pp sharing, N$880 singles. Activities included in the rate. Half-board from N$610 pp sharing. Closed 1 Dec-1 Feb.
Meals: Full board included. Half-board possible (excluding activities). Lunch N$60.
Directions: Accessible from Kamanjab on C35 towards Ruacana. After approx 36km, Kavita Lion Lodge signed to the right. Follow yellow lion 'pugmarks' for about 5km until you reach the lodge.

Hobatere Lodge

Steve and Louise Braine
Next to Otjovasandu gate, Etosha west, Kamanjab
Tel: 067-687-066 Fax: 067-687-067
Email: hobatere@mweb.com.na Web: www.exclusive.com.na/hobatere.htm

The property of Hobatere, a concession area of 32,000 hectares bordering on the Etosha National Park, is pleasantly undulating and, when I arrived after the rains, the grasslands were vibrantly green and carpeted with yellow flowers. Steve and Louise, who have operated the concession for the past 16 years, are the soul of the place and their warm and informal welcome assures that, once found (Hobatere means 'find me') it is a place you will want to return to. Steve has a great sense of humour and is passionate about nature. No creature is small or insignificant in his book and he shares his knowledge of birds, butterflies and insects as well as the larger beasts with infectious enthusiasm. He also organises birding trips in Namibia. During day game drives you have a good chance of seeing numerous elephant, lion, hyena, zebra, eland, kudu and giraffe. Night game drives are quite a rarity in Namibia and ours, on a clear and starlit night, was highly atmospheric, spring hares jumping from their holes, nightjars landing on the track in front of our vehicle and, out there somewhere, lions roaring. The rallying point in the evenings is the pleasant stone terrace in front of the reception surrounded by a rock garden, where you dine well under Louise's discreet but watchful eye. The swimming pool, concealed behind the foliage, overlooks a waterhole about 300m away where elephants come to quench their thirst.

Rooms: 12: 6 chalets and 6 double rooms, all with en-suite shower. 1 rustic Tree-house overlooking a waterhole.
Price: N$711.13 pp sharing & singles N$771.65 half board. N$771.65 pp sharing & singles N$842.26 full board. Children sadly cannot go on guided walks or night drives due to lions.
Meals: Breakfast and dinner included in half-board. Breakfast, lunch and dinner included in full board.
Directions: On the C35, drive for 64km north of Kamanjab towards Opuwo. Just 1km past the Otjovasandu entrance to Etosha Park turn left at the entrance to Hobatere property. From there follow the dirt road for 16km to the lodge.

Map Number: 23

Serra Cafema

Tanya Bern and Eric Reinhard
At the foot of the Harman's Valley, Kaokoland
Tel: 064-404-459 or 064-402-434 Fax: 064-404-664
Email: travel@palmwag.com.na or reservations@palmwag.com.na Web: www.wilderness-safaris.com or www.palmwag.com.na Cell: 081-269-7271 (after hours)

Last, but very much not least, in the Hartmann Valley of Kaokoland, between the dunes and the Kunene River and overlooking the mountains of Angola, Serra Cafema, the most romantic camp in Namibia, the most remote, the most astonishing because of its setting and its architecture, seems like a mirage. This is luxury at a price, but if you can afford it you will not be disappointed and that's a promise! The memory will stay with you. The camp is raised off the ground on stilts in the midst of huge, sinuous albida trees. Wooden walkways link the tents of canvas, wood, glass and thatch, which you enter through marvellously sculptured doors. The interiors are immense and designed for you to revel in the views - river or dunes - from the bed, shower or from the hammock on the terrace! A two-day stay is essential in order to appreciate everything: exploring the spectacular dune landscape, kopjes emerging occasionally like islets on an iridescent sea of sand; or observing the desert fauna and the birds and crocodiles on the Kunene with very knowledgeable guides. Your adventure can be made in a 4x4, on foot or by boat. After a sundowner in a small inlet, you have your meal with the managers and guides. After a day at Serra Cafema, conversation is never dull. The camp is only accessible by plane, but having negotiated a few dunes you will be quite happy not to have to drive yourself.

Rooms: 8 canvas-wrapped, grass-thatched chalets with en-suite shower. Rooms 1 & 2 can be used together as a family room.
Price: N$3,443 pp sharing all-inclusive (meals, drinks, activities, daily laundry service). Single supplement N$1,771. Activities include nature drives, walks, boating, visits to Himba villages.
Meals: Full breakfast, light lunch, 3-course dinner, all local drinks and alcohol included.
Directions: Not a self-drive destination. Access is by light aircraft only. Total flying time from Windhoek approx 3hrs 20 mins direct. From Swakopmund approx 2 hrs 45 mins.

Map Number: 22

Indexes

Index by town name

For our rural properties, we have listed the nearest town.

NAMIBIA

Index by house name

Index of Activities

Here is a simple way to find entries within the book catering for specialist interests. The numbers under each category represent the entry numbers of places where the owners/managers are themselves interested in the subject or can organise for these activities to take place on or near their property.

Horse-riding
Available on site.
18, 61, 69, 78, 105, 112, 113, 123, 124, 133, 136, 149, 160, 161, 162, 170, 174, 183, 188, 191, 193, 196, 197, 211, 212, 215, 218, 219, 220, 224, 231, 232, 234, 238, 239, 240, 247, 250, 251, 253, 255, 256, 257, 260, 262, 265, 269, 284, 290, 311, 313, 314, 315, 332, 337, 339, 346, 348.

Whale-watching
Available from the property or from so near by that it makes little difference.
1, 2, 3, 4, 5, 6, 7, 8, 21, 59, 62, 63, 64, 65, 102, 106, 107, 108, 110, 111, 113, 115, 116, 117, 118, 122, 123, 140, 141, 142, 148, 150, 153, 154, 162, 164, 165, 172, 188, 208, 209, 227, 230, 231, 232, 233, 240, 243, 318, 319.

Boat charter
Property owns boats or can organise charters.
1, 2, 3, 4, 5, 8, 9, 10, 12, 13, 16, 17, 19, 20, 21, 24, 29, 33, 34, 35, 37, 39, 40, 43, 46, 51, 54, 59, 60, 62, 63, 64, 65, 101, 102, 108, 110, 113, 116, 117, 118, 119, 120, 121, 122, 123, 125, 140, 141, 142, 144, 146, 150, 153, 156, 157, 159, 160, 161, 162, 163, 165, 171, 172, 178, 188, 189, 190, 191, 192, 201, 203, 208, 210, 211, 213, 214, 215, 216, 225, 230, 233, 234, 237, 238, 240, 241, 243, 244, 245, 246, 263, 272, 281, 301, 310, 317, 318, 319, 320, 321, 330, 335, 337, 338, 348, 349, 350, 360.

Canoeing
Canoes owned or organised by the property.
1, 2, 3, 4, 5, 6, 7, 8, 10, 17, 19, 21, 29, 33, 35, 37, 39, 40, 43, 46, 51, 60, 61, 62, 63, 64, 65, 68, 69, 75, 102, 103, 106, 107, 108, 110, 113, 116, 117, 119, 120, 121, 123, 127, 130, 131, 137, 139, 140, 141, 142, 144, 146, 150, 151, 152, 153, 155, 156, 157, 158, 160, 161, 162, 163, 164, 165, 167, 171, 172, 178, 181, 189, 190, 191, 195, 201, 202, 203, 206, 209, 210, 211, 212, 213, 214, 215, 216, 217, 218, 221, 237, 238, 239, 240, 241, 243, 244, 245, 246, 252, 253, 254, 255, 258, 261, 262, 263, 266, 275, 281, 284, 290, 291, 294, 302, 313, 318, 320, 321, 335, 337, 338, 349.

Historic house
These places are historic buildings.
1, 32, 33, 34, 36, 37, 43, 47, 61, 66, 71, 72, 73, 75, 76, 78, 80, 81, 82, 86, 88, 90, 91, 93, 97, 101, 102, 103, 104, 105, 112, 118, 127, 130, 132, 134, 138, 145, 148, 173, 175, 179, 180, 181, 182, 183, 186, 193, 195, 201, 202, 204, 207, 212, 218, 220, 221, 222, 224, 237, 253, 256, 259, 263, 265, 266, 268, 275, 288, 309.

History tours
Organised here (including battlefields).
1, 12, 36, 37, 43, 73, 77, 78, 79, 88, 101, 105, 138, 181, 182, 183, 198, 202, 204, 205, 206, 207, 208, 210, 211, 213, 215, 218, 224, 235, 237, 245, 246, 247, 248, 249, 250, 252, 253, 254, 257, 263, 266, 268, 275, 280, 284, 299, 309, 313, 314, 315, 321, 323, 342.

Self-catering option available here.
1, 2, 3, 4, 5, 8, 9, 10, 11, 14, 16, 17, 18, 19, 20, 21, 25, 26, 29, 33, 34, 35, 39, 42, 44, 45, 47, 48, 49, 50, 53, 54, 56, 57, 58, 59, 61, 63, 67, 68, 70, 73, 74, 75, 76, 80, 81, 82, 87, 88, 89, 90, 91, 95, 98, 99, 100, 101, 102, 105, 106, 107, 111, 112, 116, 118, 119, 128, 130, 133, 135, 137, 139, 141, 142, 146, 147, 148, 154, 155, 156,

157, 159, 161, 166, 168, 174, 176, 178, 185, 187, 188, 189, 192, 199, 205, 207, 210, 213, 217, 218, 219, 221, 225, 228, 230, 231, 234, 235, 239, 242, 245, 246, 249, 250, 253, 254, 258, 259, 260, 261, 262, 263, 267, 269, 270, 271, 273, 274, 277, 279, 280, 281, 287, 288, 289, 292, 295, 300, 310, 311, 313, 317, 318, 319, 330, 331, 333, 343, 353.

Bird-watching
Owners are enthusiasts.
3, 4, 5, 8, 10, 12, 14, 16, 17, 24, 54, 56, 57, 59, 60, 61, 62, 63, 64, 65, 66, 67, 68, 69, 70, 72, 73, 74, 75, 76, 77, 81, 82, 83, 87, 88, 90, 91, 92, 94, 95, 98, 101, 103, 104, 105, 106, 107, 108, 110, 112, 113, 116, 117, 118, 119, 120, 121, 122, 123, 124, 125, 128, 131, 132, 133, 134, 136, 137, 138, 139, 140, 141, 143, 144, 146, 147, 148, 149, 151, 152, 153, 156, 157, 158, 159, 160, 161, 162, 164, 167, 168, 170, 171, 172, 173, 174, 175, 176, 178, 179, 180, 181, 182, 183, 185, 186, 187, 188, 189, 190, 191, 193, 194, 196, 197, 198, 200, 201, 202, 203, 205, 206, 208, 209, 210, 211, 212, 214, 215, 216, 217, 218, 219, 220, 222, 224, 225, 228, 231, 233, 234, 235, 236, 237, 238, 240, 241, 242, 243, 244, 245, 246, 247, 248, 249, 250, 251, 252, 253, 254, 255, 256, 258, 259, 260, 262, 263, 264, 265, 266, 267, 268, 270, 272, 274, 275, 279, 280, 281, 282, 283, 284, 285, 286, 288, 289, 290, 291, 292, 294, 295, 297, 298, 299, 300, 301, 302, 303, 304, 305, 306, 307, 309, 310, 311, 312, 313, 314, 315, 316, 317, 320, 321, 322, 323, 325, 326, 327, 331, 333, 335, 337, 340, 342, 343, 344, 345, 346, 349, 350, 352, 354, 355, 356, 357, 358, 359, 360.

Beach House
1, 2, 3, 26, 59, 60, 62, 63, 64, 65, 102, 107, 111, 113, 117, 118, 122, 123, 148, 154, 155, 165, 172, 188, 189, 208, 216, 230, 231, 243, 318, 319, 320, 321.

White-water rafting
Can be arranged in-house.
40, 43, 86, 106, 107, 108, 110, 131, 171, 188, 221, 248, 252, 253, 254, 255, 257, 261, 290, 291, 292, 294, 301, 302, 303.

Fishing
Can be arranged.
2, 3, 4, 5, 8, 9, 13, 17, 19, 20, 21, 29, 35, 37, 39, 40, 43, 51, 54, 59, 60, 62, 63, 64, 65, 66, 67, 68, 69, 70, 72, 73, 74, 75, 77, 78, 82, 83, 84, 85, 86, 87, 88, 90, 94, 95, 96, 101, 102, 105, 106, 108, 110, 112, 113, 116, 118, 119, 120, 121, 122, 123, 125, 128, 130, 137, 138, 139, 140, 141, 142, 143, 144, 145, 146, 152, 153, 155, 156, 157, 159, 160, 161, 162, 163, 164, 165, 167, 169, 170, 171, 172, 178, 180, 181, 186, 187, 188, 189, 190, 191, 195, 196, 201, 202, 205, 208, 209, 210, 211, 213, 214, 215, 216, 217, 218, 219, 220, 225, 227, 230, 233, 234, 236, 237, 238, 239, 240, 243, 244, 245, 246, 247, 249, 250, 251, 252, 253, 254, 255, 256, 257, 258, 260, 261, 262, 263, 266, 267, 268, 272, 281, 284, 285, 286, 288, 290, 291, 294, 295, 309, 310, 312, 313, 314, 315, 317, 318, 319, 320, 321, 335, 336, 337, 338, 348, 349, 350, 360.

Fully child-friendly
Places where children will be particularly well looked after.
3, 8, 10, 11, 16, 17, 18, 21, 25, 32, 35, 38, 39, 43, 54, 65, 68, 77, 78, 82, 84, 90, 96, 101, 105, 107, 113, 116, 117, 118, 119, 127, 128, 135, 139, 140, 143, 147, 157, 160, 168, 169, 171, 174, 178, 186, 187, 189, 190, 191, 193, 197, 199, 200, 201, 202, 207, 209, 210, 216, 218, 219, 221, 224, 230, 231, 234, 235, 237, 238, 239, 241, 243, 244, 245, 246, 250, 252, 253, 254, 255, 260, 261, 262, 263, 265, 267, 268, 269, 270, 273, 274, 276, 279, 280, 282, 284, 296, 297, 304, 306, 310, 312, 313, 314, 315, 318, 319, 323, 325, 326, 328, 331, 334, 345, 349, 356.

SOUTH AFRICAN HIGHLIGHTS

Hand-picked Things to Do and Places to Eat

This is a brand-new Greenwood Guide, detailing those places to eat and things to do across the whole of South Africa that sit most cosily with our professed likes and dislikes, i.e. a strong leaning towards the small, family-run, unusual, off-the-beaten track, and, above all, friendly and charming.

This book is designed for holiday-makers, both South African and from overseas, who want to travel independently, avoid mass tourism and meet friendly, humorous and hospitable people. To this end we have chosen small wineries, family-run restaurants where natural friendliness and character are as important as the food itself; wonderful walks and bird-watching excursions; small, even one-man or woman, tour operators to lend expertise if you want it; we have included the best things to do with kids; we have found the best gardens, both private and municipal. Among establishments or activities that are already well known we have only included the truly worthy.

Basically if you like the sort of accommodation we have chosen, then you will find the new book a treat!

www.greenwoodguides.com

To order a copy

If you would like to order a copy of ***South African Highlights, Hand-Picked Things to Do and Places to Eat*** or any of our books, please fill in the coupon and send it with payment to Greenwood Guides, 12 Avalon Rd, London SW6 2EX. Payment can be made by UK cheque made out to 'Greenwood Guides Ltd', or by Visa/Mastercard. We will not process payments until the book is sent out.

Greenwood Guides order form

	copy(ies)	price (each)	subtotal
SOUTH AFRICAN HIGHLIGHTS **Hand-picked things to do and places to eat** (1ST EDITION)		£13.95	
THE GREENWOOD GUIDE TO SOUTH AFRICA **Hand-picked accommodation** (5TH EDITION)		£13.95	
THE GREENWOOD GUIDE TO AUSTRALIA **Hand-picked accommodation** (2ND EDITION)		£9.95	
THE GREENWOOD GUIDE TO NEW ZEALAND **Hand-picked accommodation** (4TH EDITION - OCT 06)		£9.95	
THE GREENWOOD GUIDE TO CANADA **Hand-picked accommodation** (1ST EDITION)		£9.95	
post and packing costs			
£2 per order in the UK or South Africa £3 per order within Europe £4 per order elsewhere		**Total**	

Name ....

Address to send the book to ....

....

....

Payment is by UK sterling cheque to 'Greenwood Guides Ltd' or by VISA/Mastercard (only)

Card number

Expiry date

CCV number

Please send this coupon to

12 Avalon Road, Fulham, London, SW6 2EX, UK

simon@greenwoodguides.com

THE GREENWOOD GUIDE TO

NEW ZEALAND

hand-picked accommodation

Fourth Edition due October 2006

The Greenwood Guide to New Zealand (now in 3rd edition) currently contains over 100 B&Bs, lodges, farms and self-catering cottages. The 4th edition is due out in October 2006. We are also adding sections to the guide this year on things to do and places to eat.

For more information or to order any of our guides see our web site at **www.greenwoodguides.com** or email us at **simon@greenwoodguides.com**

Notes

Notes

Notes

Notes